AF599077

THE FOUR GOSPELS
for Young Catholics

Edited by:
Andrea Ciucci, SSP
Matteo Fossati
Giacomo Perego, SSP
Paolo Sartor, SSP

BOOKS & MEDIA
Boston

Nihil Obstat:
Reverend Thomas W. Buckley, S.T.D., S.S.L.

Imprimatur:
✠ Seán Cardinal O'Malley, O.F.M. Cap.
Archbishop of Boston
October 24, 2019

Library of Congress Cataloging-in-Publication Data: 2019953824

ISBN-10: 0-8198-2751-7
ISBN-13: 978-0-8198-2751-7

Originally published by Edizioni San Paolo, Milan in Italian as *I Quattro Vangeli: Una "bella notizia" da leggere insieme*

Piazza Soncino, 5 - 20092 Cinisello Balsamo (Milano)—ITALIA,
www.edizionisanpaolo.it

Illustrations: Michela Ameti and Glifo Design
Graphic Design and Layouts: Delia Cazzulani
Graphic Revision: Laura Sansotera

Published by Pauline Books & Media, 50 Saint Pauls Avenue, Boston, MA 02130-3491

Printed in China

FGFYC LPGCHNHKKLN12-4100013 2751-7

www.pauline.org

Pauline Books & Media is the publishing house of the Daughters of St. Paul, an international congregation of women religious serving the Church with the communications media.

1 2 3 4 5 6 7 8 9 24 23 22 21 20

Contents

Dear Children,

The book you have in your hands is very precious because it contains a message that makes our life—and the lives of billions of people for the last two thousand years—beautiful.

This book is called the "Gospel." It is a word from the Greek language (the language in which it was probably written) and means "Good News."

Really, it is better to speak of "Gospels" in the plural, because—as you will discover as you turn these pages—four similar but different "Good News" stories make up this book. They are the Gospel of Matthew (abbreviated Mt), the Gospel of Mark (Mk), the Gospel of Luke (Lk), and the Gospel of John (Jn).

These four men are commonly called ***evangelists.*** *They each wrote their account or "book" with a different style for a specific group of people. They wrote about the life, acts, and words of Jesus of Nazareth. Jesus was a man who lived in Palestine at the beginning of the first century. He was raised, or resurrected, from the dead after having been unjustly crucified. We, along with his friends, recognize Jesus as the Son of God.*

These four books were written almost 2000 years ago. Because it was written so long ago, they often use symbolic language and words that may be hard to grasp. To help you understand what you are reading, we have placed explanations of difficult words beside the gospel text. We have also imagined what questions a child like you may have for each evangelist and answered them. Where words fail, the beautiful illustrations by Michela will explain what written language is not able to express.

Even though it's okay if you keep this book just for yourself, the Gospel—or the Good News—is really meant to be shared. One of the most beautiful things you can do is read the Gospel at home with your parents. Then, perhaps, you can share it with your friends and catechist. So that you and the adults in your life can enjoy this book together, there are introductions to the various sections and footnotes at the bottom of most pages. At the end of the book there are appendices and maps to help you discover some of the precious treasures hidden in these texts.

You need to know one more thing before you begin reading. Each book of the Bible is divided into chapters and verses. This allows a reader to quickly find stories or phrases which are of interest. Each Gospel—like all the other books of the Bible—is divided into ***chapters****, and each* ***chapter*** *into many* ***verses****. When, for example, you find a citation like Mk 8:28 that means it can be found in the Gospel of Mark (Mk) in chapter 8 and the verse that has a 29 before it. A—citation like Lk 15:11–32 indicates a group of verses—those contained in the Gospel of Luke (Lk) in chapter 15 from verse 11 through verse 32. Lastly, if you find a comma instead of the dash (for example Jn 9: 11, 17) means that you should look in the Gospel of John (Jn) for two verses which are found in chapter 9: verse 11 and verse 17.*

We wish you "happy reading." We hope this book helps you to discover how much Jesus loves you, and that you choose to become his friend.

Father Andrea, Father Giacomo, Matteo, and Father Paolo

GOSPEL ACCORDING TO

Matthew

AUTHOR: ANONYMOUS, LIKELY MATTHEW, THE TAX COLLECTOR WHO BECAME A DISCIPLE OF JESUS

AUDIENCE: CHRISTIANS MAINLY OF JEWISH ORIGIN

TIME AND PLACE: 80–90 AD, MAY HAVE BEEN WRITTEN IN SYRIA

THEMES: JESUS IS THE FULFILLMENT OF THE HEBREW SCRIPTURE, THE NEW MOSES, TRUE MASTER OF ALL HUMANITY; THE CHURCH IS THE IMAGE OF THE KINGDOM OF HEAVEN.

The Scribe's Treasure

Before you dive into my story, I want to tell you a little secret that will help you to understand what you are about to read. Right at the center of my Gospel—around the end of chapter 13—I described a speech, or discourse, in which Jesus used a very beautiful image that blew me away. It was like he made a picture by just using his words that described my experience of Judaism. In moments of difficulty this image helped me find the right words and motivations to preach the Good News to all men, women, and children. The image Jesus used was of a treasure.

Jesus was on a boat that was anchored near the shore of the sea of Galilee. He spoke about the kingdom of God to the crowd that had gathered there to hear him. At the end of his discourse Jesus said, "Therefore every scribe who has been trained for the kingdom of heaven is like the master of a household who brings out of his treasure what is new and what is old" (Mt 13:52).

That was exactly what I needed to hear!

At that moment, I knew that the things our religious leaders wanted us to believe about Jesus weren't true. It was not true that Jesus wanted to destroy Israel's ancient stories. Nor was it true that he had come to get rid of the Law that God had given us through Moses (the Ten Commandments). On the contrary, Jesus believed our past is a treasure. But he also did not want us to keep our treasure hidden in Jerusalem's Temple. A treasure hidden and sealed in a lockbox is useless.

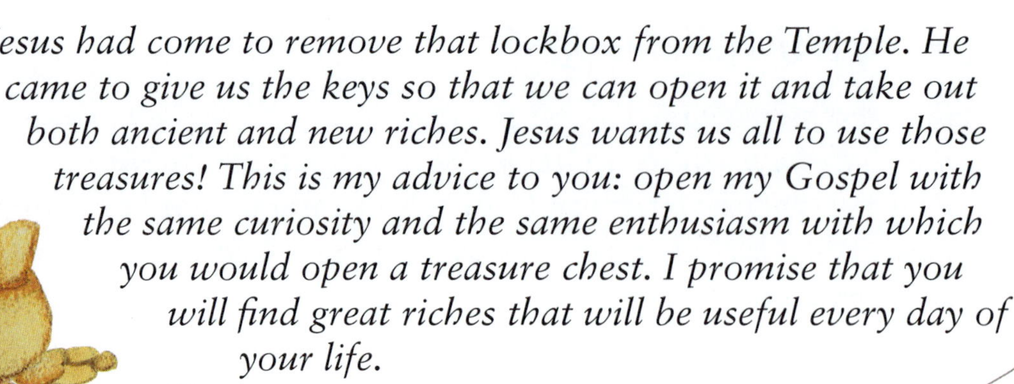

Jesus had come to remove that lockbox from the Temple. He came to give us the keys so that we can open it and take out both ancient and new riches. Jesus wants us all to use those treasures! This is my advice to you: open my Gospel with the same curiosity and the same enthusiasm with which you would open a treasure chest. I promise that you will find great riches that will be useful every day of your life.

Evangelist Matthew

A Gospel . . . from a Jewish Perspective

The most important key to reading the Gospel of Matthew is Matthew's Jewish background. A community of Jews who had converted to Christianity wrote it. This community left many fingerprints in this piece of writing:

~ First, there are many citations of the Old Testament (forty-one direct quotes, but if we include all other mentions as well, there are about seventy). Matthew's Gospel is interested in showing the connection between the old covenant and the new one.

~ Second, the many similarities between Moses and Jesus are emphasized. When they are infants, both Moses and Jesus escape a mass killing of Jewish babies; Jesus' first sermon occurs on a mountain, which would remind most Jews of the mountain on which Moses received the tablets of the Law, or the Ten Commandments; Jesus gives five sermons, the same as the number of books of the Mosaic Law tradition—the Pentateuch. All of these details told the Jewish reader (and tell us today) to see Jesus as the new Moses, as the bearer of the new Law, as the true Master and Teacher of Israel and all of humanity.

~ Third, this Gospel begins with Jesus' genealogy. His "family tree" shows the reader that Jesus is fully a part of human history. Having Jesus' story begin with Abraham is significant because Abraham is considered the father of the people of Israel. Matthew's gospel focuses on the humanity of Jesus, pointing to the importance of God becoming human in the person of Jesus Christ. For this reason, in art, Matthew is often depicted with an image of a winged man.

~ Lastly, there are several places in the text that show a deep knowledge of the Jewish world. For example, Matthew's Gospel mentions: paying tithes—making voluntary payments—for the Temple; wearing clothes with ritual tassels; ritual ablutions or washings; ways of offering one's sacrifice at the altar; and the practices of taking oaths. These are things the other three Gospels ignore, or if these actions are included the other three Gospels explain them in greater detail.

Complete the Scriptures

Matthew's Gospel shows that the bridge between the old Law and the new one is the key to the complete fulfillment of the Law. In Matthew's Gospel, Jesus says at the very beginning of his first discourse: "Do not think that I have come to abolish the law or the prophets; I have come not to abolish but to **fulfill**" (5:17).

The goal of fulfilling and of perfecting the old Law is necessary for understanding the first Gospel. Matthew's account emphasizes the continuity of the Old and New Testaments while pointing out ways the new Law breaks away from the traditions of Israel. For example, Jesus does not ignore Israel's past, but he must renew it. Jesus does not intend to abolish the old Law: but, instead he gives it a new, more profound meaning—one that the Jews of his day failed to see. In a certain sense, Matthew reads the Old Testament with Christian "reading glasses." He was among the first to take a path that is important to this very day: the awareness that only the New Testament reveals the *full* significance of the Old Testament, and that only by starting from the Old Testament can the New Testament be understood.

Structure of the Writing

Matthew divided the central part of the Gospel into five sections. Each section contains one of Jesus' important discourses as well as narration of related events. These five sections are bookended with the stories of Christmas and Easter.

~ **The Christmas stories. A king is born in Bethlehem (1:1–2:23)**: These chapters present the extraordinary events surrounding Jesus' birth.

~ **Book I. Big news (3:1–7:27)**: John the Baptist paves the way and introduces Jesus, who chooses the first disciples and proclaims his first discourse which sets the tone for the rest of the Gospel.

~ **Book II. A whole world to heal (7:28–10:42)**: Jesus sends his twelve Apostles out. Ten stories of Jesus healing people precede his second discourse, which has a missionary theme.

~ **Book III. The mystery of his kingdom (11:1–13:52)**: We see the reactions of the people and the religious leaders to Jesus' words and works. In his third discourse Jesus uses parables to explain God's kingdom.

~ **Book IV. Disciples (13:53–18:35)**: Jesus addresses his closest collaborators; his identity and his mission appear with always greater clarity.

~ **Book V. An already-present future (19:1–25:46)**: Jesus heads decidedly toward Jerusalem. He speaks openly about the destiny reserved for himself and his followers.

~ **The stories of Easter. Here at last is the now-present kingdom (26:1–28:20)**: These chapters describe the events of the last hours of Jesus' earthly life, the apparitions of the resurrected Christ to his disciples, and the sending of the disciples to teach all the nations about Jesus.

GOSPEL ACCORDING TO Matthew

The Christmas Stories (Mt 1: 1–2:23)

Matthew begins his Gospel with a family tree. It is hard for readers today to understand the long list of names of Jesus' ancestors. Yet Matthew's choice to begin this way is extremely significant. The evangelist's intention is to give maximum importance to the incredible news that God himself became man and entered fully into the story of the people of Israel. The context in which Matthew writes the Christmas stories is extremely solemn. The repeated annunciations of the angel to Joseph, the apparition of the star and the visit of the Magi, the interest of King Herod, the flight into Egypt, the massacre of the innocent, all show the greatness of baby Jesus. Jesus was born in circumstances that were similar to those of the birth of the most prominent person in the history of Israel, Moses. This emphasis on Jesus being the new Moses is intended to direct our attention to the divine dignity of Jesus, who is the undisputed protagonist of the Matthean work.

1:1 Why did you start with this series of strange names?

I wanted to reconstruct an ordered list of all Jesus' ancestors to show that he did not come from nothing. He is the fulfillment of a story willed by God that began with Abraham, the father of the people of Israel.

A King Is Born in Bethlehem

The Genealogy of Jesus the Messiah

1 An account of the genealogy[a] of Jesus the
Messiah,[b] the son of David, the son of Abraham.
2 Abraham was the father of Isaac, and Isaac
the father of Jacob, and Jacob the father of
Judah and his brothers, 3and Judah the father of
Perez and Zerah by Tamar, and Perez the father
of Hezron, and Hezron the father of Aram,
4and Aram the father of Aminadab, and
Aminadab the father of Nahshon, and Nahshon

a **1.1** Or *birth*
b **1.1** Or *Jesus Christ*

the father of Salmon, [5]and Salmon the father of Boaz by Rahab, and Boaz the father of Obed by Ruth, and Obed the father of Jesse, [6]and Jesse the father of King David.

And David was the father of Solomon by the wife of Uriah, [7]and Solomon the father of Rehoboam, and Rehoboam the father of Abijah, and Abijah the father of Asaph,[c] [8]and Asaph[d] the father of Jehoshaphat, and Jehoshaphat the father of Joram, and Joram the father of Uzziah, [9]and Uzziah the father of Jotham, and Jotham the father of Ahaz, and Ahaz the father of Hezekiah, [10]and Hezekiah the father of Manasseh, and Manasseh the father of Amos,[e] and Amos[f] the father of Josiah, [11]and Josiah the father of Jechoniah and his brothers, at the time of the deportation to Babylon.

12 And after the deportation to Babylon: Jechoniah was the father of Salathiel, and Salathiel the father of Zerubbabel, [13]and Zerubbabel the father of Abiud, and Abiud the father of Eliakim, and Eliakim the father of Azor, [14]and Azor the father of Zadok, and Zadok the father of Achim, and Achim the father of Eliud, [15]and Eliud the father of

1:1 Messiah, Son of David, Son of Abraham

These are three titles of Jesus. "Christ" indicates that Jesus was the Messiah, the anointed one, waited for by Israel to fulfill God's plan of salvation. "Son of David" tells us that he was the descendent of King David (from whom the Messiah was to come). "Son of Abraham" tells us the fulfillment of God's promise to Abraham, father of all believers.

1:4–6 Tamar, Rahab, Ruth, and the wife of Uriah? Why mention these four women?

I have singled out these non-Hebrew women to remind my readers that the whole world is involved in the story of salvation. You can read their very adventurous stories in Genesis 38 (Tamar); Joshua 2:1–21 (Rahab); the Book of Ruth; and in 2 Samuel 11–12 (wife of Uriah).

c **1.7** Other ancient authorities read *Asa*
d **1.8** Other ancient authorities read *Asa*
e **1.10** Other ancient authorities read *Amon*
f **1.10** Other ancient authorities read *Amon*

1:18 What does "from the Holy Spirit" mean?
Jesus was not conceived like every other baby. God himself intervened by means of his Spirit of life that, welcomed by Mary, brought about the conception of Jesus in her womb and made her his mother.

1:23 Emmanuel
This is one of Jesus' other names and it indicates that he is God. In Hebrew "Emmanuel" means "God is with us." This is confirmed in the last phrase of my Gospel (see 28:20).

Eleazar, and Eleazar the father of Matthan, and
Matthan the father of Jacob, 16and Jacob the
father of Joseph the husband of Mary, of whom
Jesus was born, who is called the Messiah.[g]
17 So all the generations from Abraham to
David are fourteen generations; and from
David to the deportation to Babylon, fourteen
generations; and from the deportation to
Babylon to the Messiah,[h] fourteen generations.

The Birth of Jesus the Messiah

18 Now the birth of Jesus the Messiah[i] took
place in this way. When his mother Mary
had been engaged to Joseph, but before
they lived together, she was found to be
with child from the Holy Spirit. 19Her husband Joseph, being a righteous man and
unwilling to expose her to public disgrace,
planned to dismiss her quietly. 20But just
when he had resolved to do this, an angel of
the Lord appeared to him in a dream and said,
"Joseph, son of David, do not be afraid to take
Mary as your wife, for the child conceived in
her is from the Holy Spirit. 21She will bear a
son, and you are to name him Jesus, for he will
save his people from their sins." 22All this took
place to fulfill what had been spoken by the Lord
through the prophet:

g **1.16** Or *the Christ*
h **1.17** Or *the Christ*
i **1.18** Or *Jesus Christ*

[23] "Look, the virgin shall conceive
and
bear a son,
and they shall name him
Emmanuel,"
which means, "God is with us."
[24]When Joseph awoke from
sleep, he did as the angel of the
Lord commanded him; he took
her as his wife, [25]but had no
marital relations with her until
she had borne a son;[j] and he
named him Jesus.

The Visit of the Wise Men

2 In the time of King Herod, after
Jesus was born in Bethlehem of
Judea, wise men[k] from the East
came to Jerusalem, [2]asking,
"Where is the child who has been
born king of the Jews? For we observed
his star at its rising,[l] and have come to pay
him homage." [3]When King Herod heard
this, he was frightened, and all Jerusalem
with him; [4]and calling together all the
chief priests and scribes of the people, he
inquired of them where the Messiah[m] was
to be born. [5]They told him, "In Bethlehem
of Judea; for so it has been written by the
prophet:

2:1 Why wasn't Jesus born in Nazareth where his parents lived?

The prophecy that verse 6 cites (2 Sam 5:2 and Mi 5:1–2) foretold that the Messiah would be born in Bethlehem, the city of King David. Mary and Joseph went back to that city because it is where Joseph was from, and the Romans wanted to count the number of people from each city.

2:1 Wise Men

Popular tradition says that there were three Magi and that they were kings. They were neither kings nor three in number. They were simply wise men who sought to understand the secret of life by watching the stars. The Magi were not Jewish but their presence in the Nativity story and arrival to the stable, which we celebrate on the day of Epiphany, highlights that Jesus came to save all people.

j **1.25** Other ancient authorities read *her firstborn son*
k **2.1** Or *astrologers*; Gk *magi*
l **2.2** Or *in the East*
m **2.4** Or *the Christ*

6 'And you, Bethlehem, in the land of Judah,
are by no means least among the rulers of Judah;
for from you shall come a ruler
who is to shepherd[n] my people Israel.'"

7 Then Herod secretly called for the
wise men[o] and learned from them the
exact time when the star had appeared.
8Then he sent them to Bethlehem, saying,
"Go and search diligently for the child;
and when you have found him, bring me
word so that I may also go and pay him
homage." 9When they had heard the king,
they set out; and there, ahead of them, went
the star that they had seen at its rising,[p] until
it stopped over the place where the child
was. 10When they saw that the star had
stopped,[q] they were overwhelmed with joy.
11On entering the house, they saw the child
with Mary his mother; and they knelt down
and paid him homage. Then, opening their
treasure chests, they offered him gifts of
gold, frankincense, and myrrh. 12And
having been warned in a dream not to
return to Herod, they left for their own
country by another road.

2:7 Herod

Called Herod "the Great," he was the king of the region at the time of Jesus' birth. His obsessive desire to be great, his cruelty . . . and his fear that someone would take his throne was well-known.

n **2.6** Or *rule*
o **2.7** Or *astrologers*; Gk *magi*
p **2.9** Or *in the East*
q **2.10** Gk *saw the star*

2:13 Why did Joseph have dreams with angels of the Lord in them?

Joseph was a good and just man, who always sought to do the Lord's will. In my time it was thought that God did not speak directly to men, but that God used dreams and the angels to make his will known.

2:18 Why do you continually refer to the passages of the prophets?

When I wrote this Gospel, I was thinking of my Jewish brothers and sisters who recognized Jesus as the Messiah. They knew well the texts of what you today call the Old Testament. With these passages, I have shown that Jesus fulfilled all the "old" promises, or covenants, of God to his people.

The Escape to Egypt

13 Now after they had left, an angel of the
Lord appeared to Joseph in a dream and
said, "Get up, take the child and his
mother, and flee to Egypt, and remain
there until I tell you; for Herod is
about to search for the child, to
destroy him." 14Then Joseph[r]
got up, took the child and his
mother by night, and went to
Egypt, 15and remained there
until the death of Herod. This
was to fulfill what had been
spoken by the Lord through the
prophet, "Out of Egypt I have
called my son."

The Massacre of the Infants

16 When Herod saw that he had
been tricked by the wise men,[s]
he was infuriated, and he sent and
killed all the children in and around
Bethlehem who were two years old
or under, according to the time that he

r **2.14** Gk *he*
s **2.16** Or *astrologers*; Gk *magi*
t **2.16** Or *astrologers*; Gk *magi*
u **2.21** Gk *he*

had learned from the wise men.[t] 17Then was fulfilled what had
been spoken through the prophet Jeremiah:

18 "A voice was heard in Ramah,
 wailing and loud lamentation,
Rachel weeping for her children;
 she refused to be consoled, because they are no
 more."

The Return from Egypt

19 When Herod died, an angel of the Lord suddenly appeared
in a dream to Joseph in Egypt and said, 20"Get up, take
the child and his mother, and go to the land of Israel, for
those who were seeking the child's life are dead." 21Then
Joseph[u] got up, took the child and his mother, and
went to the land of Israel. 22But when he heard that
Archelaus was ruling over Judea in place of his father
Herod, he was afraid to go there. And after being
warned in a dream, he went away to the district of
Galilee. 23There he made his home in a town called
Nazareth, so that what had been spoken through
the prophets might be fulfilled, "He will be called
a Nazorean."

The Five Books of the New Law

Book I: Big News (Mt 3:1–7:27)

John the Baptist is a “bridge” between the Jewish world and the Christian one, between the old covenant and the new, everlasting covenant. He preached conversion and prepared the men and women of his time to welcome the “big news” of the arrival of Jesus, who makes everything new. This first narrative section (3:1–4:25) is followed by the opening discourse—also known as the Sermon on the Mount—Jesus’ most important preaching. This teaching, to which the Gospel dedicates three long chapters (from 5–7), opens with the proclamation of the beatitudes (which are a portrait of Christ himself). Jesus goes on to describe how he will interpret the Mosaic Law, how he will renew it without abolishing it, and reveals its true and profound significance.

3:4 Did John the Baptist really dress like that and eat strange things?

Yes. It was the custom of some of the prophets of Israel to wear clothing made from camel hair, while the wild honey and the locusts (rich in protein) were simple foods available in the desert.

The Proclamation of John the Baptist

3 In those days John the Baptist appeared in
the wilderness of Judea, proclaiming, 2“Repent,
for the kingdom of heaven has come near.”[v] 3This
is the one of whom the prophet Isaiah spoke
when he said,

“The voice of one crying out in the
wilderness:
‘Prepare the way of the Lord,
make his paths straight.’”

4Now John wore clothing of camel’s hair with
a leather belt around his waist, and his food
was locusts and wild honey. 5Then the people
of Jerusalem and all Judea were going out to him,

v **3.2** Or *is at hand*

and all the region along the Jordan, 6 and they
were baptized by him in the river Jordan,
confessing their sins.

7 But when he saw many Pharisees
and Sadducees coming for baptism, he
said to them, "You brood of vipers!
Who warned you to flee from the wrath
to come? 8 Bear fruit worthy of repentance. 9 Do not presume to say to yourselves, 'We have Abraham as our
ancestor'; for I tell you, God is able from
these stones to raise up children to
Abraham. 10 Even now the ax is lying at the
root of the trees; every tree therefore that
does not bear good fruit is cut down and thrown
into the fire.

11 "I baptize you with[w] water for
repentance, but one who is more
powerful than I is coming after me; I
am not worthy to carry his sandals.
He will baptize you with[x] the Holy
Spirit and fire. 12 His winnowing fork
is in his hand, and he will clear his
threshing floor and will gather his
wheat into the granary; but the chaff he
will burn with unquenchable fire."

w **3.11** Or *in*
x **3.11** Or *in*

3:6–11 So Jesus did not invent Baptism!

You have a point! Washing yourself with water to ask forgiveness for your sins was a common practice even before Jesus was born. Christians have transformed this ritual to celebrate the new life given to us by Jesus at Easter in his resurrection.

3:7 Pharisees and Sadducees

These were the two main groups of Jews at the time. The Pharisees followed the Jewish Law with great attention. The Sadducees, tied to the families of priests, emphasized Sacred Scripture over the Law, and did not believe in the resurrection of the dead or even angels.

3:12 The Winnowing Fork
It lifts the grain to sift out any impurities (the "chaff").

3:15 Did Jesus have sins that needed to be forgiven?
No, Jesus did not have Original Sin or any personal sins. In fact, for this reason, John did not want to baptize him. But Jesus wanted to share in the experiences of sinners and be a friend of all men and women. Jesus is a Messiah who was close to his people from the start.

3:17 Whose voice was it?
It was God the Father who spoke (he will speak one other time, during the Transfiguration in chapter 17) and confirmed to all that Jesus was his Son, and we must follow him.

The Baptism of Jesus

13 Then Jesus came from Galilee to
John at the Jordan, to be baptized by
him. 14John would have prevented
him, saying, "I need to be baptized
by you, and do you come to me?"
15But Jesus answered him, "Let it
be so now; for it is proper for us
in this way to fulfill all righteousness." Then he consented. 16And
when Jesus had been baptized,
just as he came up from the
water, suddenly the heavens were
opened to him and he saw the
Spirit of God descending like a
dove and alighting on him. 17And
a voice from heaven said, "This is
my Son, the Beloved,[y] with whom
I am well pleased."

y **3.17** Or *my beloved Son*

The Temptation of Jesus

4 Then Jesus was led up by the Spirit into the wilderness to
be tempted by the devil. 2He fasted forty days and forty
nights, and afterwards he was famished. 3The tempter
came and said to him, "If you are the Son of God,
command these stones to become loaves of
bread." 4But he answered, "It is written,

'One does not live by bread alone,
but by every word that comes from
the mouth of God.'"

5 Then the devil took him to the holy city
and placed him on the pinnacle of the
temple, 6saying to him, "If you are the Son
of God, throw yourself down; for it is written,

'He will command his angels
concerning you,'
and 'On their hands they will bear
you up,
so that you will not dash your foot
against a stone.'"

7Jesus said to him, "Again it is written, 'Do not
put the Lord your God to the test.'"

8 Again, the devil took him to a very high mountain and showed him all the kingdoms of the world
and their splendor; 9and he said to him, "All these I
will give you, if you will fall down and worship me."
10Jesus said to him, "Away with you, Satan! for it is
written,

'Worship the Lord your God,
and serve only him.'"

4:1–11
Even Jesus was tempted?
Certainly! The devil tried convincing him to be Messiah in a different way than what God wanted. The devil wanted Jesus to seek riches, power, and glory. Jesus chased the devil away, declaring his only wish was and is to trust in God and in his word.

11Then the devil left him, and suddenly angels
came and waited on him.

Jesus Begins His Ministry in Galilee

12 Now when Jesus[z] heard that John had
been arrested, he withdrew to Galilee.
13He left Nazareth and made his home in
Capernaum by the sea, in the territory of
Zebulun and Naphtali, 14so that what had
been spoken through the prophet Isaiah
might be fulfilled:

15 "Land of Zebulun, land of
Naphtali,
on the road by the sea, across
the Jordan, Galilee of the
Gentiles—
16 the people who sat in darkness
have seen a great light,
and for those who sat in the region
and shadow of death
light has dawned."

17From that time Jesus began to proclaim, "Repent, for the kingdom of
heaven has come near."[a]

4:13–15 Capernaum, Zebulun, Naphtali

Jesus began his preaching in Galilee, a region inhabited by descendants of the tribes of Zebulun and Naphtali (two of the twelve sons of Jacob) but also inhabited by many foreigners, because his message was for all.

4:17 Kingdom of Heaven

When God's perfect love, which is manifested in Jesus, is genuinely experienced and lived then the kingdom of heaven is present. It is called the kingdom "of heaven" not because it cannot exist on the earth but to distinguish it from human kingdoms.

z **4.12** Gk *he*
a **4.17** Or *is at hand*

Jesus Calls the First Disciples

18 As he walked by the Sea of Galilee, he saw two
brothers, Simon, who is called Peter, and Andrew
his brother, casting a net into the sea—for they were
fishermen. [19]And he said to them, "Follow me, and
I will make you fish for people." [20]Immediately
they left their nets and followed him. [21]As he
went from there, he saw two other brothers,
James son of Zebedee and his brother John,
in the boat with their father Zebedee,
mending their nets, and he called them.
[22]Immediately they left the boat and
their father, and followed him.

Jesus Ministers to Crowds of People

23 Jesus[b] went throughout Galilee,
teaching in their synagogues and
proclaiming the good news[c] of the
kingdom and curing every disease
and every sickness among the people.
[24]So his fame spread throughout all
Syria, and they brought to him all the
sick, those who were afflicted with various
diseases and pains, demoniacs, epileptics,
and paralytics, and he cured them. [25]And
great crowds followed him from Galilee, the
Decapolis, Jerusalem, Judea, and from beyond
the Jordan.

4:18 Sea of Galilee
A large fishing lake known as the Lake of Gennesaret, also called Tiberias

4:20–22 Why did they not think about it for a while before following Jesus?
Of course they thought about it . . . but quickly Jesus became more important than anything else and any other person dear to them.

4:23 Good News
My entire story, which contains the testimonies of many people who encountered Jesus, announces the Good News—the kingdom of heaven is present here on earth.

b **4.23** Gk *He*
c **4.23** Gk *gospel*

The Beatitudes

5 When Jesus[d] saw the crowds, he
went up the mountain; and after he
sat down, his disciples came to him.
2 Then he began to speak, and taught
them, saying:

3 "Blessed are the poor in spirit, for theirs is the kingdom of heaven.

4 "Blessed are those who mourn, for they will be comforted.

5 "Blessed are the meek, for they will inherit the earth.

6 "Blessed are those who hunger and thirst for righteousness, for they will be filled.

7 "Blessed are the merciful, for they will receive mercy.

8 "Blessed are the pure in heart, for they will see God.

9 "Blessed are the peacemakers, for they will be called children of God.

5:1 It seems like the beginning of an official speech of a great man!

It's true! Unlike the other evangelists who scatter Jesus' teachings throughout their Gospels, I wanted to gather Jesus' teachings into five great discourses. This is the first and most famous sermon, in which Jesus described how he lived and how his disciples were called to live.

5:3 Blessed

Happy. Full of peace. Jesus started his sermon declaring that the people in the kingdom of heaven are truly happy.

5:3–11 The poor, the sick, the persecuted are sad, not happy!

The kingdom of God described by Jesus is the opposite of what the world thinks heaven should be. The people in the kingdom of heaven are happy not because being poor and sick is good, but because they are favored by God. They are favored like Jesus, the beloved Son, who became poor and meek by taking on frail human flesh and suffering—even until death on the cross.

d **5.1** Gk *he*

5:13–14 Why does Jesus want us to be salt and light of the world?

Those who choose to follow Jesus choose to live a life that is flavorful and vibrant. Their lives make the world more beautiful. Jesus' friends are responsible for preserving the taste of their life and not hiding the grace they have received.

5:15 Bushel Basket

The bushel is a large wooden container used for measuring the quantity of cereals or grains.

10 "Blessed are those who are persecuted for righteousness' sake, for theirs
is the kingdom of heaven.

11 "Blessed are you when people
revile you and persecute you and
utter all kinds of evil against you
falsely[e] on my account. 12Rejoice
and be glad, for your reward is great
in heaven, for in the same way they
persecuted the prophets who were
before you.

Salt and Light

13 "You are the salt of the earth; but if
salt has lost its taste, how can its saltiness be restored? It is no longer good for
anything, but is thrown out and trampled
under foot.

14 "You are the light of the world. A city
built on a hill cannot be hid. 15No one after
lighting a lamp puts it under the bushel basket,
but on the lampstand, and it gives light to all in
the house. 16In the same way, let your light shine
before others, so that they may see your good
works and give glory to your Father in heaven.

e **5.11** Other ancient authorities lack *falsely*

The Law and the Prophets

17 "Do not think that I have come
to abolish the law or the prophets; I
have come not to abolish but to fulfill. 18For truly I tell you, until heaven
and earth pass away, not one letter,[f]
not one stroke of a letter, will pass
from the law until all is accomplished.
19Therefore, whoever breaks[g] one of
the least of these commandments, and
teaches others to do the same, will be
called least in the kingdom of heaven;
but whoever does them and teaches
them will be called great in the kingdom
of heaven. 20For I tell you, unless your
righteousness exceeds that of the scribes
and Pharisees, you will never enter the
kingdom of heaven.

Concerning Anger

21 "You have heard that it was said to those
of ancient times, 'You shall not murder'; and
'whoever murders shall be liable to judgment.'

5:17 Law, Prophets
These two words summarize the "Sacred Scriptures" of Judaism. Jesus took some precepts of the Law, not to get rid of them, but to help the disciples know the deeper meaning.

5:18 Not One Stroke of a Letter
Jesus wanted to make it clear that he was not going to change the old Law; not a single letter or even any part of a letter.

f **5.18** Gk *one iota*
g **5.19** Or *annuls*

5:22 What happens to those who say bad words?

Jesus did not mean to say that because of a bad word one goes to hell. Loving another person means not only avoiding homicide but avoiding even the slightest insult.

5:22 Hell

Hell is a place of punishment for those who *choose* not to apologize to God for their sins. God respects everyone's freedom, so he so does not stop people from condemning themselves to eternal punishment.

5:27 Adultery

An act in which one of two spouses cheats on the other.

22 But I say to you that if you are angry
with a brother or sister,[h] you will be
liable to judgment; and if you insult[i] a
brother or sister,[j] you will be liable to
the council; and if you say, 'You fool,'
you will be liable to the hell[k] of fire.
23 So when you are offering your gift
at the altar, if you remember that your
brother or sister[l] has something against
you, 24 leave your gift there before the
altar and go; first be reconciled to your
brother or sister,[m] and then come
and offer your gift. 25 Come to terms
quickly with your accuser while
you are on the way to court[n] with
him, or your accuser may hand
you over to the judge, and the
judge to the guard, and you will
be thrown into prison. 26 Truly
I tell you, you will never get out
until you have paid the last penny.

Concerning Adultery

27 "You have heard that it was said, 'You
shall not commit adultery.' 28 But I say to
you that everyone who looks at a woman
with lust has already committed adultery

h **5.22** Gk *a brother*; other ancient authorities add *without cause*
i **5.22** Gk *say Raca to* (an obscure term of abuse)
j **5.22** Gk *a brother*
k **5.22** Gk *Gehenna*
l **5.23** Gk *your brother*
m **5.24** Gk *your brother*
n **5.25** Gk lacks *to court*

with her in his heart. 29If your right eye causes you
to sin, tear it out and throw it away; it is better for
you to lose one of your members than for your
whole body to be thrown into hell.[o] 30And if
your right hand causes you to sin, cut it off
and throw it away; it is better for you to lose
one of your members than for your whole
body to go into hell.[p]

5:29 Tear out your eye! For so little?

Jesus used a strong image—which is not to be taken literally—to teach that each part of the body is created to love, not to possess. If you use it badly, it loses its value.

Concerning Divorce

31 "It was also said, 'Whoever divorces his
wife, let him give her a certificate of divorce.'
32But I say to you that anyone who divorces his
wife, except on the ground of unchastity, causes
her to commit adultery; and whoever marries a
divorced woman commits adultery.

Concerning Oaths

33 "Again, you have heard that it was said to those
of ancient times, 'You shall not swear falsely, but carry
out the vows you have made to the Lord.' 34But I say to you,
Do not swear at all, either by heaven, for it is the throne of God, 35or
by the earth, for it is his footstool, or by Jerusalem, for it is the city of the
great King. 36And do not swear by your head, for you cannot make one
hair white or black. 37Let your word be 'Yes, Yes' or 'No, No'; anything
more than this comes from the evil one.[q]

o **5.29** Gk *Gehenna*
p **5.30** Gk *Gehenna*
q **5.37** Or *evil*

Concerning Retaliation

38 "You have heard that it was said, 'An eye for an
eye and a tooth for a tooth.' 39But I say to you, Do
not resist an evildoer. But if anyone strikes you on the
right cheek, turn the other also; 40and if anyone wants to
sue you and take your coat, give your cloak as well; 41and
if anyone forces you to go one mile, go also the second
mile. 42Give to everyone who begs from you, and do not
refuse anyone who wants to borrow from you.

Love for Enemies

43 "You have heard that it was said, 'You shall
love your neighbor and hate your enemy.'
44But I say to you, Love your enemies and pray
for those who persecute you, 45so that you
may be children of your Father in heaven; for
he makes his sun rise on the evil and on the
good, and sends rain on the righteous and on
the unrighteous. 46For if you love those who
love you, what reward do you have? Do not
even the tax collectors do the same? 47And
if you greet only your brothers and sisters,[r]
what more are you doing than others? Do not
even the Gentiles do the same? 48Be perfect,
therefore, as your heavenly Father is perfect.

5:38–48 Who is capable of loving one's enemies and turning the other cheek?

Jesus lived like this, to the point of forgiving those who killed him. Like him, each of his disciples is called to live a life of forgiveness and love. slowly becoming perfect like the Father in heaven.

r **5.47** Gk *your brothers*

Concerning Almsgiving

6 "Beware of practicing your piety before
others in order to be seen by them; for then
you have no reward from your Father in
heaven.

2 "So whenever you give alms, do
not sound a trumpet before you, as
the hypocrites do in the synagogues
and in the streets, so that they may
be praised by others. Truly I tell you,
they have received their reward.
3 But when you give alms, do not let
your left hand know what your right
hand is doing, 4 so that your alms
may be done in secret; and your
Father who sees in secret will reward
you.[s]

6:1–6, 16–18

Why hide the good things?

Almsgiving, prayer, and fasting were the three principle works of every good Jew. Jesus invited the Jews of his time and invites us today to live them in silence, expressing our love of God, without bragging in front of others.

Concerning Prayer

5 "And whenever you pray, do not be like
the hypocrites; for they love to stand and pray
in the synagogues and at the street corners, so that
they may be seen by others. Truly I tell you, they have
received their reward. 6 But whenever you pray, go into your
room and shut the door and pray to your Father who is in secret;
and your Father who sees in secret will reward you.[t]

s **6.4** Other ancient authorities add *openly*
t **6.6** Other ancient authorities add *openly*

6:7–8 So now we should only pray the Our Father? What about the other prayers?

Jesus showed us how he prayed by teaching us the Our Father as a model of prayer. For this reason, during the Mass and in Christian prayer the Our Father is never missing. The Our Father should, in some way, inspire and guide every other prayer.

6:9 Father

Jesus called God: *Abba* Jesus teaches us to speak to God the Father just as we addressed our earthly father when we were small children.

7 "When you are praying, do not heap up
empty phrases as the Gentiles do; for they
think that they will be heard because
of their many words. 8 Do not be like
them, for your Father knows what
you need before you ask him.

9 "Pray then in this way:

Our Father in heaven,
hallowed be your name.
10 Your kingdom come.
Your will be done,
on earth as it is in heaven.
11 Give us this day our daily
bread.[u]
12 And forgive us our debts,
as we also have forgiven
our debtors.
13 And do not bring us to the
time of trial,[v]
but rescue us from the
evil one.[w]

14 For if you forgive others their trespasses, your heavenly Father will also forgive you; 15 but if you do not
forgive others, neither will your Father forgive your
trespasses.

u **6.11** Or *our bread for tomorrow*

v **6.13** Or *us into temptation*

w **6.13** Or *from evil.* Other ancient authorities add, in some form, *For the kingdom and the power and the glory are yours forever. Amen.*

Concerning Fasting

16 "And whenever you fast, do not look dismal, like the
hypocrites, for they disfigure their faces so as to show
others that they are fasting. Truly I tell you, they have
received their reward. 17But when you fast, put oil on
your head and wash your face, 18so that your fasting
may be seen not by others but by your Father who is in
secret; and your Father who sees in secret will reward
you.[x]

Concerning Treasures

19 "Do not store up for yourselves treasures on earth,
where moth and rust[y] consume and where thieves
break in and steal; 20but store up for yourselves
treasures in heaven, where neither moth nor
rust[z] consumes and where thieves do not
break in and steal. 21For where your treasure is, there your heart will be also.

The Sound Eye

22 "The eye is the lamp of the body. So, if
your eye is healthy, your whole body will
be full of light; 23but if your eye is unhealthy,
your whole body will be full of darkness. If then the light in you
is darkness, how great is
the darkness!

6:19 Moth
A small insect that ruins plants by eating them from within.

x **6.18** Other ancient authorities add *openly*
y **6.19** Gk *eating*
z **6.20** Gk *eating*

6:24 Wealth

The Greek has "mammon," which is the name of an idol who impersonated wealth.

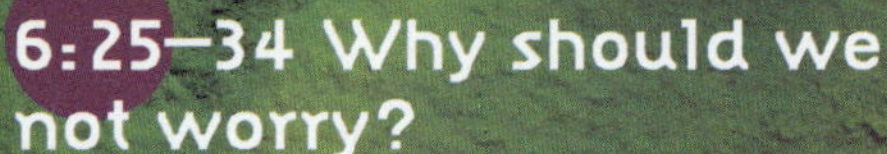

6:25–34 Why should we not worry?

Jesus repeats the invitation to not worry about four times, inviting his disciples to not be preoccupied and frightened. The Father, in fact, watches over us, considering not only our individual needs, but the needs of all his people.

Serving Two Masters

24 "No one can serve two masters; for a slave
will either hate the one and love the other, or be
devoted to the one and despise the other. You
cannot serve God and wealth.[a]

Do Not Worry

25 "Therefore I tell you, do not worry about your
life, what you will eat or what you will drink,[b] or
about your body, what you will wear. Is not life
more than food, and the body more than clothing?
26Look at the birds of the air; they neither sow nor
reap nor gather into barns, and yet your heavenly
Father feeds them. Are you not of more value
than they? 27And can any of you by worrying
add a single hour to your span of life?[c] 28And
why do you worry about clothing? Consider
the lilies of the field, how they grow; they
neither toil nor spin, 29yet I tell you, even
Solomon in all his glory was not clothed
like one of these. 30But if God so clothes
the grass of the field, which is alive today
and tomorrow is thrown into the oven,
will he not much more clothe you—you
of little faith? 31Therefore do not worry,
saying, 'What will we eat?' or 'What will
we drink?' or 'What will we wear?' 32For it
is the Gentiles who strive for all these things;

a **6.24** Gk *mammon*
b **6.25** Other ancient authorities lack *or what you will drink*
c **6.27** Or *add one cubit to your height*

and indeed your heavenly Father knows that you need all
these things. 33But strive first for the kingdom of God[d]
and his[e] righteousness, and all these things will be
given to you as well.

34 "So do not worry about tomorrow, for
tomorrow will bring worries of its own. Today's
trouble is enough for today.

Judging Others

7 "Do not judge, so that you may not be
judged. 2For with the judgment you make you
will be judged, and the measure you give will
be the measure you get. 3Why do you see the
speck in your neighbor's[f] eye, but do not notice
the log in your own eye? 4Or how can you say to
your neighbor,[g] 'Let me take the speck out of your eye,'
while the log is in your own eye? 5You hypocrite, first
take the log out of your own eye, and then you will see
clearly to take the speck out of your neighbor's[h] eye.

7:3 I do not have logs in my eyes!
Jesus used this image to remind us that, before judging another it is necessary to recognize ourselves as being sinners, just like that other person. In this way, we look to and trust together in the Lord's mercy.

Profaning the Holy

6 "Do not give what is holy to dogs; and do not throw your
pearls before swine, or they will trample them under foot and turn
and maul you.

d **6.33** Other ancient authorities lack *of God*
e **6.33** Or *its*
f **7.3** Gk *brother's*
g **7.4** Gk *brother*
h **7.5** Gk *brother's*

Ask, Search, Knock

7 "Ask, and it will be given you; search, and you will
find; knock, and the door will be opened for you. 8For
everyone who asks receives, and everyone who
searches finds, and for everyone who knocks, the
door will be opened. 9Is there anyone among
you who, if your child asks for bread, will give a
stone? 10Or if the child asks for a fish, will give
a snake? 11If you then, who are evil, know how
to give good gifts to your children, how much
more will your Father in heaven give good things
to those who ask him!

The Golden Rule

12 "In everything do to others as you would have
them do to you; for this is the law and the prophets.

The Narrow Gate

13 "Enter through the narrow gate; for the gate is wide
and the road is easy[i] that leads to destruction, and
there are many who take it. 14For the gate is narrow
and the road is hard that leads to life, and there are
few who find it.

A Tree and Its Fruit

15 "Beware of false prophets, who come to you in
sheep's clothing but inwardly are ravenous wolves.
16You will know them by their fruits. Are grapes gathered from thorns, or figs from thistles? 17In the same
way, every good tree bears good fruit, but the bad tree

7:12 I have already heard this phrase! Did Jesus invent this or did he copy it?

You are right. Words more or less similar to these are found in many religious or philosophical texts. But truth is truth, and we know Jesus is the Truth. So, Jesus has always loved us and he lived this rule to the fullest.

7:15 False Prophets

They not only say things that are wrong, but they also don't act in accordance with their teachings. They are often called "hypocrites."

i **7.13** Other ancient authorities read *for the road is wide and easy*

bears bad fruit. 18A good tree cannot bear bad fruit, nor can a
bad tree bear good fruit. 19Every tree that does not bear good
fruit is cut down and thrown into the fire. 20Thus you will
know them by their fruits.

Concerning Self-Deception

21 "Not everyone who says to me, 'Lord, Lord,' will enter
the kingdom of heaven, but only the one who does the will
of my Father in heaven. 22On that day many will say to me,
'Lord, Lord, did we not prophesy in your name, and cast
out demons in your name, and do many deeds of power
in your name?' 23Then I will declare to them, 'I never knew
you; go away from me, you evildoers.'

Hearers and Doers

24 "Everyone then who hears these words of mine and acts on
them will be like a wise man who built his house on rock.
25The rain fell, the floods came, and the winds blew and
beat on that house, but it did not fall, because it had
been founded on rock. 26And everyone who hears
these words of mine and does not act on them will
be like a foolish man who built his house on sand.
27The rain fell, and the floods came, and the winds
blew and beat against that house, and it fell—and
great was its fall!"

7:23 Evildoers
These are people who prefer, in their hearts, to do bad and unjust works over the good and just works of God.

7:24 Is it not more exhausting to build a house on rock?
True, digging in sand is easier, but sand castles are not very strong. Jesus reminds us that only by putting into practice his teachings, even if they are tiring, is it possible to build a solid life that remains strong in times of difficulty.

Book II: A Whole World to Heal (Mt 7:28–10:42)

This "second book" of Matthew's Gospel opens with a narrative section (7:28–9:38) which shows a surprising series of miracles performed by Jesus: we can count ten of them! This book gives the undeniable "good news" of Jesus entering into the world and revealing himself to be a powerful prophet in words and deeds. More importantly, he reveals himself to be the Messiah who came to re-establish order to creation and to give back to every man and woman a full life. Jesus passes this same power on to the twelve Apostles, who are sent to the "lost sheep of the house of Israel," (10:6) now having "authority over unclean spirits, to cast them out, and to cure every disease and every sickness" (10:1). Jesus entrusts the Apostles in the context of his second great teaching, the missionary discourse, to which chapter 10 is dedicated.

7:28 In hearing Jesus, were they really "astounded"?

Yes. Jesus had spoken so clearly, revealing to the crowd the deeper meaning of the beautiful and true laws, that the people were astounded or amazed at his wisdom. This made them wonder who Jesus was.

28 Now when Jesus had finished saying these
things, the crowds were astounded at his
teaching, 29for he taught them as one having
authority, and not as their scribes.

Jesus Cleanses a Leper

8 When Jesus[j] had come down from
the mountain, great crowds followed
him; 2and there was a leper[k] who came to
him and knelt before him, saying, "Lord,
if you choose, you can make me clean."
3He stretched out his hand and touched
him, saying, "I do choose. Be made clean!"
Immediately his leprosy[l] was cleansed. 4Then
Jesus said to him, "See that you say nothing to

j 8.1 Gk *he*
k 8.2 The terms *leper* and *leprosy* can refer to several diseases
l 8.3 The terms *leper* and *leprosy* can refer to several diseases

anyone; but go, show yourself to the priest, and offer the gift that Moses commanded, as a testimony to them."

Jesus Heals a Centurion's Servant

5 When he entered Capernaum, a centurion came to
him, appealing to him [6]and saying, "Lord, my servant is
lying at home paralyzed, in terrible distress." [7]And he
said to him, "I will come and cure him." (8) [8]The centurion answered, "Lord, I am not worthy to have you
come under my roof; but only speak the word, and
my servant will be healed. [9]For I also am a man
under authority, with soldiers under me; and I
say to one, 'Go,' and he goes, and to another,
'Come,' and he comes, and to my slave, 'Do
this,' and the slave does it." [10]When Jesus
heard him, he was amazed and said to
those who followed him, "Truly I tell
you, in no one[m] in Israel have I found
such faith. [11]I tell you, many will come
from east and west and will eat with
Abraham and Isaac and Jacob in the
kingdom of heaven, [12]while the heirs of
the kingdom will be thrown into the outer
darkness, where there will be weeping and
gnashing of teeth." [13]And to the centurion
Jesus said, "Go; let it be done for you according
to your faith." And the servant was healed in that
hour.

8:5 Centurion
A Roman soldier, usually a pagan, who commands one hundred soldiers.

8:8 I have heard these words before!
That's true! During Mass, before receiving Holy Communion, all the participants pray with the same words as the centurion, announcing their faith in Jesus who saves.

m **8.10** Other ancient authorities read *Truly I tell you, not even*

8:14 Peter was married?
Certainly, he was, just like some of the other disciples. Over time, it became the practice of the Roman Catholic Church to ordain to the priesthood men who were unmarried. That is why you are used to seeing priests and bishops who are not married.

8:16 Cast out the Spirits
Jesus has the power to free people from the harmful influence of evil spirits.

Jesus Heals Many at Peter's House

14 When Jesus entered Peter's house, he saw
his mother-in-law lying in bed with a fever;
15 he touched her hand, and the fever left
her, and she got up and began to serve him.
16 That evening they brought to him many
who were possessed with demons; and he
cast out the spirits with a word, and cured
all who were sick. 17 This was to fulfill what had been spoken through the
prophet Isaiah, "He took our infirmities
and bore our diseases."

Would-Be Followers of Jesus

18 Now when Jesus saw great crowds
around him, he gave orders to go
over to the other side. 19 A scribe then
approached and said, "Teacher, I will
follow you wherever you go." 20 And
Jesus said to him, "Foxes have holes,

and birds of the air have nests; but the Son of
Man has nowhere to lay his head." 21Another
of his disciples said to him, "Lord, first let me
go and bury my father." 22But Jesus said to
him, "Follow me, and let the dead
bury their own dead."

Jesus Stills the Storm

23 And when he
got into the boat, his disciples followed him.
24A windstorm arose on the sea, so great that
the boat was being swamped by the waves; but
he was asleep. 25And they went and woke him
up, saying, "Lord, save us! We are perishing!"
26And he said to them, "Why are you afraid,
you of little faith?" Then he got up and
rebuked the winds and the sea; and there

8:23 How was he able to sleep in the middle of the storm?

Jesus, unlike his disciples, trusted completely *in God, his Father, and he knew he was safe even in the scariest situations.*

8:26 Dead Calm
The absolute calm of the sea, brought about by Jesus, shows that he is the Lord of nature.

8:28 Gadarenes
They were a pagan population that lived in the region of the Decapolis, outside the borders of Israel. Jesus even went there to bring salvation, revealing yet again that salvation is meant for everyone, not just the Jews.

was a dead calm. 27They were amazed, saying, "What sort of man is this, that even the winds and the sea obey him?"

Jesus Heals the Gadarene Demoniacs

28 When he came to the other side, to the
country of the Gadarenes,[n] two demoniacs
coming out of the tombs met him. They
were so fierce that no one could pass that
way. 29Suddenly they shouted, "What
have you to do with us, Son of God? Have
you come here to torment us before the
time?" 30Now a large herd of swine was
feeding at some distance from them.
31The demons begged him, "If you cast
us out, send us into the herd of swine."
32And he said to them, "Go!" So they
came out and entered the swine; and
suddenly, the whole herd rushed down
the steep bank into the sea and perished
in the water. 33The swineherds ran off,
and on going into the town, they told the
whole story about what had happened
to the demoniacs. 34Then the whole town
came out to meet Jesus; and when they
saw him, they begged him to leave their
neighborhood.

n **8.28** Other ancient authorities read *Gergesenes*; others, *Gerasenes*

9 And after getting into a boat he crossed the sea and
came to his own town.

Jesus Heals a Paralytic

2 And just then some people were carrying a paralyzed man lying on a bed. When Jesus saw their faith,
he said to the paralytic, "Take heart, son; your sins
are forgiven." 3Then some of the scribes said to themselves, "This man is blaspheming." 4But Jesus, per-
ceiving their thoughts, said, "Why do you think evil in
your hearts? 5For which is easier, to say, 'Your sins are
forgiven,' or to say, 'Stand up and walk'? 6But so that
you may know that the Son of Man has authority on
earth to forgive sins"—he then said to the paralytic—
"Stand up, take your bed and go to your home." 7And
he stood up and went to his home. 8When the crowds
saw it, they were filled with awe, and they glorified
God, who had given such authority to human beings.

The Call of Matthew

9 As Jesus was walking along, he saw a man called Matthew sitting at the tax
booth; and he said to him, "Follow me." And he got up and followed him.
10 And as he sat at dinner[o] in the house, many tax collectors and sinners
came and were sitting[p] with him and his disciples. 11When
the Pharisees saw this, they said to his disciples,
"Why does your teacher eat with tax collectors
and sinners?" 12But when he heard this, he
said, "Those who are well have no need of
a physician, but those who are sick. 13Go
and learn what this means, 'I desire
mercy, not sacrifice.' For I have come
to call not the righteous but sinners."

9:9–13 Are you and Mathew the tax collector the same person?

Yes! Before encountering Jesus, I did a job every Jew despised. I collected the taxes for the Roman rulers. I experienced face-to-face the look of love and compassion that Jesus offers sinners like me.

The Question about Fasting

14 Then the disciples of John came
to him, saying, "Why do we and
the Pharisees fast often,[q] but your
disciples do not fast?" 15And Jesus
said to them, "The wedding guests
cannot mourn as long as the bridegroom is with them, can they? The
days will come when the bridegroom
is taken away from them, and then
they will fast. 16No one sews a piece
of unshrunk cloth on an old cloak, for
the patch pulls away from the cloak, and

o **9.10** Gk *reclined*
p **9.10** Gk *were reclining*
q **9.14** Other ancient authorities lack *often*

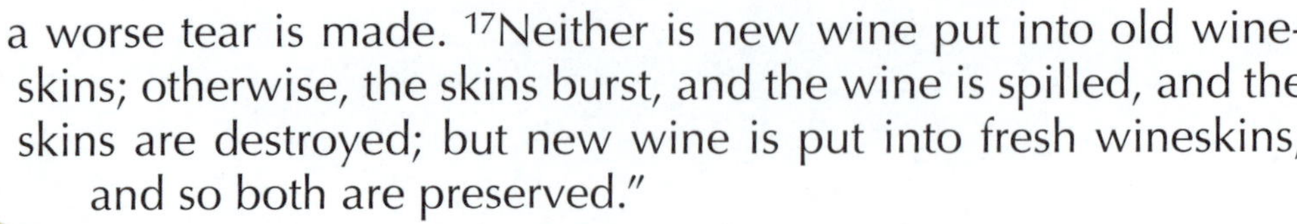

a worse tear is made. [17]Neither is new wine put into old wineskins; otherwise, the skins burst, and the wine is spilled, and the
skins are destroyed; but new wine is put into fresh wineskins,
and so both are preserved."

A Girl Restored to Life and a Woman Healed

18 While he was saying these things to them, suddenly a leader of the synagogue[r] came in and
knelt before him, saying, "My daughter has just
died; but come and lay your hand on her, and
she will live." [19]And Jesus got up and followed
him, with his disciples. [20]Then suddenly a
woman who had been suffering from hemorrhages for twelve years came up behind him
and touched the fringe of his cloak, [21]for she
said to herself, "If I only touch his cloak, I
will be made well." [22]Jesus turned, and seeing
her he said, "Take heart, daughter; your
faith has made you well." And instantly the
woman was made well. [23]When Jesus came
to the leader's house and saw the flute players
and the crowd making a commotion, [24]he said,
"Go away; for the girl is not dead but sleeping."
And they laughed at him. [25]But when the crowd
had been put outside, he went in and took her by
the hand, and the girl got up. [26]And the report of this
spread throughout that district.

9:21 Was it a magic cloak?
Absolutely not! Jesus was not a magician. Salvation is not in any cloak or object, but in the person of Jesus!

9:22 *Jesus identifies the attitude of the woman (the need to touch Jesus' cloak) as an outward sign of her belief. Faith—or belief—alone makes salvation possible.*

r **9.18** Gk lacks *of the synagogue*

Jesus Heals Two Blind Men

27 As Jesus went on from there, two blind men followed him, crying loudly,
"Have mercy on us, Son of David!" 28When he entered the house, the blind
men came to him; and Jesus said to them, "Do you believe that I am able
to do this?" They said to him, "Yes, Lord." 29Then he touched their eyes and
said, "According to your faith let it be done to you." 30And their eyes
were opened. Then Jesus sternly ordered them, "See that no
one knows of this." 31But they went away and spread the
news about him throughout that district.

Jesus Heals One Who Was Mute

32 After they had gone away, a demoniac who
was mute was brought to him. 33And when
the demon had been cast out, the one who
had been mute spoke; and the crowds were
amazed and said, "Never has anything like
this been seen in Israel." 34But the Pharisees
said, "By the ruler of the demons he casts out
the demons."[s]

The Harvest Is Great, the Laborers Few

35 Then Jesus went about all the cities
and villages, teaching in their synagogues,
and proclaiming the good news of the
kingdom, and curing every disease and
every sickness. 36When he saw the crowds,

9:34 Why were the Pharisees unhappy?

The Pharisees did not believe that Jesus was the awaited Messiah. Because stubborn unbelief and jealousy often led to violence, Jesus asked those who had received the miracles to not tell anyone about them.

s **9.34** Other ancient authorities lack this verse

9:37 Harvest
Jesus used the image of gathering crops from a field to indicate that humanity was now ready to welcome the gift of God.

10:2 Twelve Apostles
They are twelve in number like the tribes of Israel. They are divided into six pairs so that one Apostle can always hold the other Apostle accountable to the truth as witnesses to Jesus. "Apostle" is a term that comes from the Greek language and means "sent."

10:5 Samaritans
They are Jews who lived in the region of Samaria, but were disliked because in the past they had mixed with pagans.

he had compassion for them, because they were
harassed and helpless, like sheep without a
shepherd. 37Then he said to his disciples, "The
harvest is plentiful, but the laborers are few;
38therefore ask the Lord of the harvest to send
out laborers into his harvest."

The Twelve Apostles

10 Then Jesus[t] summoned his
twelve disciples and gave them authority
over unclean spirits, to cast them out,
and to cure every disease and every sickness. 2These are the names of the twelve
apostles: first, Simon, also known as
Peter, and his brother Andrew; James son
of Zebedee, and his brother John; 3Philip
and Bartholomew; Thomas and Matthew
the tax collector; James son of Alphaeus,
and Thaddaeus;[u] 4Simon the Cananaean,
and Judas Iscariot, the one who betrayed
him.

The Mission of the Twelve

5 These twelve Jesus sent out with the following instructions: "Go nowhere among

t **10.1** Gk *he*
u **10.3** Other ancient authorities read *Lebbaeus*, or *Lebbaeus called Thaddaeus*

the Gentiles, and enter no town of the
Samaritans, 6but go rather to the lost
sheep of the house of Israel. 7As you go,
proclaim the good news, 'The kingdom
of heaven has come near.'[v] 8Cure the sick,
raise the dead, cleanse the lepers,[w] cast out
demons. You received without payment;
give without payment. 9Take no gold,
or silver, or copper in your belts, 10no
bag for your journey, or two tunics,
or sandals, or a staff; for laborers
deserve their food. 11Whatever town
or village you enter, find out who in
it is worthy, and stay there until you
leave. 12As you enter the house, greet
it. 13If the house is worthy, let your
peace come upon it; but if it is not
worthy, let your peace return to you. 14If
anyone will not welcome you or listen to
your words, shake off the dust from your
feet as you leave that house or town. 15Truly I
tell you, it will be more tolerable for the land of
Sodom and Gomorrah on the day of judgment
than for that town.

10:9–10 How does one go on a journey without packing a suitcase?

Jesus wanted his Apostles to only trust in God and to be free from any material interest.

10:15 Sodom and Gomorrah

These are two cities described in the Book of Genesis (18:20–19:29) that were destroyed by God because of the grave sins done by those who lived there.

v **10.7** Or *is at hand*

w **10.8** The terms *leper* and *leprosy* can refer to several diseases

Coming Persecutions

16 "See, I am sending you out like sheep into the midst
of wolves; so be wise as serpents and innocent as
doves. 17Beware of them, for they will hand you
over to councils and flog you in their synagogues;
18and you will be dragged before governors and
kings because of me, as a testimony to them
and the Gentiles. 19When they hand you over,
do not worry about how you are to speak or
what you are to say; for what you are to say
will be given to you at that time; 20for it is not
you who speak, but the Spirit of your Father
speaking through you. 21 Brother will betray
brother to death, and a father his child, and
children will rise against parents and have
them put to death; 22and you will be hated
by all because of my name. But the one who
endures to the end will be saved. 23When
they persecute you in one town, flee to the
next; for truly I tell you, you will not have
gone through all the towns of Israel before
the Son of Man comes.

24 "A disciple is not above the
teacher, nor a slave above the master;
25it is enough for the disciple to be like
the teacher, and the slave like the
master. If they have called the master

10:16 How is a person a serpent and a dove at the same time?

Being Apostles of the Lord was not easy. While carrying a message of peace, we were often persecuted; because of this we needed to be like Jesus: on the one hand mild and meek, and on the other careful and not foolish.

of the house Beelzebul, how much more will they malign those
of his household!

Whom to Fear

26 “So have no fear of them; for nothing is covered up that will not be uncovered, and nothing secret that will not become known.
27 What I say to you in the dark, tell in the light; and what you hear whispered, proclaim from the housetops.
28 Do not fear those who kill the body but cannot kill the soul; rather fear him who can destroy both soul and body in hell.[x]
29 Are not two sparrows sold for a penny? Yet not one of them will fall to the ground apart from your Father.
30 And even the hairs of your head are all counted.
31 So do not be afraid; you are of more value than many sparrows.

32 “Everyone therefore who acknowledges me before others, I also will acknowledge before my Father in heaven;
33 but whoever denies me before others, I also will deny before my Father in heaven.

10:21–23, 34–36 But Jesus said that we must honor our parents and live as brothers and sisters . . .

Certainly, but with these very strong words he wanted to warn us that not everyone would welcome him and his message, and that our preaching would produce crisis, separation, and fights—even in the same family.

10:27 Do I really have to go to the housetop?

Not anymore. When there were no microphones it was necessary to go to a high place to be heard. Jesus wanted his message to be heard by all.

x **10.28** Gk *Gehenna*

10:37 Love Jesus more than my parents? What does Jesus want of me?

Those who love Jesus, and recognize him as the best friend one could ever have, discover the greatest way to love even one's parents, every other person, and everything else—to the point of giving one's life for them, just as Jesus did.

Not Peace, but a Sword

34 "Do not think that I have come to bring peace to the earth; I have not come to bring peace, but a sword.

35 For I have come to set a man against his father,
and a daughter against her mother,
and a daughter-in-law against her mother-in-law;
36 and one's foes will be members of one's own household.

37 Whoever loves father or mother more than me is not worthy of me; and whoever loves son or daughter more than me is not worthy of me; 38 and whoever does not take up the cross and follow me is not worthy of me. 39 Those who find their life will lose it, and those who lose their life for my sake will find it.

Rewards

40 "Whoever welcomes you welcomes me, and whoever welcomes me welcomes the one who sent me. 41 Whoever welcomes a prophet in the name of a prophet will receive a prophet's reward; and whoever welcomes a righteous person in the name of a righteous person will receive the reward of the righteous; 42 and whoever gives even a cup of cold water to one of these little ones in the name of a disciple—truly I tell you, none of these will lose their reward."

Book III: The Mystery of His Kingdom (Mt 11:1–13:52)

Jesus begins to speak about himself. His works and his sermons attract attention. In chapters 11 and 12, Matthew begins to describe the first reactions of those who meet Jesus. It was not easy for anyone to understand what Jesus was teaching. It was difficult for John the Baptist, the crowds, the scribes, the Pharisees, and often even Jesus' closest disciples. One of the ways Jesus taught was by parables—stories that contain lessons and often more lessons than one might think. This third section of Matthew's Gospel ends with several great parables (13: 1–52). In these parables, Jesus describes the characteristics of the kingdom of heaven. The true King has a lordship that avoids the weapons of power, greatness, and violence. Instead, he relies on the humble strength of a small seed placed in the earth . . . and in each person's heart!

11 Now when Jesus had finished instructing his
twelve disciples, he went on from there to teach and
proclaim his message in their cities.

Messengers from John the Baptist

2 When John heard in prison what the
Messiah[y] was doing, he sent word by his[z]
disciples (3) and said to him, "Are you the
one who is to come, or are we to wait
for another?" 4 Jesus answered them, "Go
and tell John what you hear and see:

11:3 Not even John the Baptist understood who Jesus was?

Like many other people after Jesus' first miracles and sermons, even John asked himself who Jesus was. Nobody expected the Messiah to be like a humble servant. Jesus invited everyone to see and judge his works.

y **11.2** Or *the Christ*

z **11.2** Other ancient authorities read *two of his*

[5]the blind receive their sight, the lame
walk, the lepers[a] are cleansed, the deaf
hear, the dead are raised, and the poor
have good news brought to them. [6]And
blessed is anyone who takes no offense
at me."

Jesus Praises John the Baptist

7 As they went away, Jesus began to speak to
the crowds about John: "What did you go out
into the wilderness to look at? A reed shaken
by the wind? [8]What then did you go out to see?
Someone[b] dressed in soft robes? Look, those who
wear soft robes are in royal palaces. [9]What then did
you go out to see? A prophet?[c] Yes, I tell you, and
more than a prophet. [10]This is the one about whom
it is written,

'See, I am sending my messenger ahead of you,
who will prepare your way before you.'

[11]Truly I tell you, among those born of women no one
has arisen greater than John the Baptist; yet the least
in the kingdom of heaven is greater than he. [12]From
the days of John the Baptist until now the kingdom
of heaven has suffered violence,[d] and the violent

a **11.5** The terms *leper* and *leprosy* can refer to several diseases
b **11.8** Or *Why then did you go out? To see someone*
c **11.9** Other ancient authorities read *Why then did you go out? To see a prophet?*
d **11.12** Or *has been coming violently*

take it by force. 13For all the prophets and the
law prophesied until John came; 14and if you
are willing to accept it, he is Elijah who is to
come. 15Let anyone with ears[e] listen!
16 "But to what will I compare this generation? It is like children sitting in the marketplaces and calling to one another,
17 'We played the flute for you, and you
did not dance;
we wailed, and you did not
mourn.'
18For John came neither eating nor
drinking, and they say, 'He has a
demon'; 19the Son of Man came eating
and drinking, and they say, 'Look, a
glutton and a drunkard, a friend of tax
collectors and sinners!' Yet wisdom is vindicated by her deeds."[f]

Woes to Unrepentant Cities

20 Then he began to reproach the cities
in which most of his deeds of power
had been done, because they did not

11:14 Elijah

He was the great prophet who, according to Jewish custom, would return to prepare the Messiah's coming. Jesus confirms that the wait for the new Elijah is fulfilled in John the Baptist.

11:16–17 Were the children bored?

In a way, yes. The children Jesus talks about were bored, but more than that they could not make the decision to escape their boredom. The same was also true for many adults—for whom Jesus was making the comparison—who could not decide on anything, especially on faith, who were always unsatisfied and never convinced of any religious idea.

e **11.15** Other ancient authorities add *to hear*
f **11.19** Other ancient authorities read *children*

11:21–24 Chorazin, Bethsaida, Capernaum
They were villages in which Jesus performed different miracles but where the people refused to turn back to God, even after seeing the miracles.

11:21–24 Tyre, Sidon, Sodom
According to Jesus, these foreign and pagan cities would have listened more closely to his preaching and would have repented. In saying this, he is expressing great disappointment in the people of Chorazin, Bethsaida, and Capernaum.

11:25–27 It is one of Jesus' prayers!
The Our Father is one of the few prayers of Jesus that we have. Jesus called God "Father" because he knew himself to be the beloved Son. He knew God loved him like he loves all the little ones of the earth who see God as the one who made them.

repent. 21"Woe to you, Chorazin! Woe to you,
Bethsaida! For if the deeds of power done in
you had been done in Tyre and Sidon, they
would have repented long ago in sackcloth and
ashes. 22But I tell you, on the day of judgment it
will be more tolerable for Tyre and Sidon than
for you. 23And you, Capernaum,
will you be exalted to heaven?
No, you will be brought down to Hades.
For if the deeds of power done in you
had been done in Sodom, it would have
remained until this day. 24But I tell you that
on the day of judgment it will be more tolerable for the land of Sodom than for you."

Jesus Thanks His Father

25 At that time Jesus said, "I thank[g] you,
Father, Lord of heaven and earth, because
you have hidden these things from the
wise and the intelligent and have revealed
them to infants; 26yes, Father, for such was
your gracious will.[h] 27All things have been
handed over to me by my Father; and no
one knows the Son except the Father, and
no one knows the Father except the Son and
anyone to whom the Son chooses to reveal
him.

g **11.25** Or *praise*
h **11.26** Or *for so it was well-pleasing in your sight*

28 "Come to me, all you that are weary and are carrying heavy
burdens, and I will give you rest. 29Take my yoke upon
you, and learn from me; for I am gentle and humble
in heart, and you will find rest for your souls. 30For
my yoke is easy, and my burden is light."

Plucking Grain on the Sabbath

12 At that time Jesus went through the grainfields
on the sabbath; his disciples were hungry, and they
began to pluck heads of grain and to eat. 2When
the Pharisees saw it, they said to him, "Look,
your disciples are doing what is not lawful to
do on the sabbath." 3He said to them, "Have
you not read what David did when he and his
companions were hungry? 4He entered the
house of God and ate the bread of the Presence, which it was not lawful for him or his
companions to eat, but only for the priests. 5Or
have you not read in the law that on the
sabbath the priests in the temple break
the sabbath and yet are guiltless? 6I tell

11:29 Yoke
This heavy, wooden tool is attached to a plow and is placed on the neck of two oxen, which pull the plow through the fields.

12:1 Sabbath
That was the day dedicated to God, on which no type of unnecessary work could be done.

12:6 Temple
It was the most important place for Jews. The sacred breads represented the twelve tribes of Israel before God and could not be eaten except by priests. But now there was Jesus, the Son of God, who was and is far more important than the Temple and every law.

12:9 Synagogue
A place of prayer and learning for the Jews

you, something greater than the temple is here.
7But if you had known what this means, 'I desire
mercy and not sacrifice,' you would not have
condemned the guiltless. 8For the Son of Man is
lord of the sabbath."

The Man with a Withered Hand

9 He left that place and entered their synagogue;
10 a man was there with a withered hand, and
they asked him, "Is it lawful to cure on the
sabbath?" so that they might accuse him.
11He said to them, "Suppose one of you has
only one sheep and it falls into a pit on the
sabbath; will you not lay hold of it and lift it
out? 12How much more valuable is a human
being than a sheep! So it is lawful to do
good on the sabbath." 13Then he said to the
man, "Stretch out your hand." He stretched
it out, and it was restored, as sound as the
other. 14But the Pharisees went out and
conspired against him, how to destroy him.

God's Chosen Servant

15 When Jesus became aware of this, he departed.
Many crowds[i] followed him, and he cured all of
them, 16and he ordered them not to make him
known. 17This was to fulfill what had been spoken
through the prophet Isaiah:
18 "Here is my servant, whom I have chosen,
my beloved, with whom my soul is well pleased.

i **12.15** Other ancient authorities lack *crowds*

I will put my Spirit upon him,
and he will proclaim justice to the Gentiles.
19 He will not wrangle or cry aloud,
nor will anyone hear his voice in the streets.
20 He will not break a bruised reed
or quench a smoldering wick
until he brings justice to victory.
21 And in his name the Gentiles will
hope."

Jesus and Beelzebul

22 Then they brought to him a demoniac who
was blind and mute; and he cured him, so
that the one who had been mute could speak
and see. 23All the crowds were amazed and
said, "Can this be the Son of David?" 24But
when the Pharisees heard it, they said, "It is
only by Beelzebul, the ruler of the demons, that
this fellow casts out the demons." 25He knew
what they were thinking and said to them, "Every
kingdom divided against itself is laid waste, and
no city or house divided against itself will stand. 26If
Satan casts out Satan, he is divided against himself;
how then will his kingdom stand? 27If I cast out demons
by Beelzebul, by whom do your own exorcists[j] cast them
out? Therefore they will be your judges. 28But if it is by the
Spirit of God that I cast out demons, then the kingdom of God has
come to you. 29Or how can one enter a strong man's house and plunder

12:10 What was wrong with healing on the Sabbath?

Jesus clashed with a very strong tradition by saying the work of God can be done at all times. To heal someone is to do God's work and is different from the unnecessary work that Jewish Law banned. Therefore, to heal is lawful on the Sabbath.

12:18 Who is being spoken about?

Jesus, himself. Notice that these words are similar to the ones that God said after Jesus' baptism.

j **12.27** Gk *sons*

his property, without first tying up the strong man? Then indeed the
house can be plundered. 30Whoever is not with me is against me,
and whoever does not gather with me scatters. 31Therefore I tell you,
people will be forgiven for every sin and blasphemy, but blasphemy against the Spirit will not be forgiven. 32Whoever
speaks a word against the Son of Man will be forgiven, but whoever speaks against the Holy Spirit
will not be forgiven, either in this age or in the
age to come.

12:31 What is the blasphemy against the Spirit?

Jesus was not talking about a vulgar word, but about some people's total rejection of God and stubborn refusal to recognize the signs of his presence. God, in his love, respects our freedom, even when it goes against his will.

A Tree and Its Fruit

33 "Either make the tree good, and its fruit
good; or make the tree bad, and its fruit
bad; for the tree is known by its fruit.
34You brood of vipers! How can you
speak good things, when you are evil?
For out of the abundance of the heart
the mouth speaks. 35The good person
brings good things out of a good treasure, and the evil person brings evil
things out of an evil treasure. 36I tell
you, on the day of judgment you will
have to give an account for every care-
less word you utter; 37for by your words
you will be justified, and by your words
you will be condemned."

The Sign of Jonah

38 Then some of the scribes and Pharisees said to him, "Teacher,
we wish to see a sign from you." 39But he answered them, "An
evil and adulterous generation asks for a sign, but no sign will be
given to it except the sign of the prophet Jonah. 40For just as Jonah
was three days and three nights in the belly of the sea monster,
so for three days and three nights the Son of
Man will be in the heart of the earth. 41The
people of Nineveh will rise up at the judgment with this generation and condemn it,
because they repented at the proclamation
of Jonah, and see, something greater than
Jonah is here! 42The queen of the South will
rise up at the judgment with this generation and condemn it, because she came from the ends of the earth to listen to the wisdom of Solomon, and see, something greater than Solomon is here!

12:42 Queen of the South, Solomon

The first Book of Kings (10:1–10) contains a story about a famous queen who makes a long trip to meet the very wise King Solomon. Jesus recalls this story and affirms that he is much more important than Solomon or Jonah.

12:47 Brothers
When Jews used this word they also meant cousins and other close relatives.

The Return of the Unclean Spirit

43 "When the unclean spirit has gone out of a
person, it wanders through waterless regions looking
for a resting place, but it finds none. 44Then it says,
'I will return to my house from which I came.' When
it comes, it finds it empty, swept, and put in order.
45Then it goes and brings along seven other spirits
more evil than itself, and they enter and live there;
and the last state of that person is worse than the
first. So will it be also with this evil generation."

The True Kindred of Jesus

46 While he was still speaking to the crowds, his
mother and his brothers were standing outside,
wanting to speak to him. 47Someone told him,
"Look, your mother and your brothers are
standing outside, wanting to speak to you."[k]
48But to the one who had told him this,
Jesus[l] replied, "Who is my mother, and
who are my brothers?" 49And pointing
to his disciples, he said, "Here are my
mother and my brothers! 50For whoever does the will of my Father in
heaven is my brother and sister and
mother."

k **12.47** Other ancient authorities lack verse 47
l **12.48** Gk *he*

The Parable of the Sower

13 That same day Jesus went out of the house
and sat beside the sea. 2Such great crowds gathered around him that he got into a boat and sat
there, while the whole crowd stood on the beach.
3And he told them many things in parables,
saying: "Listen! A sower went out to sow. 4And
as he sowed, some seeds fell on the path, and the
birds came and ate them up. 5Other seeds fell on
rocky ground, where they did not have much soil,
and they sprang up quickly, since they had no
depth of soil. 6But when the sun rose, they
were scorched; and since they had no
root, they withered away. 7Other seeds
fell among thorns, and the thorns grew
up and choked them. 8Other seeds
fell on good soil and brought forth
grain, some a hundredfold, some
sixty, some thirty. 9Let anyone with
ears[m] listen!"

13:3 Parables

Jesus often used these little stories to illustrate his teaching. I have gathered many of these in this third great discourse by Jesus.

13:3 Who is this sower?

It was Jesus himself who was the sower because he announced the word of the kingdom. He later explains the meaning of the parable (read verses 18–23).

m **13.9** Other ancient authorities add *to hear*

The Purpose of the Parables

10 Then the disciples came and asked him, "Why do you
speak to them in parables?" 11He answered, "To you it has
been given to know the secrets[n] of the kingdom of heaven,
but to them it has not been given. 12For to those who have,
more will be given, and they will have an abundance;
but from those who have nothing, even what they have
will be taken away. 13The reason I speak to them in
parables is that 'seeing they do not perceive, and
hearing they do not listen, nor do they understand.'
14With them indeed is fulfilled the prophecy of
Isaiah that says:

'You will indeed listen, but never understand,
and you will indeed look, but never perceive.
15 For this people's heart has grown dull,
and their ears are hard of hearing,
and they have shut their eyes;
so that they might not look with their eyes,
and listen with their ears,
and understand with their heart and turn—
and I would heal them.'

16But blessed are your eyes, for they see, and
your ears, for they hear. 17Truly I tell you, many
prophets and righteous people longed to see what you
see, but did not see it, and to hear what you hear, but did
not hear it.

13:11–12 Why be so hard on those who already have so little?

Those who trust in Jesus understand and have everything. Those who do not welcome him as a friend do not understand what he is saying and lose what he is offering.

n **13.11** Or *mysteries*

The Parable of the Sower Explained

18 "Hear then the parable of the sower. [19]When
anyone hears the word of the kingdom and
does not understand it, the evil one comes and
snatches away what is sown in the heart; this is
what was sown on the path. [20]As for what was
sown on rocky ground, this is the one who
hears the word and immediately receives it
with joy; [21]yet such a person has no root, but
endures only for a while, and when trouble or
persecution arises on account of the word, that
person immediately falls away.[o] [22]As for what was
sown among thorns, this is the one who hears the
word, but the cares of the world and the lure of
wealth choke the word, and it yields nothing.
[23]But as for what was sown on good soil, this
is the one who hears the word and understands it, who indeed bears fruit and yields, in
one case a hundredfold, in another sixty, and
in another thirty."

The Parable of Weeds among the Wheat

24 He put before them another parable: "The kingdom of
heaven may be compared to someone who sowed good
seed in his field; [25]but while everybody was asleep, an
enemy came and sowed weeds among the wheat, and

13:25 Weeds

This useless plant ruins the harvest by taking up space and nutrients where other plants—like wheat—grow. It is used as a symbol of discord among Christ's disciples.

o **13.21** Gk *stumbles*

13:28 Those slaves are right! Would it not have been better to intervene immediately?

First, you may have noticed the word "slaves." Slavery in the Bible was actually very different than what slavery was like in early America. "Slaves" in the Bible were more like servants who had their needs taken care of by their master (such as home, food, etc.). With this story, Jesus wants to caution us that judgment should be left to God alone and that our role is to preach repentance with patience and love.

13:31 How large is a mustard seed?

It is very small, about the size of the head of a pin. That is how the kingdom of God grows here on earth—it starts very small, but when it grows it is capable of bearing great fruit.

then went away. 26So when the plants came up and bore grain,
then the weeds appeared as well. 27And the slaves of the
householder came and said to him, 'Master, did you not
sow good seed in your field? Where, then, did these
weeds come from?' 28He answered, 'An enemy
has done this.' The slaves said to him, 'Then do
you want us to go and gather them?' 29But he
replied, 'No; for in gathering the weeds you
would uproot the wheat along with them.
30Let both of them grow together until the
harvest; and at harvest time I will tell
the reapers, Collect the weeds first and
bind them in bundles to be burned, but
gather the wheat into my barn.'"

The Parable of the Mustard Seed

31 He put before them another parable: "The kingdom of heaven is
like a mustard seed that someone
took and sowed in his field; 32it is the
smallest of all the seeds, but when it
has grown it is the greatest of shrubs and
becomes a tree, so that the birds of the
air come and make nests in its branches."

The Parable of the Yeast

33 He told them another parable: "The kingdom of heaven
is like yeast that a woman took and mixed in with[p] three
measures of flour until all of it was leavened."

The Use of Parables

34 Jesus told the crowds all these things in parables; without
a parable he told them nothing. 35This was to fulfill what had
been spoken through the prophet:[q]

"I will open my mouth to speak in parables;
I will proclaim what has been hidden from the foundation of the world."[r]

Jesus Explains the Parable of the Weeds

36 Then he left the crowds and went into the house. And his disciples approached him, saying, "Explain to us the parable of the
weeds of the field." 37He answered, "The one who sows the good
seed is the Son of Man; 38the field is the world, and the good seed
are the children of the kingdom; the weeds are the children of the
evil one, 39and the enemy who sowed them is the devil; the harvest is the end of the age, and the reapers are angels. 40Just as the
weeds are collected and burned up with fire, so will it be at the
end of the age. 41The Son of Man will send his angels, and they
will collect out of his kingdom all causes of sin and all evildoers,
42and they will throw them into the furnace of fire, where there
will be weeping and gnashing of teeth. 43Then the righteous will
shine like the sun in the kingdom of their Father. Let anyone with
ears[s] listen!

p **13.33** Gk *hid in*
q **13.35** Other ancient authorities read *the prophet Isaiah*
r **13.35** Other ancient authorities lack *of the world*
s **13.43** Other ancient authorities add *to hear*

Three Parables

44 "The kingdom of heaven is like treasure hidden in a field, which someone found and hid; then in his joy he goes and sells all that he has and buys that field.

45 "Again, the kingdom of heaven is like a merchant in search of fine pearls; 46on finding one pearl of great value, he went and sold all that he had and bought it.

47 "Again, the kingdom of heaven is like a
net that was thrown into the sea and caught
fish of every kind; 48when it was full, they
drew it ashore, sat down, and put the good
into baskets but threw out the bad. 49So it
will be at the end of the age. The angels
will come out and separate the evil from
the righteous 50and throw them into the
furnace of fire, where there will be weeping
and gnashing of teeth.

Treasures New and Old

51 "Have you understood all this?" They answered,
"Yes." 52And he said to them, "Therefore every scribe
who has been trained for the kingdom of heaven is like
the master of a household who brings out of his treasure
what is new and what is old." 53When Jesus had finished these
parables, he left that place.

13:47–50 Isn't this parable similar to the one about the weeds?

Yes! Jesus repeats that the moment of sorting and judgment will take place at the end of time.

13:52 Who were the scribes?

They were people who really knew the Scriptures. Some of them welcomed Jesus' teaching and were able to unite Israel's wisdom (the ancient things) with Jesus' message (the new things).

Book IV: The Life of a Brother [Mt 13:53-18:35]

The fourth book into which Matthew divides his Gospel opens with a section—chapters thirteen to seventeen—which addresses the question of Jesus' identity. This question is brought up many times. The answers vary greatly depending on who is answering. For the people of Nazareth, Jesus remains "the carpenter's son" (13:55). For Herod, he is "John the Baptist . . . raised from the dead" (14:2). For the Canaanite woman, he is "Son of David" (15:22). For his disciples Jesus is "truly . . . the Son of God" (14:33)—a belief confirmed by the voice of God himself during the transfiguration when God says of Jesus "This is my Son, the Beloved; with him I am well pleased" (17:5). Next is a speech about Christian behavior (18: 1–35) addressed to the circle of Jesus' closest friends and followers. Jesus tells them how the Christians' life ought to be guided by understanding, loving correction, forgiveness, and attention to those far from God.

The Rejection of Jesus at Nazareth

54 He came to his hometown and began to teach
the people[t] in their synagogue, so that they were
astounded and said, "Where did this man get this
wisdom and these deeds of power? 55Is not this the
carpenter's son? Is not his mother called Mary? And
are not his brothers James and Joseph and Simon and
Judas? 56And are not all his sisters with us? Where
then did this man get all this?" 57And they took
offense at him. But Jesus said to them, "Prophets
are not without honor except in their own country
and in their own house." 58And he did not do many
deeds of power there, because of their unbelief.

t **13.54** Gk *them*

The Death of John the Baptist

14 At that time Herod the ruler[u] heard reports about
Jesus; 2and he said to his servants, "This is John the Baptist; he has been raised from the dead, and for this reason
these powers are at work in him." 3For Herod had arrested
John, bound him, and put him in prison on account of
Herodias, his brother Philip's wife,[v] 4because John
had been telling him, "It is not lawful for you
to have her." 5Though Herod[w] wanted to put
him to death, he feared the crowd, because
they regarded him as a prophet. 6But when
Herod's birthday came, the daughter of
Herodias danced before the company, and
she pleased Herod 7so much that he promised on oath to grant her whatever she
might ask. 8Prompted by her mother, she
said, "Give me the head of John the Baptist
here on a platter." 9The king was grieved, yet
out of regard for his oaths and for the guests,
he commanded it to be given; 10he sent and
had John beheaded in the prison. 11The head
was brought on a platter and given to the girl,
who brought it to her mother. 12His disciples came
and took the body and buried it; then they went and
told Jesus.

14:4 Why couldn't Herod have Herodias for a wife?

John the Baptist pointed out that Herod's relationship with Herodias was illegal because she was still his brother's wife. For this reason, Herodias has John killed by taking advantage of the king's weakness.

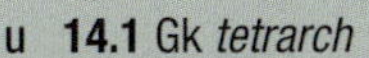

u **14.1** Gk *tetrarch*
v **14.3** Other ancient authorities read *his brother's wife*
w **14.5** Gk *he*

Feeding the Five Thousand

13 Now when Jesus heard this, he withdrew from there in a boat
to a deserted place by himself. But when the crowds heard it, they
followed him on foot from the towns. 14When he went ashore,
he saw a great crowd; and he had compassion for them and
cured their sick. 15When it was evening, the disciples came
to him and said, "This is a deserted place, and the hour
is now late; send the crowds away so that they may go
into the villages and buy food for themselves." 16Jesus
said to them, "They need not go away; you give
them something to eat." 17They replied, "We have
nothing here but five loaves and two fish." 18And he
said, "Bring them here to me." 19Then he ordered
the crowds to sit down on the grass. Taking the five
loaves and the two fish, he looked up to heaven, and
blessed and broke the loaves, and gave them to the
disciples, and the disciples gave them to the crowds.
20And all ate and were filled; and they took up what was
left over of the broken pieces, twelve baskets full. 21And
those who ate were about five thousand men, besides women
and children.

14:19 I've seen these gestures before!

You are right! In the celebration of the Mass the priest repeats these gestures and these words.

Jesus Walks on the Water

22 Immediately he made the disciples get into
the boat and go on ahead to the other side,
while he dismissed the crowds. 23And after
he had dismissed the crowds, he went up
the mountain by himself to pray. When
evening came, he was there alone, 24but
by this time the boat, battered by the
waves, was far from the land,[x] for the
wind was against them. 25And early in
the morning he came walking toward
them on the sea. 26But when the disciples saw him walking on the sea, they
were terrified, saying, "It is a ghost!"
And they cried out in fear. 27But immediately Jesus spoke to them and said, "Take
heart, it is I; do not be afraid."
28 Peter answered him, "Lord, if it is you,
command me to come to you on the water."
29He said, "Come." So Peter got out of the boat,
started walking on the water, and came toward
Jesus. 30But when he noticed the strong wind,[y] he
became frightened, and beginning to sink, he cried out,
"Lord, save me!" 31Jesus immediately reached out his hand and
caught him, saying to him, "You of little faith, why did you doubt?" 32When
they got into the boat, the wind ceased. 33And those in the boat worshiped
him, saying, "Truly you are the Son of God."

14:29 How was Peter able to walk on water?

He simply trusted in the words of Jesus, the only one who could do such a miracle. When Peter became distracted he, out of fear, doubted and began to sink.

x **14.24** Other ancient authorities read *was out on the sea*
y **14.30** Other ancient authorities read *the wind*

Jesus Heals the Sick in Gennesaret

34 When they had crossed over, they came to land at
Gennesaret. 35 After the people of that place recognized
him, they sent word throughout the region and brought
all who were sick to him, 36 and begged him that they
might touch even the fringe of his cloak; and all
who touched it were healed.

The Tradition of the Elders

15 Then Pharisees and scribes came to
Jesus from Jerusalem and said, 2 "Why do your
disciples break the tradition of the elders?
For they do not wash their hands before
they eat." 3 He answered them, "And why do
you break the commandment of God for the
sake of your tradition? 4 For God said,[z] 'Honor
your father and your mother,' and, 'Whoever
speaks evil of father or mother must surely die.'
5 But you say that whoever tells father or mother,
'Whatever support you might have had from me
is given to God,'[a] then that person need not honor
the father.[b] 6 So, for the sake of your tradition, you
make void the word[c] of God. 7 You hypocrites! Isaiah
prophesied rightly about you when he said:

15:2 Did you not wash your hands before eating?

In the time of Jesus, we washed our hands not only for hygienic reasons but also for religious ones. Jesus, however, was more concerned with the cleaning of our hearts than of our hands. But we should still wash our hands before eating!

15:7 Hypocrites

False people; liars.

z **15.4** Other ancient authorities read *commanded, saying*
a **15.5** Or *is an offering*
b **15.5** Other ancient authorities add *or the mother*
c **15.6** Other ancient authorities read *law*; others, *commandment*

8 'This people honors me with their lips,
but their hearts are far from me;
9 in vain do they worship me,
teaching human precepts as doctrines.'"

Things That Defile

10 Then he called the crowd to him and said to them,
"Listen and understand: 11it is not what goes into the
mouth that defiles a person, but it is what comes
out of the mouth that defiles." 12Then the disciples
approached and said to him, "Do you know that the
Pharisees took offense when they heard what you said?"
13He answered, "Every plant that my heavenly Father
has not planted will be uprooted. 14Let them alone;
they are blind guides of the blind.[d] And if one blind
person guides another, both will fall into a pit." 15But
Peter said to him, "Explain this parable to us." 16Then
he said, "Are you also still without understanding?
17Do you not see that whatever goes into the mouth
enters the stomach, and goes out into the sewer? 18But
what comes out of the mouth proceeds from
the heart, and this is what defiles. 19For
out of the heart come evil intentions,
murder, adultery, fornication, theft, false
witness, slander. 20These are what defile
a person, but to eat with unwashed hands
does not defile."

15:19 Heart

In the first century, people associated the heart with man's capacity to decide between good and evil. Jesus saw that contact with situations was not the origin of the heart's impurity, but rather the heart's response to those situations.

d **15.14** Other ancient authorities lack *of the blind*

15:22 Canaanite
Non-Jewish person born in Phoenicia (also called Canaan)

15:23, 26 Why was Jesus so rude to that woman?
Jesus wanted to give priority to his people . . . following the plan of God as revealed by the prophets. The insistence and the faith of the woman convinced Jesus to do a miracle. The Father gives a glimpse that the Son's mission is open also to the pagan world.

The Canaanite Woman's Faith

21 Jesus left that place and went away to the district of Tyre
and Sidon. 22Just then a Canaanite woman from that region
came out and started shouting, "Have mercy on me, Lord,
Son of David; my daughter is tormented by a demon." 23But
he did not answer her at all. And his disciples came and
urged him, saying, "Send her away, for she keeps shouting
after us." 24He answered, "I was sent only to the lost
sheep of the house of Israel." 25But she came and knelt
before him, saying, "Lord, help me." 26He answered, "It
is not fair to take the children's food and throw it
to the dogs." 27She said, "Yes, Lord, yet even the
dogs eat the crumbs that fall from their masters'
table." 28Then Jesus answered her, "Woman,
great is your faith! Let it be done for you as
you wish." And her daughter was healed
instantly.

Jesus Cures Many People

29 After Jesus had left that place, he passed
along the Sea of Galilee, and he went up
the mountain, where he sat down. 30Great
crowds came to him, bringing with them

the lame, the maimed, the blind, the mute, and many others. They put them
at his feet, and he cured them, [31]so that the crowd was amazed when they
saw the mute speaking, the maimed whole, the lame walking, and the blind
seeing. And they praised the God of Israel.

Feeding the Four Thousand

32 Then Jesus called his disciples to him and said, "I have
compassion for the crowd, because they have been with
me now for three days and have nothing to eat; and
I do not want to send them away hungry, for they
might faint on the way." [33]The disciples said to him,
"Where are we to get enough bread in the desert to
feed so great a crowd?" [34]Jesus asked them, "How
many loaves have you?" They said, "Seven, and a few
small fish." [35]Then ordering the crowd to sit down
on the ground, [36]he took the seven loaves and the
fish; and after giving thanks he broke them and gave
them to the disciples, and the disciples gave them
to the crowds. [37]And all of them ate and were filled;
and they took up the broken pieces left over, seven
baskets full. [38]Those who had eaten were four thousand
men, besides women and children. [39]After sending away
the crowds, he got into the boat and went to the region of
Magadan.[e]

e **15.39** Other ancient authorities read *Magdala* or *Magdalan*

16:2–4 Even my grandma has a similar proverb!

Sometimes, knowing how to recognize so many signs will make a person miss the most important one.

16:6 Was it a special yeast?

The yeast of the Pharisees and Sadducees ruined the flour. In other words, their teachings had bad effects on the people.

The Demand for a Sign

16 The Pharisees and Sadducees came, and to test
Jesus[f] they asked him to show them a sign from
heaven. 2 He answered them, "When it is evening,
you say, 'It will be fair weather, for the sky is red.'
3 And in the morning, 'It will be stormy today, for
the sky is red and threatening.' You know how
to interpret the appearance of the sky, but you
cannot interpret the signs of the times.[g] 4 An
evil and adulterous generation asks for a
sign, but no sign will be given to it except
the sign of Jonah." Then he left them and
went away.

The Yeast of the Pharisees and Sadducees

5 When the disciples reached the other side,
they had forgotten to bring any bread. 6 Jesus
said to them, "Watch out, and beware of the
yeast of the Pharisees and Sadducees." 7 They
said to one another, "It is because we have
brought no bread." 8 And becoming aware of it,
Jesus said, "You of little faith, why are you talking
about having no bread? 9 Do you still not perceive?
Do you not remember the five loaves for the five
thousand, and how many baskets you gathered? 10 Or

f **16.1** Gk *him*
g **16.3** Other ancient authorities lack 2*When it is . . . of the times*

the seven loaves for the four thousand, and how many baskets you gathered?
11How could you fail to perceive that I was not speaking about bread? Beware
of the yeast of the Pharisees and Sadducees!" 12Then they understood that he
had not told them to beware of the yeast of bread, but of the teaching of the
Pharisees and Sadducees.

Peter's Declaration about Jesus

13 Now when Jesus came into the district of Caesarea Philippi, he asked his
disciples, "Who do people say that the Son of Man is?" 14And they
said, "Some say John the Baptist, but others Elijah, and still
others Jeremiah or one of the prophets." 15He said to
them, "But who do you say that I am?" 16Simon Peter
answered, "You are the Messiah,[h] the Son of the
living God." 17And Jesus answered him, "Blessed
are you, Simon son of Jonah! For flesh and blood
has not revealed this to you, but my Father in
heaven. 18And I tell you, you are Peter,[i] and
on this rock[j] I will build my church, and the
gates of Hades will not prevail against it.
19I will give you the keys of the kingdom of
heaven, and whatever you bind on earth will
be bound in heaven, and whatever you loose
on earth will be loosed in heaven." 20Then he
sternly ordered the disciples not to tell anyone
that he was[k] the Messiah.[l]

16:17–18 What was Saint Peter's real name?

His name was Simon, but Jesus changed his name to Peter to indicate the mission with which he would be entrusted. Peter would be the solid rock—"petra" is Greek for rock—upon which the Church was built.

h **16.16** Or *the Christ*
i **16.18** Gk *Petros*
j **16.18** Gk *petra*
k **16.20** Other ancient authorities add *Jesus*
l **16.20** Or *the Christ*

Jesus Foretells His Death and Resurrection

21 From that time on, Jesus began to show his disciples that he must
go to Jerusalem and undergo great suffering at the hands of the elders
and chief priests and scribes, and be killed, and on the third day be
raised. 22And Peter took him aside and began to rebuke him,
saying, "God forbid it, Lord! This must never happen to
you." 23But he turned and said to Peter, "Get behind
me, Satan! You are a stumbling block to me; for you
are setting your mind not on divine things but on
human things."

The Cross and Self-Denial

24 Then Jesus told his disciples, "If any want
to become my followers, let them deny themselves and take up their cross and follow me.
25For those who want to save their life will lose
it, and those who lose their life for my sake will
find it. 26For what will it profit them if they gain the
whole world but forfeit their life? Or what will they
give in return for their life?

27 "For the Son of Man is to come with his angels in
the glory of his Father, and then he will repay everyone for
what has been done. 28Truly I tell you, there are some standing
here who will not taste death before they see the Son of Man
coming in his kingdom."

16:21–23 Why does Jesus begin to speak about his death?

Little by little Jesus began to reveal that remaining faithful to God would lead to his death. The Apostles (especially Peter) did not want to consider this as a possibility.

The Transfiguration

17 Six days later, Jesus took with him Peter and James and his
brother John and led them up a high mountain, by themselves.
2And he was transfigured before them, and his face shone like
the sun, and his clothes became dazzling white. 3Suddenly there
appeared to them Moses and Elijah, talking with him. 4Then
Peter said to Jesus, "Lord, it is good for us to be here; if you
wish, I[m] will make three dwellings[n] here, one for you, one for
Moses, and one for Elijah." 5While he was still speaking,
suddenly a bright cloud overshadowed them, and
from the cloud a voice said, "This is my Son, the
Beloved;[o] with him I am well pleased; listen to
him!" 6When the disciples heard this, they fell
to the ground and were overcome by fear. 7But
Jesus came and touched them, saying, "Get
up and do not be afraid." 8And when they
looked up, they saw no one except Jesus
himself alone.

9 As they were coming down the mountain, Jesus ordered them, "Tell no one about
the vision until after the Son of Man has been
raised from the dead." 10And the disciples asked
him, "Why, then, do the scribes say that Elijah
must come first?" 11He replied, "Elijah is indeed
coming and will restore all things; 12but I tell you that
Elijah has already come, and they did not recognize

17:6 Did Jesus really become so radiant?

Yes. Jesus showed himself in all his glory as Son of God to three of us. It was bright and absolutely unexpected by the disciples who were, in all honesty, frightened by what they saw.

m **17.4** Other ancient authorities read *we*
n **17.4** Or *tents*
o **17.5** Or *my beloved Son*

him, but they did to him whatever they pleased. So also
the Son of Man is about to suffer at their hands." 13Then
the disciples understood that he was speaking to
them about John the Baptist.

Jesus Cures a Boy with a Demon

14 When they came to the crowd, a man came
to him, knelt before him, 15and said, "Lord,
have mercy on my son, for he is an epileptic
and he suffers terribly; he often falls into the
fire and often into the water. 16And I brought
him to your disciples, but they could not cure
him." 17Jesus answered, "You faithless and
perverse generation, how much longer must I
be with you? How much longer must I put up
with you? Bring him here to me." 18And Jesus
rebuked the demon,[p] and it[q] came out of
him, and the boy was cured instantly.
19Then the disciples came to Jesus privately and said, "Why could we not

p **17.18** Gk *it* or *him*
q **17.18** Gk *the demon*

17:20 Is it really enough to have just a little faith to perform a miracle?
Even just a little faith in our all-powerful God is enough for God to work through the person to do miraculous deeds.

17:23 Why were you sad if after he would resurrect?
We heard Jesus speak about "resurrection," but did not understand what it meant. We were sad because all we understood was that he had to die.

cast it out?" 20He said to them, "Because of your little
faith. For truly I tell you, if you have faith the size
of a[r] mustard seed, you will say to this mountain,
'Move from here to there,' and it will move; and
nothing will be impossible for you."[s]

Jesus Again Foretells His Death and Resurrection

22 As they were gathering[t] in Galilee,
Jesus said to them, "The Son of Man is
going to be betrayed into human hands,
23and they will kill him, and on the third
day he will be raised." And they were
greatly distressed.

Jesus and the Temple Tax

24 When they reached Capernaum, the
collectors of the temple tax[u] came to
Peter and said, "Does your teacher not pay
the temple tax?"[v] 25He said, "Yes, he does."
And when he came home, Jesus spoke of it
first, asking, "What do you think, Simon? From
whom do kings of the earth take toll or tribute?
From their children or from others?" 26When Peter[w]

r **17.20** Gk *faith as a grain of*
s **17.20** Other ancient authorities add verse 21, *But this kind does not come out except by prayer and fasting*
t **17.22** Other ancient authorities read *living*
u **17.24** Gk *didrachma*
v **17.24** Gk *didrachma*
w **17.26** Gk *he*

said, "From others," Jesus said to him, "Then the children are free.
27However, so that we do not give offense to them, go to the sea
and cast a hook; take the first fish that comes up; and when you
open its mouth, you will find a coin;[x] take that and give it
to them for you and me."

True Greatness

18 At that time the disciples came to Jesus
and asked, "Who is the greatest in the
kingdom of heaven?" 2He called a child,
whom he put among them, 3and said,
"Truly I tell you, unless you change
and become like children, you will
never enter the kingdom of heaven.
4Whoever becomes humble like this
child is the greatest in the kingdom
of heaven. 5Whoever welcomes one
such child in my name welcomes
me.

17:27 Jesus paid taxes?

Certainly, even though, being the Son of God, Jesus was not obligated. He always did everything that the law required of everyone else, in order not to offend the "little" and just ones.

18:1–4, 10 Finally, we talk about us, children!

Jesus never spoke directly to children, but he loved you and could not bear anyone treating you badly. Moreover, he taught that only those who become small—like a child—are able to welcome the Good News of God's kingdom.

x **17.27** Gk *stater*; the stater was worth two didrachmas

Temptations to Sin

6 "If any of you put a stumbling block before one of these
little ones who believe in me, it would be better for you
if a great millstone were fastened around your neck
and you were drowned in the depth of the sea.
7Woe to the world because of stumbling blocks!
Occasions for stumbling are bound to
come, but woe to the one by whom
the stumbling block comes!

8 "If your hand or your foot causes
you to stumble, cut it off and throw it
away; it is better for you to enter life
maimed or lame than to have two hands
or two feet and to be thrown into the
eternal fire. 9And if your eye causes you to
stumble, tear it out and throw it away; it is
better for you to enter life with one eye
than to have two eyes and to be thrown
into the hell[y] of fire.

The Parable of the Lost Sheep

10 "Take care that you do not despise
one of these little ones; for, I tell you, in
heaven their angels continually see the face of my
Father in heaven.[z] 12What do you think? If a shepherd
has a hundred sheep, and one of them has gone astray,

y **18.9** Gk *Gehenna*

z **18.10** Other ancient authorities add verse 11, *For the Son of Man came to save the lost*

does he not leave the ninety-nine on the mountains and
go in search of the one that went astray? 13And if he
finds it, truly I tell you, he rejoices over it more than
over the ninety-nine that never went astray. 14So it
is not the will of your[a] Father in heaven that one
of these little ones should be lost.

Reproving Another Who Sins

15 "If another member of the church[b] sins
against you,[c] go and point out the fault when
the two of you are alone. If the member listens
to you, you have regained that one.[d] 16But if
you are not listened to, take one or two others
along with you, so that every word may be confirmed by the evidence of two or three witnesses.
17If the member refuses to listen to them, tell it to
the church; and if the offender refuses to listen
even to the church, let such a one be to you as
a Gentile and a tax collector. 18Truly I tell you,
whatever you bind on earth will be bound in
heaven, and whatever you loose on earth will be
loosed in heaven. 19Again, truly I tell you, if two
of you agree on earth about anything you ask,
it will be done for you by my Father in heaven.

18:12 I would have left it. I would already have so many sheep with ninety-nine!
God the Father never abandons anyone; God never gives up.

18:17 Church
In Greek, the language in which I wrote my Gospel, I used the word *ekklesia*, which means a community of believers. The word "Church" is derived from it.

a **18.14** Other ancient authorities read *my*
b **18.15** Gk *If your brother*
c **18.15** Other ancient authorities lack *against you*
d **18.15** Gk *the brother*

18:20 Is Jesus really among us when we gather?
Yes. Where the community of believers gathers, he reveals himself truly as God with us.

18:22 So I must forgive seventy-seven times?
No, much more than that! Seventy-seven is a way of saying "a limitless number of times."

20 For where two or three are gathered in my name,
I am there among them."

Forgiveness

21 Then Peter came and said to him, "Lord, if
another member of the church[e] sins against
me, how often should I forgive? As many
as seven times?" 22 Jesus said to him, "Not
seven times, but, I tell you, seventy-seven[f]
times.

The Parable of the Unforgiving Servant

23 "For this reason the kingdom of
heaven may be compared to a king who
wished to settle accounts with his slaves.
24 When he began the reckoning, one
who owed him ten thousand talents[g]
was brought to him; 25 and, as he could
not pay, his lord ordered him to be sold,
together with his wife and children and
all his possessions, and payment to be
made. 26 So the slave fell on his knees
before him, saying, 'Have patience with
me, and I will pay you everything.' 27 And
out of pity for him, the lord of that slave

e **18.21** Gk *if my brother*
f **18.22** Or *seventy times seven*
g **18.24** A talent was worth more than fifteen years' wages of a laborer

released him and forgave him the debt. [28]But
that same slave, as he went out, came upon
one of his fellow slaves who owed him a
hundred denarii;[h] and seizing him by the
throat, he said, 'Pay what you owe.' [29]Then
his fellow slave fell down and pleaded with
him, 'Have patience with me, and I will
pay you.' [30]But he refused; then he went
and threw him into prison until he would
pay the debt. [31]When his fellow slaves
saw what had happened, they were
greatly distressed, and they went and
reported to their lord all that had taken
place. [32]Then his lord summoned him
and said to him, 'You wicked slave! I
forgave you all that debt because you
pleaded with me. [33]Should you not
have had mercy on your fellow slave,
as I had mercy on you?' [34]And in
anger his lord handed him over to be
tortured until he would pay his entire
debt. [35]So my heavenly Father will
also do to every one of you, if you do
not forgive your brother or sister[i] from
your heart."

18:24–28 Talents, Denarii

They were the money of that time. A talent was a huge amount, hundreds of thousands of dollars. A denarius, however, had the value of only ten dollars. Jesus used the great difference between the two amounts in the parable to remind us that among the forgiven—we Christians—there can be no other law than that of shared forgiveness.

h **18.28** The denarius was the usual day's wage for a laborer
i **18.35** Gk *brother*

Book V: A Future that is Already Present (Mt 19:1–25:46)

The growing tension between Jesus and the religious authorities of official Judaism is clear in the narrative section of this fifth book (19:1–23:39). The Master, however, does not avoid giving a decisive testimony to the newness of the kingdom. The theme of the presence of the kingdom is taken up again even in the last of the Master's great teachings, the talks on the end of the world, which wind through chapters 24 and 25. Under a layer of typically apocalyptical language—similar to the language used in the book of the prophet Daniel and in John's Apocalypse (the Book of Revelation)—Matthew shows us what matters to Jesus. It is not so much "the day and the hour," since no one—"neither the angels of heaven, nor the Son, but only the Father" (24:36)—know what that might be. Jesus wants us to know that we need to be always vigilant. Just knowing that one day each person will meet God face-to-face should \ lead believers to be determined in following and living the teachings and the example of our Lord Jesus.

19:5 What passage is Jesus referring to?

He is referring to the second chapter of Genesis where God's will in making man and woman capable of loving each other faithfully is clear.

Teaching about Divorce

19 When Jesus had finished saying these
things, he left Galilee and went to the region of
Judea beyond the Jordan. 2Large crowds followed
him, and he cured them there.
3 Some Pharisees came to him, and to test
him they asked, "Is it lawful for a man to divorce
his wife for any cause?" 4He answered, "Have
you not read that the one who made them at the
beginning 'made them male and female,' 5and
said, 'For this reason a man shall leave his father

and mother and be joined to his wife, and the two shall
become one flesh'? 6So they are no longer two, but one
flesh. Therefore what God has joined together, let no
one separate." 7They said to him, "Why then did Moses
command us to give a certificate of dismissal and to
divorce her?" 8He said to them, "It was because
you were so hard-hearted that Moses allowed
you to divorce your wives, but from the beginning it was not so. 9And I say to you, whoever divorces his wife, except for unchastity,
and marries another commits adultery."[j]

10 His disciples said to him, "If such is
the case of a man with his wife, it is better
not to marry." 11But he said to them, "Not
everyone can accept this teaching, but
only those to whom it is given. 12For there
are eunuchs who have been so from birth,
and there are eunuchs who have been
made eunuchs by others, and there are
eunuchs who have made themselves
eunuchs for the sake of the kingdom of
heaven. Let anyone accept this who can."

19:12 Eunuchs

A term used for men who have been made physically incapable of having children. Jesus used this word to explain that the kingdom of heaven is such a great gift that for its sake, a person could even renounce the gift of having a family.

j **19.9** Other ancient authorities read *except on the ground of unchastity, causes her to commit adultery*; others add at the end of the verse *and he who marries a divorced woman commits adultery*

19:16 Why did this young man give up on following Jesus?

Maybe he had thought that to be a good disciple it was enough to simply do some good deeds. Instead, Jesus asked the young man to make a gift of his own life—to love Jesus and others in the same way that Jesus did. Sadly, the young man did not have the courage to leave everything for Jesus' sake.

Jesus Blesses Little Children

13 Then little children were being brought to him in order
that he might lay his hands on them and pray. The disciples spoke sternly to those who brought them; 14but
Jesus said, "Let the little children come to me, and
do not stop them; for it is to such as these that
the kingdom of heaven belongs." 15And he
laid his hands on them and went on his way.

The Rich Young Man

16 Then someone came to him and said,
"Teacher, what good deed must I do
to have eternal life?" 17And he said to
him, "Why do you ask me about what
is good? There is only one who is good.
If you wish to enter into life, keep the
commandments." 18He said to him,
"Which ones?" And Jesus said, "You shall
not murder; You shall not commit adultery;
You shall not steal; You shall not bear false
witness; 19Honor your father and mother; also,
You shall love your neighbor as yourself." 20The
young man said to him, "I have kept all these;[k] what
do I still lack?" 21Jesus said to him, "If you wish to be
perfect, go, sell your possessions, and give the money[l] to the

k **19.20** Other ancient authorities add *from my youth*
l **19.21** Gk lacks *the money*

poor, and you will have treasure in heaven; then come, follow
me." 22When the young man heard this word, he went away
grieving, for he had many possessions.
23 Then Jesus said to his disciples, "Truly I tell you, it will
be hard for a rich person to enter the kingdom of heaven.
24Again I tell you, it is easier for a camel to go through the
eye of a needle than for someone who is rich to enter the
kingdom of God." 25When the disciples heard this, they
were greatly astounded and said, "Then who can be
saved?" 26But Jesus looked at them and said, "For mortals it is impossible, but for God all things are possible."
27 Then Peter said in reply, "Look, we have left everything and followed you. What then will we have?"
28Jesus said to them, "Truly I tell you, at the
renewal of all things, when the Son of Man is
seated on the throne of his glory, you who
have followed me will also sit on twelve
thrones, judging the twelve tribes of Israel.
29And everyone who has left houses or
brothers or sisters or father or mother or
children or fields, for my name's sake,
will receive a hundredfold,[m] and will
inherit eternal life. 30But many who are
first will be last, and the last will be first.

m **19.29** Other ancient authorities read *manifold*

The Laborers in the Vineyard

20 "For the kingdom of heaven is like a landowner who went out early in
the morning to hire laborers for his vineyard. 2After agreeing with the laborers
for the usual daily wage,[n] he sent them into his vineyard. 3When
he went out about nine o'clock, he saw others standing
idle in the marketplace; 4and he said to them, 'You also
go into the vineyard, and I will pay you whatever is
right.' So they went. 5When he went out again about
noon and about three o'clock, he did the same.
6And about five o'clock he went out and found
others standing around; and he said to them,
'Why are you standing here idle all day?' 7They
said to him, 'Because no one has hired us.' He
said to them, 'You also go into the vineyard.'
8When evening came, the owner of the vineyard said to his manager, 'Call the laborers
and give them their pay, beginning with the
last and then going to the first.' 9When those
hired about five o'clock came, each of them
received the usual daily wage.[o] 10Now when
the first came, they thought they would receive
more; but each of them also received the usual
daily wage.[p] 11And when they received it, they
grumbled against the landowner, 12saying, 'These
last worked only one hour, and you have made them
equal to us who have borne the burden of the day and the
scorching heat.' 13But he replied to one of them, 'Friend, I am
doing you no wrong; did you not agree with me for the usual
daily wage?[q] 14Take what belongs to you and go; I choose to

20:11 The owner in the story does act unfairly. *With this story, Jesus wanted to remind those who thought that they were righteous that God's love is even greater than humans can understand. Jesus wants us to remember that he wants to save everyone, even someone who does not deserve it. It may seem unfair, but God's mercy and love is beyond our capacity.*

n **20.2** Gk *a denarius*
o **20.9** Gk *a denarius*
p **20.10** Gk *a denarius*
q **20.13** Gk *a denarius*

give to this last the same as I give to you. 15Am I not
allowed to do what I choose with what belongs to
me? Or are you envious because I am generous?'[r]
16So the last will be first, and the first will be
last."[s]

A Third Time Jesus Foretells His Death and Resurrection

17 While Jesus was going up to Jerusalem, he
took the twelve disciples aside by themselves,
and said to them on the way, 18"See, we are going
up to Jerusalem, and the Son of Man will be handed
over to the chief priests and scribes, and they will
condemn him to death; 19then they will hand him over
to the Gentiles to be mocked and flogged and crucified; and on the third day he will be raised."

The Request of the Mother of James and John

20 Then the mother of the sons of Zebedee came
to him with her sons, and kneeling before him,
she asked a favor of him. 21And he said to her,
"What do you want?" She said to him, "Declare
that these two sons of mine will sit, one at your
right hand and one at your left, in your kingdom."
22But Jesus answered, "You do not know what
you are asking. Are you able to drink the cup
that I am about to drink?"[t] They said to him,
"We are able." 23He said to them, "You will

r **20.15** Gk *is your eye evil because I am good?*

s **20.16** Other ancient authorities add *for many are called but few are chosen*

t **20.22** Other ancient authorities add *or to be baptized with the baptism that I am baptized with?*

20:22 Cup

Often, this word is translated as **chalice,** which is a precious goblet used for the celebration of Passover. Jesus uses "cup" as a symbol of the passion and death that Jesus—and after him, many disciples—would face.

indeed drink my cup, but to sit at my right hand and at my left,
this is not mine to grant, but it is for those for whom it has been
prepared by my Father."
24 When the ten heard it, they were angry with the two brothers.
25But Jesus called them to him and said, "You know that the
rulers of the Gentiles lord it over them, and their great
ones are tyrants over them. 26It will not be so among
you; but whoever wishes to be great among you
must be your servant, 27and whoever wishes to
be first among you must be your slave; 28just as
the Son of Man came not to be served but to
serve, and to give his life a ransom for many."

20:26–27 Like a slave? Isn't it enough to help one another?

Jesus did not limit himself to helping others only every now and then. Instead he became the servant, or slave, of all people, even to the point of dying on the cross for us.

Jesus Heals Two Blind Men

29 As they were leaving Jericho, a large crowd
followed him. 30There were two blind men sitting by the roadside. When they heard that Jesus
was passing by, they shouted, "Lord,[u] have mercy
on us, Son of David!" 31The crowd sternly ordered
them to be quiet; but they shouted even more loudly,
"Have mercy on us, Lord, Son of David!" 32Jesus stood
still and called them, saying, "What do you want me to do
for you?" 33They said to him, "Lord, let our eyes be opened."
34Moved with compassion, Jesus touched their eyes. Immediately
they regained their sight and followed him.

u **20.30** Other ancient authorities lack *Lord*

Jesus' Triumphal Entry into Jerusalem

21 When they had come near Jerusalem and had reached Bethphage, at
the Mount of Olives, Jesus sent two disciples, 2saying to them, "Go into the village ahead of you, and immediately you will find a donkey
tied, and a colt with her; untie them and bring them to me.
3If anyone says anything to you, just say this, 'The Lord
needs them.' And he will send them immediately."[v] 4This
took place to fulfill what had been spoken through the
prophet, saying,

5 "Tell the daughter of Zion,
Look, your king is coming to you,
humble, and mounted on a donkey,
and on a colt, the foal of a
donkey."

6The disciples went and did as Jesus had directed
them; 7they brought the donkey and the colt, and
put their cloaks on them, and he sat on them. 8A
very large crowd[w] spread their cloaks on the road,
and others cut branches from the trees and spread
them on the road. 9The crowds that went ahead of
him and that followed were shouting,

"Hosanna to the Son of David!
Blessed is the one who comes in the name of
the Lord!
Hosanna in the highest heaven!"

10When he entered Jerusalem, the whole city was in tur-
moil, asking, "Who is this?" 11The crowds were saying,
"This is the prophet Jesus from Nazareth in Galilee."

21:5 Daughter of Zion
Zion is another name for Jerusalem—the city Jesus enters to fulfill his mission and which welcomes him as a king.

21:9 Hosanna
This word is Aramaic, the language Jesus and his followers spoke. It is a term of joy and praise. Here, as the people of Jerusalem welcome Jesus, it means "Save us!" Using this word showed their joy and hope in him as their Savior.

v **21.3** Or *'The Lord needs them and will send them back immediately.'*
w **21.8** Or *Most of the crowd*

Jesus Cleanses the Temple

12 Then Jesus entered the temple[x] and drove out
all who were selling and buying in the temple,
and he overturned the tables of the money
changers and the seats of those who sold doves.
13 He said to them, "It is written,
'My house shall be called a house of prayer';
but you are making it a den of robbers."
14 The blind and the lame came to him in the
temple, and he cured them. 15 But when the chief
priests and the scribes saw the amazing things
that he did, and heard[y] the children crying out in
the temple, "Hosanna to the Son of David," they
became angry 16 and said to him, "Do you hear
what these are saying?" Jesus said to them, "Yes;
have you never read,

> 'Out of the mouths of infants and nursing
> babies
> you have prepared praise for yourself'?"

17 He left them, went out of the city to Bethany,
and spent the night there.

Jesus Curses the Fig Tree

18 In the morning, when he returned to the city,
he was hungry. 19 And seeing a fig tree by the side
of the road, he went to it and found nothing at

x **21.12** Other ancient authorities add *of God*
y **21.15** Gk lacks *heard*

all on it but leaves. Then he said to it, "May no fruit
ever come from you again!" And the fig tree withered at once. 20When the disciples saw it, they
were amazed, saying, "How did the fig tree
wither at once?" 21Jesus answered them,
"Truly I tell you, if you have faith and do
not doubt, not only will you do what
has been done to the fig tree, but
even if you say to this mountain, 'Be
lifted up and thrown into the sea,' it
will be done. 22Whatever you ask
for in prayer with faith, you will
receive."

The Authority of Jesus Questioned

23 When he entered the temple,
the chief priests and the elders
of the people came to him as
he was teaching, and said, "By
what authority are you doing these
things, and who gave you this
authority?" 24Jesus said to them, "I
will also ask you one question; if you
tell me the answer, then I will also tell

21:12 There was a marketplace in the Temple?

Yes, but this was normal. In fact, it was necessary so that certain Temple rituals could be carried out. Jesus was not angry with the merchants because of their noisy presence. He was challenging the lack of understanding of people who based their relationship with God only on exterior offerings and sacrifices.

21:19 Why did he get so angry with that poor fig tree?

In the Bible, the fig tree is often used as a symbol for the people of Israel. In my story, this fig tree was a sign of a lifeless and unfruitful faith. This was what provoked Jesus' reaction.

you by what authority I do these things. 25Did
the baptism of John come from heaven, or was
it of human origin?" And they argued with one
another, "If we say, 'From heaven,' he will say to
us, 'Why then did you not believe him?' 26But if
we say, 'Of human origin,' we are afraid of the
crowd; for all regard John as a prophet." 27So they
answered Jesus, "We do not know." And he said
to them, "Neither will I tell you by what authority
I am doing these things.

The Parable of the Two Sons

28 "What do you think? A man had two sons;
he went to the first and said, 'Son, go and work
in the vineyard today.' 29He answered, 'I will not';
but later he changed his mind and went. 30The father[z]
went to the second and said the same; and he answered, 'I
go, sir'; but he did not go. 31Which of the two did the will of
his father?" They said, "The first." Jesus said to them, "Truly I
tell you, the tax collectors and the prostitutes are going into
the kingdom of God ahead of you. 32For John came to you
in the way of righteousness and you did not believe him, but
the tax collectors and the prostitutes believed him; and even
after you saw it, you did not change your minds and believe
him.

z **21.30** Gk *He*

The Parable of the Wicked Tenants

33 "Listen to another parable. There was a landowner
who planted a vineyard, put a fence around it, dug a
wine press in it, and built a watchtower. Then he leased
it to tenants and went to another country. 34When the
harvest time had come, he sent his slaves to the tenants to collect his produce. 35But the tenants seized
his slaves and beat one, killed another, and stoned
another. 36Again he sent other slaves, more than the
first; and they treated them in the same way. 37Finally
he sent his son to them, saying, 'They will respect my
son.' 38But when the tenants saw the son, they said to
themselves, 'This is the heir; come, let us kill him and
get his inheritance.' 39So they seized him, threw him out
of the vineyard, and killed him. 40Now when the owner of the
vineyard comes, what will he do to those tenants?" 41They said to
him, "He will put those wretches to a miserable death, and lease
the vineyard to other tenants who will give him the produce at the
harvest time."

42 Jesus said to them, "Have you never read in the scriptures:

'The stone that the builders rejected
    has become the cornerstone;[a]
this was the Lord's doing,
    and it is amazing in our eyes'?

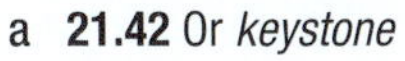

a **21.42** Or *keystone*

43 Therefore I tell you, the kingdom of God will be taken
away from you and given to a people that produces the
fruits of the kingdom.[b] 44 The one who falls on this stone
will be broken to pieces; and it will crush anyone on whom
it falls."[c]
45 When the chief priests and the Pharisees heard his
parables, they realized that he was speaking about
them. 46 They wanted to arrest him, but they
feared the crowds, because they regarded him
as a prophet.

The Parable of the Wedding Banquet

22 Once more Jesus spoke to them
in parables, saying: 2 "The kingdom of
heaven may be compared to a king
who gave a wedding banquet for his
son. 3 He sent his slaves to call those
who had been invited to the wedding
banquet, but they would not come.
4 Again he sent other slaves, saying,
'Tell those who have been invited:
Look, I have prepared my dinner, my
oxen and my fat calves have been slaugh-
tered, and everything is ready; come to
the wedding banquet.' 5 But they made
light of it and went away, one to his farm,
another to his business, 6 while the rest seized
his slaves, mistreated them, and killed them. 7 The

22:2 Is heaven like a banquet?

Yes, a delicious banquet which all people are invited to. But some people will refuse to come (the first ones invited). Others will not be allowed to attend because they did not listen well to the invitation and are not clothed in a wedding robe (the conversion to which Jesus calls every person).

b **21.43** Gk *the fruits of it*
c **21.44** Other ancient authorities lack verse 44

king was enraged. He sent his troops, destroyed those
murderers, and burned their city. 8Then he said to his
slaves, 'The wedding is ready, but those invited were
not worthy. 9Go therefore into the main streets, and invite
everyone you find to the wedding banquet.' 10Those
slaves went out into the streets and gathered all whom
they found, both good and bad; so the wedding hall
was filled with guests.

11 "But when the king came in to see the guests,
he noticed a man there who was not wearing a wedding robe, 12and he said to him, 'Friend, how did you
get in here without a wedding robe?' And he was
speechless. 13Then the king said to the attendants,
'Bind him hand and foot, and throw him into the
outer darkness, where there will be weeping
and gnashing of teeth.' 14For many are called,
but few are chosen."

The Question about Paying Taxes

15 Then the Pharisees went and plotted
to entrap him in what he said. 16So they
sent their disciples to him, along with
the Herodians, saying, "Teacher,
we know that you are sincere, and
teach the way of God in accordance
with truth, and show deference to no
one; for you do not regard people with

22:17 Emperor
The Roman emperor, at that time, Tiberius, was also called by the title "Caesar."

22:18 Malice
To think and do what is evil, with cunning and deceit.

partiality. 17Tell us, then, what you think. Is it lawful to
pay taxes to the emperor, or not?" 18But Jesus, aware
of their malice, said, "Why are you putting me to the
test, you hypocrites? 19Show me the coin used for the
tax." And they brought him a denarius. 20Then he
said to them, "Whose head is this, and whose title?"
21They answered, "The emperor's." Then he said to
them, "Give therefore to the emperor the things that
are the emperor's, and to God the things that are
God's." 22When they heard this, they were amazed;
and they left him and went away.

The Question about the Resurrection

23 The same day some Sadducees came to him,
saying there is no resurrection;[d] and they asked him
a question, saying, 24"Teacher, Moses said, 'If a man
dies childless, his brother shall marry the widow,
and raise up children for his brother.' 25Now there
were seven brothers among us; the first married,
and died childless, leaving the widow to his brother.
26The second did the same, so also the third, down
to the seventh. 27Last of all, the woman herself died.
28In the resurrection, then, whose wife of the seven
will she be? For all of them had married her."

d **22.23** Other ancient authorities read *who say that there is no resurrection*

29 Jesus answered them, "You are wrong, because
you know neither the scriptures nor the power of
God. 30 For in the resurrection they neither
marry nor are given in marriage, but are like
angels[e] in heaven. 31 And as for the resurrection of the dead, have you not read what
was said to you by God, 32 'I am the God
of Abraham, the God of Isaac, and the
God of Jacob'? He is God not of the
dead, but of the living." 33 And when
the crowd heard it, they were
astounded at his teaching.

The Greatest Commandment

34 When the Pharisees heard that
he had silenced the Sadducees,
they gathered together, 35 and one of
them, a lawyer, asked him a question to test him. 36 "Teacher, which
commandment in the law is the
greatest?" 37 He said to him, " 'You
shall love the Lord your God with all
your heart, and with all your soul, and
with all your mind.' 38 This is the greatest
and first commandment. 39 And a second
is like it: 'You shall love your neighbor as
yourself.' 40 On these two commandments
hang all the law and the prophets."

22:30 Will we have wings in heaven?

When Jesus said that those in heaven are like angels, he did not mean that they have wings. He meant that we will be "similar" to the angels—in being perfected—but not the "same" as the angels because we will have our bodies too. Angels do not have bodies at all—or wings (although they are often shown this way in art).

22:37 Are these two more commandments?

Love for God and neighbor is the foundation of the whole Law of God, including the Ten Commandments which you know. So, these two commandments are not really new as much as they explain the purpose of all the other commandments.

e **22.30** Other ancient authorities add *of God*

The Question about David's Son

41 Now while the Pharisees were gathered together, Jesus
asked them this question: 42"What do you think of the
Messiah?[f] Whose son is he?" They said to him, "The
son of David." 43He said to them, "How is it then
that David by the Spirit[g] calls him Lord, saying,
44 'The Lord said to my Lord,
"Sit at my right hand,
until I put your enemies under your
feet"'?
45If David thus calls him Lord, how can
he be his son?" 46No one was able to
give him an answer, nor from that day
did anyone dare to ask him any more
questions.

22:45 What does this line mean?

The person of Jesus is gradually revealed in a completely unexpected way. Only when Jesus dies on the cross and is resurrected will he be definitively understood as the Messiah, the Son of David.

Jesus Denounces Scribes and Pharisees

23 Then Jesus said to the crowds
and to his disciples, 2"The scribes and
the Pharisees sit on Moses' seat; 3there-
fore, do whatever they teach you and
follow it; but do not do as they do, for
they do not practice what they teach.

f **22.42** Or *Christ*
g **22.43** Gk *in spirit*

4They tie up heavy burdens, hard to bear,[h] and lay them on the shoulders
of others; but they themselves are unwilling to lift a finger to move them.
5They do all their deeds to be seen by others; for they make their phylacteries
broad and their fringes long. 6They love to have the place of honor at banquets and the best seats in the synagogues, 7and to be greeted with respect
in the marketplaces, and to have people
call them rabbi. 8But you are not to be
called rabbi, for you have one teacher,
and you are all students.[i] 9And call no
one your father on earth, for you have
one Father—the one in heaven. 10Nor
are you to be called instructors, for
you have one instructor, the Messiah.[j]
11The greatest among you will be your
servant. 12All who exalt themselves
will be humbled, and all who humble
themselves will be exalted.

13 "But woe to you, scribes and
Pharisees, hypocrites! For you lock
people out of the kingdom of heaven. For
you do not go in yourselves, and when

23:5 Phylacteries, Fringes

Phylacteries are leather straps connected to a little box that contains some Scripture verses. These are wrapped around the arms and forehead. Fringes, instead, hang from the corners of the observant Jew's garments, as a reminder of the commandments of the Jewish Law. Both phylacteries and fringes are still used today.

h **23.4** Other ancient authorities lack *hard to bear*

i **23.8** Gk *brothers*

j **23.10** Or *the Christ*

k **23.13** Other authorities add here (or after verse 12) verse 14, *Woe to you, scribes and Pharisees, hypocrites! For you devour widows' houses and for the sake of appearance you make long prayers; therefore you will receive the greater condemnation*

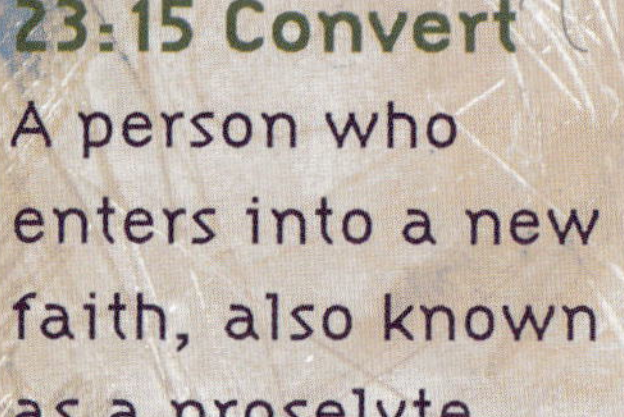

23:15 Convert
A person who enters into a new faith, also known as a proselyte

others are going in, you stop them.[k] 15Woe to you, scribes
and Pharisees, hypocrites! For you cross sea and land to
make a single convert, and you make the new convert
twice as much a child of hell[l] as yourselves.
16 "Woe to you, blind guides, who say, 'Whoever
swears by the sanctuary is bound by nothing, but whoever
swears by the gold of the sanctuary is bound by the oath.'
17You blind fools! For which is greater, the gold or the
sanctuary that has made the gold sacred? 18And you say,
'Whoever swears by the altar is bound by nothing, but
whoever swears by the gift that is on the altar is bound by
the oath.' 19How blind you are! For which is greater, the
gift or the altar that makes the gift sacred? 20So whoever swears by the altar, swears by it and by everything on it; 21and whoever swears by the
sanctuary, swears by it and by the one
who dwells in it; 22and whoever
swears by heaven, swears by the
throne of God and by the one
who is seated upon it.
23 "Woe to you, scribes and
Pharisees, hypocrites! For you
tithe mint, dill, and cummin, and
have neglected the weightier
matters of the law: justice and
mercy and faith. It is these you

l **23.15** Gk *Gehenna*

ought to have practiced without neglecting
the others. 24You blind guides! You strain out
a gnat but swallow a camel!
25 "Woe to you, scribes and Pharisees,
hypocrites! For you clean the outside of the
cup and of the plate, but inside they are full
of greed and self-indulgence. 26You blind
Pharisee! First clean the inside of the cup,[m] so
that the outside also may become clean.
27 "Woe to you, scribes and Pharisees, hypocrites! For you are like whitewashed tombs,
which on the outside look beautiful, but inside
they are full of the bones of the dead and of all
kinds of filth. 28So you also on the outside look
righteous to others, but inside you are full of
hypocrisy and lawlessness.
29 "Woe to you, scribes and Pharisees, hypocrites! For you build the tombs of the prophets and
decorate the graves of the righteous, 30and you say, 'If
we had lived in the days of our ancestors, we would
not have taken part with them in shedding the blood of
the prophets.' 31Thus you testify against yourselves that
you are descendants of those who murdered the prophets.
32Fill up, then, the measure of your ancestors. 33You snakes, you
brood of vipers! How can you escape being sentenced to hell?[n]

m **23.26** Other ancient authorities add *and of the plate*
n **23.33** Gk *Gehenna*

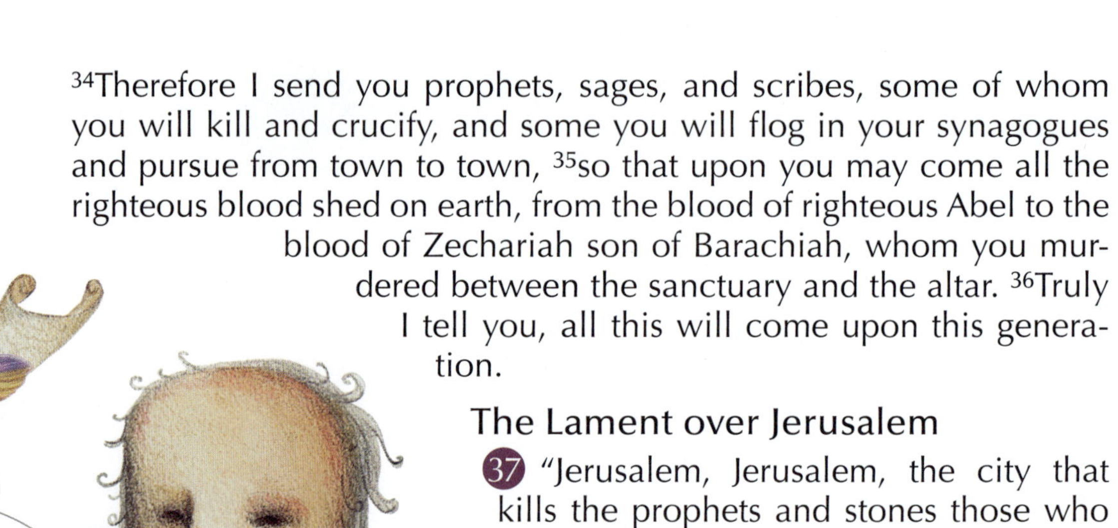

34Therefore I send you prophets, sages, and scribes, some of whom
you will kill and crucify, and some you will flog in your synagogues
and pursue from town to town, 35so that upon you may come all the
righteous blood shed on earth, from the blood of righteous Abel to the
blood of Zechariah son of Barachiah, whom you mur-
dered between the sanctuary and the altar. 36Truly
I tell you, all this will come upon this generation.

The Lament over Jerusalem

37 "Jerusalem, Jerusalem, the city that
kills the prophets and stones those who
are sent to it! How often have I desired
to gather your children together as a hen
gathers her brood under her wings, and
you were not willing! 38See, your house
is left to you, desolate.o 39For I tell you,
you will not see me again until you say,
'Blessed is the one who comes in the
name of the Lord.'"

23:37 Why did they persecute the prophets?

Because their message was uncomfortable and required listeners to change their life.

o **23.38** Other ancient authorities lack *desolate*

The Destruction of the Temple Foretold

24 As Jesus came out of the temple and was going away, his disciples came to point out to him the buildings of the temple. 2 Then he asked them, "You see all these, do you not? Truly I tell you, not one stone will be left here upon another; all will be thrown down."

Signs of the End of the Age

3 When he was sitting on the Mount of Olives, the disciples came to him privately, saying, "Tell us, when will this be, and what will be the sign of your coming and of the end of the age?" 4 Jesus answered them, "Beware that no one leads you astray. 5 For many will come in my name, saying, 'I am the Messiah!'[p] and they will lead many astray. 6 And you will hear of wars and rumors of wars; see that you are not alarmed; for this must take place, but the end is not yet. 7 For nation will rise against nation, and kingdom against kingdom, and there will be famines[q] and earthquakes in various places: 8 all this is but the beginning of the birth pangs.

24:1 How big was this Temple?

It was a complex of different buildings which took up an entire hilltop. It had been under construction for many years and still was not finished. I begin the last great discourse of my Gospel with Jesus' prediction about the temple's destruction, which worried his listeners.

p **24.5** Or *the Christ*
q **24.7** Other ancient authorities add *and pestilences*

Persecutions Foretold

9 "Then they will hand you over to be tortured and will
put you to death, and you will be hated by all nations
because of my name. 10Then many will fall away,[r] and
they will betray one another and hate one another.
11And many false prophets will arise and lead many
astray. 12And because of the increase of lawlessness, the love of many will grow cold. 13But the
one who endures to the end will be saved. 14And
this good news[s] of the kingdom will be proclaimed
throughout the world, as a testimony to all the
nations; and then the end will come.

The Desolating Sacrilege

15 "So when you see the desolating sacrilege
standing in the holy place, as was spoken of
by the prophet Daniel (let the reader understand), 16then those in Judea must flee to the
mountains; 17the one on the housetop must
not go down to take what is in the house;
18the one in the field must not turn back to get
a coat. 19Woe to those who are pregnant and
to those who are nursing infants in those days!
20Pray that your flight may not be in winter
or on a sabbath. 21For at that time there will
be great suffering, such as has not been from
the beginning of the world until now, no, and
never will be. 22And if those days had not been

r **24.10** Or *stumble*
s **24.14** Or *gospel*

24:13 What does it mean to endure
To remain faithful to Jesus, while not being afraid of what might happen

24:15, 21 Desolating Sacrilege, Suffering
Sacrilege here means misusing something holy. Desolating means to leave something empty or without life. A desolating sacrilege, therefore, is a misuse of something holy, like a temple, which causes God to leave the place empty. The emptiness—the absence of God—leads to much sadness and suffering.

cut short, no one would be saved; but for the sake of the elect those days will
be cut short. 23 Then if anyone says to you, 'Look! Here is the Messiah!'[t] or
'There he is!'—do not believe it. 24 For false messiahs[u] and false prophets will
appear and produce great signs and omens, to lead astray, if possible, even
the elect. 25 Take note, I have told you beforehand. 26 So, if they say to you,
'Look! He is in the wilderness,' do not go out. If they say, 'Look!
He is in the inner rooms,' do not believe it. 27 For as the lightning comes from the east and flashes as far as the west,
so will be the coming of the Son of Man. 28 Wherever
the corpse is, there the vultures will gather.

The Coming of the Son of Man

29 "Immediately after the suffering of those days
the sun will be darkened,
and the moon will not give its light;
the stars will fall from heaven,
and the powers of heaven will be shaken.
30 Then the sign of the Son of Man will
appear in heaven, and then all the tribes
of the earth will mourn, and they will see
'the Son of Man coming on the clouds of
heaven' with power and great glory. 31 And
he will send out his angels with a loud
trumpet call, and they will gather his elect
from the four winds, from one end of heaven
to the other.

24:28 Corpses eaten by vultures! Ewwww!

Jesus wanted to use such an ugly image to say that the person who is not ready to welcome him at his coming will not have any other fate than the destruction of his or her life.

t **24.23** Or *the Christ*
u **24.24** Or *christs*

24:36 What about people who say they know when the world will end? *They are frauds! Do not trust them. Not even Jesus knew when the end of the world would come.*

The Lesson of the Fig Tree

32 "From the fig tree learn its lesson: as soon as
its branch becomes tender and puts forth its
leaves, you know that summer is near. 33 So
also, when you see all these things, you
know that he[v] is near, at the very gates.
34 Truly I tell you, this generation will not
pass away until all these things have taken
place. 35 Heaven and earth will pass away,
but my words will not pass away.

The Necessity for Watchfulness

36 "But about that day and hour no one
knows, neither the angels of heaven, nor
the Son,[w] but only the Father. 37 For as the
days of Noah were, so will be the coming of
the Son of Man. 38 For as in those days before
the flood they were eating and drinking, marrying
and giving in marriage, until the day Noah entered
the ark, 39 and they knew nothing until the flood came and
swept them all away, so too will be the coming of the Son of
Man. 40 Then two will be in the field; one will be taken and one
will be left. 41 Two women will be grinding meal together; one

v **24.33** Or *it*
w **24.36** Other ancient authorities lack *nor the Son*

will be taken and one will be left. 42Keep awake therefore, for you do not
know on what day[x] your Lord is coming. 43But understand this: if the owner
of the house had known in what part of the night the thief was coming, he
would have stayed awake and would not have let his house be broken into.
44Therefore you also must be ready, for the Son of Man is coming
at an unexpected hour.

The Faithful or the Unfaithful Slave

45 "Who then is the faithful and wise slave, whom
his master has put in charge of his household, to
give the other slaves[y] their allowance of food
at the proper time? 46Blessed is that slave
whom his master will find at work when he
arrives. 47Truly I tell you, he will put that
one in charge of all his possessions. 48But
if that wicked slave says to himself, 'My
master is delayed,' 49and he begins to beat
his fellow slaves, and eats and drinks with
drunkards, 50the master of that slave will
come on a day when he does not expect
him and at an hour that he does not know.
51He will cut him in pieces[z] and put him with
the hypocrites, where there will be weeping and
gnashing of teeth.

24:42 We have to stay awake all the time?

Go ahead and sleep at night, Jesus knows our bodies need to rest. But keep your heart awake at all times, and don't forget Jesus.

x **24.42** Other ancient authorities read *at what hour*
y **24.45** Gk *to give them*
z **24.51** Or *cut him off*

25:5 Who is this slowpoke bridegroom?
It's Jesus! Since it is Jesus who we are waiting for, we cannot risk being unprepared for his coming, even if the wait is long and we are tired.

The Parable of the Ten Bridesmaids

25 "Then the kingdom of heaven will be like
this. Ten bridesmaids[a] took their lamps and
went to meet the bridegroom.[b] 2Five of them
were foolish, and five were wise. 3When
the foolish took their lamps, they took no
oil with them; 4but the wise took flasks of
oil with their lamps. 5As the bridegroom
was delayed, all of them became drowsy
and slept. 6But at midnight there was a
shout, 'Look! Here is the bridegroom!
Come out to meet him.' 7Then all those
bridesmaids[c] got up and trimmed their
lamps. 8The foolish said to the wise,
'Give us some of your oil, for our lamps
are going out.' 9But the wise replied, 'No!
there will not be enough for you and for us;
you had better go to the dealers and buy some
for yourselves.' 10And while they went to buy it,
the bridegroom came, and those who were ready
went with him into the wedding banquet; and the door
was shut. 11Later the other bridesmaids[d] came also, saying,
'Lord, lord, open to us.' 12But he replied, 'Truly I tell you, I do not know you.'
13Keep awake therefore, for you know neither the day nor the hour.[e]

a **25.1** Gk *virgins*
b **25.1** Other ancient authorities add *and the bride*
c **25.7** Gk *virgins*
d **25.11** Gk *virgins*
e **25.13** Other ancient authorities add *in which the Son of Man is coming*

The Parable of the Talents

14 "For it is as if a man, going on a journey,
summoned his slaves and entrusted his property to them; 15to one he gave five talents,[f] to
another two, to another one, to each according
to his ability. Then he went away. 16The one who
had received the five talents went off at once and
traded with them, and made five more talents.
17In the same way, the one who had the two talents made two more talents. 18But the one who had
received the one talent went off and dug a hole in the
ground and hid his master's money. 19After a long time
the master of those slaves came and settled accounts
with them. 20Then the one who had received the five
talents came forward, bringing five more talents, saying,
'Master, you handed over to me five talents; see, I have
made five more talents.' 21His master said to him, 'Well
done, good and trustworthy slave; you have been trustworthy in a few things, I will put you in charge of many
things; enter into the joy of your master.' 22And the one
with the two talents also came forward, saying, 'Master,
you handed over to me two talents; see, I have made two
more talents.' 23His master said to him, 'Well done, good
and trustworthy slave; you have been trustworthy in a few
things, I will put you in charge of many things; enter into
the joy of your master.' 24Then the one who had received
the one talent also came forward, saying, 'Master, I knew

f **25.15** A talent was worth more than fifteen years' wages of a laborer

that you were a harsh man, reaping where you
did not sow, and gathering where you did not
scatter seed; 25so I was afraid, and I went and
hid your talent in the ground. Here you have
what is yours.' 26But his master replied, 'You
wicked and lazy slave! You knew, did you,
that I reap where I did not sow, and gather
where I did not scatter? 27Then you ought to
have invested my money with the bankers,
and on my return I would have received
what was my own with interest. 28So take
the talent from him, and give it to the one
with the ten talents. 29For to all those who
have, more will be given, and they will
have an abundance; but from those who
have nothing, even what they have will
be taken away. 30As for this worthless slave,
throw him into the outer darkness, where
there will be weeping and gnashing of teeth.'

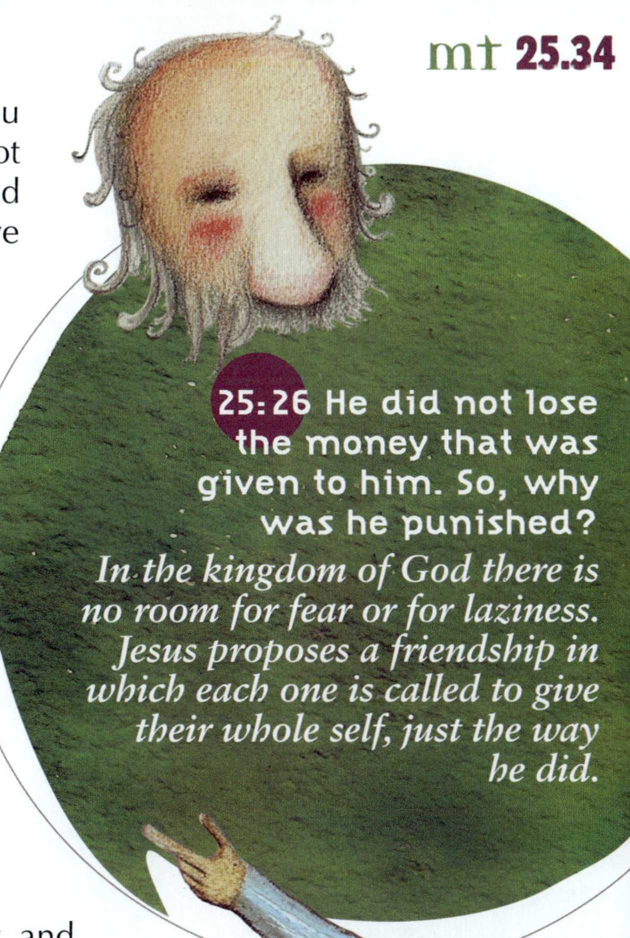

25:26 He did not lose the money that was given to him. So, why was he punished?

In the kingdom of God there is no room for fear or for laziness. Jesus proposes a friendship in which each one is called to give their whole self, just the way he did.

The Judgment of the Nations

31 "When the Son of Man comes in his glory, and
all the angels with him, then he will sit on the throne
of his glory. 32All the nations will be gathered before him,
and he will separate people one from another as a shepherd separates the sheep from the goats, 33and he will put the
sheep at his right hand and the goats at the left. 34Then the king
will say to those at his right hand, 'Come, you that are blessed by my

Father, inherit the kingdom prepared for you from the foundation of the world; 35for I was hungry and you gave me food, I
was thirsty and you gave me something to drink, I was a stranger
and you welcomed me, 36I was naked and you gave me clothing,
I was sick and you took care of me, I was in prison and you
visited me.' 37Then the righteous will answer him, 'Lord, when
was it that we saw you hungry and gave you food, or thirsty and
gave you something to drink? 38And when was it that we saw
you a stranger and welcomed you, or naked and gave you
clothing? 39And when was it that we saw you sick or in
prison and visited you?' 40And the king will answer
them, 'Truly I tell you, just as you did it to one of
the least of these who are members of my family,[g]
you did it to me.' 41Then he will say to those at
his left hand, 'You that are accursed, depart
from me into the eternal fire prepared for the
devil and his angels; 42for I was hungry and you
gave me no food, I was thirsty and you gave
me nothing to drink, 43I was a stranger and you
did not welcome me, naked and you did not
give me clothing, sick and in prison and you did
not visit me.' 44Then they also will answer, 'Lord,
when was it that we saw you hungry or thirsty or
a stranger or naked or sick or in prison, and did not
take care of you?' 45Then he will answer them, 'Truly
I tell you, just as you did not do it to one of the least of
these, you did not do it to me.' 46And these will go away into
eternal punishment, but the righteous into eternal life."

25:40–45 So then, every time we see a poor person we see Jesus?

Yes, and we will be judged on how we welcomed, helped, and loved him or her. Sometimes it is hard to know what the right thing to do is. For example, sometimes it might make sense to give a poor person food instead of money.

g **25.40** Gk *these my brothers*

The Easter Accounts (Mt 26:1–28:20)

Here the Gospel account reaches its peak: the good news preached and lived by Jesus is rejected by the people of Israel. The high priests and the elders come together and secretly plot to arrest the Master and they decide to have him killed (26:3–4). The Lord's passion and death, however, are not failures of his teaching but rather its completion. Matthew's Gospel—more than the others—shows Jesus as one who teaches and lives out his teaching all the way until his death. It also adds to every page of this last section citations from the Old Testament. Matthew does this to confirm the fact that the Law and the Prophets are truly being fulfilled. The Resurrection confirms what the Lord had announced to his disciples. It was also necessary so that he could continue to be the Emmanuel (1:23)—that is, God with us—"always, to the end of the age" (28:20).

The Plot to Kill Jesus

26 When Jesus had finished saying all these things, he said
to his disciples, 2"You know that after two days the Passover is
coming, and the Son of Man will be handed over to be
crucified."
3 Then the chief priests and the elders of the people
gathered in the palace of the high priest, who was
called Caiaphas, 4and they conspired to arrest Jesus
by stealth and kill him. 5But they said, "Not during the
festival, or there may be a riot among the people."

26:2 Passover
A sacred festival in which Jewish people remember how God freed them from slavery in Egypt.

26:9 Weren't your disciples right?

Jesus praised the woman's seemingly wasteful act because what she did reminded everyone that Jesus is the most precious treasure. In turn, he poured himself out completely on the cross for us.

26:15 Why thirty pieces of silver?

It was the cost to buy a slave. That is how much the life of the Son of God was thought to be worth!

The Anointing at Bethany

6 Now while Jesus was at Bethany in the house of Simon
the leper,[h] 7a woman came to him with an alabaster
jar of very costly ointment, and she poured it on
his head as he sat at the table. 8But when the disciples saw it, they were angry and said, "Why
this waste? [9] 9For this ointment could have been
sold for a large sum, and the money given to
the poor." 10But Jesus, aware of this, said to
them, "Why do you trouble the woman? She
has performed a good service for me. 11For
you always have the poor with you, but you
will not always have me. 12By pouring this
ointment on my body she has prepared
me for burial. 13Truly I tell you, wherever
this good news[i] is proclaimed in the whole
world, what she has done will be told in
remembrance of her."

Judas Agrees to Betray Jesus

14 Then one of the twelve, who was called
Judas Iscariot, went to the chief priests 15and
said, "What will you give me if I betray him to
you?" They paid him thirty pieces of silver. 16And
from that moment he began to look for an opportunity to betray him.

h **26.6** The terms *leper* and *leprosy* can refer to several diseases
i **26.13** Or *gospel*

The Passover with the Disciples

17 On the first day of Unleavened Bread the disciples came to Jesus, saying, "Where do you want us to make the preparations for you to eat the Passover?"
18He said, "Go into the city to a certain man, and say to him, 'The Teacher says, My time is near; I will keep the Passover at your house with my disciples.'"
19So the disciples did as Jesus had directed them, and they prepared the Passover meal.

20 When it was evening, he took his place with the twelve;[j]
21and while they were eating, he said, "Truly I tell you, one of you will betray me."
22And they became greatly distressed and began to say to him one after another, "Surely not I, Lord?"
23He answered, "The one who has dipped his hand into the bowl with me will betray me.
24The Son of Man goes as it is written of him, but woe to that one by whom the Son of Man is betrayed! It would have been better for that one not to have been born."
25Judas, who betrayed him, said, "Surely not I, Rabbi?" He replied, "You have said so."

26:17 Unleavened Bread
Bread made without yeast, eaten throughout the week of Passover as a reminder of the flight from Egypt.

26:21
How did he know that someone would betray him?
Jesus knew his friends well, and he knew how to look into each person's heart. Even though he was betrayed, that did not stop him from giving his life for us and for everyone.

j **26.20** Other ancient authorities add *disciples*

The Institution of the Lord's Supper

26 While they were eating, Jesus took a loaf of bread, and after
blessing it he broke it, gave it to the disciples, and said, "Take, eat;
this is my body." 27Then he took a cup, and after giving thanks he
gave it to them, saying, "Drink from it, all of you; 28for this is my
blood of the[k] covenant, which is poured out for many for
the forgiveness of sins. 29I tell you, I will never again
drink of this fruit of the vine until that day when I
drink it new with you in my Father's kingdom."
30 When they had sung the hymn, they
went out to the Mount of Olives.

26:28 What is the "blood of the covenant"?

In the Old Testament, Jews sacrificed animals to establish a solemn promise of friendship. Jesus began the new and eternal covenant between God and people by sacrificing himself. This is what we recall every time we celebrate the Mass.

Peter's Denial Foretold

31 Then Jesus said to them, "You will all
become deserters because of me this night;
for it is written,

'I will strike the shepherd,
and the sheep of the flock will be
scattered.'

32But after I am raised up, I will go ahead
of you to Galilee." 33Peter said to him,
"Though all become deserters because of
you, I will never desert you." 34Jesus said
to him, "Truly I tell you, this very night,

k **26.28** Other ancient authorities add *new*
l **26.41** Or *into temptation*

before the cock crows, you will deny me three times." 35Peter said
to him, "Even though I must die with you, I will not deny you." And
so said all the disciples.

Jesus Prays in Gethsemane

36 Then Jesus went with them to a place called
Gethsemane; and he said to his disciples, "Sit
here while I go over there and pray." 37He took
with him Peter and the two sons of Zebedee,
and began to be grieved and agitated. 38Then
he said to them, "I am deeply grieved, even
to death; remain here, and stay awake with
me." 39And going a little farther, he threw
himself on the ground and prayed, "My
Father, if it is possible, let this cup pass from
me; yet not what I want but what you want."
40Then he came to the disciples and found
them sleeping; and he said to Peter, "So, could
you not stay awake with me one hour? 41Stay
awake and pray that you may not come into the
time of trial;[l] the spirit indeed is willing, but the
flesh is weak." 42Again he went away for the second
time and prayed, "My Father, if this cannot pass unless
I drink it, your will be done." 43Again he came and found

26:39 So, Jesus did not want to die!

He certainly did not! He, too, felt very much afraid. Ultimately, though, he decided to continue doing the Father's will, loving his friends to the point of total self-offering, and entrusting himself to God's promise.

them sleeping, for their eyes were heavy. 44So leaving them again, he went
away and prayed for the third time, saying the same words. 45Then he came
to the disciples and said to them, "Are you still sleeping and taking your rest?
See, the hour is at hand, and the Son of Man is betrayed into the hands of
sinners. 46Get up, let us be going. See, my betrayer is at hand."

The Betrayal and Arrest of Jesus

47 While he was still speaking, Judas,
one of the twelve, arrived; with him was
a large crowd with swords and clubs,
from the chief priests and the elders of
the people. 48Now the betrayer had given
them a sign, saying, "The one I will kiss
is the man; arrest him." 49At once he
came up to Jesus and said, "Greetings,
Rabbi!" and kissed him. 50Jesus said to
him, "Friend, do what you are here to
do." Then they came and laid hands
on Jesus and arrested him. 51Suddenly,
one of those with Jesus put his hand
on his sword, drew it, and struck the
slave of the high priest, cutting off his
ear. 52Then Jesus said to him, "Put your
sword back into its place; for all who

take the sword will perish by the sword. 53Do you think that
I cannot appeal to my Father, and he will at once send me
more than twelve legions of angels? 54But how then would
the scriptures be fulfilled, which say it must happen in this
way?" 55At that hour Jesus said to the crowds, "Have
you come out with swords and clubs to arrest me
as though I were a bandit? Day after day I sat in
the temple teaching, and you did not arrest me.
56But all this has taken place, so that the scriptures of the prophets may be fulfilled." Then
all the disciples deserted him and fled.

Jesus before the High Priest

57 Those who had arrested Jesus took
him to Caiaphas the high priest, in whose
house the scribes and the elders had gathered. 58But Peter was following him at a
distance, as far as the courtyard of the high
priest; and going inside, he sat with the
guards in order to see how this would
end. 59Now the chief priests and the
whole council were looking for false
testimony against Jesus so that they
might put him to death, 60but they
found none, though many false witnesses came forward. At last two came

26:53 Why didn't Jesus call on the angels to save him?
Because he wanted to save the world by an act of love, not by imposing an army of heavenly angels.

26:57, 59 High Priest
The highest religious position among the people of Israel. He was the head of the Sanhedrin, a high court composed of scribes, elders, and chief priests.

forward [61]and said, "This fellow said, 'I am able to destroy the temple of God
and to build it in three days.'" [62]The high priest stood up and said, "Have you
no answer? What is it that they testify against you?" [63]But Jesus was silent.
Then the high priest said to him, "I put you under oath before the living God,
tell us if you are the Messiah,[m] the Son of God." [64]Jesus said to him, "You have
said so. But I tell you,

From now on you will see the Son of Man
seated at the right hand of Power
and coming on the clouds of heaven."

[65]Then the high priest tore his clothes and
said, "He has blasphemed! Why do we still
need witnesses? You have now heard his
blasphemy. [66]What is your verdict?" They
answered, "He deserves death." [67]Then they
spat in his face and struck him; and some
slapped him, [68]saying, "Prophesy to us, you
Messiah![n] Who is it that struck you?"

26:65 Was Jesus really condemned to death for blasphemy?

When Jesus replied, "You have said so," he affirmed that he was the Messiah, the Son of God. For an Israelite, this claim was blasphemy and it called for the death penalty.

m **26.63** Or *Christ*
n **26.68** Or *Christ*

26:75 Why did Peter deny Jesus?
Unlike his Master, Peter was overcome by his fear. However, Peter's great love for Jesus remained true. That is why, as soon as he realized his weakness, Peter burst into tears.

Peter's Denial of Jesus

69 Now Peter was sitting outside in the courtyard.
A servant-girl came to him and said, "You also
were with Jesus the Galilean." 70But he denied it
before all of them, saying, "I do not know what
you are talking about." 71When he went out to
the porch, another servant-girl saw him, and
she said to the bystanders, "This man was
with Jesus of Nazareth."[o] 72Again he denied
it with an oath, "I do not know the man."
73After a little while the bystanders came
up and said to Peter, "Certainly you are
also one of them, for your accent betrays
you." 74Then he began to curse, and he
swore an oath, "I do not know the man!"
At that moment the cock crowed. 75Then
Peter remembered what Jesus had said:
"Before the cock crows, you will deny me
three times." And he went out and wept
bitterly.

Jesus Brought before Pilate

27 When morning came, all the chief
priests and the elders of the people conferred together against Jesus in order to
bring about his death. 2They bound him,
led him away, and handed him over to
Pilate the governor.

27:2 Pilate
He was the governor of Judea and a representative of the Roman emperor in Palestine. At the time of Jesus, he was the only one who could order a death sentence.

o **26.71** Gk *the Nazorean*

The Suicide of Judas

3 When Judas, his betrayer, saw that Jesus[p] was
condemned, he repented and brought back
the thirty pieces of silver to the chief priests
and the elders. 4He said, "I have sinned by
betraying innocent[q] blood." But they said,
"What is that to us? See to it yourself."
5 Throwing down the pieces of silver in
the temple, he departed; and he went
and hanged himself. 6But the chief
priests, taking the pieces of silver, said,
"It is not lawful to put them into the
treasury, since they are blood money."
7After conferring together, they used
them to buy the potter's field as a place
to bury foreigners. 8For this reason that
field has been called the Field of Blood to
this day. 9Then was fulfilled what had been
spoken through the prophet Jeremiah,[r] "And
they took[s] the thirty pieces of silver, the price of
the one on whom a price had been set,[t] on whom
some of the people of Israel had set a price, 10and they
gave[u] them for the potter's field, as the Lord commanded
me."

27:5 What a terrible death Judas had!

Judas' suicide is sad and is the rotten fruit of his betrayal of the Creator of all life. Jesus, however, gave his life even for Judas. For this reason, we can hope that Jesus' love reached his betrayer.

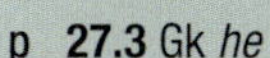

p **27.3** Gk *he*
q **27.4** Other ancient authorities read *righteous*
r **27.9** Other ancient authorities read *Zechariah* or *Isaiah*
s **27.9** Or *I took*
t **27.9** Or *the price of the precious One*
u **27.10** Other ancient authorities read *I gave*

Pilate Questions Jesus

11 Now Jesus stood before the governor; and the governor asked him, "Are
you the King of the Jews?" Jesus said, "You say so." 12But when he was accused
by the chief priests and elders, he did not answer.
13Then Pilate said to him, "Do you not hear how
many accusations they make against you?"
14 But he gave him no answer, not even to
a single charge, so that the governor was
greatly amazed.

Barabbas or Jesus?

15 Now at the festival the governor
was accustomed to release a prisoner
for the crowd, anyone whom they
wanted. 16At that time they had a noto-
rious prisoner, called Jesus[v] Barabbas.
17So after they had gathered, Pilate said
to them, "Whom do you want me to
release for you, Jesus[w] Barabbas or Jesus
who is called the Messiah?"[x] 18For he
realized that it was out of jealousy that
they had handed him over. 19 While he
was sitting on the judgment seat, his wife
sent word to him, "Have nothing to do with
that innocent man, for today I have suffered
a great deal because of a dream about him."

27:14 Why didn't Jesus defend himself?

Jesus was the king of the Jews, but not in the way that Pilate could have imagined. Jesus chooses to subject his divine authority to human authority, represented by Pilate. With this in mind Jesus does not continue the discussion with Pilate.

27:19 Why didn't Pilate listen to his wife?

Pilate preferred not to listen to the intuition of his wife out of pure political calculation and convenience. Pilate wanted to avoid the possibility of a revolt.

v **27.16** Other ancient authorities lack *Jesus*
w **27.17** Other ancient authorities lack *Jesus*
x **27.17** Or *the Christ*
y **27.22** Or *the Christ*
z **27.24** Other ancient authorities read *this righteous blood*, or *this righteous man's blood*
a **27.27** Gk *the praetorium*

[20]Now the chief priests and the elders per-
suaded the crowds to ask for Barabbas
and to have Jesus killed. [21]The governor again said to them, "Which
of the two do you want me to
release for you?" And they said,
"Barabbas." [22]Pilate said to them,
"Then what should I do with Jesus
who is called the Messiah?"[y] All of
them said, "Let him be crucified!"
[23]Then he asked, "Why, what evil has
he done?" But they shouted all the more, "Let
him be crucified!"

Pilate Hands Jesus over to Be Crucified

24 So when Pilate saw that he could do nothing, but rather that a riot
was beginning, he took some water and washed his hands before the crowd,
saying, "I am innocent of this man's blood;[z] see to it yourselves."
[25]Then the people as a whole answered, "His blood be on
us and on our children!" [26]So he released Barabbas for
them; and after flogging Jesus, he handed him over to
be crucified.

The Soldiers Mock Jesus

27 Then the soldiers of the governor took Jesus
into the governor's headquarters,[a] and they
gathered the whole cohort around him. [28]They
stripped him and put a scarlet robe on him, [29]and
after twisting some thorns into a crown, they put
it on his head. They put a reed in his right hand

27:28–29 They dressed him up like a king!
Jesus truly is the King, but the Jews and the Romans mocked him and did not care about who they were putting to death.

and knelt before him and mocked him, saying, "Hail, King of the Jews!"
30They spat on him, and took the reed and struck him on the head. 31After
mocking him, they stripped him of the robe and put his own clothes on him.
Then they led him away to crucify him.

The Crucifixion of Jesus

32 As they went out, they came upon a man from Cyrene
named Simon; they compelled this man to carry his
cross. 33And when they came to a place called Golgotha
(which means Place of a Skull), 34they offered him
wine to drink, mixed with gall; but when he tasted
it, he would not drink it. 35And when they had crucified him, they divided his clothes among themselves
by casting lots;[b] 36then they sat down there and kept
watch over him. 37Over his head they put the charge
against him, which read, "This is Jesus, the King of
the Jews."

38 Then two bandits were crucified with him, one
on his right and one on his left. 39Those who passed by
derided[c] him, shaking their heads 40and saying, "You who
would destroy the temple and build it in three days, save
yourself! If you are the Son of God, come down from the cross."
41In the same way the chief priests also, along with the scribes and
elders, were mocking him, saying, 42"He saved others; he cannot save
himself.[d] He is the King of Israel; let him come down from the cross now, and
we will believe in him. 43He trusts in God; let God deliver him now, if he
wants to; for he said, 'I am God's Son.'" 44The bandits who were crucified
with him also taunted him in the same way.

27:40 Why didn't he save himself?

Jesus came to love, not to astound people with amazing deeds. Jesus saved us by giving his life, not by keeping it for himself.

b **27.35** Other ancient authorities add *in order that what had been spoken through the prophet might be fulfilled, "They divided my clothes among themselves, and for my clothing they cast lots."*

c **27.39** Or *blasphemed*

d **27.42** Or *is he unable to save himself?*

The Death of Jesus

45 From noon on, darkness came over the whole land[e] until three in the
afternoon. 46And about three o'clock Jesus cried with a loud voice, "Eli, Eli,
lema sabachthani?" that is, "My God, my God, why have you forsaken me?"
47When some of the bystanders heard it, they said, "This man is calling
for Elijah." 48At once one of them ran and got a sponge, filled it
with sour wine, put it on a stick, and gave it to him to drink.
49But the others said, "Wait, let us see whether Elijah
will come to save him."[f] 50Then Jesus cried again
with a loud voice and breathed his last.[g] 51At that
moment the curtain of the temple was torn in
two, from top to bottom. The earth shook, and
the rocks were split. 52The tombs also were
opened, and many bodies of the saints who
had fallen asleep were raised. 53After his
resurrection they came out of the tombs
and entered the holy city and appeared
to many. 54Now when the centurion and
those with him, who were keeping watch
over Jesus, saw the earthquake and what
took place, they were terrified and said,
"Truly this man was God's Son!"[h]

55 Many women were also there, looking
on from a distance; they had followed Jesus
from Galilee and had provided for him.
56Among them were Mary Magdalene, and
Mary the mother of James and Joseph, and the
mother of the sons of Zebedee.

27:51 What was the curtain of the temple?

It was a cloth in the temple that separated the space reserved for God from the space where the people could be. With his passion and death, Jesus took away this separation.

27:53 Why was there an earthquake? Did the dead really rise?

I used these images to show the power of Jesus' gift; His death and resurrection (after which the dead rose) brought life into the world and that life has unimaginable power.

e **27.45** Or *earth*

f **27.49** Other ancient authorities add *And another took a spear and pierced his side, and out came water and blood*

g **27.50** Or *gave up his spirit*

h **27.54** Or *a son of God*

The Burial of Jesus

57 When it was evening, there came a rich man from Arimathea,
named Joseph, who was also a disciple of Jesus. 58He went to Pilate
and asked for the body of Jesus; then Pilate ordered it to be given
to him. 59So Joseph took the body and wrapped it in a clean linen
cloth 60and laid it in his own new tomb, which he had hewn in the
rock. He then rolled a great stone to the door of the tomb and went
away. 61Mary Magdalene and the other Mary were there, sitting
opposite the tomb.

The Guard at the Tomb

62 The next day, that is, after the day of Preparation, the chief
priests and the Pharisees gathered before Pilate 63and said,
"Sir, we remember what that impostor said while he was
still alive, 'After three days I will rise again.' 64Therefore
command the tomb to be made secure until the third
day; otherwise his disciples may go and steal him
away, and tell the people, 'He has been raised
from the dead,' and the last deception would
be worse than the first." 65Pilate said to them,
"You have a guard[i] of soldiers; go, make it
as secure as you can."[j] 66So they went with
the guard and made the tomb secure by
sealing the stone.

i **27.65** Or *Take a guard*
j **27.65** Gk *you know how*

The Resurrection of Jesus

28 After the sabbath, as the first day of the week was
dawning, Mary Magdalene and the other Mary went to see the
tomb. 2And suddenly there was a great earthquake; for an angel
of the Lord, descending from heaven, came and rolled back the
stone and sat on it. 3His appearance was like lightning, and
his clothing white as snow. 4For fear of him the guards
shook and became like dead men. 5But the angel
said to the women, "Do not be afraid; I know that
you are looking for Jesus who was crucified.
6He is not here; for he has been raised, as he
said. Come, see the place where he[k] lay.
7Then go quickly and tell his disciples,
'He has been raised from the dead,[l] and
indeed he is going ahead of you to
Galilee; there you will see him.' This
is my message for you." 8So they
left the tomb quickly with fear and
great joy, and ran to tell his disciples. 9Suddenly Jesus met them
and said, "Greetings!" And they
came to him, took hold of his
feet, and worshiped him. 10Then
Jesus said to them, "Do not be
afraid; go and tell my brothers to
go to Galilee; there they will see
me."

28:1 So, what day was it?

The resurrection of Jesus happened the day after the Sabbath—the holy day of the Jews. The Sabbath is on Saturday so the resurrection happened on a Sunday, or the Lord's Day. Christians gather on Sunday to remember Jesus' Passover.

28:8 How can somebody be joyful and fearful at the same time?

The news that the women heard was absolutely unexpected and unbelievable. This is why they felt such a mixture of contradictory feelings.

k **28.6** Other ancient authorities read *the Lord*

l **28.7** Other ancient authorities lack *from the dead*

The Report of the Guard

11 While they were going, some of the guard went into
the city and told the chief priests everything that had
happened. 12 After the priests[m] had assembled with
the elders, they devised a plan to give a large
sum of money to the soldiers, 13telling them,
"You must say, 'His disciples came by night
and stole him away while we were asleep.'
14If this comes to the governor's ears, we
will satisfy him and keep you out of
trouble." 15So they took the money and
did as they were directed. And this story
is still told among the Jews to this day.

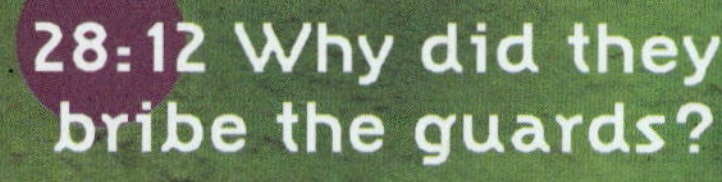

When I was writing this Gospel, the lie that Jesus' body had been stolen during the night was pretty widespread. That is why I wanted to make very clear just what happened.

m **28.12** Gk *they*

The Commissioning of the Disciples

16 Now the eleven disciples went to Galilee, to the
mountain to which Jesus had directed them.
17When they saw him, they worshiped him;
but some doubted. 18And Jesus came and
said to them, "All authority in heaven
and on earth has been given to me.
19Go therefore and make disciples
of all nations, baptizing them in
the name of the Father and of the
Son and of the Holy Spirit, 20and
teaching them to obey everything
that I have commanded you. And
remember, I am with you always,
to the end of the age."[n]

28:18–20 Are these Jesus' last words?

Yes! With them, Jesus entrusts us with a mission. We are called to tell everyone what Jesus did (preach) and to bring others into his friendship, which never diminishes and always saves (baptize).

n **28.20** Other ancient authorities add *Amen*

THE GOSPEL ACCORDING TO Mark

AUTHOR: ANONYMOUS,
LIKELY MARK,
DISCIPLE OF PETER AND PAUL

AUDIENCE: CHRISTIANS,
MOSTLY THOSE OF PAGAN ORIGIN

TIME AND PLACE: 65–70 AD,
PROBABLY WRITTEN IN ROME

THEMES: THE CENTRALITY
OF THE CROSS

The Story of a Young Man Who Ran Away Naked . . .

When I began to describe the story of Jesus' arrest, I decided to report a curious episode that one of the Apostles told me In it one of the important characters, or protagonists, was a courageous young man. When a crowd of men carrying swords and sticks came to arrest Jesus, the disciples ran away as fast as they could. All of them ran except Peter and one young man. I wrote about this event in chapter 14, verses 51 and 52: this "certain young man was following him [Jesus], wearing nothing but a linen cloth. They caught hold of him, but he left the linen cloth and ran off naked."

Many scholars have tried, like attentive detectives, to discover who the young man was. Some think it was me; others identify him as the Apostle John, or Lazarus, or even Paul! I don't know who it was, but I saw in the story of that young man the image of everyone who desires to follow Jesus. It is not an easy choice. At some point, every disciple of Jesus feels the temptation to run away. At the beginning of my missionary journey, I was afraid too. Try reading what Luke wrote about me in the Acts of the Apostles, in chapter 15, between verses 36 and 40!

But in the end, those who love Jesus are able to overcome every fear. This is the reason that I assigned the announcement of the resurrection on Easter morning not to an angel, but to that young man who had run away naked just a few days before. The women who went to Jesus' tomb "saw a young man, dressed in a white robe, sitting on the right side. . . . he said to them, 'Do not be alarmed; you are looking for Jesus of Nazareth, who was crucified. He has been raised; he is not here.'" (16:5–6). The shame and fear he felt after running away without his linen cloth is replaced by the glory of Jesus' resurrection in the white robe.

Evangelist Mark

Two Cries That Pierce the Heavens

Mark sandwiches the ministry of Jesus between two loud cries: first, the cry of John the Baptist at the beginning of the gospel narration (1:3) and, second, the cry of Jesus from the cross at the end of the of his earthly life (15:37). Already from this framework it is possible to see some stylistic elements of the second Gospel: a strong tone; drama; detailed descriptions of places and people; attention to major themes like failure, fear, betrayal, the effort to understand, and rejection. Because of these elements, Mark is identified with the symbol of a lion, since his Gospel lets out a "roar" that pierces even the chaos of our lives.

Three Occasions of Revelation

While composing the narrative for his Gospel, Mark emphasizes three important moments of revelation. These moments allow us to overcome the confusion that often marks the relationship between Jesus and his disciples. These three moments are placed at the beginning, the center, and the end of the story.

The first moment is Jesus' baptism in the Jordan River (1:9–11). Here the Father's voice solemnly proclaims Jesus' identity and the fulfillment of all the ancient Scriptures. The Torah, the Prophets, and the Writings are realized in the words inspired by God who "steps" out of the heavens to reveal himself. The second moment is the transfiguration (9:2–8) where Jesus is speaking with Moses and Elijah—two figures associated with Israel's wait for the Messiah. In this scene the Father's voice reconfirms the revelation that first happened in the Jordan—only now God invites everyone to listen through the figures of Peter, James, and John. The third moment happens at Golgotha, the place where both the death cry resounds (15:34–37) and where the resurrection is announced (16:1–8). Here, however, the Father is silent, giving humankind the chance to proclaim the greatness of Jesus' gift—first recognized by a pagan centurion (15:39) and then proclaimed by a young man dressed in white (16:5–7).

Four Narrative Sections

The attentive reader will notice that the Gospel of Mark is divided into four narrative sections.

~ The prologue (1:1–13). It begins the Gospel by presenting Jesus' public ministry as the quenching water for the thirst for salvation always present in the human heart. Moreover, it offers the possibility of restoring the harmony humans enjoyed with God at the beginning.

~ The section on identity (1:14–8:30). The question of Jesus' identity runs through this section. But Jesus is not easily labeled, despite the attempts of those who wanted to reduce him to either a worker of miracles, an influential political figure, or a made-up character to fulfill the messianic expectations of the people.

~ The section on following Christ (8:31–14:50). It highlights the demands of discipleship. All the while the looming shadow of the cross is present which will eventually cause all of the disciples to abandon Jesus.

~ The paschal mystery (14:51–16:8). This section contains the fulfillment of Jesus' ministry in the paschal mystery or his passion, death, and resurrection. It reveals how his gift transforms the believer, here represented by the young man in 14:51–52 and 16:5–7. In an attempt to respond to the questions that Mark had willingly left open at the end of his account in 16:8, the evangelist or one of his friends added verses 9–20.

THE GOSPEL ACCORDING TO

Mark

Prologue (Mk 1:1–13)

After declaring that his written account is "the good news of Jesus Christ, the Son of God," Mark opens his narrative with three scenes: the crowds going out to John the Baptist (1:2–8); Jesus' baptism in the Jordan River (1:9–11); and Jesus in the desert (1:12–13). There are many themes in these three scenes that make a sort of lens through which one should read the rest of Mark's Gospel. The gathering crowds prepare us for the public ministry of Jesus, who alone can fulfill every human being's need and desire for salvation (1:14–14–50). Also, Jesus' baptism begins a process that makes God's will present in the flesh and will find its total fulfilment in his passion and death (14:1–15:47). Lastly, the angels serving Christ in the desert show a new creation which will come to be after the resurrection and will be made available for everyone (16:1–8).

The Proclamation of John the Baptist

1 The beginning of the good news[a] of Jesus Christ, the Son of God.[b]

2 As it is written in the prophet Isaiah,[c]
"See, I am sending my messenger ahead of you,[d]
who will prepare your way;
3 the voice of one crying out in the wilderness:
'Prepare the way of the Lord,
make his paths straight,'"

1:1 Is it not a little strange to begin a book this way?
With this first verse, I wanted to give you the meaning of my Gospel: to help you discover who Jesus truly is.

a **1.1** Or *gospel*
b **1.1** Other ancient authorities lack *the Son of God*
c **1.2** Other ancient authorities read *in the prophets*
d **1.2** Gk *before your face*

1:5 Baptism is a Christian sacrament, right?

Certainly! John the Baptist's baptism was only a penitential gesture—recognizing and turning away from one's sins. The sacrament Christians celebrate unites us forever to Jesus whose death and resurrection helps us to continue moving away from sin.

1:9 Did Jesus have to be baptized?

Jesus had no sins, but he still wanted to share fully in our human experience. When he was baptized the Father definitively declared him to be the beloved Son of God.

4 John the baptizer appeared[e] in the wilderness, proclaiming a baptism of repentance for the forgiveness
of sins. 5 And people from the whole Judean countryside and all the people of Jerusalem were going
out to him, and were baptized by him in the
river Jordan, confessing their sins. 6 Now John
was clothed with camel's hair, with a leather
belt around his waist, and he ate locusts and
wild honey. 7 He proclaimed, "The one who
is more powerful than I is coming after me; I
am not worthy to stoop down and untie the
thong of his sandals. 8 I have baptized you
with[f] water; but he will baptize you with[g] the
Holy Spirit."

The Baptism of Jesus

9 In those days Jesus came from Nazareth
of Galilee and was baptized by John in the
Jordan. 10 And just as he was coming up out of
the water, he saw the heavens torn apart and the
Spirit descending like a dove on him. 11 And a voice
came from heaven, "You are my Son, the Beloved;[h]
with you I am well pleased."

The Temptation of Jesus

12 And the Spirit immediately drove him out into the wilderness. 13 He was in the wilderness forty days, tempted by Satan; and
he was with the wild beasts; and the angels waited on him.

e **1.4** Other ancient authorities read *John was baptizing*
f **1.8** Or *in*
g **1.8** Or *in*
h **1.11** Or *my beloved Son*

Who is Jesus? (Mk 1:14–8:30)

From the beginning of Jesus' public ministry, the people who meet him often ask themselves: "Who is this?" The crowds (and others too) wonder about his identity. An identity which is known by the demons but veiled to all those who follow Jesus—including his own disciples. This section expresses in three parts the developing formation of the Twelve Apostles.

In the first part (1:14–3:6), Jesus calls his first disciples and affirms the traditions of their Jewish faith, but also slowly teaches them that God is present and can act outside the "holy places." Salvation engages human beings not only in synagogues, but also in homes, places of daily work, and spaces that nature offers (deserts, lakes, hills). Salvation even comes for the people whom Mosaic Law labeled almost un-savable—the possessed.

In the second part (3:7–6:6a), Jesus distinguishes his teaching from that of the rabbis of his time. The Twelve are not simply "disciples" learning from him to then go off and create their own versions. Rather, they are men called "to remain with him" and to grow in friendship with Jesus, a relationship that goes beyond even family bonds. They are to become co-protagonists in the proclamation of salvation.

The third part (6:6b–8:30) focuses on the question, "Who is Jesus?" This question is posed to the disciples. The answer develops and is contained in a simple yet eloquent sign—the bread broken and shared, which is the key to entering into the Master's mystery—but, for now, the Twelve Apostles do not see this clearly.

From Amazement to Indignation Mk 1:14–3:6

The Beginning of the Galilean Ministry

14 Now after John was arrested, Jesus came to Galilee, proclaiming the good news[i] of God,[j] 15 and saying, "The time is fulfilled, and the kingdom of God has come near;[k] repent, and believe in the good news."[l]

Jesus Calls the First Disciples

16 As Jesus passed along the Sea of Galilee, he saw Simon and his brother Andrew casting a net into the

1:15 The kingdom of God

The realization of God's plan which is fulfilled by our openness and efforts to have friendship with Jesus—the one awaited by Israel and by every human being

i **1.14** Or *gospel*
j **1.14** Other ancient authorities read *of the kingdom*
k **1.15** Or *is at hand*
l **1.15** Or *gospel*

1:21 Synagogue
The place where the Jews meet for prayer and instruction

1:24 Holy One of God
Holiness is a feature of God which sets him apart. The demons knew that Jesus is the Son of God.

1:21–39 What did Jesus do all day?
In these few verses I tried to tell you about a typical day for Jesus. He preached publicly, healed the sick, ate meals, met with the local people, and prayed.

sea—for they were fishermen. 17 And Jesus said to them,
"Follow me and I will make you fish for people." 18 And
immediately they left their nets and followed him. 19 As
he went a little farther, he saw James son of Zebedee
and his brother John, who were in their boat mending
the nets. 20 Immediately he called them; and they left
their father Zebedee in the boat with the hired men,
and followed him.

The Man with an Unclean Spirit

21 They went to Capernaum; and when the sabbath
came, he entered the synagogue and taught. 22 They
were astounded at his teaching, for he taught them
as one having authority, and not as the scribes. 23 Just
then there was in their synagogue a man with an
unclean spirit, 24 and he cried out, "What have you
to do with us, Jesus of Nazareth? Have you come to
destroy us? I know who you are, the Holy One of
God." 25 But Jesus rebuked him, saying, "Be silent,
and come out of him!" 26 And the unclean spirit,
convulsing him and crying with a loud voice,
came out of him. 27 They were all amazed, and
they kept on asking one another, "What is this?
A new teaching—with authority! He[m] commands
even the unclean spirits, and they obey him." 28 At
once his fame began to spread throughout the surrounding region of Galilee.

m **1.27** Or *A new teaching! With authority he*

Jesus Heals Many at Simon's House

29 As soon as they[n] left the synagogue, they entered the
house of Simon and Andrew, with James and John. 30 Now
Simon's mother-in-law was in bed with a fever, and they told
him about her at once. 31 He came and took her by the hand
and lifted her up. Then the fever left her, and she began to
serve them.

32 That evening, at sunset, they brought to him all who were
sick or possessed with demons. 33 And the whole city was gathered around the door. 34 And he cured many who were sick
with various diseases, and cast out many demons; and he
would not permit the demons to speak, because they
knew him.

A Preaching Tour in Galilee

35 In the morning, while it was still very dark, he
got up and went out to a deserted place, and there
he prayed. 36 And Simon and his companions
hunted for him. 37 When they found him, they
said to him, "Everyone is searching for you."
38 He answered, "Let us go on to the neighboring
towns, so that I may proclaim the message there
also; for that is what I came out to do." 39 And he
went throughout Galilee, proclaiming the message in their synagogues and casting out demons.

Jesus Cleanses a Leper

40 A leper[o] came to him begging him, and kneeling[p] he said to him, "If you choose, you can make
me clean." 41 Moved with pity,[q] Jesus[r] stretched out

1:40 Leper

Unlike other people of his day, Jesus was very attentive to lepers. Since their sickness was contagious, they were not allowed to live with others. Lepers were excluded, abandoned, and treated as though they were already dead by everyone—except Jesus.

n **1.29** Other ancient authorities read *he*
o **1.40** The terms *leper* and *leprosy* can refer to several diseases
p **1.40** Other ancient authorities lack *kneeling*
q **1.41** Other ancient authorities read *anger*
r **1.41** Gk *he*

his hand and touched him, and said to him, "I do choose. Be made clean!"
42 Immediately the leprosy[s] left him, and he was made clean. 43 After sternly
warning him he sent him away at once, 44 saying to him, "See that you say
nothing to anyone; but go, show yourself to the priest, and offer for your
cleansing what Moses commanded, as a testimony to them." 45 But he
went out and began to proclaim it freely, and to spread the word, so
that Jesus[t] could no longer go into a town openly, but stayed out
in the country; and people came to him from every quarter.

1:44 Why did Jesus not want them to know that he could heal lepers?
Jesus did not want to cause a frenzy. He was God's answer to what the people were waiting for, but Jesus was not what the people of his time imagined the Messiah to be.

2:5 Why did Jesus not heal the paralytic right away?
Jesus wanted them to understand that physical healing is only a sign of the more important healing from sin and evil—which only God can accomplish.

Jesus Heals a Paralytic

2 When he returned to Capernaum after some
days, it was reported that he was at home. 2 So
many gathered around that there was no longer
room for them, not even in front of the door;
and he was speaking the word to them. 3 Then
some people[u] came, bringing to him a paralyzed man, carried by four of them. 4 And
when they could not bring him to Jesus
because of the crowd, they removed the roof
above him; and after having dug through it,
they let down the mat on which the paralytic
lay. 5 When Jesus saw their faith, he said to
the paralytic, "Son, your sins are forgiven."
6 Now some of the scribes were sitting there,
questioning in their hearts, 7 "Why does this
fellow speak in this way? It is blasphemy! Who
can forgive sins but God alone?" 8 At once Jesus

s **1.42** The terms *leper* and *leprosy* can refer to several diseases
t **1.45** Gk *he*
u **2.3** Gk *they*

perceived in his spirit that they were discussing
these questions among themselves; and he said
to them, "Why do you raise such questions in
your hearts? 9Which is easier, to say to the paralytic, 'Your sins are forgiven,' or to say, 'Stand
up and take your mat and walk'? 10But so
that you may know that the Son of Man has
authority on earth to forgive sins"—he said
to the paralytic— 11"I say to you, stand up,
take your mat and go to your home." 12And
he stood up, and immediately took the mat
and went out before all of them; so that
they were all amazed and glorified God,
saying, "We have never seen anything like
this!"

Jesus Calls Levi

13 Jesus[v] went out again beside the sea; the
whole crowd gathered around him, and he
taught them. 14As he was walking along, he
saw Levi son of Alphaeus sitting at the tax
booth, and he said to him, "Follow me." And
he got up and followed him.

15 And as he sat at dinner[w] in Levi's[x] house,
many tax collectors and sinners were also sitting[y] with Jesus and his disciples—for there were

2:10 Son of Man

This is another one of Jesus' titles. It refers to a passage (Dn 7:13–14) where it speaks of a man who is presented to God and is tasked with the care of all creation. This scene is interpreted as being the moment of the final judgment.

2:15 Tax Collectors

The Hebrews hated tax collectors and labeled them sinners because they worked for the Roman Empire and often collected more than was due.

v **2.13** Gk *He*
w **2.15** Gk *reclined*
x **2.15** Gk *his*
y **2.15** Gk *reclining*

2:16 Pharisees

This was a group of Israelites who greatly respected the Law. Jesus entered into several arguments with them because most of them only wanted to *appear* holy rather than actually *be* holy.

2:18 Disciples

The word disciple means pupil or student, a person who goes to the school of a master teacher. Jesus does even more than this. He invites his disciples to follow him, to become his friends, and to be part of his family.

2:19 But there is no wedding here!

Jesus was speaking about himself. He is the bridegroom, the one people have waited for and the reason for which the people are able to feast.

many who followed him. 16When the scribes
of[z] the Pharisees saw that he was eating with
sinners and tax collectors, they said to his disciples, "Why does he eat[a] with tax collectors
and sinners?" 17When Jesus heard this, he said
to them, "Those who are well have no need of a
physician, but those who are sick; I have come
to call not the righteous but sinners."

The Question about Fasting

18 Now John's disciples and the Pharisees were
fasting; and people[b] came and said to him,
"Why do John's disciples and the disciples of the
Pharisees fast, but your disciples do not fast?"
19Jesus said to them, "The wedding guests cannot
fast while the bridegroom is with them, can they?
As long as they have the bridegroom with them,
they cannot fast. 20The days will come when the
bridegroom is taken away from them, and then
they will fast on that day.

21 "No one sews a piece of unshrunk cloth on
an old cloak; otherwise, the patch pulls away from
it, the new from the old, and a worse tear is made.
22And no one puts new wine into old wineskins;
otherwise, the wine will burst the skins, and the
wine is lost, and so are the skins; but one puts new
wine into fresh wineskins."[c]

z **2.16** Other ancient authorities read *and*
a **2.16** Other ancient authorities add *and drink*
b **2.18** Gk *they*
c **2.22** Other ancient authorities lack *but one puts new wine into fresh wineskins*

Pronouncement about the Sabbath

23 One sabbath he was going through the
grainfields; and as they made their way
his disciples began to pluck heads of grain.
24 The Pharisees said to him, "Look, why are
they doing what is not lawful on the sabbath?"
25 And he said to them, "Have you never read
what David did when he and his companions
were hungry and in need of food? 26 He entered
the house of God, when Abiathar was high priest,
and ate the bread of the Presence, which it is not
lawful for any but the priests to eat, and he gave
some to his companions." 27 Then he said to
them, "The sabbath was made for humankind,
and not humankind for the sabbath; 28 so the
Son of Man is lord even of the sabbath."

The Man with a Withered Hand

3 Again he entered the synagogue, and a
man was there who had a withered hand. 2 They
watched him to see whether he would cure him on
the sabbath, so that they might accuse him. 3 And he
said to the man who had the withered hand, "Come
forward." 4 Then he said to them, "Is it lawful to do
good or to do harm on the sabbath, to save life or
to kill?" But they were silent. 5 He looked around
at them with anger; he was grieved at their hard-
ness of heart and said to the man, "Stretch out

2:24 Why were the Pharisees so worried about the Sabbath?

The Pharisees, above all, obeyed all aspects of the laws and rarely allowed exceptions. In this and the following scene, Jesus reminds everyone that God's Law is for the good of people.

2:26 Bread of the Presence

These were the breads that, according to the Old Testament, were offered to God and could be eaten only by priests.

3:6 Herodians
These were friends and supporters of King Herod and his policies. They are mentioned in some of the events of Jesus' public life because they plotted against him, seeking a way to kill him.

3:14 Why twelve?
Twelve is an important number for Jews since historically there were twelve tribes in Israel. Jesus' twelve disciples symbolize the twelve tribes in the New Covenant and form a new people of God.

your hand." He stretched it out, and his hand was
restored. 6The Pharisees went out and immediately
conspired with the Herodians against him, how to
destroy him.

A Multitude at the Seaside

7 Jesus departed with his disciples to the sea, and a
great multitude from Galilee followed him; 8hearing
all that he was doing, they came to him in great
numbers from Judea, Jerusalem, Idumea, beyond the
Jordan, and the region around Tyre and Sidon. 9He told
his disciples to have a boat ready for him because of
the crowd, so that they would not crush him; 10for he
had cured many, so that all who had diseases pressed
upon him to touch him. 11Whenever the unclean spirits
saw him, they fell down before him and shouted, "You
are the Son of God!" 12But he sternly ordered them not to
make him known.

Jesus Appoints the Twelve

13 He went up the mountain and called to him those whom
he wanted, and they came to him. 14And he appointed
twelve, whom he also named apostles,[d] to be with him, and
to be sent out to proclaim the message, 15and to have authority
to cast out demons. 16So he appointed the twelve:[e] Simon (to
whom he gave the name Peter); 17James son of Zebedee and

d **3.14** Other ancient authorities lack *whom he also named apostles*
e **3.16** Other ancient authorities lack *So he appointed the twelve*

John the brother of James (to whom he gave the name Boanerges, that is,
Sons of Thunder); 18and Andrew, and Philip, and Bartholomew, and Matthew,
and Thomas, and James son of Alphaeus, and Thaddaeus, and Simon the
Cananaean, 19and Judas Iscariot, who betrayed him.

Jesus and Beelzebul

Then he went home; 20and the crowd came together
again, so that they could not even eat. 21When
his family heard it, they went out to restrain him,
for people were saying, "He has gone out of his
mind." 22And the scribes who came down from
Jerusalem said, "He has Beelzebul, and by the
ruler of the demons he casts out demons." 23And
he called them to him, and spoke to them in
parables, "How can Satan cast out Satan? 24If a
kingdom is divided against itself, that kingdom
cannot stand. 25And if a house is divided
against itself, that house will not be able to
stand. 26And if Satan has risen up against
himself and is divided, he cannot stand, but
his end has come. 27But no one can enter a
strong man's house and plunder his property without first tying up the strong man;
then indeed the house can be plundered.

3:22 Scribes

At the time of Jesus, they were scholars of the Law. They were important people in Israel, but they did not appreciate Jesus because of his influential preaching and his criticism in regard to the religious leaders.

3:22–23 Satan, Beelzebul, demons

These are some of the names given to evil spirits, which are always active in human history.

28 "Truly I tell you, people will be forgiven for their sins and
whatever blasphemies they utter; 29but whoever blasphemes against
the Holy Spirit can never have forgiveness, but is guilty of an eternal
sin"— 30for they had said, "He has an unclean spirit."

The True Kindred of Jesus

31 Then his mother and his brothers came; and standing
outside, they sent to him and called him. 32A crowd was
sitting around him; and they said to him, "Your mother
and your brothers and sisters[f] are outside, asking for
you." 33And he replied, "Who are my mother and my
brothers?" 34And looking at those who sat around
him, he said, "Here are my mother and my brothers!
35Whoever does the will of God is my brother and
sister and mother."

3:31 I thought Jesus was an only child?
Sometimes one word can mean many things. In Jesus' time the word "brothers" meant siblings but it could also mean cousins and relatives in general.

The Parable of the Sower

4 Again he began to teach beside the sea. Such a
very large crowd gathered around him that he got into
a boat on the sea and sat there, while the whole crowd
was beside the sea on the land. 2He began to teach
them many things in parables, and in his teaching
he said to them: 3"Listen! A sower went out to sow.
4And as he sowed, some seed fell on the path, and
the birds came and ate it up. 5Other seed fell on rocky
ground, where it did not have much soil, and it sprang

f **3.32** Other ancient authorities lack *and sisters*

up quickly, since it had no depth of soil. [6]And when the sun rose, it was
scorched; and since it had no root, it withered away. [7]Other seed
fell among thorns, and the thorns grew up and choked it, and
it yielded no grain. [8]Other seed fell into good soil and
brought forth grain, growing up and increasing and
yielding thirty and sixty and a hundredfold." [9]And
he said, "Let anyone with ears to hear listen!"

The Purpose of the Parables

10 When he was alone, those who were around
him along with the twelve asked him about
the parables. [11]And he said to them, "To you
has been given the secret[g] of the kingdom
of God, but for those outside, everything
comes in parables; [12]in order that

'they may indeed look, but not
perceive,
and may indeed listen, but not
understand;
so that they may not turn again and
be forgiven.'"

4:4 This sower is not very good; he throws seeds everywhere!

Jesus wanted to remind us that his word is for everyone, everywhere. He knew, of course, that not everyone would receive it in the same way; but even so, God never tires of sowing.

4:12 Did Jesus want people to understand him or not?

In order to understand the Good News, it is not enough to just listen to Jesus. We must follow him and become his disciples. This is what he means when he cited this passage from Isaiah.

g **4.11** Or *mystery*

13 And he said to them, "Do you not understand this parable? Then how
will you understand all the parables? 14The sower sows the word. 15These are
the ones on the path where the word is sown: when they hear, Satan immediately comes and takes away the word that is sown in them. 16And these are
the ones sown on rocky ground: when they hear the word,
they immediately receive it with joy. 17But they have no
root, and endure only for a while; then, when trouble or
persecution arises on account of the word, immediately
they fall away.[h] 18And others are those sown among the
thorns: these are the ones who hear the word, 19but the
cares of the world, and the lure of wealth, and the desire
for other things come in and choke the word, and it
yields nothing. 20And these are the ones sown on the
good soil: they hear the word and accept it and bear
fruit, thirty and sixty and a hundredfold."

4:21 Bushel basket

This was a kind of bucket used to measure the quantity of materials like flour and milk.

A Lamp under a Bushel Basket

21 He said to them, "Is a lamp brought in to be put
under the bushel basket, or under the bed, and not on
the lampstand? 22For there is nothing hidden, except
to be disclosed; nor is anything secret, except to
come to light. 23Let anyone with ears to hear listen!"
24And he said to them, "Pay attention to what you
hear; the measure you give will be the measure you
get, and still more will be given you. 25For to those

h **4.17** Or *stumble*

who have, more will be given; and from those who have nothing, even what
they have will be taken away."

The Parable of the Growing Seed

26 He also said, "The kingdom of God is as if someone would scatter seed
on the ground, 27and would sleep and rise night and day, and the seed would
sprout and grow, he does not know how. 28The earth produces of itself, first
the stalk, then the head, then the full grain in the head. 29But when
the grain is ripe, at once he goes in with his sickle, because
the harvest has come."

The Parable of the Mustard Seed

30 He also said, "With what can we compare
the kingdom of God, or what parable will we
use for it? 31It is like a mustard seed, which,
when sown upon the ground, is the smallest
of all the seeds on earth; 32yet when it is
sown it grows up and becomes the greatest
of all shrubs, and puts forth large branches,
so that the birds of the air can make nests
in its shade."

The Use of Parables

33 With many such parables he spoke the
word to them, as they were able to hear it;
34he did not speak to them except in parables, but he explained everything in private to
his disciples.

4:31 But how can a kingdom be compared with a small seed?

A kingdom is not built in a day. It starts small, like a seed, with a building. Then, it grows like a tree, with another building, and another. More than once, Jesus reminds us that God's ways are not ours. Sometimes what is small is big and vice versa.

Jesus Stills a Storm

35 On that day, when evening had come, he said to them, "Let
us go across to the other side." 36And leaving the crowd
behind, they took him with them in the boat, just as he
was. Other boats were with him. 37A great windstorm
arose, and the waves beat into the boat, so that the
boat was already being swamped. 38But he was in
the stern, asleep on the cushion; and they woke
him up and said to him, "Teacher, do you not care
that we are perishing?" 39He woke up and rebuked
the wind, and said to the sea, "Peace! Be still!"
Then the wind ceased, and there was a dead calm.
40He said to them, "Why are you afraid? Have you
still no faith?" 41And they were filled with great awe
and said to one another, "Who then is this, that even
the wind and the sea obey him?"

4:38 Wasn't Jesus afraid of the storm?

Whoever is united to God the Father, as Jesus was, knows that his life is in secure hands. This is why Jesus accuses his disciples of not having enough faith, and they in turn question each other about who Jesus really is.

Jesus Heals the Gerasene Demoniac

5 They came to the other side of the sea, to the country
of the Gerasenes.[i] 2And when he had stepped out of
the boat, immediately a man out of the tombs with an
unclean spirit met him. 3He lived among the tombs; and no
one could restrain him any more, even with a chain; 4for he
had often been restrained with shackles and chains, but the chains
he wrenched apart, and the shackles he broke in pieces; and no one had
the strength to subdue him. 5Night and day among the tombs and on the
mountains he was always howling and bruising himself with stones. 6When

i **5.1** Other ancient authorities read *Gergesenes*; others, *Gadarenes*

he saw Jesus from a distance, he ran and bowed down
before him; 7and he shouted at the top of his voice,
"What have you to do with me, Jesus, Son of the Most
High God? I adjure you by God, do not torment me."
8For he had said to him, "Come out of the man, you
unclean spirit!" 9Then Jesus[j] asked him, "What is
your name?" He replied, "My name is Legion; for
we are many." 10He begged him earnestly not to
send them out of the country. 11Now there on
the hillside a great herd of swine was feeding;
12and the unclean spirits[k] begged him, "Send
us into the swine; let us enter them." 13So he
gave them permission. And the unclean spirits
came out and entered the swine; and the herd,
numbering about two thousand, rushed down
the steep bank into the sea, and were drowned
in the sea.

14 The swineherds ran off and told it in the
city and in the country. Then people came to see
what it was that had happened. 15They came to Jesus
and saw the demoniac sitting there, clothed and in his
right mind, the very man who had had the legion; and they were
afraid. 16Those who had seen what had happened to the demoniac and to the
swine reported it. 17Then they began to beg Jesus[l] to leave their neighborhood. 18As he was getting into the boat, the man who had been possessed by
demons begged him that he might be with him. 19But Jesus[m] refused, and said

5:7 This event is like something from a horror film!

Evil spirits are real and have been present throughout human history. Sometimes they make trouble for people in a destructive way.

j **5.9** Gk *he*
k **5.12** Gk *they*
l **5.17** Gk *him*
m **5.19** Gk *he*

to him, "Go home to your friends, and tell them how much the Lord has
done for you, and what mercy he has shown you." 20And he went away
and began to proclaim in the Decapolis how much Jesus had done for him;
and everyone was amazed.

A Girl Restored to Life and a Woman Healed

21 When Jesus had crossed again in the boat[n] to the other side, a great
crowd gathered around him; and he was by the sea. 22Then one of the
leaders of the synagogue named Jairus came and, when he saw him, fell
at his feet 23and begged him repeatedly, "My little daughter
is at the point of death. Come and lay your hands on her,
so that she may be made well, and live." 24So he went
with him.

And a large crowd followed him and pressed in on
him. 25Now there was a woman who had been suffering from hemorrhages for twelve years. 26She had
endured much under many physicians, and had
spent all that she had; and she was no better, but
rather grew worse. 27She had heard about Jesus,
and came up behind him in the crowd and
touched his cloak, 28for she said, "If I but touch
his clothes, I will be made well." 29Immediately
her hemorrhage stopped; and she felt in her
body that she was healed of her disease.
30Immediately aware that power had gone forth
from him, Jesus turned about in the crowd and

n **5.21** Other ancient authorities lack *in the boat*

5:41 What language did Jesus speak?

These words are in Aramaic, the language used in Israel at the time of Jesus. For some of the most important moments of Jesus' life I wanted to quote the words he spoke in his native Aramaic.

said, "Who touched my clothes?" 31 And his disciples said to
him, "You see the crowd pressing in on you; how can you
say, 'Who touched me?'" 32 He looked all around to see
who had done it. 33 But the woman, knowing what
had happened to her, came in fear and trembling,
fell down before him, and told him the whole
truth. 34 He said to her, "Daughter, your faith has
made you well; go in peace, and be healed of
your disease."

35 While he was still speaking, some people
came from the leader's house to say, "Your
daughter is dead. Why trouble the teacher any
further?" 36 But overhearing[o] what they said, Jesus
said to the leader of the synagogue, "Do not fear,
only believe." 37 He allowed no one to follow him
except Peter, James, and John, the brother of James.
38 When they came to the house of the leader of the
synagogue, he saw a commotion, people weeping and
wailing loudly. 39 When he had entered, he said to them, "Why
do you make a commotion and weep? The child is not dead but sleeping."
40 And they laughed at him. Then he put them all outside, and took the child's
father and mother and those who were with him, and went in where the child
was. 41 He took her by the hand and said to her, "Talitha cum," which means,
"Little girl, get up!" 42 And immediately the girl got up and began to walk
about (she was twelve years of age). At this they were overcome with amazement. 43 He strictly ordered them that no one should know this, and told them
to give her something to eat.

o **5.36** Or *ignoring*; other ancient authorities read *hearing*

The Rejection of Jesus at Nazareth

6 He left that place and came to his hometown, and his disciples followed
him. 2On the sabbath he began to teach in the synagogue, and many who
heard him were astounded. They said, "Where did this man get all this? What
is this wisdom that has been given to him? What deeds of power are being
done by his hands! 3Is not this the carpenter, the son of Mary[p] and brother of
James and Joses and Judas and Simon, and are not his sisters here with us?"
And they took offense[q] at him. 4Then Jesus said to them, "Prophets are not
without honor, except in their hometown, and among their own kin, and in
their own house." 5And he could do no deed of power there, except that he
laid his hands on a few sick people and cured them. 6And he was amazed at
their unbelief.

The Mission of the Twelve

Then he went about among the villages teaching. 7He
called the twelve and began to send them out two
by two, and gave them authority over the unclean
spirits. 8He ordered them to take nothing for their
journey except a staff; no bread, no bag, no
money in their belts; 9but to wear sandals and
not to put on two tunics. 10He said to them,
"Wherever you enter a house, stay there
until you leave the place. 11If any place will
not welcome you and they refuse to hear
you, as you leave, shake off the dust that is
on your feet as a testimony against them."

6:7–8 Why two by two and without taking anything on the journey?

Jesus wanted to teach his friends and all those who would continue his mission, that it is necessary to trust, not in one's own means, but in God above all else when proclaiming the Gospel. This mission is not for loners, it is to be shared with others.

p **6.3** Other ancient authorities read *son of the carpenter and of Mary*
q **6.3** Or *stumbled*

12 So they went out and proclaimed that all should repent. 13 They cast out
many demons, and anointed with oil many who were sick and cured them.

The Death of John the Baptist

14 King Herod heard of it, for Jesus'[r] name had become known. Some were[s]
saying, "John the baptizer has been raised from the dead; and for this reason
these powers are at work in him." 15 But others said, "It is Elijah." And others
said, "It is a prophet, like one of the prophets of old."
16 But when Herod heard of it, he said, "John, whom I
beheaded, has been raised."

17 For Herod himself had sent men who arrested
John, bound him, and put him in prison on account of
Herodias, his brother Philip's wife, because Herod[t] had
married her. 18 For John had been telling Herod, "It is not
lawful for you to have your brother's wife." 19 And
Herodias had a grudge against him, and wanted to kill
him. But she could not, 20 for Herod feared John, knowing
that he was a righteous and holy man, and he protected
him. When he heard him, he was greatly perplexed;[u] and
yet he liked to listen to him. 21 But an opportunity came
when Herod on his birthday gave a banquet for his court-
iers and officers and for the leaders of Galilee. 22 When his
daughter Herodias[v] came in and danced, she pleased Herod and his guests;
and the king said to the girl, "Ask me for whatever you wish, and I will give
it." 23 And he solemnly swore to her, "Whatever you ask me, I will give you,
even half of my kingdom." 24 She went out and said to her mother, "What

6:14 King Herod
This is Herod Antipas, son of Herod the Great, who was king at the time Jesus was born.

r **6.14** Gk *his*
s **6.14** Other ancient authorities read *He was*
t **6.17** Gk *he*
u **6.20** Other ancient authorities read *he did many things*
v **6.22** Other ancient authorities read *the daughter of Herodias herself*
w **6.27** Gk *his*

should I ask for?" She replied, "The head of John the baptizer." 25Immediately
she rushed back to the king and requested, "I want you to give me at once the
head of John the Baptist on a platter." 26The king was deeply grieved; yet out
of regard for his oaths and for the guests, he did not want to refuse her.
27Immediately the king sent a soldier of the guard with orders to bring John's[w]
head. He went and beheaded him in the prison, 28brought his head on a
platter, and gave it to the girl. Then the girl gave it to her mother. 29When his
disciples heard about it, they came and took his body, and laid it in a tomb.

Feeding the Five Thousand

30 The apostles gathered around Jesus, and told him
all that they had done and taught. 31He said to them,
"Come away to a deserted place all by yourselves
and rest a while." For many were coming and
going, and they had no leisure even to eat.
32And they went away in the boat to a deserted
place by themselves. 33Now many saw them
going and recognized them, and they hurried
there on foot from all the towns and arrived
ahead of them. 34As he went ashore, he saw a
great crowd; and he had compassion for them,
because they were like sheep without a shepherd;
and he began to teach them many things. 35When it
grew late, his disciples came to him and said, "This is a
deserted place, and the hour is now very late; 36send them
away so that they may go into the surrounding country and

6:26 Could Herod have refused to put John the Baptist to death?
He certainly could have, but as often happens, he did not have the courage or the strength to stand up for what is right. Herod preferred to choose the easiest way out.

6:34 Compassion

Jesus was not indifferent to the condition of all the hungry people. Instead, he was deeply moved. One of the psalms in the Old Testament refers to God as a mother who cannot help but love her children and who never abandons them.

6:43 Could Jesus have been more careful and avoided all these leftovers?

This miracle is a different way of presenting the reality of the kingdom that Jesus was referring to. In the kingdom of God there is an abundance of food for everyone, without end.

villages and buy something for themselves to eat."
37 But he answered them, "You give them something
to eat." They said to him, "Are we to go and buy
two hundred denarii[x] worth of bread, and give
it to them to eat?" 38 And he said to them, "How
many loaves have you? Go and see." When they
had found out, they said, "Five, and two fish."
39 Then he ordered them to get all the people to
sit down in groups on the green grass. 40 So they
sat down in groups of hundreds and of fifties.
41 Taking the five loaves and the two fish, he
looked up to heaven, and blessed and broke
the loaves, and gave them to his disciples to
set before the people; and he divided the two
fish among them all. 42 And all ate and were
filled; (43) and they took up twelve baskets full
of broken pieces and of the fish. 44 Those
who had eaten the loaves numbered five
thousand men.

Jesus Walks on the Water

45 Immediately he made his disciples get
into the boat and go on ahead to the other
side, to Bethsaida, while he dismissed the
crowd. 46 After saying farewell to them, he
went up on the mountain to pray.

x **6.37** The denarius was the usual day's wage for a laborer

47 When evening came, the boat was out on the sea, and he was alone on
the land. [48]When he saw that they were straining at the oars against an
adverse wind, he came towards them early in the morning,
walking on the sea. He intended to pass them by. [49]But
when they saw him walking on the sea, they thought it
was a ghost and cried out; [50]for they all saw him and were
terrified. But immediately he spoke to them and said, "Take
heart, it is I; do not be afraid." [51]Then he got into the boat
with them and the wind ceased. And they were utterly
astounded, [52]for they did not understand about the
loaves, but their hearts were hardened.

Healing the Sick in Gennesaret

53 When they had crossed over, they came
to land at Gennesaret and moored the boat.
[54]When they got out of the boat, people at
once recognized him, [55]and rushed about
that whole region and began to bring the sick
on mats to wherever they heard he was. [56]And
wherever he went, into villages or cities or
farms, they laid the sick in the marketplaces,
and begged him that they might touch even
the fringe of his cloak; and all who touched it
were healed.

The Tradition of the Elders

7 Now when the Pharisees and some of the scribes who had come from
Jerusalem gathered around him, 2 they noticed that some of his disciples were
eating with defiled hands, that is, without washing them. 3 (For the Pharisees,
and all the Jews, do not eat unless they thoroughly wash their
hands,[y] thus observing the tradition of the elders; 4 and they
do not eat anything from the market unless they wash it;[z]
and there are also many other traditions that they observe,
the washing of cups, pots, and bronze kettles.[a]) 5 So
the Pharisees and the scribes asked him, "Why do
your disciples not live[b] according to the tradition
of the elders, but eat with defiled hands?" 6 He
said to them, "Isaiah prophesied rightly about
you hypocrites, as it is written,

'This people honors me with their lips,
but their hearts are far from me;
7 in vain do they worship me,
teaching human precepts as doctrines.'

8 You abandon the commandment of God
and hold to human tradition."

9 Then he said to them, "You have a fine
way of rejecting the commandment of God
in order to keep your tradition! 10 For Moses

7:2–4 Why did the Pharisees have so many rules throughout the day?

In Jesus' time, some of the customs for observing the Law of God were unquestioned. Doing these things without knowing why meant the people were forgetting the true meaning of the commandments. Here, Jesus tried to help the Israelites remember the true intent of the Law, just as he did with the Sabbath (Mk 2:23–28).

y **7.3** Meaning of Gk uncertain

z **7.4** Other ancient authorities read *and when they come from the marketplace, they do not eat unless they purify themselves*

a **7.4** Other ancient authorities add *and beds*

b **7.5** Gk *walk*

said, 'Honor your father and your mother';
and, 'Whoever speaks evil of father or
mother must surely die.' 11 But you say that
if anyone tells father or mother, 'Whatever
support you might have had from me is
Corban' (that is, an offering to God[c])—
12 then you no longer permit doing anything for a father or mother, 13 thus making
void the word of God through your tradition
that you have handed on. And you do many
things like this."
14 Then he called the crowd again and said to
them, "Listen to me, all of you, and understand:
15 there is nothing outside a person that by going in
can defile, but the things that come out are what
defile."[d]
17 When he had left the crowd and entered the house,
his disciples asked him about the parable. 18 He said to them,
"Then do you also fail to understand? Do you not see that whatever goes into a person from outside cannot defile, 19 since it enters,
not the heart but the stomach, and goes out into the sewer?" (Thus he declared
all foods clean.) 20 And he said, "It is what comes out of a person that defiles.

7:19 Why does Jesus speak about impure foods?

Many cultures and religions have bans on certain foods. Here, however, Jesus reminds everyone that evil is not found within things *but, rather, it is found in the human heart. By saying this, "he declared all foods clean" and, therefore, removed all bans on foods.*

c **7.11** Gk lacks *to God*

d **7.15** Other ancient authorities add verse 16, *"Let anyone with ears to hear listen"*

7:21–22 Fornication, adultery, licentiousness
With these words, Jesus is referring to actions which indicate an unhealthy and unholy relationship between a man and a woman.

7:24 Were Tyre and Sidon in Israel?
No, they were in Phoenicia (present-day Lebanon) and, in fact, the woman who is the protagonist, or main character, in this story was both Syrophoenician and a pagan. In this passage, Jesus reveals a shift in his mission. Now it was not only for the Israelites, but for all men and women who recognize, believe, and come to him.

21 For it is from within, from the human heart, that
evil intentions come: fornication, theft, murder,
22 adultery, avarice, wickedness, deceit, licentiousness, envy, slander, pride, folly. 23 All these
evil things come from within, and they defile a
person."

The Syrophoenician Woman's Faith

24 From there he set out and went away to the
region of Tyre.[e] He entered a house and did not
want anyone to know he was there. Yet he could
not escape notice, 25 but a woman whose little
daughter had an unclean spirit immediately
heard about him, and she came and bowed
down at his feet. 26 Now the woman was a
Gentile, of Syrophoenician origin. She begged
him to cast the demon out of her daughter.
27 He said to her, "Let the children be fed first,
for it is not fair to take the children's food and
throw it to the dogs." 28 But she answered him,
"Sir,[f] even the dogs under the table eat the
children's crumbs." 29 Then he said to her, "For
saying that, you may go—the demon has left
your daughter." 30 So she went home, found the
child lying on the bed, and the demon gone.

e **7.24** Other ancient authorities add *and Sidon*
f **7.28** Or *Lord*; other ancient authorities prefix *Yes*

Jesus Cures a Deaf Man

31 Then he returned from the region of Tyre, and went by
way of Sidon towards the Sea of Galilee, in the region of
the Decapolis. 32 They brought to him a deaf man who
had an impediment in his speech; and they begged
him to lay his hand on him. 33 He took him aside
in private, away from the crowd, and put his
fingers into his ears, and he spat and touched
his tongue. 34 Then looking up to heaven, he
sighed and said to him, "Ephphatha," that is,
"Be opened." 35 And immediately his ears were
opened, his tongue was released, and he spoke
plainly. 36 Then Jesus[g] ordered them to tell no
one; but the more he ordered them, the more
zealously they proclaimed it. 37 They were
astounded beyond measure, saying, "He has
done everything well; he even makes the deaf to
hear and the mute to speak."

7:32–37 From all Jesus' miracles, why did you choose to tell us about this one?

Because the man who was healed of his inability to hear or speak is the perfect symbol for the reader who recognizes his or her own inability to hear the Good News and to proclaim that Jesus is Lord.

Feeding the Four Thousand

8 In those days when there was again a great crowd without
anything to eat, he called his disciples and said to them, 2 "I
have compassion for the crowd, because they have been with
me now for three days and have nothing to eat. 3 If I send them
away hungry to their homes, they will faint on the way—and some

g **7.36** Gk *he*

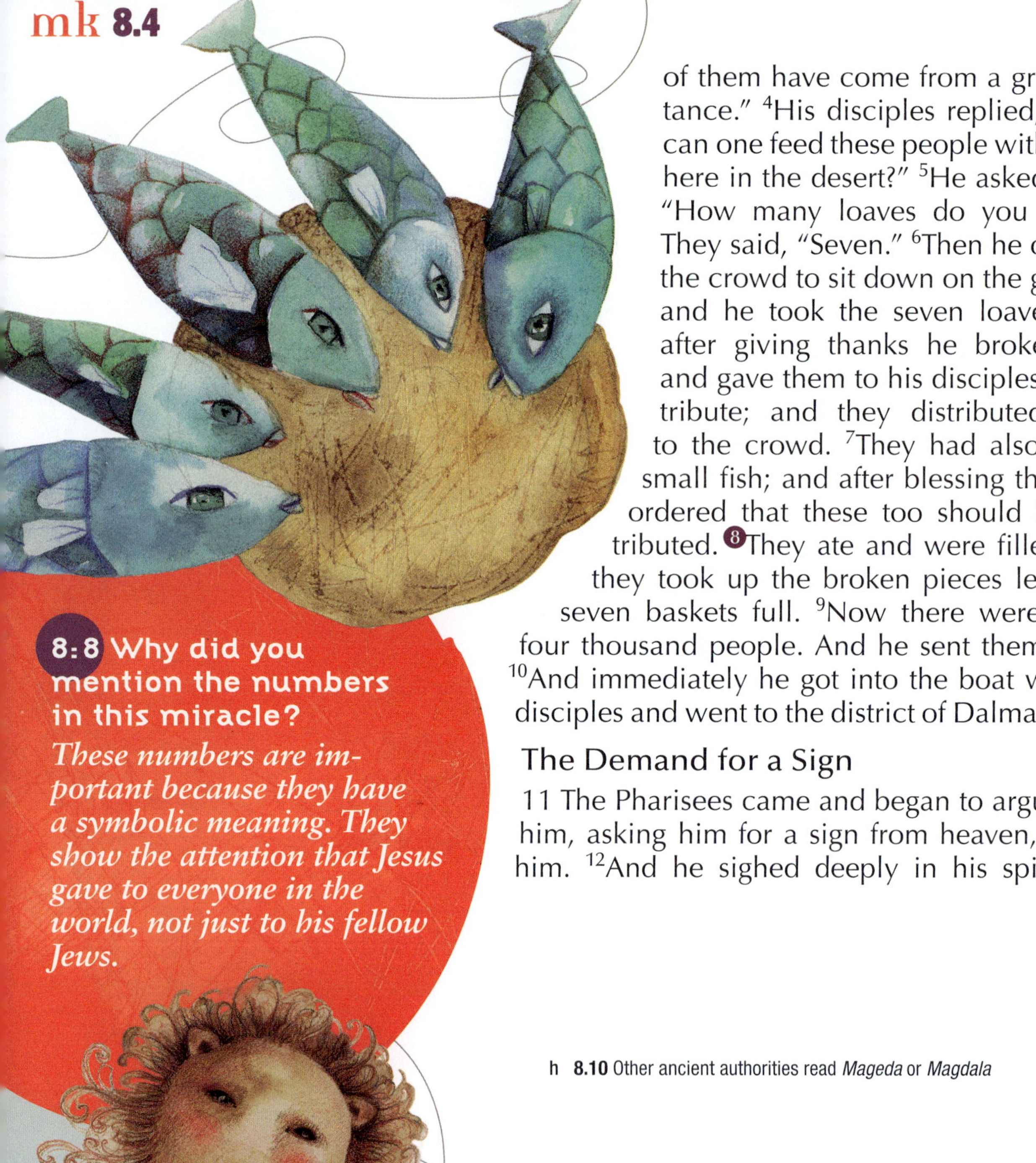

of them have come from a great distance." [4]His disciples replied, "How
can one feed these people with bread
here in the desert?" [5]He asked them,
"How many loaves do you have?"
They said, "Seven." [6]Then he ordered
the crowd to sit down on the ground;
and he took the seven loaves, and
after giving thanks he broke them
and gave them to his disciples to distribute; and they distributed them
to the crowd. [7]They had also a few
small fish; and after blessing them, he
ordered that these too should be distributed. [8]They ate and were filled; and
they took up the broken pieces left over,
seven baskets full. [9]Now there were about
four thousand people. And he sent them away.
[10]And immediately he got into the boat with his
disciples and went to the district of Dalmanutha.[h]

8:8 Why did you mention the numbers in this miracle?

These numbers are important because they have a symbolic meaning. They show the attention that Jesus gave to everyone in the world, not just to his fellow Jews.

The Demand for a Sign

11 The Pharisees came and began to argue with
him, asking him for a sign from heaven, to test
him. [12]And he sighed deeply in his spirit and

h **8.10** Other ancient authorities read *Mageda* or *Magdala*

said, "Why does this generation ask for a sign?
Truly I tell you, no sign will be given to this generation." 13And he left them, and getting into the
boat again, he went across to the other side.

The Yeast of the Pharisees and of Herod

14 Now the disciples[i] had forgotten to bring
any bread; and they had only one loaf with
them in the boat. 15And he cautioned them,
saying, "Watch out—beware of the yeast of
the Pharisees and the yeast of Herod."[j] 16They
said to one another, "It is because we have
no bread." 17And becoming aware of it, Jesus
said to them, "Why are you talking about having
no bread? Do you still not perceive or understand? Are
your hearts hardened? 18Do you have eyes, and fail to
see? Do you have ears, and fail to hear? And do you
not remember? 19When I broke the five loaves
for the five thousand, how many baskets full of
broken pieces did you collect?" They said to
him, "Twelve." 20"And the seven for the four
thousand, how many baskets full of broken
pieces did you collect?" And they said to him,
"Seven." 21Then he said to them, "Do you not
yet understand?"

8:15 Yeast of the Pharisees

Here, yeast is something that ruins dough by causing it to ferment.

8:17–21 Why did Jesus get so angry? What should the disciples have understood?

They did not yet understand that when Jesus was with them, they had everything. They had forgotten to bring enough bread, but they had with them the only Bread capable of satisfying every need: Jesus. The "one loaf" they had with them in the boat is symbolic of Jesus.

i **8.14** Gk *they*
j **8.15** Other ancient authorities read *the Herodians*

8:25 Why didn't the miracle work the first time?
That blind man represents every disciple. Jesus helps him to understand little by little, without forcing him and without rushing, that he is the Son of God.

8:29 Messiah

Some people think Christ is Jesus' last name, but it is not. "Christ" is a Greek term that means "anointed one" or "consecrated." It's meaning is similar to the Hebrew word for Messiah. At the time of Jesus, the Jews were waiting for the Messiah to free them from the Romans.

Jesus Cures a Blind Man at Bethsaida

22 They came to Bethsaida. Some people[k]
brought a blind man to him and begged him to
touch him. 23 He took the blind man by the hand
and led him out of the village; and when he had
put saliva on his eyes and laid his hands on him,
he asked him, "Can you see anything?" 24 And
the man[l] looked up and said, "I can see people,
but they look like trees, walking." 25 Then Jesus[m]
laid his hands on his eyes again; and he looked
intently and his sight was restored, and he saw
everything clearly. 26 Then he sent him away to his
home, saying, "Do not even go into the village."[n]

Peter's Declaration about Jesus

27 Jesus went on with his disciples to the villages
of Caesarea Philippi; and on the way he asked his
disciples, "Who do people say that I am?" 28 And
they answered him, "John the Baptist; and others,
Elijah; and still others, one of the prophets." 29 He
asked them, "But who do you say that I am?" Peter
answered him, "You are the Messiah."[o] 30 And he
sternly ordered them not to tell anyone about him.

k **8.22** Gk *They*
l **8.24** Gk *he*
m **8.25** Gk *he*
n **8.26** Other ancient authorities add *or tell anyone in the village*
o **8.29** Or *the Christ*

How to Follow Jesus? (Mk 8:31–14:50)

The demands of Jesus' teachings inspire and strengthen the disciples' desire to follow Jesus more radically. This section dedicated to this theme can be articulated in three parts.

The first part (8:31–10:52) is made up of three announcements of the paschal mystery. Along the path from Galilee to the gates of Jerusalem Jesus tells the disciples what awaits him is his death and resurrection. Each of the three times the Twelve Apostles react with an attitude of incomprehension, resistance, and refusal.

The second part (11:1–13:37), which takes place in Jerusalem and the Temple, presents the confrontation between Jesus and his people. It shows a difficult and complex relationship which involves the disciples themselves. The symbols of the fig tree, the vine, and the Temple foreshadow Jesus' destiny that looms on the horizon.

The last part (14:1–50) clearly describes the destination of Jesus Master's path, which is expressed by three highly evocative gestures: the alabaster jar broken in Bethany, the bread broken during the Last Supper, and Jesus' broken heart in the prayer at Gethsemane. The section concludes with Jesus' disciples abandoning him. Those who had left everything to follow him still find it too hard to follow him to the death and flee.

Jesus Foretells His Death and Resurrection

31 Then he began to teach them that the
Son of Man must undergo great suffering, and be rejected by the elders,
the chief priests, and the scribes, and
be killed, and after three days rise

8:31 Did Jesus know that he would rise after three days?

Jesus knew that love is stronger than death and that the Father would not abandon him. Jesus took the image of the three days from some verses of the prophets Hosea (6:2) and Joel (2:1).

8:32 Did Peter really yell at Jesus?

Yes! For Peter—like many of the Jews of his day—it was unthinkable to have a suffering and persecuted Messiah. Peter needed to learn to reason like God.

8:38 Glory

In the Hebrew world, the "glory" of God was the way of speaking about God's presence and his manifestation in history.

again. 32 He said all this quite openly. And Peter
took him aside and began to rebuke him. 33 But
turning and looking at his disciples, he rebuked
Peter and said, "Get behind me, Satan! For you
are setting your mind not on divine things but
on human things."

34 He called the crowd with his disciples,
and said to them, "If any want to become my
followers, let them deny themselves and take
up their cross and follow me. 35 For those who
want to save their life will lose it, and those
who lose their life for my sake, and for the sake
of the gospel,[p] will save it. 36 For what will it profit
them to gain the whole world and forfeit their life?
37 Indeed, what can they give in return for their life?
38 Those who are ashamed of me and of my words[q]
in this adulterous and sinful generation, of them
the Son of Man will also be ashamed when he
comes in the glory of his Father with the holy
angels."

9 1 And he said to them, "Truly I tell you, there
are some standing here who will not taste death
until they see that the kingdom of God has come
with[r] power."

p **8.35** Other ancient authorities read *lose their life for the sake of the gospel*
q **8.38** Other ancient authorities read *and of mine*
r **9.1** Or *in*

The Transfiguration

2 Six days later, Jesus took with him Peter and
James and John, and led them up a high mountain apart, by themselves. And he was transfigured before them, (3) and his clothes became
dazzling white, such as no one[s] on earth
could bleach them. 4And there appeared
to them Elijah with Moses, who were
talking with Jesus. 5Then Peter said
to Jesus, "Rabbi, it is good for us to
be here; let us make three dwellings,[t]
one for you, one for Moses, and one for
Elijah." 6He did not know what to say,
for they were terrified. 7Then a cloud
overshadowed them, and from the cloud
there came a voice, "This is my Son, the
Beloved;[u] listen to him!" 8Suddenly when
they looked around, they saw no one with
them any more, but only Jesus.

9:3 Why did Jesus' clothes become so white?

Right at the halfway point in his public life, Jesus reveals himself to the disciples as who he really is the Son of God. The first time Jesus is referred to as God's son is at his baptism (1:9–11). It will be repeated by the centurion when Jesus is on the cross (15:39). The extremely white clothes are a sign of Jesus' divine identity.

9:7 Cloud

This is one of the symbols by which God mysteriously makes himself present. Read Exodus 14:15–20 which tells the story about God guiding his people out of Egypt.

s **9.3** Gk *no fuller*
t **9.5** Or *tents*
u **9.7** Or *my beloved Son*

The Coming of Elijah

9 As they were coming down the mountain, he ordered them to tell no one
about what they had seen, until after the Son of Man had risen from the dead.
10 So they kept the matter to themselves, questioning what this rising from the
dead could mean. 11 Then they asked him, "Why do the scribes say that Elijah
must come first?" 12 He said to them, "Elijah is indeed coming first to restore
all things. How then is it written about the Son of Man, that he
is to go through many sufferings and be treated with contempt? 13 But I tell you that Elijah has come, and they did
to him whatever they pleased, as it is written about him."

The Healing of a Boy with a Spirit

14 When they came to the disciples, they saw a great
crowd around them, and some scribes arguing with
them. 15 When the whole crowd saw him, they were
immediately overcome with awe, and they ran forward to greet him. 16 He asked them, "What are
you arguing about with them?" 17 Someone from
the crowd answered him, "Teacher, I brought you
my son; he has a spirit that makes him unable
to speak; 18 and whenever it seizes him, it dashes
him down; and he foams and grinds his teeth and
becomes rigid; and I asked your disciples to cast it
out, but they could not do so." 19 He answered them,
"You faithless generation, how much longer must I
be among you? How much longer must I put up with
you? Bring him to me." 20 And they brought the boy[v]
to him. When the spirit saw him, immediately it con-
vulsed the boy,[w] and he fell on the ground and rolled

9:14–29

There is so much evil in the world. What is God doing about it?

This scene reminds us that Jesus drew closer to each suffering person he met. Oftentimes, those who suffer are closer to God than others and, by healing them, Jesus shows that God always wills the good of all people.

v **9.20** Gk *him*
w **9.20** Gk *him*

about, foaming at the mouth. 21 Jesus[x] asked the father, "How long
has this been happening to him?" And he said, "From childhood. 22 It has often cast him into the fire and into the water,
to destroy him; but if you are able to do anything, have
pity on us and help us." 23 Jesus said to him, "If you are
able!—All things can be done for the one who believes."
24 Immediately the father of the child cried out,[y] "I believe;
help my unbelief!" 25 When Jesus saw that a crowd came
running together, he rebuked the unclean spirit, saying
to it, "You spirit that keeps this boy from speaking and
hearing, I command you, come out of him, and never
enter him again!" 26 After crying out and convulsing him
terribly, it came out, and the boy was like a corpse, so
that most of them said, "He is dead." 27 But Jesus took him
by the hand and lifted him up, and he was able to stand.
28 When he had entered the house, his disciples asked him
privately, "Why could we not cast it out?" 29 He said to them,
"This kind can come out only through prayer."[z]

Jesus Again Foretells His Death and Resurrection

30 They went on from there and passed through
Galilee. He did not want anyone to know it; 31 for he
was teaching his disciples, saying to them, "The Son
of Man is to be betrayed into human hands, and
they will kill him, and three days after being killed,
he will rise again." 32 But they did not understand
what he was saying and were afraid to ask him.

x **9.21** Gk *He*
y **9.24** Other ancient authorities add *with tears*
z **9.29** Other ancient authorities add *and fasting*

Who Is the Greatest?

33 Then they came to Capernaum; and when he was in the
house he asked them, "What were you arguing about
on the way?" 34But they were silent, for on the way
they had argued with one another who was the
greatest. 35He sat down, called the twelve,
and said to them, "Whoever wants to be
first must be last of all and servant of all."
36Then he took a little child and put it
among them; and taking it in his arms, he
said to them, 37"Whoever welcomes one
such child in my name welcomes me,
and whoever welcomes me welcomes
not me but the one who sent me."

Another Exorcist

38 John said to him, "Teacher, we
saw someone[a] casting out demons in
your name, and we tried to stop him,
because he was not following us." 39But
Jesus said, "Do not stop him; for no one
who does a deed of power in my name
will be able soon afterward to speak evil
of me. 40Whoever is not against us is for us.
41For truly I tell you, whoever gives you a cup
of water to drink because you bear the name of
Christ will by no means lose the reward.

9:36 Why did Jesus place a child in the midst of the disciples?

In Jesus' day, children received little attention from adults. But Jesus presents the child as a model for faith and for receiving Jesus' word with trust and enthusiasm.

9:38 Why were there so many people possessed by the devil at that time?

It was sometimes difficult to tell the difference between someone who was possessed by the devil and someone who was just ill. Some of these "possessed" people could have had a mental or physical sickness not caused by an evil spirit.

a **9.38** Other ancient authorities add *who does not follow us*

9:43, 45, and 47 Cut off your hand, your foot? Tear out your eye?! Does Jesus really ask people to do that?

Languages in eastern lands often use strong images in order to shock the listener. Jesus does not want anyone to to hurt oneself in any way. What Jesus is saying is that sin should be avoided at all times. His disciples should reject every form of evil.

10:2 Divorce
A decree that a marriage has legally ended.

Temptations to Sin

42 "If any of you put a stumbling block before one
of these little ones who believe in me,[b] it would
be better for you if a great millstone were hung
around your neck and you were thrown into the
sea. 43 If your hand causes you to stumble, cut
it off; it is better for you to enter life maimed
than to have two hands and to go to hell,[c]
to the unquenchable fire.[d] 45 And if your foot
causes you to stumble, cut it off; it is better
for you to enter life lame than to have two
feet and to be thrown into hell.[e] [f] 47 And if
your eye causes you to stumble, tear it out; it
is better for you to enter the kingdom of God
with one eye than to have two eyes and to
be thrown into hell,[g] 48 where their worm never
dies, and the fire is never quenched.
49 "For everyone will be salted with fire.[h] 50 Salt
is good; but if salt has lost its saltiness, how can you
season it?[i] Have salt in yourselves, and be at peace with
one another."

Teaching about Divorce

10 He left that place and went to the region of Judea
and[j] beyond the Jordan. And crowds again gathered
around him; and, as was his custom, he again taught them.
2 Some Pharisees came, and to test him they asked, "Is it

b **9.42** Other ancient authorities lack *in me*
c **9.43** Gk *Gehenna*
d **9.43** Verses 44 and 46 (which are identical with verse 48) are lacking in the best ancient authorities
e **9.45** Gk *Gehenna*
f **9.45** Verses 44 and 46 (which are identical with verse 48) are lacking in the best ancient authorities
g **9.47** Gk *Gehenna*
h **9.49** Other ancient authorities either add or substitute *and every sacrifice will be salted with salt*
i **9.50** Or *how can you restore its saltiness?*
j **10.1** Other ancient authorities lack *and*

lawful for a man to divorce his wife?" 3He answered them, "What did Moses
command you?" 4They said, "Moses allowed a man to write a certificate of
dismissal and to divorce her." 5But Jesus said to them, "Because of your hard-
ness of heart he wrote this commandment for you. 6But from the beginning of
creation, 'God made them male and female.' 7'For this reason a
man shall leave his father and mother and be joined to his wife,[k]
8and the two shall become one flesh.' So they are no longer two,
but one flesh. 9Therefore what God has joined together, let no
one separate."

10 Then in the house the disciples asked him again
about this matter. 11He said to them, "Whoever
divorces his wife and marries another commits
adultery against her; 12and if she divorces her
husband and marries another, she commits
adultery."

Jesus Blesses Little Children

13 People were bringing little children to
him in order that he might touch them; and
the disciples spoke sternly to them. 14But
when Jesus saw this, he was indignant and
said to them, "Let the little children come
to me; do not stop them; for it is to such
as these that the kingdom of God belongs.
15Truly I tell you, whoever does not receive the
kingdom of God as a little child will never enter
it." 16And he took them up in his arms, laid his
hands on them, and blessed them.

10:1–45 If we want to be people who trust Jesus and accept God's kingdom, what do we have to do?

This chapter contains the actions and teachings that answer your question. We must live like Jesus, who loves faithfully, becomes little (is humble), is not governed by earthly riches, and serves others.

k **10.7** Other ancient authorities lack *and be joined to his wife*

10:19 Defraud
To cheat; to behave dishonestly

10:25 What do camels have to do with needles?
It is possible that Jesus used a different, but still exaggerated, image. (The Greek word kamelos can also mean "thick rope.") Regardless of the exact image, it is still clear that Jesus is explaining that only those who trust in God and enter into relationship with him can be saved. Jesus communicated the same message to the rich man when Jesus looked at him with great love and invited him to renounce his earthly possessions for Jesus' sake.

The Rich Man

17 As he was setting out on a journey, a man ran up and
knelt before him, and asked him, "Good Teacher, what must
I do to inherit eternal life?" 18Jesus said to him, "Why do
you call me good? No one is good but God alone. 19You
know the commandments: 'You shall not murder; You shall
not commit adultery; You shall not steal; You shall not bear
false witness; You shall not defraud; Honor your father
and mother.' " 20He said to him, "Teacher, I have
kept all these since my youth." 21Jesus, looking at
him, loved him and said, "You lack one thing;
go, sell what you own, and give the money[l]
to the poor, and you will have treasure in
heaven; then come, follow me." 22When he
heard this, he was shocked and went away
grieving, for he had many possessions.

23 Then Jesus looked around and said
to his disciples, "How hard it will be for
those who have wealth to enter the
kingdom of God!" 24And the disciples
were perplexed at these words. But Jesus
said to them again, "Children, how hard it
is[m] to enter the kingdom of God! 25It is easier
for a camel to go through the eye of a needle
than for someone who is rich to enter the
kingdom of God." 26They were greatly astounded
and said to one another,[n] "Then who can be saved?"

l **10.21** Gk lacks *the money*
m **10.24** Other ancient authorities add *for those who trust in riches*
n **10.26** Other ancient authorities read *to him*

27 Jesus looked at them and said, "For mortals it is impossible,
but not for God; for God all things are possible."
28 Peter began to say to him, "Look, we have
left everything and followed you." 29 Jesus said,
"Truly I tell you, there is no one who has left
house or brothers or sisters or mother or
father or children or fields, for my sake and
for the sake of the good news,[o] 30 who will
not receive a hundredfold now in this age—
houses, brothers and sisters, mothers and
children, and fields, with persecutions—and
in the age to come eternal life. 31 But many
who are first will be last, and the last will be
first."

A Third Time Jesus Foretells His Death and Resurrection

32 They were on the road, going up to Jerusalem,
and Jesus was walking ahead of them; they were
amazed, and those who followed were afraid. He
took the twelve aside again and began to tell them
what was to happen to him, 33 saying, "See, we are
going up to Jerusalem, and the Son of Man will be
handed over to the chief priests and the scribes, and
they will condemn him to death; then they will hand
him over to the Gentiles; 34 they will mock him, and spit
upon him, and flog him, and kill him; and after three
days he will rise again."

10:33 Chief priests
These religious leaders of Israel were the heads of the various priestly families who directed Jewish religious life.

o **10.29** Or *gospel*

The Request of James and John

35 James and John, the sons of Zebedee, came forward to him and said to him, "Teacher, we want
you to do for us whatever we ask of you." 36And
he said to them, "What is it you want me to
do for you?" 37And they said to him, "Grant
us to sit, one at your right hand and one
at your left, in your glory." 38But Jesus said
to them, "You do not know what you are
asking. Are you able to drink the cup that I
drink, or be baptized with the baptism that
I am baptized with?" 39They replied, "We
are able." Then Jesus said to them, "The cup
that I drink you will drink; and with the baptism with which I am baptized, you will be
baptized; 40but to sit at my right hand or at my
left is not mine to grant, but it is for those for
whom it has been prepared."
41 When the ten heard this, they began to be angry
with James and John. 42So Jesus called them and said to
them, "You know that among the Gentiles those whom they recognize as
their rulers lord it over them, and their great ones are tyrants over them. 43But
it is not so among you; but whoever wishes to become great among you must
be your servant, 44and whoever wishes to be first among you must be slave of

10:38 What was Jesus referring to when speaking of a chalice and baptism?

In the face of two brothers' dreams of greatness, Jesus is speaking of the chalice of self-offering and baptism of suffering that he himself will undergo. Glory can be reached only through the cross.

all. 45For the Son of Man came not to be served
but to serve, and to give his life a ransom for
many."

The Healing of Blind Bartimaeus

46 They came to Jericho. As he and his disciples and a large crowd were leaving Jericho,
Bartimaeus son of Timaeus, a blind beggar,
was sitting by the roadside. 47When he heard
that it was Jesus of Nazareth, he began to shout
out and say, "Jesus, Son of David, have mercy
on me!" 48Many sternly ordered him to be
quiet, but he cried out even more loudly, "Son
of David, have mercy on me!" 49Jesus stood still
and said, "Call him here." And they called the
blind man, saying to him, "Take heart; get up,
he is calling you." 50So throwing off his cloak, he
sprang up and came to Jesus. 51Then Jesus said
to him, "What do you want me to do for you?"
The blind man said to him, "My teacher,[p] let me
see again." 52Jesus said to him, "Go; your faith
has made you well." Immediately he regained
his sight and followed him on the way.

p **10.51** Aramaic *Rabbouni*

Jesus' Triumphal Entry into Jerusalem

11 When they were approaching Jerusalem, at Bethphage and Bethany, near the Mount of Olives, he sent
two of his disciples 2and said to them, "Go into the village ahead of you, and immediately as you enter
it, you will find tied there a colt that has never
been ridden; untie it and bring it. 3If anyone
says to you, 'Why are you doing this?' just say
this, 'The Lord needs it and will send it back here
immediately.'" 4They went away and found a colt
tied near a door, outside in the street. As they were
untying it, 5some of the bystanders said to them,
"What are you doing, untying the colt?" 6They told
them what Jesus had said; and they allowed them
to take it. 7Then they brought the colt to Jesus
and threw their cloaks on it; and he sat on it.
8Many people spread their cloaks on the road,
and others spread leafy branches that they had
cut in the fields. 9Then those who went ahead
and those who followed were shouting,

"Hosanna!
Blessed is the one who comes in
the name of the Lord!
10 Blessed is the coming kingdom of
our ancestor David!
Hosanna in the highest heaven!"

11:4 Why did he ride a donkey?

Because, as the prophet Zechariah had foretold (Zec 9:9), the donkey is a sign of Jesus' humility. And Jesus is a humble and peaceful Messiah who came to save and not to dominate.

11 Then he entered Jerusalem and went into the temple; and when he had looked around at everything, as it was already late, he went out to Bethany with the twelve.

Jesus Curses the Fig Tree

12 On the following day, when they came from Bethany,
he was hungry. 13 Seeing in the distance a fig tree in leaf,
he went to see whether perhaps he would find anything on it. When he came to it, he found nothing but
leaves, for it was not the season for figs. 14 He said to
it, "May no one ever eat fruit from you again." And his disciples heard it.

Jesus Cleanses the Temple

15 Then they came to Jerusalem. And he entered the temple and began to drive out those who were selling and those who were buying in the temple, and he overturned the tables of the money changers and the seats of those who sold doves;
16 and he would not allow anyone to carry anything through the temple.
17 He was teaching and saying, "Is it not
written,

> 'My house shall be called a house of prayer for all the nations'?
> But you have made it a den of robbers."

11:9 Hosanna

This word, which we sing during the Mass, means "Save us!" Those who cried out this word as Jesus entered Jerusalem were proclaiming him as Savior and Messiah.

11:13, 15

Jesus curses a fig tree, and he angrily drives out the sellers from the Temple. Was he truly that angry?

Jesus did these two things to show that Jewish rituals performed without awareness of God's presence bore no fruit. Jesus is the new Temple. He has become the meeting place, and he renews the rituals which serve to reunite God and his people.

18 And when the chief priests and the scribes heard it, they
kept looking for a way to kill him; for they were afraid
of him, because the whole crowd was spellbound by his
teaching. 19 And when evening came, Jesus and his disciples[q] went out of the city.

The Lesson from the Withered Fig Tree

20 In the morning as they passed by, they saw the fig tree
withered away to its roots. 21 Then Peter remembered and said to
him, "Rabbi, look! The fig tree that you cursed has withered." 22 Jesus answered
them, "Have[r] faith in God. 23 Truly I tell you, if you say to this mountain, 'Be
taken up and thrown into the sea,' and if you do not doubt in your heart, but
believe that what you say will come to pass, it will be done for you. 24 So I tell
you, whatever you ask for in prayer, believe that you have received[s] it, and it
will be yours.

25 "Whenever you stand praying, forgive, if you have anything against
anyone; so that your Father in heaven may also forgive you your trespasses."[t]

Jesus' Authority Is Questioned

27 Again they came to Jerusalem. As he was walking in the temple, the chief
priests, the scribes, and the elders came to him 28 and said, "By what authority
are you doing these things? Who gave you this authority to do them?" 29 Jesus
said to them, "I will ask you one question; answer me, and I will tell you by
what authority I do these things. 30 Did the baptism of John come from heaven,
or was it of human origin? Answer me." 31 They argued with one another, "If we
say, 'From heaven,' he will say, 'Why then did you not believe him?' 32 But shall
we say, 'Of human origin'?"—they were afraid of the crowd, for all regarded

q **11.19** Gk *they*: other ancient authorities read *he*
r **11.22** Other ancient authorities read *"If you have*
s **11.24** Other ancient authorities read *are receiving*
t **11.25** Other ancient authorities add verse 26, *"But if you do not forgive, neither will your Father in heaven forgive your trespasses."*

John as truly a prophet. [33]So they answered Jesus, "We do not
know." And Jesus said to them, "Neither will I tell you by what
authority I am doing these things."

The Parable of the Wicked Tenants

12 Then he began to speak to them in parables. "A
man planted a vineyard, put a fence around it, dug a
pit for the wine press, and built a watchtower; then
he leased it to tenants and went to another country.
[2]When the season came, he sent a slave to the tenants to collect from them his share of the produce
of the vineyard. [3]But they seized him, and beat
him, and sent him away empty-handed. [4]And
again he sent another slave to them; this one
they beat over the head and insulted. [5]Then he
sent another, and that one they killed. And so it
was with many others; some they beat, and others
they killed. [6]He had still one other, a beloved son.
Finally he sent him to them, saying, 'They will
respect my son.' [7]But those tenants said to one
another, 'This is the heir; come, let us kill him,
and the inheritance will be ours.' [8]So they seized
him, killed him, and threw him out of the vineyard.

12:1–9 What was Jesus thinking about when he told this parable?

Jesus was reminding his listeners about the history of the people of Israel and its leaders. Historically, the people did not listen to the prophets and now they will even reject him, the Son, who will die outside the city.

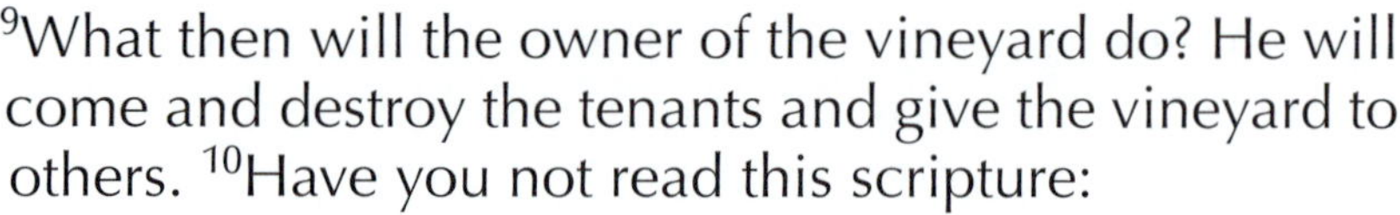

12:10 Cornerstone
This is the most important stone in construction because it is the one that supports the whole building.

12:14 Who is the emperor?
At that time the emperor, or Caesar, of the Roman empire was Tiberius.

9 What then will the owner of the vineyard do? He will
come and destroy the tenants and give the vineyard to
others. 10 Have you not read this scripture:
'The stone that the builders rejected
has become the cornerstone;[u]
11 this was the Lord's doing,
and it is amazing in our eyes'?"
12 When they realized that he had told this parable against them, they wanted to arrest him, but they feared the crowd. So they left him and went away.

The Question about Paying Taxes

13 Then they sent to him some Pharisees and some
Herodians to trap him in what he said. 14 And they
came and said to him, "Teacher, we know that you
are sincere, and show deference to no one; for you
do not regard people with partiality, but teach the
way of God in accordance with truth. Is it lawful to
pay taxes to the emperor, or not? 15 Should we pay
them, or should we not?" But knowing their hypocrisy, he said to them, "Why are you putting me to the
test? Bring me a denarius and let me see it." 16 And they
brought one. Then he said to them, "Whose head is this,
and whose title?" They answered, "The emperor's." 17 Jesus
said to them, "Give to the emperor the things that are the
emperor's, and to God the things that are God's." And they
were utterly amazed at him.

u **12.10** Or *keystone*

The Question about the Resurrection

18 Some Sadducees, who say there is no resurrection, came to him and asked him a question,
saying, 19"Teacher, Moses wrote for us that if a
man's brother dies, leaving a wife but no child, the
man[v] shall marry the widow and raise up children
for his brother. 20There were seven brothers; the first
married and, when he died, left no children; 21and
the second married the widow[w] and died, leaving
no children; and the third likewise; 22none of the
seven left children. Last of all the woman herself
died. 23In the resurrection[x] whose wife will she be?
For the seven had married her."

24 Jesus said to them, "Is not this the reason you
are wrong, that you know neither the scriptures nor
the power of God? 25For when they rise from the
dead, they neither marry nor are given in marriage,
but are like angels in heaven. 26And as for the
dead being raised, have you not read in the book
of Moses, in the story about the bush, how God
said to him, 'I am the God of Abraham, the God
of Isaac, and the God of Jacob'? 27He is God not
of the dead, but of the living; you are quite
wrong."

12:18 Sadducees
This Hebrew aristocratic group was in favor of Roman rule in Israel and denied the resurrection of the body after death.

12:19–22 A woman who has to marry seven brothers . . . What a strange law!
According to Jewish tradition, if a married man died without having children, his brother had to marry his widow in order to give the deceased brother heirs and ensure the continuation of the family.

v **12.19** Gk *his brother*
w **12.21** Gk *her*
x **12.23** Other ancient authorities add *when they rise*

12:29 Jesus' answer is not a part of the Ten Commandments!

The Law of love which Jesus presents is a summary of all the commandments. Jesus spent his whole life loving others, even to the point of making a gift of himself.

12:35 Why was it important that Jesus belong to the tribe of David?

King David wanted to build the Temple in Jerusalem as soon as the city was conquered. At that time, the prophet Nathan (2 Sm 7) told him that God does not dwell in one location. Rather, God would remain close to his people through David's descendants.

The First Commandment

28 One of the scribes came near and heard them dis-
puting with one another, and seeing that he answered
them well, he asked him, "Which commandment
is the first of all?" 29 Jesus answered, "The first is,
'Hear, O Israel: the Lord our God, the Lord is
one; 30 you shall love the Lord your God with
all your heart, and with all your soul, and with
all your mind, and with all your strength.'
31 The second is this, 'You shall love your
neighbor as yourself.' There is no other
commandment greater than these."
32 Then the scribe said to him, "You are
right, Teacher; you have truly said that 'he
is one, and besides him there is no other';
33 and 'to love him with all the heart, and
with all the understanding, and with all
the strength,' and 'to love one's neighbor
as oneself,'—this is much more important
than all whole burnt offerings and sacrifices." 34 When Jesus saw that he answered
wisely, he said to him, "You are not far from
the kingdom of God." After that no one dared
to ask him any question.

The Question about David's Son

35 While Jesus was teaching in the temple, he
said, "How can the scribes say that the Messiah[y]
is the son of David? 36David himself, by the Holy
Spirit, declared,

'The Lord said to my Lord,
"Sit at my right hand,
until I put your enemies under
your feet."'

37David himself calls him Lord; so
how can he be his son?" And the
large crowd was listening to him
with delight.

Jesus Denounces the Scribes

38 As he taught, he said, "Beware of the
scribes, who like to walk around in long robes, and to
be greeted with respect in the marketplaces, 39and to
have the best seats in the synagogues and places of
honor at banquets! 40They devour widows' houses and
for the sake of appearance say long prayers. They will
receive the greater condemnation."

The Widow's Offering

41 He sat down opposite the treasury, and watched
the crowd putting money into the treasury. Many rich

12:41 Treasury
This was where all the Jews were to deposit their offerings for the Temple.

y **12.35** Or *the Christ*

13:1 Temple

This most important place for faithful Jews was composed of various buildings and courtyards. It was a magnificent, richly decorated construction. A little under forty years after Jesus said this, it was destroyed by the Romans in the year 70 AD.

13:1–27 Why does Jesus speak about all these terrible events?

Evil is present in the world and we often hear about terrible incidents. Jesus wants to remind us that, even when facing the end of the world, there is no need to fear because the salvation that he brought us is more powerful than any tragedy.

people put in large sums. 42A poor widow came
and put in two small copper coins, which are
worth a penny. 43Then he called his disciples
and said to them, "Truly I tell you, this poor
widow has put in more than all those who are
contributing to the treasury. 44For all of them
have contributed out of their abundance; but
she out of her poverty has put in everything
she had, all she had to live on."

The Destruction of the Temple Foretold

13 As he came out of the temple, one of
his disciples said to him, "Look, Teacher,
what large stones and what large buildings!"
2Then Jesus asked him, "Do you see
these great buildings? Not one stone will be
left here upon another; all will be thrown
down."

3 When he was sitting on the Mount of
Olives opposite the temple, Peter, James,
John, and Andrew asked him privately,
4"Tell us, when will this be, and what will
be the sign that all these things are about to
be accomplished?" 5Then Jesus began to say
to them, "Beware that no one leads you
astray. 6Many will come in my name and say,
'I am he!'[z] and they will lead many astray.
7When you hear of wars and rumors of wars,

z **13.6** Gk *I am*

do not be alarmed; this must take place, but the
end is still to come. 8For nation will rise against
nation, and kingdom against kingdom; there
will be earthquakes in various places; there
will be famines. This is but the beginning of
the birth pangs.

Persecution Foretold

9 "As for yourselves, beware; for they will
hand you over to councils; and you will
be beaten in synagogues; and you will
stand before governors and kings because
of me, as a testimony to them. 10And the
good news[a] must first be proclaimed to
all nations. 11When they bring you to trial
and hand you over, do not worry beforehand about what you are to say; but say
whatever is given you at that time, for it is
not you who speak, but the Holy Spirit. 12Brother
will betray brother to death, and a father his child, and children will rise against parents and have them put to death; 13and you will be
hated by all because of my name. But the one who endures to the end will
be saved.

13:9 Councils

This passage is referring to the Sanhedrin, the supreme court for the Hebrews. It was overseen by the high priest, and it dealt with questions of a religious and civil nature—judging them according to Jewish Law. At the time of Jesus, this court was not allowed to condemn anyone to death.

The Desolating Sacrilege

14 "But when you see the desolating sacrilege set up where it ought not to be
(let the reader understand), then those in Judea must flee to the mountains;
15the one on the housetop must not go down or enter the house to take anything away; 16the one in the field must not turn back to get a coat. 17Woe to

a **13.10** Gk *gospel*

those who are pregnant and to those who are nursing infants in those days!
[18]Pray that it may not be in winter. [19]For in those days there will be suffering,
such as has not been from the beginning of the creation that God created
until now, no, and never will be. [20]And if the Lord had not cut short those
days, no one would be saved; but for the sake of the elect, whom he chose,
he has cut short those days. [21]And if anyone says to you at that time, 'Look!
Here is the Messiah!'[b] or 'Look! There he is!'—do not believe it. [22]False messiahs[c] and false prophets will appear and produce signs and omens, to lead
astray, if possible, the elect. [23]But be alert; I have already
told you everything.

13:27 Four winds
This image refers to all the ends of the earth.

The Coming of the Son of Man

24 "But in those days, after that suffering,
the sun will be darkened,
and the moon will not give its light,
[25]and the stars will be falling from heaven,
and the powers in the heavens will be shaken.
[26]Then they will see 'the Son of Man
coming in clouds' with great power
and glory. [27]Then he will send out the
angels, and gather his elect from the
four winds, from the ends of the earth
to the ends of heaven.

b **13.21** Or *the Christ*
c **13.22** Or *christs*

The Lesson of the Fig Tree

28 "From the fig tree learn its lesson: as soon as its
branch becomes tender and puts forth its leaves,
you know that summer is near. 29So also, when
you see these things taking place, you know that
he[d] is near, at the very gates. 30Truly I tell you,
this generation will not pass away until all these
things have taken place. 31Heaven and earth will
pass away, but my words will not pass away.

The Necessity for Watchfulness

32 "But about that day or hour no one knows,
neither the angels in heaven, nor the Son,
but only the Father. 33Beware, keep alert;[e]
for you do not know when the time
will come. 34It is like a man going on
a journey, when he leaves home and
puts his slaves in charge, each with his
work, and commands the doorkeeper
to be on the watch. 35Therefore, keep
awake—for you do not know when
the master of the house will come, in
the evening, or at midnight, or at cock-
crow, or at dawn, 36or else he may find
you asleep when he comes suddenly. 37And
what I say to you I say to all: Keep awake."

13:32 Son, Father

Jesus speaks of himself as the Son and of God as the Father.

13:35 What does it mean to keep awake?

Jesus' disciples need to be alert and attentive to everything that happens and to the signs of the Lord's presence throughout history. As disciples we are called to be full of hope and never distracted from carrying out God's will.

d **13.29** Or *it*

e **13.33** Other ancient authorities add *and pray*

14:1 Passover

This was the most important Jewish festival. It recalls Israel's liberation from Egyptian slavery. During the week-long celebration of this feast, the faithful went on pilgrimage to Jerusalem, where the Passover meal was eaten.

14:3 Nard

A very precious and very expensive perfumed oil

The Plot to Kill Jesus

14 It was two days before the Passover
and the festival of Unleavened Bread. The chief
priests and the scribes were looking for a way
to arrest Jesus[f] by stealth and kill him; 2for they
said, "Not during the festival, or there may be a
riot among the people."

The Anointing at Bethany

3 While he was at Bethany in the house of Simon
the leper,[g] as he sat at the table, a woman came
with an alabaster jar of very costly ointment of
nard, and she broke open the jar and poured
the ointment on his head. 4But some were there
who said to one another in anger, "Why was the
ointment wasted in this way? 5For this ointment
could have been sold for more than three hundred
denarii,[h] and the money given to the poor." And
they scolded her. 6But Jesus said, "Let her alone;
why do you trouble her? She has performed a good
service for me. 7For you always have the poor with
you, and you can show kindness to them whenever
you wish; but you will not always have me. 8She has
done what she could; she has anointed my body beforehand for its burial. 9Truly I tell you, wherever the good
news[i] is proclaimed in the whole world, what she has
done will be told in remembrance of her."

f **14.1** Gk *him*
g **14.3** The terms *leper* and *leprosy* can refer to several diseases
h **14.5** The denarius was the usual day's wage for a laborer
i **14.9** Or *gospel*

Judas Agrees to Betray Jesus

10 Then Judas Iscariot, who was one of the twelve,
went to the chief priests in order to betray him to
them. 11 When they heard it, they were greatly
pleased, and promised to give him money. So
he began to look for an opportunity to betray
him.

The Passover with the Disciples

12 On the first day of Unleavened Bread,
when the Passover lamb is sacrificed, his
disciples said to him, "Where do you want
us to go and make the preparations for you
to eat the Passover?" 13 So he sent two of his
disciples, saying to them, "Go into the
city, and a man carrying a jar of water
will meet you; follow him, 14 and wherever he enters, say to the owner of the
house, 'The Teacher asks, Where is my guest room
where I may eat the Passover with my disciples?'
15 He will show you a large room upstairs, furnished
and ready. Make preparations for us there." 16 So the
disciples set out and went to the city, and found
everything as he had told them; and they prepared
the Passover meal.

17 When it was evening, he came with the
twelve. 18 And when they had taken their places
and were eating, Jesus said, "Truly I tell you, one

14:12 Unleavened Bread

This was bread without yeast, used during the paschal meal and throughout the week of the Jewish Passover.

14:22–23 Bread, cup, blessing

During the Passover meal the unleavened bread and the cup, or chalice, of wine were blessed according to a precise rite that Jesus and his friends followed that evening.

of you will betray me, one who is eating
with me." 19They began to be distressed and
to say to him one after another, "Surely, not
I?" 20He said to them, "It is one of the twelve,
one who is dipping bread[j] into the bowl[k]
with me. 21For the Son of Man goes as it is
written of him, but woe to that one by whom
the Son of Man is betrayed! It would have
been better for that one not to have been
born."

The Institution of the Lord's Supper

22 While they were eating, he took a loaf of
bread, and after blessing it he broke it, gave
it to them, and said, "Take; this is my body."
23Then he took a cup, and after giving thanks
he gave it to them, and all of them drank from
it. 24He said to them, "This is my blood of the[l]
covenant, which is poured out for many. 25Truly
I tell you, I will never again drink of the fruit of
the vine until that day when I drink it new in the
kingdom of God."

j **14.20** Gk lacks *bread*
k **14.20** Other ancient authorities read *same bowl*
l **14.24** Other ancient authorities add *new*

Peter's Denial Foretold

26 When they had sung the hymn, they went out to the
Mount of Olives. 27And Jesus said to them, "You will all
become deserters; for it is written,

'I will strike the shepherd,
and the sheep will be scattered.'

28But after I am raised up, I will go before you to Galilee."
29Peter said to him, "Even though all become deserters, I
will not." 30Jesus said to him, "Truly I tell you, this day,
this very night, before the cock crows twice, you will
deny me three times." 31But he said vehemently,
"Even though I must die with you, I will not deny
you." And all of them said the same.

Jesus Prays in Gethsemane

32 They went to a place called Gethsemane;
and he said to his disciples, "Sit here while I
pray." 33He took with him Peter and James and
John, and began to be distressed and agitated.
34And he said to them, "I am deeply grieved,
even to death; remain here, and keep awake."
35And going a little farther, he threw himself on
the ground and prayed that, if it were possible,
the hour might pass from him. 36He said, "Abba,[m]
Father, for you all things are possible; remove this
cup from me; yet, not what I want, but what you
want." 37He came and found them sleeping; and he
said to Peter, "Simon, are you asleep? Could you not keep

14:36 Abba

Jesus addresses God using an affectionate Aramaic word for father.

14:33–36 Jesus was afraid?

Of course! Like everyone else, Jesus did not want to suffer and die. This is why he asked God the Father to be spared from such a terrible ordeal. Nonetheless, Jesus entrusts himself entirely to God's will.

m **14.36** Aramaic for *Father*

awake one hour? 38Keep awake and pray that you may not come into the
time of trial;[n] the spirit indeed is willing, but the flesh is weak." 39And again
he went away and prayed, saying the same words. 40And once more he came
and found them sleeping, for their eyes were very heavy; and they did not
know what to say to him. 41He came a third time and said to them, "Are you
still sleeping and taking your rest? Enough! The hour has come; the Son of
Man is betrayed into the hands of sinners. 42Get up, let us
be going. See, my betrayer is at hand."

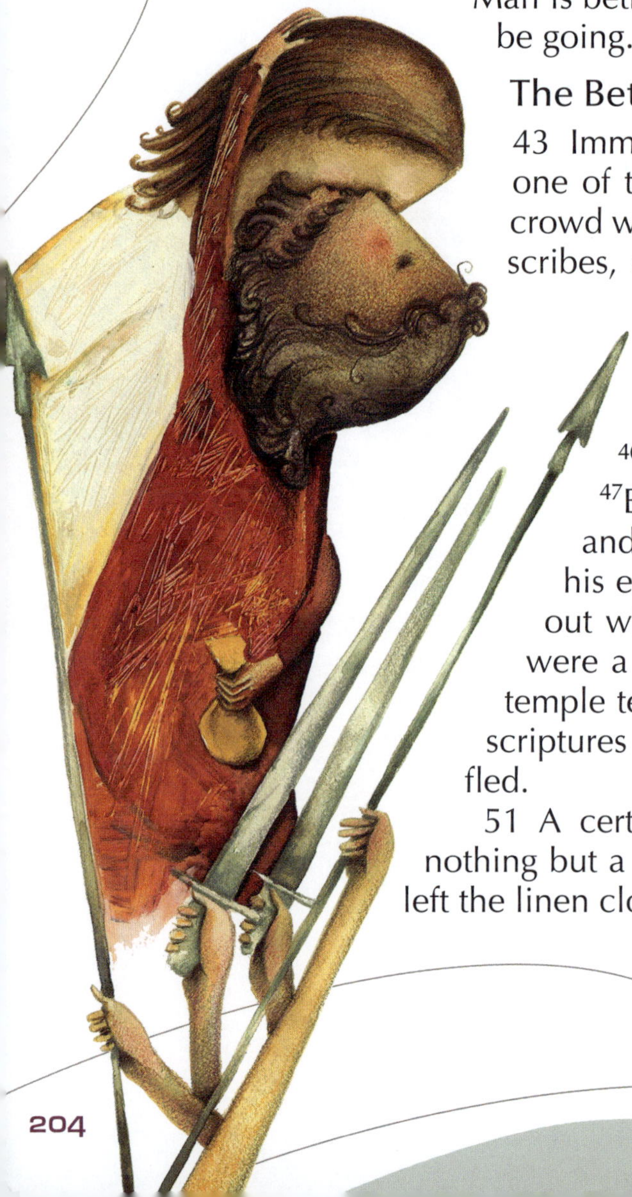

The Betrayal and Arrest of Jesus

43 Immediately, while he was still speaking, Judas,
one of the twelve, arrived; and with him there was a
crowd with swords and clubs, from the chief priests, the
scribes, and the elders. 44Now the betrayer had given
them a sign, saying, "The one I will kiss is the
man; arrest him and lead him away under
guard." 45So when he came, he went up to
him at once and said, "Rabbi!" and kissed him.
46Then they laid hands on him and arrested him.
47But one of those who stood near drew his sword
and struck the slave of the high priest, cutting off
his ear. 48Then Jesus said to them, "Have you come
out with swords and clubs to arrest me as though I
were a bandit? 49Day after day I was with you in the
temple teaching, and you did not arrest me. But let the
scriptures be fulfilled." 50All of them deserted him and
fled.

51 A certain young man was following him, wearing
nothing but a linen cloth. They caught hold of him, 52but he
left the linen cloth and ran off naked.

n **14.38** Or *into temptation*

The Paschal Mystery (Mk 14:51–16:8)

Mark creates a framework around the mysterious figure of a young man who runs away naked (14:51–52) and a young man who announces the resurrection (16:1–8). Within this framework, the evangelist tells the story of Jesus' arrest, condemnation, death, and resurrection. He sets the scene with great care, first by telling us how all the disciples leave (14:53–15:20); then he places Jesus' death at the center, emphasizing his solitude and abandonment (15:21–37); and last is the hope of the resurrection that replaces his self-offering on Golgotha (15:38–47). Three groups abandoned Jesus and are responsible for his death (the disciples, the religious authorities, and the political authorities). But Jesus' death offers these groups redemption. Joseph of Arimathea—who is both a disciple and a religious leader—and the pagan centurion are representative of the transformation that occurs in those who are willing to accept that offer.

Jesus before the Council

53 They took Jesus to the high priest; and all the chief priests, the
elders, and the scribes were assembled. 54 Peter had followed him
at a distance, right into the courtyard of the high priest; and he
was sitting with the guards, warming himself at the fire. 55 Now
the chief priests and the whole council were looking for testimony
against Jesus to put him to death; but they found none. 56 For many
gave false testimony against him, and their testimony did not
agree. 57 Some stood up and gave false testimony against him,

saying, 58"We heard him say, 'I will destroy this temple
that is made with hands, and in three days I will
build another, not made with hands.'" 59But
even on this point their testimony did not
agree. 60Then the high priest stood up
before them and asked Jesus, "Have
you no answer? What is it that they
testify against you?" 61But he was
silent and did not answer. Again
the high priest asked him, "Are
you the Messiah,[o] the Son of the
Blessed One?" 62Jesus said, "I
am; and
'you will see the Son of Man
seated at the right hand of the
Power,'
and 'coming with the clouds of
heaven.'"
63Then the high priest tore his
clothes and said, "Why do we still
need witnesses? 64You have heard his
blasphemy! What is your decision?"
All of them condemned him as deserving
death. 65Some began to spit on him, to
blindfold him, and to strike him, saying to
him, "Prophesy!" The guards also took him over
and beat him.

14:58 Could Jesus really have done this?

The reference to the Temple (13:2) is symbolic. Jesus is saying that his death and resurrection (which happened on the third day) would mark the beginning of a new relationship between God and mankind, as well as a new era in which there would be no need for the actual Temple. Today, although there are churches where we gather to pray, a Catholic community can celebrate Mass anyplace (ideally in a church) and can pray anywhere.

o **14.61** Or *the Christ*

Peter Denies Jesus

66 While Peter was below in the courtyard, one of the
servant-girls of the high priest came by. [67]When she saw
Peter warming himself, she stared at him and said,
"You also were with Jesus, the man from Nazareth."
[68]But he denied it, saying, "I do not know or understand what you are talking about." And he went
out into the forecourt.[p] Then the cock crowed.[q]
[69]And the servant-girl, on seeing him, began again
to say to the bystanders, "This man is one of them."
[70]But again he denied it. Then after a little while the
bystanders again said to Peter, "Certainly you are
one of them; for you are a Galilean." [71]But he began
to curse, and he swore an oath, "I do not know this man
you are talking about." [72]At that moment the cock crowed
for the second time. Then Peter remembered that Jesus had
said to him, "Before the cock crows twice, you will deny
me three times." And he broke down and wept.

14:63 Did Jesus blaspheme?

By saying that he is the Messiah and the Son of Man, Jesus is drawing so close to God that he scandalizes the high priest.

Jesus before Pilate

15 As soon as it was morning, the chief priests held a
consultation with the elders and scribes and the whole
council. They bound Jesus, led him away, and handed
him over to Pilate. [2]Pilate asked him, "Are you the King
of the Jews?" He answered him, "You say so." [3]Then the

15:1 Pilate

He was the representative of the Roman emperor during the time of Jesus' public ministry.

p **14.68** Or *gateway*
q **14.68** Other ancient authorities lack *Then the cock crowed*

15:12 King of the Jews

Pilate was concerned that Jesus' preaching would inspire a revolt against Roman rule. This is why he asked if Jesus considered himself a king (and therefore an enemy of the Romans).

15:15 Flogging

Flogging, or scourging, was done with a flagellum—a whip made of leather strips with small stones, bones, and/or hooks at the ends. The Romans tortured their prisoners with this extremely painful instrument.

chief priests accused him of many things. 4Pilate
asked him again, "Have you no answer? See how
many charges they bring against you." 5But Jesus
made no further reply, so that Pilate was amazed.

Pilate Hands Jesus over to Be Crucified

6 Now at the festival he used to release a prisoner for them, anyone for whom they asked.
7Now a man called Barabbas was in prison with
the rebels who had committed murder during
the insurrection. 8So the crowd came and
began to ask Pilate to do for them according
to his custom. 9Then he answered them, "Do
you want me to release for you the King of the
Jews?" 10For he realized that it was out of jealousy that the chief priests had handed him over.
11But the chief priests stirred up the crowd to
have him release Barabbas for them instead.
12Pilate spoke to them again, "Then what do
you wish me to do[r] with the man you call[s]
the King of the Jews?" 13They shouted back,
"Crucify him!" 14Pilate asked them, "Why,
what evil has he done?" But they shouted all
the more, "Crucify him!" 15So Pilate, wishing to
satisfy the crowd, released Barabbas for them;
and after flogging Jesus, he handed him over to
be crucified.

r **15.12** Other ancient authorities read *what should I do*
s **15.12** Other ancient authorities lack *the man you call*

The Soldiers Mock Jesus

16 Then the soldiers led him into the courtyard of
the palace (that is, the governor's headquarters[t]);
and they called together the whole cohort. 17And
they clothed him in a purple cloak; and after
twisting some thorns into a crown, they put it on
him. 18And they began saluting him, "Hail, King
of the Jews!" 19They struck his head with a reed,
spat upon him, and knelt down in homage to
him. 20After mocking him, they stripped him of
the purple cloak and put his own clothes on
him. Then they led him out to crucify him.

The Crucifixion of Jesus

21 They compelled a passer-by, who was coming in
from the country, to carry his cross; it was Simon of
Cyrene, the father of Alexander and Rufus. 22Then
they brought Jesus[u] to the place called Golgotha
(which means the place of a skull). 23And they
offered him wine mixed with myrrh; but he did not
take it. 24And they crucified him, and divided his
clothes among them, casting lots to decide what
each should take.

25 It was nine o'clock in the morning when they
crucified him. 26The inscription of the charge against
him read, "The King of the Jews." 27And with him they
crucified two bandits, one on his right and one on his left.[v]

15:22 Golgotha
This was a small hill, possibly extracted from a quarry, which stood outside the city walls. Those condemned to death were executed here.

15:23 Myrrh
It was an aromatic substance used to provide fragrance to the wine that helped numb the condemned person.

t **15.16** Gk *the praetorium*
u **15.22** Gk *him*
v **15.27** Other ancient authorities add verse 28, *And the scripture was fulfilled that says, "And he was counted among the lawless."*

15:29–31 Why didn't Jesus come down from the cross?

If he had tried to save himself, maybe through a great event, Jesus certainly would have acted more closely to what the Jews expected of their Messiah. But then he would have denied being the Son of God who, out of love, saves by accepting death, like every man.

15:39 Centurion

This officer of the Roman army commanded one hundred soldiers. He would have been a pagan, which is a non-Jew.

29 Those who passed by derided[w] him, shaking their
heads and saying, "Aha! You who would destroy the
temple and build it in three days, 30 save yourself,
and come down from the cross!" 31 In the same
way the chief priests, along with the scribes,
were also mocking him among themselves and
saying, "He saved others; he cannot save himself. 32 Let the Messiah,[x] the King of Israel,
come down from the cross now, so that we
may see and believe." Those who were crucified with him also taunted him.

The Death of Jesus

33 When it was noon, darkness came over the
whole land[y] until three in the afternoon. 34 At
three o'clock Jesus cried out with a loud voice,
"Eloi, Eloi, lema sabachthani?" which means,
"My God, my God, why have you forsaken me?"[z]
35 When some of the bystanders heard it, they said,
"Listen, he is calling for Elijah." 36 And someone ran, filled
a sponge with sour wine, put it on a stick, and gave it to
him to drink, saying, "Wait, let us see whether Elijah will
come to take him down." 37 Then Jesus gave a loud cry
and breathed his last. 38 And the curtain of the temple
was torn in two, from top to bottom. 39 Now when the
centurion, who stood facing him, saw that in this way
he[a] breathed his last, he said, "Truly this man was
God's Son!"[b]

w **15.29** Or *blasphemed*
x **15.32** Or *the Christ*
y **15.33** Or *earth*
z **15.34** Other ancient authorities read *made me a reproach*
a **15.39** Other ancient authorities add *cried out and*
b **15.39** Or *a son of God*

15:39 God's Son

Finally someone recognizes who Jesus truly is—the Son of God. Jesus is the only one who has seen God and truly knows him as a Father.

15:42 Day of Preparation

It was the day of preparation before a solemn Sabbath, so Jesus needed to be buried before sunset.

40 There were also women looking on from a distance; among them were Mary Magdalene, and
Mary the mother of James the younger and of Joses,
and Salome. 41 These used to follow him and provided for him when he was in Galilee; and there
were many other women who had come up with
him to Jerusalem.

The Burial of Jesus

42 When evening had come, and since it was
the day of Preparation, that is, the day before
the sabbath, 43 Joseph of Arimathea, a respected
member of the council, who was also himself
waiting expectantly for the kingdom of God,
went boldly to Pilate and asked for the body of
Jesus. 44 Then Pilate wondered if he were already
dead; and summoning the centurion, he asked him
whether he had been dead for some time. 45 When
he learned from the centurion that he was dead, he
granted the body to Joseph. 46 Then Joseph[c] bought
a linen cloth, and taking down the body,[d] wrapped
it in the linen cloth, and laid it in a tomb that had
been hewn out of the rock. He then rolled a stone
against the door of the tomb. 47 Mary Magdalene and
Mary the mother of Joses saw where the body[e] was
laid.

c **15.46** Gk *he*
d **15.46** Gk *it*
e **15.47** Gk *it*

The Resurrection of Jesus

16 When the sabbath was over, Mary Magdalene,
and Mary the mother of James, and Salome bought spices,
so that they might go and anoint him. 2And very early on the
first day of the week, when the sun had risen, they went to the
tomb. 3They had been saying to one another, "Who will roll away the
stone for us from the entrance to the tomb?" 4When they looked up,
they saw that the stone, which was very large, had already been rolled
back. 5As they entered the tomb, they saw a young man, dressed in
a white robe, sitting on the right side; and they were alarmed. 6But
he said to them, "Do not be alarmed; you are looking for Jesus of
Nazareth, who was crucified. He has been raised; he is not here.
Look, there is the place they laid him. 7But go, tell his disciples
and Peter that he is going ahead of you to Galilee; there you
will see him, just as he told you." 8So they went out and fled
from the tomb, for terror and amazement had seized them;
and they said nothing to anyone, for they were afraid.[f]

The Shorter Ending of Mark

[[And all that had been commanded them they told briefly to those around Peter. And afterward Jesus himself sent out through them, from east to west, the sacred and imperishable proclamation of eternal salvation.[g]]]

f **16.8** Some of the most ancient authorities bring the book to a close at the end of verse 8. One authority concludes the book with the shorter ending; others include the shorter ending and then continue with verses 9–20. In most authorities verses 9–20 follow immediately after verse 8, though in some of these authorities the passage is marked as being doubtful.

g **16.8** Other ancient authorities add *Amen*

The Longer Ending of Mark

Jesus Appears to Mary Magdalene

9 [[Now after he rose early on the first day of the week, he
appeared first to Mary Magdalene, from whom he had cast out
seven demons. 10 She went out and told those who had been with
him, while they were mourning and weeping. 11 But when they
heard that he was alive and had been seen by her, they would
not believe it.

Jesus Appears to Two Disciples

12 After this he appeared in another form to two of them, as they
were walking into the country. 13 And they went back and told the
rest, but they did not believe them.

Jesus Commissions the Disciples

14 Later he appeared to the eleven themselves as they were sitting at the table; and he upbraided them for their lack of faith
and stubbornness, because they had not believed those who
saw him after he had risen.[h] 15 And he said to them, "Go into
all the world and proclaim the good news[i] to the whole creation. 16 The one who believes and is baptized will be saved;

h **16.14** Other ancient authorities add, in whole or in part, *And they excused themselves, saying, "This age of lawlessness and unbelief is under Satan, who does not allow the truth and power of God to prevail over the unclean things of the spirits. Therefore reveal your righteousness now"—thus they spoke to Christ. And Christ replied to them, "The term of years of Satan's power has been fulfilled, but other terrible things draw near. And for those who have sinned I was handed over to death, that they may return to the truth and sin no more, that they may inherit the spiritual and imperishable glory of righteousness that is in heaven."*

i **16.15** Or *gospel*

but the one who does not believe will be condemned.
[17]And these signs will accompany those who believe:
by using my name they will cast out demons; they will
speak in new tongues; [18]they will pick up snakes in
their hands,[j] and if they drink any deadly thing, it will
not hurt them; they will lay their hands on the sick, and
they will recover."

The Ascension of Jesus

19 So then the Lord Jesus, after he had spoken to them,
was taken up into heaven and sat down at the right
hand of God. [20]And they went out and proclaimed the
good news everywhere, while the Lord worked with
them and confirmed the message by the signs that
accompanied it.[k]]]

j **16.18** Other ancient authorities lack *in their hands*
k **16.20** Other ancient authorities add *Amen*

THE GOSPEL ACCORDING TO

Luke

AUTHOR: ANONYMOUS, TRADITIONALLY IDENTIFIED AS LUKE, THE DOCTOR WHO TRAVELED WITH THE APOSTLE PAUL ON HIS MISSIONARY JOURNEYS

AUDIENCE: PEOPLE WHO BELIEVED IN MULTIPLE GODS (PAGANS) WHO WERE PROBABLY OF GREEK ORIGIN THAT CONVERTED TO CHRISTIANITY

TIME AND PLACE: COMPOSED ABOUT 85 AD; MAY HAVE BEEN WRITTEN IN SYRIA OR GREECE

UNDERLYING THEMES: JESUS' PREFERENCE FOR THE POOR, THE REJECTED, AND THE SINNERS; FORGIVENESS AND GOD'S MERCY; THE UNIVERSALITY OF SALVATION; THE ROLE OF THE HOLY SPIRIT IN BOTH JESUS' WORK AND THE LIFE OF THE CHURCH

A Friend of God . . .

If you open my Gospel and read the first lines, it will seem like I did not write it for children. When I began to do research about Jesus and drafted the first pages of my work, I had in mind an audience of educated adults—like my friend Theophilus. In fact, I wanted to draw these people closer to the Lord with my book.

Although my aim was to appeal to the well-educated, I wanted to make sure less-educated people (like children!) could read my work as well. In my Gospel you will meet many different personalities; you will find many impressive stories that you can remember for years to come; and I hope you will discover God's immense love for you—regardless of who you are and what you have done. God's best quality is his forgiveness, which he offers to everyone unconditionally. All we need to do is receive it. This is what I wanted to testify to in my writing.

Before you continue on to read my account of Jesus' life, I want to tell you something very important. In the first paragraph I call your attention to my friend Theophilus—the person I address in my Gospel. Theophilus was my friend and a wise pagan. But his name has a hidden meaning that includes you, too, since in Greek it means: "friend of God." Now you know that I dedicated my writings not only to him, but also to whoever is or wants to be a friend of Jesus. I pray that my work and your assistance will help the number of God's friends continue to grow so that there will always be more believers in the world. After you read my Gospel and discover in Jesus a God who desires to be our friend, share this Good News with everyone you know! This is what I hope for you and all the children of this world.

Evangelist Luke

A First-Rate Writer

The Gospel of Luke is considered the pearl of the New Testament writings. It is the longest writing in the New Testament and is also the most elegant in style and vocabulary. We know little about the author, but his writing style tells us that he was certainly a very educated man. By the end of the second century it was commonly thought that the author was Luke, a doctor who converted from a pagan faith to Christianity. We hear about Luke from another writer of New Testament writings. In some of the letters by the Apostle Paul we learn that Luke traveled with Paul for years in his missionary journeys (Col 4:14; 2 Tm 4:11; Phlm 24). Luke learned about Jesus thanks to Saint Paul's preaching, but looked for other sources too. Before writing, Luke checked several sources such as the Gospel of Mark and various eye witnesses. Luke wanted to compose a work that could be compared to those of the more serious Greek historians, who were known for providing in-depth information and rich documentation.

A Great Diptych: The Gospel and the Acts of the Apostles

The ambition and breadth of Luke's project becomes even more clear when we consider the fact that he did not limit himself to writing a single book with the story of Jesus' life—the Gospel. Instead he added a second volume—the Acts of the Apostles—in which he recounts what the Apostles and Jesus' disciples did to help the Church grow after Jesus' ascension to heaven. Both the Gospel and Acts of the Apostles tell one single story. Still it is important to clarify that this great project is not only historical. We know that his work is to be considered a catechetical aid. (He describes this intention in addressing himself to Theophilus.) By catechetical he means he intends to quench the thirst for truth of the pagans who have heard the Apostles' preaching, to support the truthfulness of what has been proclaimed, and to invite everyone to the journey of Christian life.

Jerusalem: A Steadfast Idea

The third Gospel begins in the very heart of Jerusalem—the Temple. This setting is very significant because it foreshadows, that is it reveals, how Jesus is drawn to Jerusalem and how he goes there by his own free will. The Gospel is structured like Jesus' travel log to the holy city. It is in Jerusalem that Jesus will carry out salvation. In the Old Testament, it is in this city that God's prophets were killed because of the message they preached. Luke depicts Jesus heading determinedly, humbly, and obediently toward Jerusalem, where he will be sacrificed. Because this Gospel focuses so much on the call to sacrifice, service, and strength, Luke is symbolically portrayed as an ox—an animal known for its strength and as an acceptable sacrificial animal—who also had wings.

Luke's second work, the Acts of the Apostles, shows the Apostles sowing the Good News of Jesus in Jerusalem and then "in all Judea and Samaria, and to the ends of the earth" (Acts 1:8). Using this geographical setting, we propose a structure made up of seven accounts in Luke's Gospel: the **Prologue** (Lk1:1–4); **The Infancy Narrative**, "Nothing is impossible with God" (Lk 1:5–2:52); **Preparation for Public Ministry**, "You are my Son, the Beloved" (Lk 3:1–4:13); **Ministry in Galilee**, "Good news for the world" (Lk 4:14–9:50) ; **Journey**, "Headed for Jerusalem" (Lk 9:51–19:27); **Teaching in Jerusalem**, "Blessed is the king who comes" (Lk 19:28–21:38); **The Passion**, "See how a son dies" (Lk 22:1–23-56); **The Resurrection**, "Witnesses of the Risen One" (Lk 24:1–53).

THE GOSPEL ACCORDING TO Luke

Prologue (Lk 1:1–4)

Dedication to Theophilus

1 Since many have undertaken to set down an orderly
account of the events that have been fulfilled among
us, 2just as they were handed on to us by those who
from the beginning were eyewitnesses and servants
of the word, 3I too decided, after investigating
everything carefully from the very first,[a] to
write an orderly account for you, most excel-
lent Theophilus, 4so that you may know the
truth concerning the things about which
you have been instructed.

a **1.3** Or *for a long time*

The Infancy Narrative: "Nothing is impossible with God" (Lk 1:5–2:52)

From theological, literary, and historical points of view, the first section of the Gospel of Luke is very rich. The evangelist opens his narration using language that is similar to that used in the Old Testament. For example, he inserts canticles or songs that have an ancient Jewish "flavor" in order to present to his readers typical things in the traditional Judaic world because his readers, being originally pagan, did not know much about the Jewish life. Unlike Matthew, however, Luke does not explicitly cite or make precise references to persons or events in the Old Testament. Instead, he tries to bring about an important sense of continuity with a distant yet important story, which was still being learned by his readers. From a literary point of view, one cannot help but notice the parallels between the figures of John the Baptist and Jesus. There are two annunciations, two births, two circumcisions, and two growths to adulthood and mission. Interestingly, Luke is the only evangelist who describes the events of an adolescent Jesus who stayed in Jerusalem after Passover and was found in the Temple by Mary and Joseph speaking with the teachers of the Jewish Law.

1:5 Herod
King of Judea from 37 BC to 4 AD, during which time Jesus was born.

The Birth of John the Baptist Foretold

5 In the days of King Herod of Judea, there was a
priest named Zechariah, who belonged to the priestly
order of Abijah. His wife was a descendant of Aaron,
and her name was Elizabeth. 6 Both of them were
righteous before God, living blamelessly according
to all the commandments and regulations of the
Lord. 7 But they had no children, because Elizabeth
was barren, and both were getting on in years.
8 Once when he was serving as priest before
God and his section was on duty, 9 he was chosen

by lot, according to the custom of the
priesthood, to enter the sanctuary of
the Lord and offer incense. 10Now at
the time of the incense offering, the
whole assembly of the people was
praying outside. 11Then there
appeared to him an angel of the
Lord, standing at the right side of
the altar of incense. 12When
Zechariah saw him, he was terrified; and fear overwhelmed him.
13But the angel said to him, "Do not
be afraid, Zechariah, for your prayer
has been heard. Your wife Elizabeth
will bear you a son, and you will
name him John. 14You will have joy
and gladness, and many will rejoice at
his birth, 15for he will be great in the
sight of the Lord. He must never drink
wine or strong drink; even before his
birth he will be filled with the Holy Spirit.
16He will turn many of the people of Israel
to the Lord their God. 17With the spirit and
power of Elijah he will go before him, to turn
the hearts of parents to their children, and the
disobedient to the wisdom of the righteous, to
make ready a people prepared for the Lord."

1:5–10 What did priests do in Herod's time?

They celebrated Jewish rites of worship (in this scene the offering of incense) in Jerusalem's Temple. They were all descendants of Aaron (Moses' brother) who took turns serving.

[18]Zechariah said to the angel, "How will I know that this is so? For I am an
old man, and my wife is getting on in years." [19]The angel replied, "I am
Gabriel. I stand in the presence of God, and I have been sent to speak to you
and to bring you this good news. [20]But now, because you did not believe my
words, which will be fulfilled in their time, you will become mute, unable to
speak, until the day these things occur."

21 Meanwhile the people were waiting for
Zechariah, and wondered at his delay in the sanctuary. [22]When he did come out, he could not speak
to them, and they realized that he had seen a vision
in the sanctuary. He kept motioning to them and
remained unable to speak. [23]When his time of service was ended, he went to his home.

24 After those days his wife Elizabeth conceived, and for five months she remained in
seclusion. She said, [25]"This is what the Lord has
done for me when he looked favorably on me
and took away the disgrace I have endured
among my people."

The Birth of Jesus Foretold

26 In the sixth month the angel Gabriel was sent
by God to a town in Galilee called Nazareth,
[27]to a virgin engaged to a man whose name
was Joseph, of the house of David. The virgin's

1:27 Virgin

Mary was a teenage girl when this happened. Although she was married to Joseph, according to Jewish tradition she did not yet live with him as his wife.

1:28 I've heard these words before!
Another way this verse can be translated is, "Hail, full of grace, the Lord is with you!" Now do they sound familiar? They are the words of the Hail Mary. Catholics for centuries have turned to the Blessed Mother with the Archangel Gabriel's words. Another part of the Hail Mary is taken from Elizabeth's words found in verse 42.

1:28 What does "full of grace" mean?
By greeting her this way, Gabriel told Mary that she has always been loved by God in a very special way.

1:32 Who was David?
He was Israel's greatest king and he lived about 950 years before Jesus was born. God had told his people through his prophets that the Messiah would be a descendent of this king. Joseph, a descendant of David, is the final link between David and his descendants and Jesus.

name was Mary. 28 And he came to her and said, "Greetings,
favored one! The Lord is with you."[b] 29 But she was much
perplexed by his words and pondered what sort of
greeting this might be. 30 The angel said to her, "Do
not be afraid, Mary, for you have found favor
with God. 31 And now, you will conceive in
your womb and bear a son, and you will
name him Jesus. 32 He will be great, and
will be called the Son of the Most High,
and the Lord God will give to him the
throne of his ancestor David. 33 He
will reign over the house of Jacob
forever, and of his kingdom there
will be no end." 34 Mary said to the
angel, "How can this be, since I am
a virgin?"[c] 35 The angel said to her,
"The Holy Spirit will come upon
you, and the power of the Most High
will overshadow you; therefore the
child to be born[d] will be holy; he
will be called Son of God. 36 And
now, your relative Elizabeth in her
old age has also conceived a son;
and this is the sixth month for her
who was said to be barren. 37 For nothing
will be impossible with God." 38 Then Mary
said, "Here am I, the servant of the Lord; let it
be with me according to your word." Then the
angel departed from her.

b **1.28** Other ancient authorities add *Blessed are you among women*
c **1.34** Gk *I do not know a man*
d **1.35** Other ancient authorities add *of you*

Mary Visits Elizabeth

39 In those days Mary set out and went with
haste to a Judean town in the hill country,
40where she entered the house of Zechariah
and greeted Elizabeth. 41When Elizabeth
heard Mary's greeting, the child leaped in
her womb. And Elizabeth was filled with the
Holy Spirit 42and exclaimed with a loud cry,
"Blessed are you among women, and blessed
is the fruit of your womb. 43And why has
this happened to me, that the mother of my
Lord comes to me? 44For as soon as I heard
the sound of your greeting, the child in my
womb leaped for joy. 45And blessed is she
who believed that there would be[e] a fulfillment of what was spoken to her by the Lord."

1:46 Magnifies
Here this means to give thanks or sing someone's praise. Literally, it means "to enlarge" someone; in this case, God. Mary praises God because he has done great things. God keeps his promises and undoes the sins of humanity.

Mary's Song of Praise

46 And Mary[f] said,
"My soul magnifies the Lord,
47 and my spirit rejoices in God my Savior,
48 for he has looked with favor on the lowliness of his servant.
Surely, from now on all generations will call me blessed;
49 for the Mighty One has done great things for me,
and holy is his name.

e **1.45** Or *believed, for there will be*
f **1.46** Other ancient authorities read *Elizabeth*

50 His mercy is for those who fear him
from generation to generation.
51 He has shown strength with his arm;
he has scattered the proud in the thoughts
of their hearts.
52 He has brought down the powerful from their
thrones,
and lifted up the lowly;
53 he has filled the hungry with good things,
and sent the rich away empty.
54 He has helped his servant Israel,
in remembrance of his mercy,
55 according to the promise he made to our
ancestors,
to Abraham and to his descendants
forever."

56 And Mary remained with her about three months
and then returned to her home.

The Birth of John the Baptist

57 Now the time came for Elizabeth to give birth,
and she bore a son. 58Her neighbors and relatives heard that the Lord had shown his great
mercy to her, and they rejoiced with her.
59 On the eighth day they came to circumcise the child, and they were going to

name him Zechariah after his father. 60 But his mother said,
"No; he is to be called John." 61 They said to her, "None of
your relatives has this name." 62 Then they began
motioning to his father to find out what name
he wanted to give him. 63 He asked for a
writing tablet and wrote, "His name is
John." And all of them were amazed.
64 Immediately his mouth was opened and
his tongue freed, and he began to speak,
praising God. 65 Fear came over all their
neighbors, and all these things were talked
about throughout the entire hill country of
Judea. 66 All who heard them pondered them
and said, "What then will this child become?"
For, indeed, the hand of the Lord was with him.

Zechariah's Prophecy

67 Then his father Zechariah was filled with the
Holy Spirit and spoke this prophecy:

68 "Blessed be the Lord God of Israel,
for he has looked favorably on his people and
redeemed them.
69 He has raised up a mighty savior[g] for us
in the house of his servant David,

g **1.69** Gk *a horn of salvation*

70 as he spoke through the mouth of his holy prophets from
of old,
71 that we would be saved from our enemies and
from the hand of all who hate us.
72 Thus he has shown the mercy promised to our ancestors,
and has remembered his holy covenant,
73 the oath that he swore to our ancestor Abraham,
to grant us 74that we, being rescued from the
hands of our enemies,
might serve him without fear, 75in holiness and righteousness
before him all our days.
76 And you, child, will be called the prophet of the
Most High;
for you will go before the Lord to prepare his ways,
77 to give knowledge of salvation to his people
by the forgiveness of their sins.
78 By the tender mercy of our God,
the dawn from on high will break upon[h] us,
79 to give light to those who sit in darkness and in the
shadow of death,
to guide our feet into the way of peace."
80 The child grew and became strong in spirit, and he
was in the wilderness until the day he appeared
publicly to Israel.

h **1.78** Other ancient authorities read *has broken upon*

2:1 Emperor Augustus
The Roman emperor
who was in power,
even in Palestine,
at this time.

2:2 Why is it important to know who the governor of Syria was?
I added this and other details to emphasize the fact that the birth of Jesus is an historical fact. It happened in a particular place and on a precise date; it is not a mythical fairy tale!

The Birth of Jesus

2 In those days a decree went out from
Emperor Augustus that all the world should
be registered. 2 This was the first registration
and was taken while Quirinius was governor
of Syria. 3All went to their own towns to be
registered. 4Joseph also went from the town
of Nazareth in Galilee to Judea, to the city
of David called Bethlehem, because he was
descended from the house and family of David.
5He went to be registered with Mary, to whom
he was engaged and who was expecting a child.
6While they were there, the time came for her
to deliver her child. 7And she gave birth
to her firstborn son and wrapped him in
bands of cloth, and laid him in a manger,
because there was no place for them in the
inn.

The Shepherds and the Angels

8 In that region there were shepherds
living in the fields, keeping watch over
their flock by night. 9Then an angel of
the Lord stood before them, and the
glory of the Lord shone around them,

and they were terrified. 10 But the angel said to them, "Do
not be afraid; for see—I am bringing you good news of
great joy for all the people: 11 to you is born this day
in the city of David a Savior, who is the Messiah,[i]
the Lord. 12 This will be a sign for you: you will find
a child wrapped in bands of cloth and lying in
a manger." 13 And suddenly there was with the
angel a multitude of the heavenly host,[j] praising
God and saying,
14 "Glory to God in the highest heaven,
and on earth peace among those whom
he favors!"[k]
15 When the angels had left them and gone into
heaven, the shepherds said to one another, "Let us
go now to Bethlehem and see this thing that has taken
place, which the Lord has made known to us." 16 So
they went with haste and found Mary and Joseph,
and the child lying in the manger. 17 When they saw
this, they made known what had been told them
about this child; 18 and all who heard it were amazed
at what the shepherds told them. 19 But Mary treasured all these words and pondered them in her
heart. 20 The shepherds returned, glorifying and
praising God for all they had heard and seen, as it
had been told them.

2:8 Why was the announcement made to shepherds?

Because they were poor and awake—two necessary characteristics for hearing the Good News of Jesus.

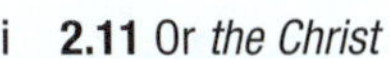

i **2.11** Or *the Christ*
j **2.13** Gk *army*
k **2.14** Other ancient authorities read *peace, goodwill among people*

2:21 Circumcise

Circumcision is the religious ritual through which each Jewish male child, even today, enters the large family of the people of Israel. The rite entails cutting a piece of the foreskin.

Jesus Is Named

21 After eight days had passed, it was time to
circumcise the child; and he was called Jesus,
the name given by the angel before he was
conceived in the womb.

Jesus Is Presented in the Temple

22 When the time came for their purification
according to the law of Moses, they brought
him up to Jerusalem to present him to the
Lord 23(as it is written in the law of the Lord,
"Every firstborn male shall be designated
as holy to the Lord"), 24and they offered a
sacrifice according to what is stated in the
law of the Lord, "a pair of turtledoves or
two young pigeons."

25 Now there was a man in Jerusalem
whose name was Simeon;[l] this man was righteous and devout, looking forward to the consolation of Israel, and the Holy Spirit rested on
him. 26It had been revealed to him by the Holy
Spirit that he would not see death before he
had seen the Lord's Messiah.[m] 27Guided by the
Spirit, Simeon[n] came into the temple; and when
the parents brought in the child Jesus, to do for

2:25 Who was Simeon waiting for?

Here Simeon represents all the people of Israel who await God's consolation. Jesus, the Messiah, is the concrete sign.

l **2.25** Gk *Symeon*
m **2.26** Or *the Lord's Christ*
n **2.27** Gk *In the Spirit, he*

him what was customary under the
law, [28]Simeon[o] took him in his arms
and praised God, saying,

29 "Master, now you are dismissing
your servant[p] in peace,
according to your word;
30 for my eyes have seen your
salvation,
31 which you have prepared
in the presence of all
peoples,
32 a light for revelation to the Gentiles
and for glory to your people
Israel."

33 And the child's father and mother were
amazed at what was being said about him.
34 Then Simeon[q] blessed them and said to his
mother Mary, "This child is destined for the falling
and the rising of many in Israel, and to be a sign that
will be opposed [35]so that the inner thoughts of many will be
revealed—and a sword will pierce your own soul too."

36 There was also a prophet, Anna[r] the daughter of Phanuel,
of the tribe of Asher. She was of a great age, having lived with her
husband seven years after her marriage, [37]then as a widow to the
age of eighty-four. She never left the temple but worshiped there

2:34 Why does Simeon, after saying these beautiful words, give such terrible news?

With the grace of God, Simeon had the insight that Jesus' salvation would not be simple or painless.

o **2.28** Gk *he*
p **2.29** Gk *slave*
q **2.34** Gk *Symeon*
r **2.36** Gk *Hanna*

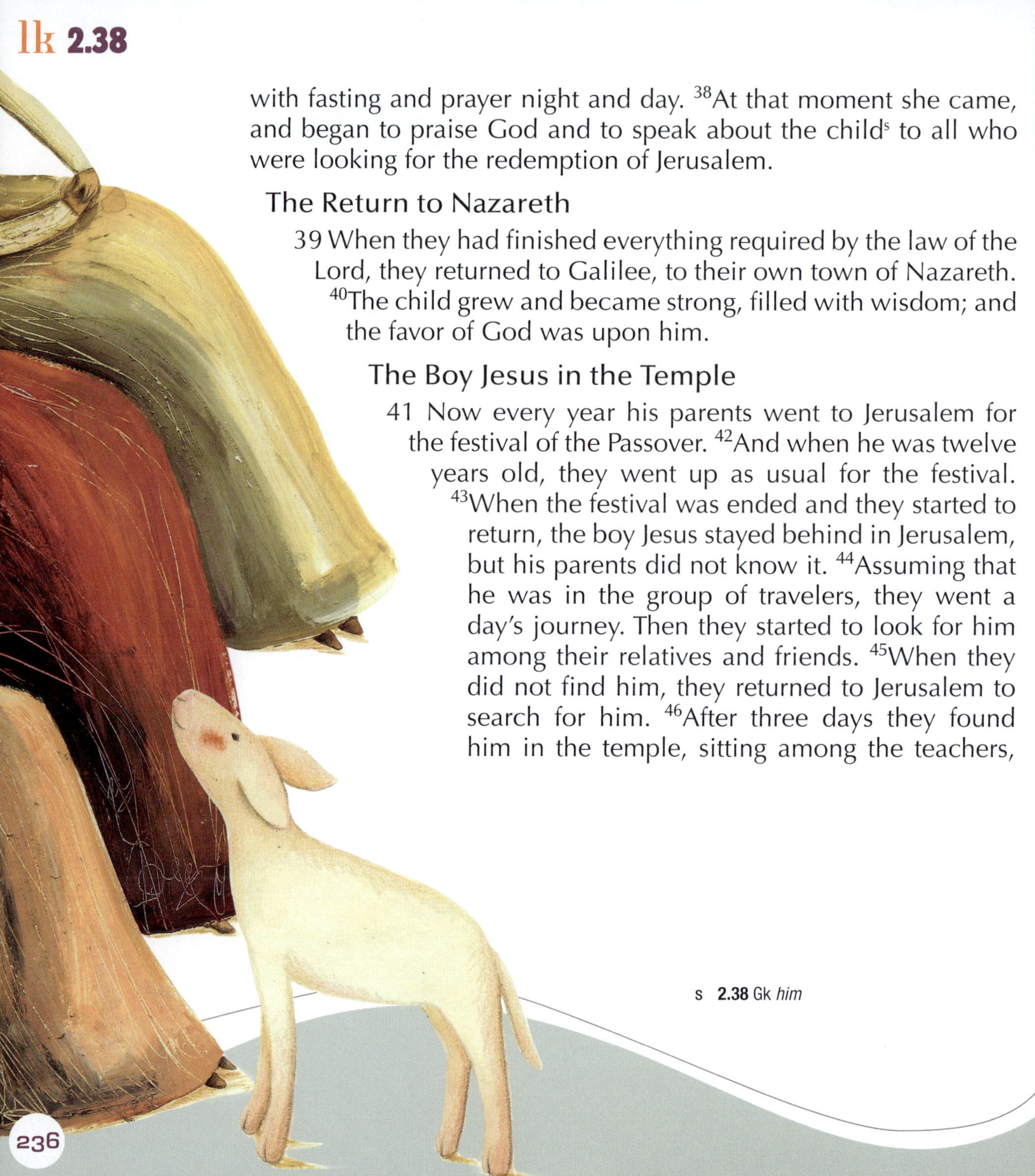

with fasting and prayer night and day. 38At that moment she came,
and began to praise God and to speak about the child[s] to all who
were looking for the redemption of Jerusalem.

The Return to Nazareth

39 When they had finished everything required by the law of the
Lord, they returned to Galilee, to their own town of Nazareth.
40The child grew and became strong, filled with wisdom; and
the favor of God was upon him.

The Boy Jesus in the Temple

41 Now every year his parents went to Jerusalem for
the festival of the Passover. 42And when he was twelve
years old, they went up as usual for the festival.
43When the festival was ended and they started to
return, the boy Jesus stayed behind in Jerusalem,
but his parents did not know it. 44Assuming that
he was in the group of travelers, they went a
day's journey. Then they started to look for him
among their relatives and friends. 45When they
did not find him, they returned to Jerusalem to
search for him. 46After three days they found
him in the temple, sitting among the teachers,

s **2.38** Gk *him*

listening to them and asking them questions. 47And all who
heard him were amazed at his understanding and his
answers. 48When his parents[t] saw him they were
astonished; and his mother said to him, "Child,
why have you treated us like this? Look,
your father and I have been searching
for you in great anxiety." 49He said to
them, "Why were you searching for
me? Did you not know that I must
be in my Father's house?"[u] 50But
they did not understand what he
said to them. 51Then he went
down with them and came to
Nazareth, and was obedient to
them. His mother treasured all
these things in her heart.
52 And Jesus increased in
wisdom and in years,[v] and in
divine and human favor.

2:49 Jesus was rude to his parents?

He definitely said things they did not expect. Jesus reveals his understanding that he is the son of not only Mary and Joseph but of God, the Father.

2:51 What does it mean that Mary treasured all these things in her heart?

Even though Mary knew who her son was, she did not know or understand everything his life would bring. She watched him grow up and remembered everything with great love and affection, sure that she would one day understand.

t **2.48** Gk *they*
u **2.49** Or *be about my Father's interests?*
v **2.52** Or *in stature*

Preparation for Public Ministry: "You are my Son, the Beloved" (Lk 3:1–4:15)

In this section, Luke reintroduces the figure of John the Baptist. Luke describes how John the Baptist prepares everyone for Jesus' entrance on the scene—which happened at his baptism in the Jordan River. Theologically speaking, these verses are very dense because they present Jesus as "more powerful" than John the Baptist (3:16), and as the beloved Son of the Father (3:22), the new Adam who has come to bring universal salvation (3:38), and the victor over the devil and every evil (4:13).

The Proclamation of John the Baptist

3 In the fifteenth year of the reign of Emperor Tiberius, when Pontius Pilate was governor of Judea, and Herod was ruler[w] of Galilee, and
his brother Philip ruler[x] of the region of Ituraea and Trachonitis, and
Lysanias ruler[y] of Abilene, [2]during the high
priesthood of Annas and Caiaphas,
the word of God came to John son of
Zechariah in the wilderness. [3]He went
into all the region around the Jordan,
proclaiming a baptism of repentance for
the forgiveness of sins, [4]as it is written in
the book of the words of the prophet Isaiah,

"The voice of one crying out in the
wilderness:
'Prepare the way of the Lord,
make his paths straight.

w **3.1** Gk *tetrarch*
x **3.1** Gk *tetrarch*
y **3.1** Gk *tetrarch*

5 Every valley shall be filled,
and every mountain and hill shall be made low,
and the crooked shall be made straight,
and the rough ways made smooth;
6 and all flesh shall see the salvation of God.'"

7 John said to the crowds that came out to
be baptized by him, "You brood of vipers!
Who warned you to flee from the wrath to
come? 8Bear fruits worthy of repentance.
Do not begin to say to yourselves, 'We
have Abraham as our ancestor'; for I tell
you, God is able from these stones to raise
up children to Abraham. 9Even now the
ax is lying at the root of the trees; every
tree therefore that does not bear good
fruit is cut down and thrown into the fire."

10 And the crowds asked him, "What then should we do?" 11In
reply he said to them, "Whoever has two coats must share with anyone who
has none; and whoever has food must do likewise." 12Even tax collectors
came to be baptized, and they asked him, "Teacher, what should we do?"
13He said to them, "Collect no more than the amount prescribed for you."
14Soldiers also asked him, "And we, what should we do?" He said to them,
"Do not extort money from anyone by threats or false accusation, and be
satisfied with your wages."

3:8 Repentance

To repent, that is to change one's mentality and way of living, can also be referred to as "conversion." John the Baptist's invitation to repent raises, for those who listen to it, the question that is repeated three times: "What then should we do?"

3:16 Does that mean there were two different baptisms?

Yes. John the Baptist's baptism was a sign of purification and conversion. The Baptism offered by Jesus brings us new life, marked by the presence of the Holy Spirit.

15 As the people were filled with expectation,
and all were questioning in their hearts concerning John, whether he might be the
Messiah,[z] 16 John answered all of them by
saying, "I baptize you with water; but one
who is more powerful than I is coming; I
am not worthy to untie the thong of his
sandals. He will baptize you with[a] the
Holy Spirit and fire. 17 His winnowing fork
is in his hand, to clear his threshing floor
and to gather the wheat into his granary;
but the chaff he will burn with unquenchable fire."
18 So, with many other exhortations, he
proclaimed the good news to the people. 19 But
Herod the ruler,[b] who had been rebuked by him
because of Herodias, his brother's wife, and
because of all the evil things that Herod had done,
20 added to them all by shutting up John in prison.

3:19 Herod the ruler

This Herod was known as Herod the Tetrarch, who ruled until the end of the year 30. He was actually the son of Herod the Great (who reigned when Jesus was born).

The Baptism of Jesus

21 Now when all the people were baptized, and
when Jesus also had been baptized and was
praying, the heaven was opened, 22 and the Holy
Spirit descended upon him in bodily form like a
dove. And a voice came from heaven, "You are my
Son, the Beloved;[c] with you I am well pleased."[d]

z **3.15** Or *the Christ*
a **3.16** Or *in*
b **3.19** Gk *tetrarch*
c **3.22** Or *my beloved Son*
d **3.22** Other ancient authorities read *You are my Son, today I have begotten you*
e **3.27** Gk *Salathiel*
f **3.32** Other ancient authorities read *Salmon*
g **3.33** Other ancient authorities read *Amminadab, son of Aram*; others vary widely

The Ancestors of Jesus

23 Jesus was about thirty years old when he began his work. He was
the son (as was thought) of Joseph son of Heli, 24son of Matthat, son
of Levi, son of Melchi, son of Jannai, son of Joseph, 25son
of Mattathias, son of Amos, son of Nahum, son of Esli,
son of Naggai, 26son of Maath, son of Mattathias, son
of Semein, son of Josech, son of Joda, 27son of Joanan,
son of Rhesa, son of Zerubbabel, son of Shealtiel,[e]
son of Neri, 28son of Melchi, son of Addi, son of
Cosam, son of Elmadam, son of Er, 29son of
Joshua, son of Eliezer, son of Jorim, son of
Matthat, son of Levi, 30son of Simeon, son
of Judah, son of Joseph, son of Jonam, son
of Eliakim, 31son of Melea, son of Menna,
son of Mattatha, son of Nathan, son of David,
32son of Jesse, son of Obed, son of Boaz, son of
Sala,[f] son of Nahshon, 33son of Amminadab, son
of Admin, son of Arni,[g] son of Hezron, son of
Perez, son of Judah, 34son of Jacob, son of Isaac,
son of Abraham, son of Terah, son of Nahor,
35son of Serug, son of Reu, son of Peleg, son of
Eber, son of Shelah, 36son of Cainan, son of
Arphaxad, son of Shem, son of Noah, son
of Lamech, 37son of Methuselah, son of
Enoch, son of Jared, son of Mahalaleel,
son of Cainan, 38son of Enos, son of
Seth, son of Adam, son of God.

The Temptation of Jesus

4 Jesus, full of the Holy Spirit, returned from the Jordan and was led by the
Spirit in the wilderness, 2where for forty days he was tempted by the devil.
He ate nothing at all during those days, and when they were over, he was
famished. 3The devil said to him, "If you are the Son of God, command this
stone to become a loaf of bread." 4Jesus answered him, "It is written, 'One
does not live by bread alone.'"
5 Then the devil[h] led him up and showed him in an instant
all the kingdoms of the world. 6And the devil[i] said to
him, "To you I will give their glory and all this
authority; for it has been given over to me, and I
give it to anyone I please. 7If you, then, will worship
me, it will all be yours." 8Jesus answered him, "It is
written,

'Worship the Lord your God,
and serve only him.'"

9 Then the devil[j] took him to Jerusalem, and placed
him on the pinnacle of the temple, saying to him, "If
you are the Son of God, throw yourself down from here,
10 for it is written,

'He will command his angels concerning you,
to protect you,'

11and

'On their hands they will bear you up,
so that you will not dash your foot against
a stone.'"

4:5 Led

Jesus lets himself be pushed, but only up to a certain point.

h **4.5** Gk *he*
i **4.6** Gk *he*
j **4.9** Gk *he*

12Jesus answered him, "It is said, 'Do not put
the Lord your God to the test.'" 13When the
devil had finished every test, he departed
from him until an opportune time.

The Beginning of the Galilean Ministry

14 Then Jesus, filled with the power
of the Spirit, returned to Galilee, and
a report about him spread through
all the surrounding country. 15He
began to teach in their synagogues
and was praised by everyone.

4:10 Why did Jesus not throw himself down if it is true that he would have been saved?

If Jesus had thrown himself down, he would have "tested" the Lord, meaning he would have expected the Lord to save him from his own reckless decision.

4:15 Synagogues

Places where Jews gather to listen to the word of God, to deepen their understanding of it, and to hear the teachings of their rabbis.

Ministering in Galilee: Good News for the World (Lk 4:16–9:50)

Jesus begins his public ministry in Nazareth among the people who saw him grow up. He starts not just in any place, but in the heart of the city—its synagogue. It is clear that he intends to focus on his fellow Jews, at least at the beginning. Among them Jesus heals, preaches, teaches, and chooses his first disciples. Despite everything he does, Jesus is not always accepted. His discussions with the Pharisees are about resting on the Sabbath, fasting, and his authority. The Lord also reaches out to people who were regarded by the Jewish authorities as "far away"—such as sinners, tax collectors, prostitutes, and pagans. Jesus places a choice before each of them: follow him or reject him. Some will follow him and experience the blessedness of the poor. Others will reject him, preferring themselves and the hell a way of life without Jesus produces for them.

The Rejection of Jesus at Nazareth

16 When he came to Nazareth, where he had been brought
up, he went to the synagogue on the sabbath day, as was his custom. He stood up to
read, 17 and the scroll of the prophet Isaiah
was given to him. He unrolled the scroll and found the place where it was written:

18 "The Spirit of the Lord is upon me,
because he has anointed me
to bring good news to the poor.
He has sent me to proclaim release to
the captives
and recovery of sight to the blind,
to let the oppressed go free,
19 to proclaim the year of the Lord's favor."

20And he rolled up the scroll, gave it back to the attendant,
and sat down. The eyes of all in the synagogue were fixed
on him. 21Then he began to say to them, "Today this
scripture has been fulfilled in your hearing."
22All spoke well of him and were amazed
at the gracious words that came from his
mouth. They said, "Is not this Joseph's
son?" 23He said to them, "Doubtless
you will quote to me this proverb,
'Doctor, cure yourself!' And you
will say, 'Do here also in your
hometown the things that we
have heard you did at Capernaum.' " 24And he said, "Truly I
tell you, no prophet is accepted in
the prophet's hometown. 25But the
truth is, there were many widows
in Israel in the time of Elijah, when
the heaven was shut up three years
and six months, and there was a severe
famine over all the land; 26yet Elijah was
sent to none of them except to a widow at
Zarephath in Sidon. 27There were also many
lepers[k] in Israel in the time of the prophet Elisha,
and none of them was cleansed except Naaman the

4:21 What does this sentence mean?

Unlike other teachers who interpreted the word of God, Jesus fulfills it. Everything proclaimed by Isaiah happens as a result of Jesus' words and actions. That is why everyone is amazed. They went to hear a teacher and found themselves in front of someone much greater!

k **4.27** The terms *leper* and *leprosy* can refer to several diseases

Syrian." 28When they heard this, all in the synagogue were
filled with rage. 29They got up, drove him out of the town,
and led him to the brow of the hill on which their town
was built, so that they might hurl him off the cliff. 30But
he passed through the midst of them and went on his
way.

The Man with an Unclean Spirit

31 He went down to Capernaum, a city in
Galilee, and was teaching them on the sabbath. 32They were astounded at his teaching,
because he spoke with authority. 33In the
synagogue there was a man who had the
spirit of an unclean demon, and he cried
out with a loud voice, 34"Let us alone! What
have you to do with us, Jesus of Nazareth?
Have you come to destroy us? I know who
you are, the Holy One of God." 35But Jesus
rebuked him, saying, "Be silent, and come
out of him!" When the demon had thrown
him down before them, he came out of him
without having done him any harm. 36They
were all amazed and kept saying to one
another, "What kind of utterance is this? For
with authority and power he commands the
unclean spirits, and out they come!" 37And a
report about him began to reach every place in
the region.

4:28 Why were they "filled with rage"?
Because they thought it was absurd that God would manifest himself to the pagans and not to the Jews.

4:38 Peter had a mother-in-law?
Yes. He was married like some of Jesus' other disciples.

4:41 Why did Jesus not allow them to speak?
Because no one can really understand who Jesus is without first acknowledging his passion, death, and resurrection.

4:43 Kingdom of God
The peace and good that God gives through Jesus Christ.

Healings at Simon's House

38 After leaving the synagogue he entered
Simon's house. Now Simon's mother-
in-law was suffering from a high fever,
and they asked him about her. 39 Then
he stood over her and rebuked the
fever, and it left her. Immediately she
got up and began to serve them.
40 As the sun was setting, all those
who had any who were sick with various kinds of diseases brought them to
him; and he laid his hands on each of
them and cured them. 41 Demons also
came out of many, shouting, "You are
the Son of God!" But he rebuked them
and would not allow them to speak,
because they knew that he was the
Messiah.[l]

Jesus Preaches in the Synagogues

42 At daybreak he departed and went into a
deserted place. And the crowds were looking
for him; and when they reached him, they
wanted to prevent him from leaving them. 43 But
he said to them, "I must proclaim the good news
of the kingdom of God to the other cities also; for
I was sent for this purpose." 44 So he continued proclaiming the message in the synagogues of Judea.[m]

l **4.41** Or *the Christ*
m **4.44** Other ancient authorities read *Galilee*

Jesus Calls the First Disciples

5 Once while Jesus[n] was standing beside the lake of Gennesaret, and the crowd was pressing in on him to hear the word of God, [2]he saw two boats there at the shore of the lake; the fishermen had gone out of them and were washing their nets. [3]He got into one of the boats, the one belonging to Simon, and asked him to put out a little way from the shore. Then he sat down and taught the crowds from the boat. [4]When he had finished speaking, he said to Simon, "Put out into the deep water and let down your nets for a catch." [5]Simon answered, "Master, we have worked all night long but have caught nothing. Yet if you say so, I will let down the nets." [6]When they had done this, they caught so many fish that their nets were beginning to break. [7]So they signaled their partners in the other boat to come and help them. And they came and filled both boats, so that they began to sink. [8]But when Simon Peter saw it, he fell down at Jesus' knees, saying, "Go away from me, Lord, for I am a sinful man!" [9]For he and all who were with him were amazed at the catch of fish that they had taken; [10]and so also were James and John, sons of Zebedee, who were partners with Simon. Then Jesus said to Simon, "Do not be afraid; from now on you will be catching people." [11]When they had brought their boats to shore, they left everything and followed him.

n **5.1** Gk *he*

5:13 Wasn't it dangerous to touch a leper?

Of course, but Jesus touched him anyway to show everyone that he has eliminated any separation between himself and those who were sick or were considered impure. With Jesus, there is no more separation between God and men and women.

5:17 Pharisees and teachers of the Law

Jewish groups of the time, composed both of scholars and strict observers of the Law and Jewish religious traditions.

Jesus Cleanses a Leper

12 Once, when he was in one of the cities,
there was a man covered with leprosy.[o]
When he saw Jesus, he bowed with
his face to the ground and begged
him, "Lord, if you choose, you can
make me clean." 13 Then Jesus[p]
stretched out his hand, touched
him, and said, "I do choose. Be
made clean." Immediately the leprosy[q] left him. 14 And he ordered
him to tell no one. "Go," he said,
"and show yourself to the priest,
and, as Moses commanded, make
an offering for your cleansing, for a
testimony to them." 15 But now more
than ever the word about Jesus[r] spread
abroad; many crowds would gather to
hear him and to be cured of their diseases. 16 But he would withdraw to deserted
places and pray.

Jesus Heals a Paralytic

17 One day, while he was teaching, Pharisees and teachers of the law were sitting near by (they had come from every village of Galilee and Judea and from Jerusalem); and the power of the Lord was with him to heal.[s]

o **5.12** The terms *leper* and *leprosy* can refer to several diseases
p **5.13** Gk *he*
q **5.13** The terms *leper* and *leprosy* can refer to several diseases
r **5.15** Gk *him*
s **5.17** Other ancient authorities read *was present to heal them*

[18]Just then some men came, carrying a paralyzed man on a bed. They were
trying to bring him in and lay him before Jesus;[t] [19]but finding no
way to bring him in because of the crowd, they went up
on the roof and let him down with his bed through the
tiles into the middle of the crowd[u] in front of Jesus.
[20]When he saw their faith, he said, "Friend,[v] your
sins are forgiven you." [21]Then the scribes and the
Pharisees began to question, "Who is this who
is speaking blasphemies? Who can forgive sins
but God alone?" [22]When Jesus perceived their
questionings, he answered them, "Why do you
raise such questions in your hearts? [23]Which
is easier, to say, 'Your sins are forgiven you,' or
to say, 'Stand up and walk'? [24]But so that you
may know that the Son of Man has authority on
earth to forgive sins"—he said to the one who
was paralyzed—"I say to you, stand up and take
your bed and go to your home." [25]Immediately he
stood up before them, took what he had been
lying on, and went to his home, glorifying God.
[26]Amazement seized all of them, and they glorified God and were filled with awe, saying,
"We have seen strange things today."

Jesus Calls Levi

27 After this he went out and saw a tax collector
named Levi, sitting at the tax booth; and he said to
him, "Follow me." [28]And he got up, left everything,
and followed him.

5:21 Why did they think Jesus was blaspheming?

By forgiving sins, Jesus revealed that he possessed a power that only God could have. For the Jews, such a claim was the highest form of blasphemy.

5:27 Tax Collector

A Jew who other Jews considered both a sinner and a traitor because he collected taxes for personal profit on behalf of the Romans.

t **5.18** Gk *him*
u **5.19** Gk *into the midst*
v **5.20** Gk *Man*

5:30 People were not allowed to eat with sinners?

According to Jewish religious laws, eating with sinners made a person impure. To spend time with a sinner implied "entering their circle." Jesus included sinners to invite them to repentance.

29 Then Levi gave a great banquet for him in his
house; and there was a large crowd of tax collectors and others sitting at the table[w] with them.
30 The Pharisees and their scribes were complaining to his disciples, saying, "Why do
you eat and drink with tax collectors and
sinners?" 31 Jesus answered, "Those who are
well have no need of a physician, but those
who are sick; 32 I have come to call not the
righteous but sinners to repentance."

The Question about Fasting

33 Then they said to him, "John's disciples, like the disciples of the Pharisees, fre-
quently fast and pray, but your disciples eat
and drink." 34 Jesus said to them, "You cannot
make wedding guests fast while the bridegroom
is with them, can you? 35 The days will come when
the bridegroom will be taken away from them, and
then they will fast in those days." 36 He also told them a
parable: "No one tears a piece from a new garment and sews
it on an old garment; otherwise the new will be torn, and the piece
from the new will not match the old. 37 And no one puts new wine into
old wineskins; otherwise the new wine will burst the skins and will be
spilled, and the skins will be destroyed. 38 But new wine must be put into
fresh wineskins. 39 And no one after drinking old wine desires new wine, but
says, 'The old is good.'"[x]

w **5.29** Gk *reclining*
x **5.39** Other ancient authorities read *better*; others lack verse 39

The Question about the Sabbath

6 One sabbath[y] while Jesus[z] was going through the grainfields, his disciples
plucked some heads of grain, rubbed them in their hands, and
ate them. 2But some of the Pharisees said, "Why are you doing
what is not lawful[a] on the sabbath?" 3Jesus answered, "Have
you not read what David did when he and his companions were hungry? 4He entered the house of God and
took and ate the bread of the Presence, which it
is not lawful for any but the priests to eat, and
gave some to his companions?" 5Then he said
to them, "The Son of Man is lord of the sabbath."

The Man with a Withered Hand

6 On another sabbath he entered the synagogue and taught, and there was a man
there whose right hand was withered. 7The
scribes and the Pharisees watched him to
see whether he would cure on the sabbath, so
that they might find an accusation against him.
8Even though he knew what they were thinking,
he said to the man who had the withered hand,
"Come and stand here." He got up and stood there.
9Then Jesus said to them, "I ask you, is it lawful to do
good or to do harm on the sabbath, to save life or to
destroy it?" 10After looking around at all of them, he
said to him, "Stretch out your hand." He did so, and
his hand was restored. 11But they were filled with
fury and discussed with one another what
they might do to Jesus.

6:8 Why does Jesus do this there in the synagogue?

Jesus knew that the scribes and Pharisees were judging him harshly. But what always matters most to Jesus is the person who is suffering. Jesus' apparent lack of concern about breaking religious traditions is why they get angry.

y **6.1** Other ancient authorities read *On the second first sabbath*
z **6.1** Gk *he*
a **6.2** Other ancient authorities add *to do*

6:12 Did Jesus pray?

Certainly. In fact, his is the most perfect prayer—the Son who calls on his Father. We Christians end every liturgical prayer with the phrase, "through Christ our Lord," because it is really through his Son Jesus that God the Father receives our requests.

Jesus Chooses the Twelve Apostles

12 Now during those days he went out to the
mountain to pray; and he spent the night
in prayer to God. 13 And when day came,
he called his disciples and chose twelve
of them, whom he also named apostles:
14 Simon, whom he named Peter, and his
brother Andrew, and James, and John, and
Philip, and Bartholomew, 15 and Matthew,
and Thomas, and James son of Alphaeus,
and Simon, who was called the Zealot,
16 and Judas son of James, and Judas Iscariot,
who became a traitor.

Jesus Teaches and Heals

17 He came down with them and stood on a
level place, with a great crowd of his disciples
and a great multitude of people from all Judea,
Jerusalem, and the coast of Tyre and Sidon. 18 They
had come to hear him and to be healed of their diseases; and those who were troubled with unclean
spirits were cured. 19 And all in the crowd were
trying to touch him, for power came out from him
and healed all of them.

6:13 Twelve Apostles

There were as many Apostles as there were tribes of Israel. This indicates that from the Apostles the new people of God—the Church—was born.

Blessings and Woes

20 Then he looked up at his disciples and said:
"Blessed are you who are poor,
for yours is the kingdom of God.
21 "Blessed are you who are hungry now,
for you will be filled.
"Blessed are you who weep now,
for you will laugh.
22 "Blessed are you when people hate
you, and when they exclude you, revile
you, and defame you[b] on account of the
Son of Man. 23 Rejoice in that day and leap
for joy, for surely your reward is great in
heaven; for that is what their ancestors did
to the prophets.
24 "But woe to you who are rich,
for you have received your consolation.
25 "Woe to you who are full now,
for you will be hungry.
"Woe to you who are laughing now,
for you will mourn and weep.
26 "Woe to you when all speak well of you, for that is
what their ancestors did to the false prophets.

6:24–26 Isn't Jesus exaggerating when he proclaims the "woes" of the rich?
Jesus warns the rich not so that they will become very poor, but so that the rich may stop thinking only of their own wealth and pleasure and see others' needs.

b **6.22** Gk *cast out your name as evil*

Love for Enemies

27 "But I say to you that listen, Love your enemies, do
good to those who hate you, 28bless those who curse
you, pray for those who abuse you. 29If anyone
strikes you on the cheek, offer the other also;
and from anyone who takes away your coat
do not withhold even your shirt. 30Give
to everyone who begs from you; and if
anyone takes away your goods, do not
ask for them again. 31Do to others as
you would have them do to you.

32 "If you love those who love
you, what credit is that to you? For
even sinners love those who love
them. 33If you do good to those who
do good to you, what credit is that to
you? For even sinners do the same.
34If you lend to those from whom you
hope to receive, what credit is that to
you? Even sinners lend to sinners, to
receive as much again. 35But love your
enemies, do good, and lend, expecting
nothing in return.[c] Your reward will be great,
and you will be children of the Most High; for he
is kind to the ungrateful and the wicked. 36Be merciful, just as your Father is merciful.

6:29 I have been taught to defend myself, not to suffer ill treatment!

To defend yourself from those who do evil is right and can also be a duty for those who are responsible for other people's lives and for the common good—like police officers. What Jesus is saying is that without love there can be no justice. We must love, or we are against God!

c **6.35** Other ancient authorities read *despairing of no one*

Judging Others

37 "Do not judge, and you will not be
judged; do not condemn, and you will not
be condemned. Forgive, and you will be
forgiven; 38 give, and it will be given to
you. A good measure, pressed down,
shaken together, running over, will
be put into your lap; for the measure
you give will be the measure you
get back."

39 He also told them a parable:
"Can a blind person guide a blind
person? Will not both fall into a pit?
40 A disciple is not above the teacher,
but everyone who is fully qualified
will be like the teacher. 41 Why do you
see the speck in your neighbor's[d] eye,
but do not notice the log in your own eye?
42 Or how can you say to your neighbor,[e]
'Friend,[f] let me take out the speck in your eye,' when
you yourself do not see the log in your own eye? You
hypocrite, first take the log out of your own eye, and
then you will see clearly to take the speck out of your
neighbor's[g] eye.

6:42 Hypocrite
Someone who is false and a liar.

d **6.41** Gk *brother's*
e **6.42** Gk *brother*
f **6.42** Gk *brother*
g **6.42** Gk *brother's*

A Tree and Its Fruit

43 "No good tree bears bad fruit, nor again does a bad tree bear good fruit;
44 for each tree is known by its own fruit. Figs are not gathered from thorns,
nor are grapes picked from a bramble bush. 45 The good person out of the
good treasure of the heart produces good, and the evil person out of evil treasure produces evil; for it is out of the abundance of the heart that the mouth
speaks.

The Two Foundations

46 "Why do you call me 'Lord, Lord,' and do not do what I tell you?
47 I will show you what someone is like who comes to me, hears
my words, and acts on them. 48 That one is like a man building
a house, who dug deeply and laid the foundation
on rock; when a flood arose, the river burst
against that house but could not shake it,
because it had been well built.[h] 49 But the one
who hears and does not act is like a man
who built a house on the ground without
a foundation. When the river burst
against it, immediately it fell,
and great was the ruin of
that house."

h **6.48** Other ancient authorities read *founded upon the rock*

Jesus Heals a Centurion's Servant

7 After Jesus[i] had finished all his sayings in
the hearing of the people, he entered Capernaum. 2A centurion there had a slave whom
he valued highly, and who was ill and close
to death. 3When he heard about Jesus, he sent
some Jewish elders to him, asking him to come
and heal his slave. 4When they came to Jesus,
they appealed to him earnestly, saying, "He is
worthy of having you do this for him, 5for he loves
our people, and it is he who built our synagogue
for us." 6And Jesus went with them, but when he
was not far from the house, the centurion sent
friends to say to him, "Lord, do not trouble yourself, for I am not worthy to have you come under my
roof; 7therefore I did not presume to come to you.
But only speak the word, and let my servant be healed. 8For I also am a man
set under authority, with soldiers under me; and I say to one, 'Go,' and he
goes, and to another, 'Come,' and he comes, and to my slave, 'Do this,' and
the slave does it." 9When Jesus heard this he was amazed at him, and turning
to the crowd that followed him, he said, "I tell you, not even in Israel have
I found such faith." 10When those who had been sent returned to the house,
they found the slave in good health.

7:2 Centurion
A Roman soldier, usually a pagan, who commands one hundred soldiers and, in this case, a person who cared deeply for others.

i **7.1** Gk *he*

Jesus Raises the Widow's Son at Nain

11 Soon afterwards[j] he went to a town called Nain, and
his disciples and a large crowd went with him. 12 As he
approached the gate of the town, a man who had died
was being carried out. He was his mother's only son,
and she was a widow; and with her was a large
crowd from the town. 13 When the Lord saw her,
he had compassion for her and said to her,
"Do not weep." 14 Then he came forward and
touched the bier, and the bearers stood still.
And he said, "Young man, I say to you,
rise!" 15 The dead man sat up and began to
speak, and Jesus[k] gave him to his mother.
16 Fear seized all of them; and they glorified God, saying, "A great prophet has
risen among us!" and "God has looked
favorably on his people!" 17 This word
about him spread throughout Judea and
all the surrounding country.

Messengers from John the Baptist

18 The disciples of John reported all these
things to him. So John summoned two of
his disciples 19 and sent them to the Lord to
ask, "Are you the one who is to come, or
are we to wait for another?" 20 When the men

7:12 The only son of a widow dies, leaving her with no one to watch out for her . . . what a tragedy!

In Jesus' time, widows were some of the poorest and most defenseless people. Without children, this woman had no one to care for her as she aged. That is why Jesus was so moved by that scene and brought the young man back to life.

7:19 Did John the Baptist have doubts about Jesus too?

Yes. Everyone, even the greatest person, must make a journey of faith. Time and effort are required to understand important things.

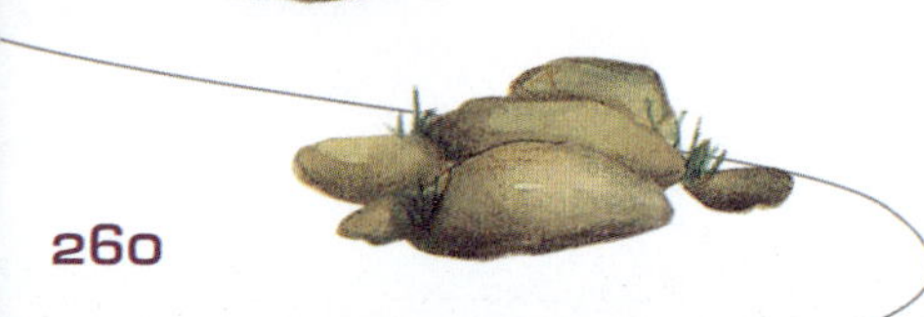

j **7.11** Other ancient authorities read *Next day*
k **7.15** Gk *he*

had come to him, they said, "John the Baptist has sent us to you to ask, 'Are
you the one who is to come, or are we to wait for another?' " 21 Jesus[l] had
just then cured many people of diseases, plagues, and evil
spirits, and had given sight to many who were blind.
22 And he answered them, "Go and tell John what you
have seen and heard: the blind receive their sight,
the lame walk, the lepers[m] are cleansed, the
deaf hear, the dead are raised, the poor have
good news brought to them. 23 And blessed is
anyone who takes no offense at me."

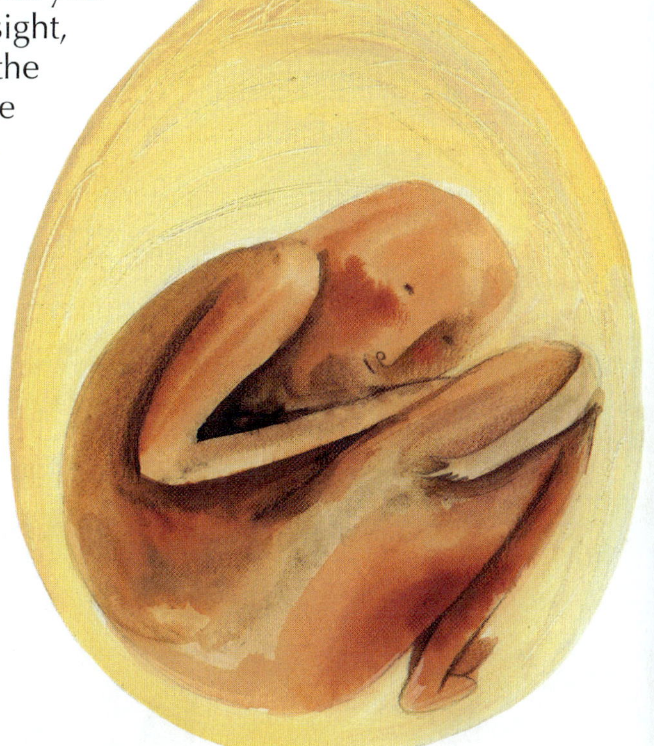

24 When John's messengers had gone,
Jesus[n] began to speak to the crowds about
John:[o] "What did you go out into the wilderness to look at? A reed shaken by the
wind? 25 What then did you go out to see?
Someone[p] dressed in soft robes? Look,
those who put on fine clothing and live in
luxury are in royal palaces. 26 What then
did you go out to see? A prophet? Yes, I tell
you, and more than a prophet. 27 This is the
one about whom it is written,

> 'See, I am sending my messenger
> ahead of you,
> who will prepare your way before
> you.'

l **7.21** Gk *He*
m **7.22** The terms *leper* and *leprosy* can refer to several diseases
n **7.24** Gk *he*
o **7.24** Gk *him*
p **7.25** Or *Why then did you go out? To see someone*

[28]I tell you, among those born of women no one is greater than John; yet the
least in the kingdom of God is greater than he." [29](And all the people who
heard this, including the tax collectors, acknowledged the justice of God,[q]
because they had been baptized with John's baptism. [30]But by refusing to be
baptized by him, the Pharisees and the lawyers rejected God's purpose for
themselves.)

31 "To what then will I compare the people of this generation, and what
are they like? [32]They are like children sitting in the marketplace and calling to
one another,

'We played the flute for you, and you did not dance;
we wailed, and you did not weep.'

[33]For John the Baptist has come eating no bread and
drinking no wine, and you say, 'He has a demon'; [34]the
Son of Man has come eating and drinking, and you
say, 'Look, a glutton and a drunkard, a friend of tax
collectors and sinners!' [35]Nevertheless, wisdom is
vindicated by all her children."

A Sinful Woman Forgiven

36 One of the Pharisees asked Jesus[r] to eat with
him, and he went into the Pharisee's house and
took his place at the table. [37]And a woman in
the city, who was a sinner, having learned that
he was eating in the Pharisee's house, brought
an alabaster jar of ointment. [38]She stood behind
him at his feet, weeping, and began to bathe his

q **7.29** Or *praised God*
r **7.36** Gk *him*

feet with her tears and to dry them with her hair. Then
she continued kissing his feet and anointing
them with the ointment. 39Now when the
Pharisee who had invited him saw it, he
said to himself, "If this man were a
prophet, he would have known who
and what kind of woman this is
who is touching him—that she is a
sinner." 40Jesus spoke up and said
to him, "Simon, I have something to say to you." "Teacher,"
he replied, "speak." 41"A certain
creditor had two debtors; one
owed five hundred denarii,[s] and
the other fifty. 42When they could
not pay, he canceled the debts
for both of them. Now which of
them will love him more?" 43Simon
answered, "I suppose the one for
whom he canceled the greater debt."
And Jesus[t] said to him, "You have judged
rightly." 44Then turning toward the woman,
he said to Simon, "Do you see this woman? I
entered your house; you gave me no water for my feet,
but she has bathed my feet with her tears and dried them with her hair.

7:38 Why did she cry so much?

Coming closer to Jesus, she understood that she wasn't just a prisoner to her sins, of those who had exploited her, and of people's judgment. She understood that she was wrapped in an immense and freely given love—God's love.

s **7.41** The denarius was the usual day's wage for a laborer
t **7.43** Gk *he*

45You gave me no kiss, but from the time I came in she has not
stopped kissing my feet. 46You did not anoint my head with oil,
but she has anointed my feet with ointment. 47Therefore, I tell
you, her sins, which were many, have been forgiven; hence she
has shown great love. But the one to whom little is forgiven,
loves little." 48Then he said to her, "Your sins are forgiven."
49But those who were at the table with him began to
say among themselves, "Who is this who even for-
gives sins?" 50And he said to the woman, "Your
faith has saved you; go in peace."

Some Women Accompany Jesus

8 Soon afterwards he went on through
cities and villages, proclaiming and
bringing the good news of the kingdom
of God. The twelve were with him, 2as
well as some women who had been
cured of evil spirits and infirmities:
Mary, called Magdalene, from whom
seven demons had gone out, 3and Joanna,
the wife of Herod's steward Chuza, and
Susanna, and many others, who provided
for them[u] out of their resources.

8:2–3 I have never heard some of these names.

Perhaps, you only know the names of the Apostles. Actually, in addition to the Twelve, there were many disciples who followed Jesus, including the women mentioned here. These same women will have a very important task in Luke 24.

u **8.3** Other ancient authorities read *him*

The Parable of the Sower

4 When a great crowd gathered and people from town after town came to him, he said in a parable: 5"A sower went out to sow his seed; and as he sowed, some fell on the path and was trampled on, and the birds of the air ate it up. 6Some fell on the rock; and as it grew up, it withered for lack of moisture. 7Some fell among thorns, and the thorns grew with it and choked it. 8Some fell into good soil, and when it grew, it produced a hundredfold." As he said this, he called out, "Let anyone with ears to hear listen!"

The Purpose of the Parables

9 Then his disciples asked him what this parable meant. 10He said, "To you it has been given to know the secrets[v] of the kingdom of God; but to others I speak[w] in parables, so that
'looking they may not perceive,
and listening they may not understand.'

The Parable of the Sower Explained

11 "Now the parable is this: The seed is the word of God. 12The ones on the path are those who have heard; then the devil comes and takes away the word from their hearts, so that they may not believe and be saved. 13The ones on the rock are those who, when they hear the word, receive it with joy. But these have no root; they believe only for a while and in a time of testing fall away. 14As for what

8:8 What does this parable mean?

The story was unclear, even for his disciples. This is why Jesus explains its meaning in verses 11–15.

v **8.10** Or *mysteries*
w **8.10** Gk lacks *I speak*

fell among the thorns, these are the ones who hear; but as they go
on their way, they are choked by the cares and riches and pleasures
of life, and their fruit does not mature. [15]But as for that in the good
soil, these are the ones who, when they hear the word, hold it fast
in an honest and good heart, and bear fruit with patient
endurance.

A Lamp under a Jar

16 "No one after lighting a lamp hides it under a jar,
or puts it under a bed, but puts it on a lampstand,
so that those who enter may see the light. [17]For
nothing is hidden that will not be disclosed, nor
is anything secret that will not become known
and come to light. [18]Then pay attention to how
you listen; for to those who have, more will be
given; and from those who do not have, even
what they seem to have will be taken away."

The True Kindred of Jesus

19 Then his mother and his brothers came to
him, but they could not reach him because of
the crowd. [20]And he was told, "Your mother
and your brothers are standing outside, wanting
to see you." [21]But he said to them, "My mother
and my brothers are those who hear the word of
God and do it."

8:24 Were they very afraid?

Yes, because in those days storms could be extremely dangerous and many fishermen died if they got caught in one while out on their boats. Also, the Apostles did not yet fully understand that if Jesus was with them, nothing bad would happen to them.

Jesus Calms a Storm

22 One day he got into a boat with his
disciples, and he said to them, "Let us
go across to the other side of the lake."
So they put out, 23 and while they were
sailing he fell asleep. A windstorm
swept down on the lake, and the boat
was filling with water, and they were in
danger. 24 They went to him and woke
him up, shouting, "Master, Master,
we are perishing!" And he woke up
and rebuked the wind and the raging
waves; they ceased, and there was a
calm. 25 He said to them, "Where is your
faith?" They were afraid and amazed,
and said to one another, "Who then is
this, that he commands even the winds
and the water, and they obey him?"

Jesus Heals the Gerasene Demoniac

26 Then they arrived at the country of the
Gerasenes,[x] which is opposite Galilee. 27 As he
stepped out on land, a man of the city who had
demons met him. For a long time he had worn[y]

x **8.26** Other ancient authorities read *Gadarenes*; others, *Gergesenes*

y **8.27** Other ancient authorities read *a man of the city who had had demons for a long time met him. He wore*

no clothes, and he did not live in a house but in the tombs. 28 When he saw
Jesus, he fell down before him and shouted at the top of his voice, "What
have you to do with me, Jesus, Son of the Most High God? I beg you, do not
torment me"— 29 for Jesus[z] had commanded the unclean spirit to come out
of the man. (For many times it had seized him; he was kept under guard and
bound with chains and shackles, but he would break the bonds and be driven
by the demon into the wilds.) 30 Jesus then asked him, "What is your name?"
He said, "Legion"; for many demons had entered him. 31 They begged him not
to order them to go back into the abyss.

32 Now there on the hillside a large herd of swine was feeding; and the
demons[a] begged Jesus[b] to let them enter these. So he gave them permission.
33 Then the demons came out of the man and entered the
swine, and the herd rushed down the steep bank into the
lake and was drowned.

34 When the swineherds saw what had happened, they ran off and told it in the city and in
the country. 35 Then people came out to see
what had happened, and when they came to Jesus, they found the man from whom the demons had gone sitting at the feet of Jesus, clothed and in his right mind. And they were
afraid. 36 Those who had seen it told them how
the one who had been possessed by demons

8:30 Legion

In the Roman army a legion was a group of 5,000 foot soldiers, joined by many cavalrymen.

z **8.29** Gk *he*
a **8.32** Gk *they*
b **8.32** Gk *him*

had been healed. 37 Then all the people of the surrounding
country of the Gerasenes[c] asked Jesus[d] to leave them;
for they were seized with great fear. So he got
into the boat and returned. 38 The man from
whom the demons had gone begged that he
might be with him; but Jesus[e] sent him
away, saying, 39 "Return to your home,
and declare how much God has done
for you." So he went away, proclaiming
throughout the city how much Jesus
had done for him.

8:37 Wouldn't you have been afraid too?
Of who? Of Jesus? Here Jesus defeats an entire legion, or army, of demons, giving the man back his freedom. It is a reason to rejoice, not to be afraid!

A Girl Restored to Life and a Woman Healed

40 Now when Jesus returned, the crowd
welcomed him, for they were all waiting
for him. 41 Just then there came a man
named Jairus, a leader of the synagogue. He
fell at Jesus' feet and begged him to come to
his house, 42 for he had an only daughter, about
twelve years old, who was dying.
As he went, the crowds pressed in on him. 43 Now there
was a woman who had been suffering from hemorrhages for twelve
years; and though she had spent all she had on physicians,[f] no one could
cure her. 44 She came up behind him and touched the fringe of his clothes,

c **8.37** Other ancient authorities read *Gadarenes*; others, *Gergesenes*
d **8.37** Gk *him*
e **8.38** Gk *he*
f **8.43** Other ancient authorities lack *and though she had spent all she had on physicians*

and immediately her hemorrhage stopped. [45]Then Jesus asked, "Who touched me?" When all denied it, Peter[g] said, "Master, the crowds surround you and press in on you." [46]But Jesus said, "Someone touched me; for I noticed that power had gone out from me." [47]When the woman saw that she could not remain hidden, she came trembling; and falling down before him, she declared in the presence of all the people why she had touched him, and how she had been immediately healed. [48]He said to her, "Daughter, your faith has made you well; go in peace."

49 While he was still speaking, someone came from the leader's house to say, "Your daughter is dead; do not trouble the teacher any longer." [50]When Jesus heard this, he replied, "Do not fear. Only believe, and she will be saved." [51]When he came to the house, he did not allow anyone to enter with him, except Peter, John, and James, and the child's father and mother. [52]They were all weeping and wailing for her; but he said, "Do not weep; for she is not dead but sleeping." [53]And they laughed at him, knowing that she was dead. [54]But he took her by the hand and called out, "Child, get up!" [55]Her spirit returned, and she got up at once. Then he directed them to give her something to eat. [56]Her parents were astounded; but he ordered them to tell no one what had happened.

8:48 Was the woman healed by the fringe of his clothes?

Jesus was not wearing magic clothes. Jesus has the power to heal and it was this power that went out. The woman expresses her faith through the very simple and tangible gesture of reaching out to touch Jesus' clothes.

g **8.45** Other ancient authorities add *and those who were with him*

The Mission of the Twelve

9 Then Jesus[h] called the twelve together and gave them power and authority
over all demons and to cure diseases, 2and he sent them out to proclaim the
kingdom of God and to heal. 3He said to them, "Take nothing for
your journey, no staff, nor bag, nor bread, nor money—not even
an extra tunic. 4Whatever house you enter, stay there, and
leave from there. 5Wherever they do not welcome you,
as you are leaving that town shake the dust off your
feet as a testimony against them." 6They departed
and went through the villages, bringing the good
news and curing diseases everywhere.

9:9 Was Herod curious?

Yes, but only in a superficial sort of way. He had already condemned John the Baptist to death, even though there was something about John the Baptist's preaching that attracted him. He would have done the same thing with Jesus.

Herod's Perplexity

7 Now Herod the ruler[i] heard about all that
had taken place, and he was perplexed,
because it was said by some that John had
been raised from the dead, 8by some that
Elijah had appeared, and by others that
one of the ancient prophets had arisen.
9Herod said, "John I beheaded; but who is
this about whom I hear such things?" And
he tried to see him.

h **9.1** Gk *he*
i **9.7** Gk *tetrarch*

Feeding the Five Thousand

10 On their return the apostles told Jesus[j] all they had done. He took them with
him and withdrew privately to a city called Bethsaida. 11When the crowds
found out about it, they followed him; and he welcomed them, and spoke to
them about the kingdom of God, and healed those who needed to be cured.
12 The day was drawing to a close, and the twelve came to him and said,
"Send the crowd away, so that they may go into the surrounding
villages and countryside, to lodge and get provisions; for we
are here in a deserted place." 13But he said to them, "You
give them something to eat." They said, "We have no
more than five loaves and two fish—unless we are
to go and buy food for all these people." 14For
there were about five thousand men. And he
said to his disciples, "Make them sit down
in groups of about fifty each." 15They did
so and made them all sit down. 16And
taking the five loaves and the two fish,
he looked up to heaven, and blessed
and broke them, and gave them to the
disciples to set before the crowd. 17And
all ate and were filled. What was left
over was gathered up, twelve baskets
of broken pieces.

9:17 Did Jesus miscalculate the number of people?

No, he knew how many people were present. Jesus was not simply preparing a normal lunch. The Lord gave everyone the banquet of the kingdom of God where food is always plentiful. There is more than enough food for everyone, including the absent.

j **9.10** Gk *him*

9:20 Messiah of God

Title by which Jesus is recognized as the Christ, or the one anointed by God.

Peter's Declaration about Jesus

18 Once when Jesus[k] was praying alone, with only
the disciples near him, he asked them, "Who do the
crowds say that I am?" 19They answered, "John the
Baptist; but others, Elijah; and still others, that one of
the ancient prophets has arisen." 20He said to them,
"But who do you say that I am?" Peter answered, "The
Messiah[l] of God."

Jesus Foretells His Death and Resurrection

21 He sternly ordered and commanded them not
to tell anyone, 22saying, "The Son of Man must
undergo great suffering, and be rejected by the
elders, chief priests, and scribes, and be killed,
and on the third day be raised."
23 Then he said to them all, "If any want
to become my followers, let them deny
themselves and take up their cross daily and
follow me. 24For those who want to save
their life will lose it, and those who lose
their life for my sake will save it. 25What does
it profit them if they gain the whole world,
but lose or forfeit themselves? 26Those who
are ashamed of me and of my words, of them

k **9.18** Gk *he*
l **9.20** Or *The Christ*

the Son of Man will be ashamed when he comes in his glory and the glory of the Father and of the holy angels. 27But truly I tell you, there are some standing here who will not taste death before they see the kingdom of God."

The Transfiguration

28 Now about eight days after these sayings Jesus[m] took with him
Peter and John and James, and went up on the mountain to
pray. 29And while he was praying, the appearance of his
face changed, and his clothes became dazzling white.
30Suddenly they saw two men, Moses and Elijah,
talking to him. 31They appeared in glory and were
speaking of his departure, which he was about
to accomplish at Jerusalem. 32Now Peter and
his companions were weighed down with
sleep; but since they had stayed awake,[n]
they saw his glory and the two men
who stood with him. 33Just as they
were leaving him, Peter said to Jesus,
"Master, it is good for us to be here;
let us make three dwellings,[o] one
for you, one for Moses, and one for
Elijah"—not knowing what he said.

9:32 Why didn't they sleep if they were tired?

Because they were witnessing an incredible event: Jesus radiating God's glory—as if he were already risen—in the company of Elijah and Moses.

m **9.28** Gk *he*
n **9.32** Or *but when they were fully awake*
o **9.33** Or *tents*

34 While he was saying this, a cloud came and overshadowed them; and they
were terrified as they entered the cloud. 35 Then from the cloud came a voice
that said, "This is my Son, my Chosen;[p] listen to him!" 36 When
the voice had spoken, Jesus was found alone. And they
kept silent and in those days told no one any of the
things they had seen.

9:45 If one does not understand, one should ask. Why do the disciples not do that?

They sensed that Jesus' answer would not be easy to accept because he would have spoken about death and suffering.

Jesus Heals a Boy with a Demon

37 On the next day, when they had come down
from the mountain, a great crowd met him.
38 Just then a man from the crowd shouted,
"Teacher, I beg you to look at my son; he
is my only child. 39 Suddenly a spirit seizes
him, and all at once he[q] shrieks. It convulses
him until he foams at the mouth; it mauls
him and will scarcely leave him. 40 I begged
your disciples to cast it out, but they could
not." 41 Jesus answered, "You faithless and
perverse generation, how much longer must I
be with you and bear with you? Bring your son
here." 42 While he was coming, the demon dashed
him to the ground in convulsions. But Jesus rebuked the
unclean spirit, healed the boy, and gave him back to his
father. 43 And all were astounded at the greatness of God.

p **9.35** Other ancient authorities read *my Beloved*
q **9.39** Or *it*

Jesus Again Foretells His Death

While everyone was amazed at all that he was doing, he said
to his disciples, 44"Let these words sink into your ears: The
Son of Man is going to be betrayed into human hands."
45But they did not understand this saying; its meaning was
concealed from them, so that they could not perceive it.
And they were afraid to ask him about this saying.

True Greatness

46 An argument arose among them as to which one of
them was the greatest. 47But Jesus, aware of their inner
thoughts, took a little child and put it by his side, 48and
said to them, "Whoever welcomes this child in my
name welcomes me, and whoever welcomes me welcomes the one who sent me; for the least among all of
you is the greatest."

Another Exorcist

49 John answered, "Master, we saw someone casting out
demons in your name, and we tried to stop him, because
he does not follow with us." 50But Jesus said to him, "Do
not stop him; for whoever is not against you is for you."

The Journey: "Headed for Jerusalem" (Lk 9:51–19:28)

We arrive at the heart of Luke's Gospel: ten chapters that present Jesus' long journey from Galilee to Jerusalem. This section is characteristic of this third Gospel. Here the evangelist offers us a lot of previously unpublished material, gleaned from sources unknown to Mark and Matthew. Luke organizes the material in the context of a great journey, which acquires a highly symbolic value. Jesus Master goes on this journey ("set his face" 9:51) with the intention of not looking back. It is a journey that will bring him to the city that, historically, marked the end of many of the prophets' lives. It is presented by Luke as the image of Christian life: a road that climbs upward, hard and tiring, but made valuable by the camaraderie with other traveling companions and, above all, by constant communion with God the Father.

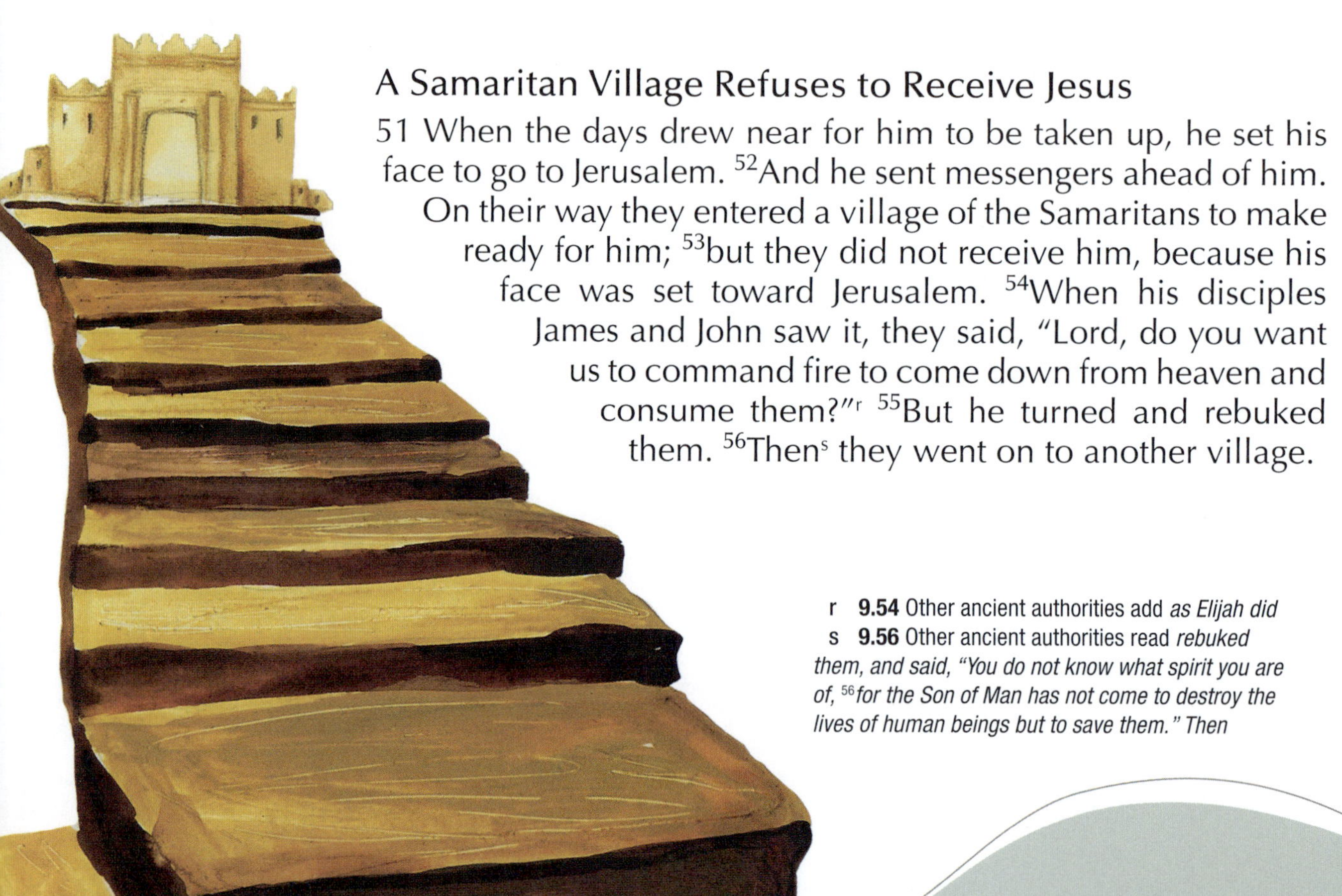

A Samaritan Village Refuses to Receive Jesus

51 When the days drew near for him to be taken up, he set his
face to go to Jerusalem. 52 And he sent messengers ahead of him.
On their way they entered a village of the Samaritans to make
ready for him; 53 but they did not receive him, because his
face was set toward Jerusalem. 54 When his disciples
James and John saw it, they said, "Lord, do you want
us to command fire to come down from heaven and
consume them?"[r] 55 But he turned and rebuked
them. 56 Then[s] they went on to another village.

r **9.54** Other ancient authorities add *as Elijah did*

s **9.56** Other ancient authorities read *rebuked them, and said, "You do not know what spirit you are of, 56 for the Son of Man has not come to destroy the lives of human beings but to save them." Then*

Would-Be Followers of Jesus

57 As they were going along the road, someone said to
him, "I will follow you wherever you go." 58And Jesus
said to him, "Foxes have holes, and birds of the
air have nests; but the Son of Man has nowhere
to lay his head." 59To another he said, "Follow
me." But he said, "Lord, first let me go and
bury my father." 60But Jesus[t] said to him,
"Let the dead bury their own dead; but as
for you, go and proclaim the kingdom of
God." 61Another said, "I will follow you,
Lord; but let me first say farewell to those at
my home." 62Jesus said to him, "No one who
puts a hand to the plow and looks back is fit
for the kingdom of God."

10:1 Why did he send out these seventy disciples?

The task of every disciple is exactly that—to be a faith-filled person who goes out to proclaim Jesus as Savior to everyone, even at the cost of being persecuted.

The Mission of the Seventy

10 After this the Lord appointed seventy[u] others
and sent them on ahead of him in pairs to every town
and place where he himself intended to go. 2He said to
them, "The harvest is plentiful, but the laborers are few; therefore
ask the Lord of the harvest to send out laborers into his harvest. 3Go
on your way. See, I am sending you out like lambs into the midst of

t **9.60** Gk *he*
u **10.1** Other ancient authorities read *seventy-two*

wolves. [4]Carry no purse, no bag, no sandals; and greet no one on the road.
[5]Whatever house you enter, first say, ‘Peace to this house!’ [6]And if anyone
is there who shares in peace, your peace will rest on that person; but if not,
it will return to you. [7]Remain in the same house, eating and drinking whatever they provide, for the laborer deserves to be paid. Do not
move about from house to house. [8]Whenever you enter
a town and its people welcome you, eat what
is set before you; [9]cure the sick who are
there, and say to them, ‘The kingdom
of God has come near to you.’[v] [10]But
whenever you enter a town and they
do not welcome you, go out into its
streets and say, [11]‘Even the dust of
your town that clings to our feet, we
wipe off in protest against you. Yet
know this: the kingdom of God has
come near.’[w] [12]I tell you, on that day
it will be more tolerable for Sodom
than for that town.

Woes to Unrepentant Cities

13 “Woe to you, Chorazin! Woe to you, Bethsaida!
For if the deeds of power done in you had been
done in Tyre and Sidon, they would have repented
long ago, sitting in sackcloth and ashes. [14]But at
the judgment it will be more tolerable for Tyre
and Sidon than for you. [15]And you, Capernaum,

v **10.9** Or *is at hand for you*
w **10.11** Or *is at hand*

will you be exalted to heaven?
No, you will be brought down to Hades.
16 "Whoever listens to you listens to me, and whoever rejects you rejects me, and whoever rejects me rejects the one who sent me."

The Return of the Seventy

17 The seventy[x] returned with joy, saying, "Lord, in
your name even the demons submit to us!" 18He
said to them, "I watched Satan fall from heaven
like a flash of lightning. 19See, I have given you
authority to tread on snakes and scorpions, and
over all the power of the enemy; and nothing
will hurt you. 20Nevertheless, do not rejoice at
this, that the spirits submit to you, but rejoice
that your names are written in heaven."

Jesus Rejoices

21 At that same hour Jesus[y] rejoiced in the Holy
Spirit[z] and said, "I thank[a] you, Father, Lord of
heaven and earth, because you have hidden
these things from the wise and the intelligent
and have revealed them to infants; yes, Father,
for such was your gracious will.[b] 22All things have
been handed over to me by my Father; and no one
knows who the Son is except the Father, or who the
Father is except the Son and anyone to whom the
Son chooses to reveal him."

x **10.17** Other ancient authorities read *seventy-two*
y **10.21** Gk *he*
z **10.21** Other authorities read *in the spirit*
a **10.21** Or *praise*
b **10.21** Or *for so it was well-pleasing in your sight*

23 Then turning to the disciples, Jesus[c] said to them privately, "Blessed are
the eyes that see what you see! 24For I tell you that many prophets and kings
desired to see what you see, but did not see it, and to hear what you hear, but
did not hear it."

The Parable of the Good Samaritan

25 Just then a lawyer stood up to test Jesus.[d] "Teacher,"
he said, "what must I do to inherit eternal life?" 26He
said to him, "What is written in the law? What
do you read there?" 27He answered, "You shall
love the Lord your God with all your heart, and
with all your soul, and with all your strength,
and with all your mind; and your neighbor as
yourself." 28And he said to him, "You have
given the right answer; do this, and you will
live."

29 But wanting to justify himself, he asked
Jesus, "And who is my neighbor?" 30Jesus
replied, "A man was going down from
Jerusalem to Jericho, and fell into the hands of
robbers, who stripped him, beat him, and went
away, leaving him half dead. 31Now by chance a
priest was going down that road; and when he saw
him, he passed by on the other side. 32So likewise a
Levite, when he came to the place and saw him, passed

10:31–32 Why did the priest and the Levite ignore the injured man?

According to the Jewish law of the time, they would have been made impure by touching the wounded man and would not have then been able to carry out their religious responsibility. They put their participation in religious rituals above helping others in need.

c **10.23** Gk *he*
d **10.25** Gk *him*

10:36 But the lawyer did not ask this . . .

The lawyer asked, "who is my neighbor?" He wanted to know who he should help. In his reply, Jesus invites the lawyer to become a neighbor to those who are suffering and in need without waiting for others to make the first move.

10:40 Didn't Martha have a right to complain about her sister?

Even though Martha needed help, she didn't understand that remaining with Jesus was the hospitality he desired most! So, in this sense, she is wrongly complaining because she doesn't see what is more important.

by on the other side. 33 But a Samaritan while traveling
came near him; and when he saw him, he was
moved with pity. 34 He went to him and ban-
daged his wounds, having poured oil and
wine on them. Then he put him on his
own animal, brought him to an inn,
and took care of him. 35 The next day
he took out two denarii,[e] gave them
to the innkeeper, and said, 'Take
care of him; and when I come
back, I will repay you whatever
more you spend.' 36 Which of
these three, do you think, was a
neighbor to the man who fell
into the hands of the robbers?"
37 He said, "The one who
showed him mercy." Jesus said
to him, "Go and do likewise."

Jesus Visits Martha and Mary

38 Now as they went on their way,
he entered a certain village, where a
woman named Martha welcomed him
into her home. 39 She had a sister named
Mary, who sat at the Lord's feet and listened
to what he was saying. 40 But Martha was

e **10.35** The denarius was the usual day's wage for a laborer

distracted by her many tasks; so she came to him and asked, "Lord, do you not care that my sister has left me to do all the work by myself? Tell her then to help me." 41But the Lord answered her, "Martha, Martha, you are worried and distracted by many things; 42there is need of only one thing.[f] Mary has chosen the better part, which will not be taken away from her."

The Lord's Prayer

11 He was praying in a certain place, and after he had finished, one of his disciples said to him, "Lord, teach us to pray, as John taught his disciples." 2He said to them, "When you pray, say:

Father,[g] hallowed be your name.
Your kingdom come.[h]
3 Give us each day our daily bread.[i]
4 And forgive us our sins,
for we ourselves forgive everyone indebted to us.
And do not bring us to the time of trial."[j]

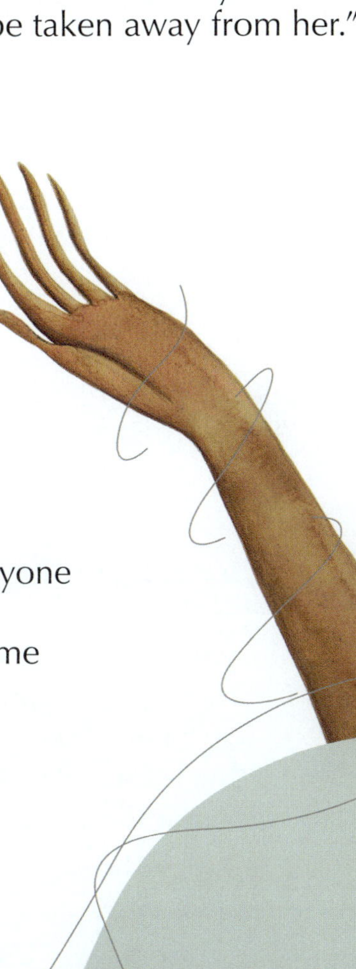

f **10.42** Other ancient authorities read *few things are necessary, or only one*

g **11.2** Other ancient authorities read *Our Father in heaven*

h **11.2** A few ancient authorities read *Your Holy Spirit come upon us and cleanse us.* Other ancient authorities add *Your will be done, on earth as in heaven*

i **11.3** Or *our bread for tomorrow*

j **11.4** Or *us into temptation.* Other ancient authorities add *but rescue us from the evil one* (or *from evil*)

Perseverance in Prayer

5 And he said to them, "Suppose one of you has a friend, and you go to him
at midnight and say to him, 'Friend, lend me three loaves of bread; 6for a
friend of mine has arrived, and I have nothing to set before him.' 7And he
answers from within, 'Do not bother me; the door has already been locked,
and my children are with me in bed; I cannot get up and give you anything.'
8I tell you, even though he will not get up and give him anything because he
is his friend, at least because of his persistence he will get up and give him
whatever he needs.

9 "So I say to you, Ask, and it will be given you; search, and you will find;
knock, and the door will be opened for you. 10For everyone who asks receives,
and everyone who searches finds, and for everyone who knocks, the door
will be opened. 11Is there anyone among you who, if your child asks for[k] a
fish, will give a snake instead of a fish? 12Or if the child asks for an egg, will
give a scorpion? 13If you then, who are evil, know how to give good gifts to
your children, how much more will the heavenly Father
give the Holy Spirit[l] to those who ask him!"

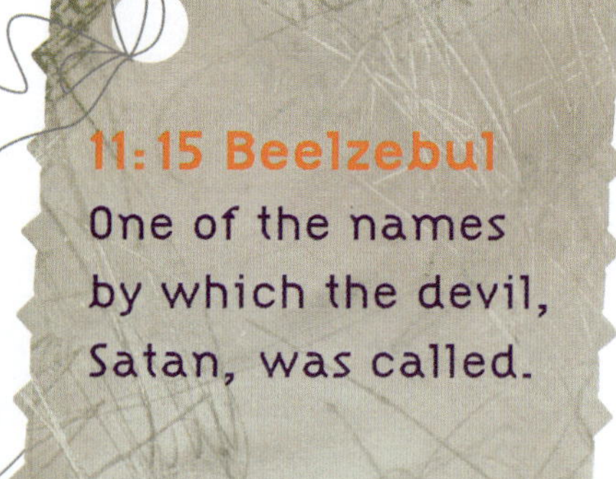

Jesus and Beelzebul

14 Now he was casting out a demon that was mute;
when the demon had gone out, the one who had been
mute spoke, and the crowds were amazed. 15But some
of them said, "He casts out demons by Beelzebul,
the ruler of the demons." 16Others, to test him, kept
demanding from him a sign from heaven. 17But he knew

k **11.11** Other ancient authorities add *bread, will give a stone; or if your child asks for*

l **11.13** Other ancient authorities read *the Father give the Holy Spirit from heaven*

what they were thinking and said to them, "Every kingdom divided against
itself becomes a desert, and house falls on house. [18]If Satan also is
divided against himself, how will his kingdom stand? —for you
say that I cast out the demons by Beelzebul. [19]Now if I cast
out the demons by Beelzebul, by whom do your exorcists[m]
cast them out? Therefore they will be your judges. [20]But if
it is by the finger of God that I cast out the demons, then
the kingdom of God has come to you. [21]When a strong
man, fully armed, guards his castle, his property is
safe. [22]But when one stronger than he attacks him and
overpowers him, he takes away his armor in which
he trusted and divides his plunder. [23]Whoever is
not with me is against me, and whoever does not
gather with me scatters.

The Return of the Unclean Spirit

24 "When the unclean spirit has gone out of a person, it
wanders through waterless regions looking for a resting
place, but not finding any, it says, 'I will return to my
house from which I came.' [25]When it comes, it finds it
swept and put in order. [26]Then it goes and brings seven
other spirits more evil than itself, and they enter and live
there; and the last state of that person is worse than the
first."

m **11.19** Gk *sons*

True Blessedness

27 While he was saying this, a woman in the crowd raised her
voice and said to him, "Blessed is the womb that bore you and
the breasts that nursed you!" 28 But he said, "Blessed rather are
those who hear the word of God and obey it!"

The Sign of Jonah

29 When the crowds were increasing, he
began to say, "This generation is an evil generation; it asks for a sign, but no sign will be
given to it except the sign of Jonah. 30 For just as
Jonah became a sign to the people of Nineveh,
so the Son of Man will be to this generation.
31 The queen of the South will rise at the judgment with the people of this generation and
condemn them, because she came from the
ends of the earth to listen to the wisdom of
Solomon, and see, something greater than
Solomon is here! 32 The people of Nineveh will
rise up at the judgment with this generation
and condemn it, because they repented at the
proclamation of Jonah, and see, something
greater than Jonah is here!

11:31 Queen of the South

She was an African queen who was not afraid to undertake a long and tiring journey to meet King Solomon, who was famous for his wisdom. Read 1 Kings 10 for more about her.

The Light of the Body

33 "No one after lighting a lamp puts it in a cellar,[n] but on the
lampstand so that those who enter may see the light. 34 Your eye
is the lamp of your body. If your eye is healthy, your whole body

n **11.33** Other ancient authorities add *or under the bushel basket*

is full of light; but if it is not healthy, your body is
full of darkness. [35]Therefore consider whether
the light in you is not darkness. [36]If then
your whole body is full of light, with no
part of it in darkness, it will be as full of
light as when a lamp gives you light
with its rays."

Jesus Denounces Pharisees and Lawyers

37 While he was speaking, a Pharisee
invited him to dine with him; so he
went in and took his place at the
table. [38]The Pharisee was amazed to
see that he did not first wash before
dinner. [39]Then the Lord said to him,
"Now you Pharisees clean the outside of
the cup and of the dish, but inside you are
full of greed and wickedness. [40]You fools! Did
not the one who made the outside make the inside
also? [41]So give for alms those things that are within; and
see, everything will be clean for you.

42 "But woe to you Pharisees! For you tithe the mint and
rue and herbs of all kinds, and neglect justice and the
love of God; it is these you ought to have practiced,

11:34 What if they put on glasses?

When people notice that they cannot see well, they get glasses to correct the problem. We must do the same when we notice a defect or failing in our behavior; we must correct the issue so that our entire life will shine brightly.

11:38 Wash before dinner

Jewish ritual cleansing required by the Law and the traditions of the time.

without neglecting the others. [43]Woe to you Pharisees!
For you love to have the seat of honor in the synagogues and to be greeted with respect in the
marketplaces. [44]Woe to you! For you are like
unmarked graves, and people walk over them
without realizing it."
45 One of the lawyers answered him, "Teacher,
when you say these things, you insult us too." [46]And
he said, "Woe also to you lawyers! For you load people
with burdens hard to bear, and you yourselves do not
lift a finger to ease them. [47]Woe to you! For you
build the tombs of the prophets whom your ancestors killed. [48]So you are witnesses and approve of
the deeds of your ancestors; for they killed them,
and you build their tombs. [49]Therefore also the
Wisdom of God said, 'I will send them prophets
and apostles, some of whom they will kill and
persecute,' [50]so that this generation may be
charged with the blood of all the prophets shed
since the foundation of the world, [51]from the
blood of Abel to the blood of Zechariah, who
perished between the altar and the sanctuary. Yes, I
tell you, it will be charged against this generation.
[52]Woe to you lawyers! For you have taken away the key
of knowledge; you did not enter yourselves, and you hindered
those who were entering."

11:51 Who are these people?
They are good men from the history of Israel who were faithful to God and unjustly killed—like Jesus, the just one, who would soon be crucified.

53 When he went outside, the scribes and the Pharisees began to be very
hostile toward him and to cross-examine him about many things, [54]lying in
wait for him, to catch him in something he might say.

A Warning against Hypocrisy

12 Meanwhile, when the crowd gathered by the thousands, so that they
trampled on one another, he began to speak first to his disciples, "Beware
of the yeast of the Pharisees, that is, their hypocrisy. [2]Nothing is covered up
that will not be uncovered, and nothing secret that will not become known.
[3]Therefore whatever you have said in the dark will be heard in the light, and
what you have whispered behind closed doors will be proclaimed from the
housetops.

Exhortation to Fearless Confession

4 "I tell you, my friends, do not fear those who kill the body, and after that can
do nothing more. [5]But I will warn you whom to
fear: fear him who, after he has killed, has authority[o] to cast into hell.[p] Yes, I tell you, fear him! [6]Are
not five sparrows sold for two pennies? Yet not

12:5 Hell
In some translations it is referred to as Gehenna—one of the valleys surrounding Jerusalem, where the city's waste was burned.

o **12.5** Or *power*
p **12.5** Gk *Gehenna*

12:7 Does God really know how many hairs I have on my head?

Not only that, He knows you so well that he also knows what is in your heart. God knows more about you than anyone else and he loves you more than anyone else.

12:10 I have never heard a blasphemy against the Holy Spirit!

This is not about cursing. Rather, it is about refusing the gift that God gives us in the Holy Spirit. When a person blasphemes against or rejects the Holy Spirit, God cannot and will not force the person to accept the gift.

one of them is forgotten in God's sight. 7But even the hairs
of your head are all counted. Do not be afraid; you are
of more value than many sparrows.
8 "And I tell you, everyone who acknowledges
me before others, the Son of Man also will
acknowledge before the angels of God; 9but
whoever denies me before others will be
denied before the angels of God. 10And
everyone who speaks a word against the
Son of Man will be forgiven; but whoever
blasphemes against the Holy Spirit will
not be forgiven. 11When they bring you
before the synagogues, the rulers, and
the authorities, do not worry about
how[q] you are to defend yourselves or
what you are to say; 12for the Holy
Spirit will teach you at that very hour
what you ought to say."

The Parable of the Rich Fool

13 Someone in the crowd said to him,
"Teacher, tell my brother to divide the
family inheritance with me." 14But he said to
him, "Friend, who set me to be a judge or arbi-
trator over you?" 15And he said to them, "Take

q **12.11** Other ancient authorities add *or what*

care! Be on your guard against all kinds of greed;
for one's life does not consist in the abundance
of possessions." [16]Then he told them a parable:
"The land of a rich man produced abundantly.
[17]And he thought to himself, 'What should I do,
for I have no place to store my crops?' [18]Then
he said, 'I will do this: I will pull down my
barns and build larger ones, and there I will
store all my grain and my goods. [19]And I will
say to my soul, Soul, you have ample goods
laid up for many years; relax, eat, drink, be
merry.' [20]But God said to him, 'You fool!
This very night your life is being demanded
of you. And the things you have prepared,
whose will they be?' [21]So it is with those who
store up treasures for themselves but are not rich toward God."

12:15 Greed
An exaggerated desire for money and possessions, that often comes from the idea that riches can solve all problems.

Do Not Worry

22 He said to his disciples, "Therefore I tell you, do not worry about your
life, what you will eat, or about your body, what you will wear. [23]For life is
more than food, and the body more than clothing. [24]Consider the ravens:
they neither sow nor reap, they have neither storehouse nor barn, and yet
God feeds them. Of how much more value are you than the birds! [25]And can
any of you by worrying add a single hour to your span of life?[r] [26]If then you
are not able to do so small a thing as that, why do you worry about the rest?

r **12.25** Or *add a cubit to your stature*

12:33 Moth
An insect that eats plants, destroying them.

27Consider the lilies, how they grow: they neither toil nor
spin;[s] yet I tell you, even Solomon in all his glory was not
clothed like one of these. 28But if God so clothes the grass
of the field, which is alive today and tomorrow is thrown
into the oven, how much more will he clothe you—you
of little faith! 29And do not keep striving for what you are
to eat and what you are to drink, and do not keep worrying. 30For it is the nations of the world that strive after
all these things, and your Father knows that you need
them. 31Instead, strive for his[t] kingdom, and these things
will be given to you as well.

32 "Do not be afraid, little flock, for it is your
Father's good pleasure to give you the kingdom.
33Sell your possessions, and give alms. Make
purses for yourselves that do not wear out,
an unfailing treasure in heaven, where no
thief comes near and no moth destroys.
34For where your treasure is, there your
heart will be also.

Watchful Slaves

35 "Be dressed for action and have your
lamps lit; 36be like those who are waiting
for their master to return from the wedding banquet, so that they may open the
door for him as soon as he comes and
knocks. 37Blessed are those slaves whom

12:37 Where are the masters available to the slaves?
Not among men, but in the kingdom of God inaugurated by Jesus, the Lord has made himself the least and the slave of all.

s **12.27** Other ancient authorities read *Consider the lilies; they neither spin nor weave*
t **12.31** Other ancient authorities read *God's*

the master finds alert when he comes; truly I tell you, he will fasten his belt
and have them sit down to eat, and he will come and serve them. 38If he
comes during the middle of the night, or near dawn, and finds them so,
blessed are those slaves.
39 "But know this: if the owner of the house had known at what hour the
thief was coming, he[u] would not have let his house be
broken into. 40You also must be ready, for the Son
of Man is coming at an unexpected hour."

The Faithful or the Unfaithful Slave

41 Peter said, "Lord, are you telling this parable for us or for everyone?" 42And the Lord
said, "Who then is the faithful and prudent
manager whom his master will put in charge
of his slaves, to give them their allowance
of food at the proper time? 43Blessed is that
slave whom his master will find at work
when he arrives. 44Truly I tell you, he will
put that one in charge of all his possessions.
45But if that slave says to himself, 'My master
is delayed in coming,' and if he begins to
beat the other slaves, men and women, and
to eat and drink and get drunk, 46the master
of that slave will come on a day when he
does not expect him and at an hour that he
does not know, and will cut him in pieces,[v]
and put him with the unfaithful. 47That slave
who knew what his master wanted, but did

u **12.39** Other ancient authorities add *would have watched and*
v **12.46** Or *cut him off*

not prepare himself or do what was wanted, will receive a severe beating.
48But the one who did not know and did what deserved a beating will receive
a light beating. From everyone to whom much has been given, much will be
required; and from the one to whom much has been entrusted, even more
will be demanded.

Jesus the Cause of Division

49 "I came to bring fire to the earth, and how I wish it were
already kindled! 50I have a baptism with which to be baptized, and what stress I am under until it is completed!
51Do you think that I have come to bring peace to the
earth? No, I tell you, but rather division! 52From now
on five in one household will be divided, three
against two and two against three; 53they will be
divided:

father against son
 and son against father,
mother against daughter
 and daughter against mother,
mother-in-law against her daughter-in-law
 and daughter-in-law against mother-in-law."

12:55 Why is Jesus talking about the weather?

He used this example to encourage people to recognize not only the seasons, but also the presence of God among them.

Interpreting the Time

54 He also said to the crowds, "When you see a
cloud rising in the west, you immediately say, 'It
is going to rain'; and so it happens. 55And when
you see the south wind blowing, you say, 'There

will be scorching heat'; and it happens. [56]You hypocrites! You know how to interpret the appearance of earth and sky, but why do you not know how to interpret the present time?

Settling with Your Opponent

57 "And why do you not judge for yourselves what is right? [58]Thus, when you go with your accuser before a magistrate, on the way make an effort to settle the case,[w] or you may be dragged before the judge, and the judge hand you over to the officer, and the officer throw you in prison. [59]I tell you, you will never get out until you have paid the very last penny."

Repent or Perish

13 At that very time there were some present who told him about the Galileans whose blood Pilate had mingled with their sacrifices. [2]He asked them, "Do you think that because these Galileans suffered in this way they were worse sinners than all other Galileans? [3]No, I tell you; but unless you repent, you will all perish as they did. [4]Or those eighteen who were killed when the tower of Siloam fell on them—do you think that they were worse offenders than all the others living in Jerusalem? [5]No, I tell you; but unless you repent, you will all perish just as they did."

The Parable of the Barren Fig Tree

6 Then he told this parable: "A man had a fig tree planted in his vineyard; and he came looking for fruit on it and found none. [7]So he said to the gardener, 'See here! For

w **12.58** Gk *settle with him*

three years I have come looking for fruit on this fig tree, and still
I find none. Cut it down! Why should it be wasting the soil?'
[8]He replied, 'Sir, let it alone for one more year, until I dig
around it and put manure on it. [9]If it bears fruit next
year, well and good; but if not, you can cut it
down.'"

13:13 Why are you the only one who narrates this miracle?

Because I like talking about Jesus as one who straightens peoples' lives and lets them hold their head high, unlike evil that keeps them enslaved and unable to contemplate heaven.

Jesus Heals a Crippled Woman

10 Now he was teaching in one of the
synagogues on the sabbath. [11]And just
then there appeared a woman with a
spirit that had crippled her for eighteen years. She was bent over and
was quite unable to stand up straight.
[12]When Jesus saw her, he called her
over and said, "Woman, you are set
free from your ailment." [13]When he
laid his hands on her, immediately she
stood up straight and began praising
God. [14]But the leader of the synagogue,
indignant because Jesus had cured on the
sabbath, kept saying to the crowd, "There
are six days on which work ought to be done;
come on those days and be cured, and not on the
sabbath day." [15]But the Lord answered him and said,
"You hypocrites! Does not each of you on the sabbath
untie his ox or his donkey from the manger, and lead

it away to give it water? [16]And ought not this woman, a
daughter of Abraham whom Satan bound for eighteen
long years, be set free from this bondage on the sabbath day?" [17]When he said this, all his opponents were
put to shame; and the entire crowd was rejoicing at all
the wonderful things that he was doing.

13:21 Measures
One measure was equivalent to approximately fifteen liters or almost four gallons.

The Parable of the Mustard Seed

18 He said therefore, "What is the kingdom of God like?
And to what should I compare it? [19]It is like a mustard
seed that someone took and sowed in the garden; it grew
and became a tree, and the birds of the air made nests in
its branches."

The Parable of the Yeast

20 And again he said, "To what should I compare
the kingdom of God? [21]It is like yeast that a woman
took and mixed in with[x] three measures of flour
until all of it was leavened."

The Narrow Door

22 Jesus[y] went through one town and village
after another, teaching as he made his way to
Jerusalem. [23]Someone asked him, "Lord, will
only a few be saved?" He said to them, [24]"Strive
to enter through the narrow door; for many, I tell

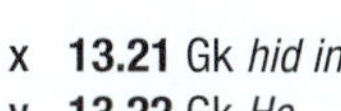

x **13.21** Gk *hid in*
y **13.22** Gk *He*

you, will try to enter and will not be able. [25]When
once the owner of the house has got up and shut
the door, and you begin to stand outside and to
knock at the door, saying, 'Lord, open to us,' then in
reply he will say to you, 'I do not know where you
come from.' [26]Then you will begin to say, 'We ate
and drank with you, and you taught in our streets.'
[27]But he will say, 'I do not know where you come
from; go away from me, all you evildoers!' [28]There
will be weeping and gnashing of teeth when you see
Abraham and Isaac and Jacob and all the prophets
in the kingdom of God, and you yourselves thrown
out. [29]Then people will come from east and west, from
north and south, and will eat in the kingdom of God.
[30]Indeed, some are last who will be first, and some are
first who will be last."

The Lament over Jerusalem

31 At that very hour some Pharisees came and said
to him, "Get away from here, for Herod wants to
kill you." [32]He said to them, "Go and tell that fox
for me,[z] 'Listen, I am casting out demons and
performing cures today and tomorrow, and on
the third day I finish my work. [33]Yet today,
tomorrow, and the next day I must be on my
way, because it is impossible for a prophet to
be killed outside of Jerusalem.' [34]Jerusalem,
Jerusalem, the city that kills the prophets and

z **13.32** Gk lacks *for me*

stones those who are sent to it! How often have I desired to gather your children together as a hen gathers her brood under her wings, and you were not
willing! 35See, your house is left to you. And I tell you, you will not see me
until the time comes when[a] you say, 'Blessed is the one who comes in the
name of the Lord.'"

Jesus Heals the Man with Dropsy

14 On one occasion when Jesus[b] was going to
the house of a leader of the Pharisees to eat a
meal on the sabbath, they were watching him
closely. 2Just then, in front of him, there was
a man who had dropsy. 3And Jesus asked the
lawyers and Pharisees, "Is it lawful to cure
people on the sabbath, or not?" 4But they were
silent. So Jesus[c] took him and healed him, and
sent him away. 5Then he said to them, "If one
of you has a child[d] or an ox that has fallen into
a well, will you not immediately pull it out on
a sabbath day?" 6And they could not reply to
this.

14:2 Dropsy
Swelling due to an accumulation of watery fluid in skin cells or soft tissues.

Humility and Hospitality

7 When he noticed how the guests chose the
places of honor, he told them a parable. 8"When
you are invited by someone to a wedding banquet,
do not sit down at the place of honor, in case someone
more distinguished than you has been invited by your host;

a **13.35** Other ancient authorities lack *the time comes when*
b **14.1** Gk *he*
c **14.4** Gk *he*
d **14.5** Other ancient authorities read *a donkey*

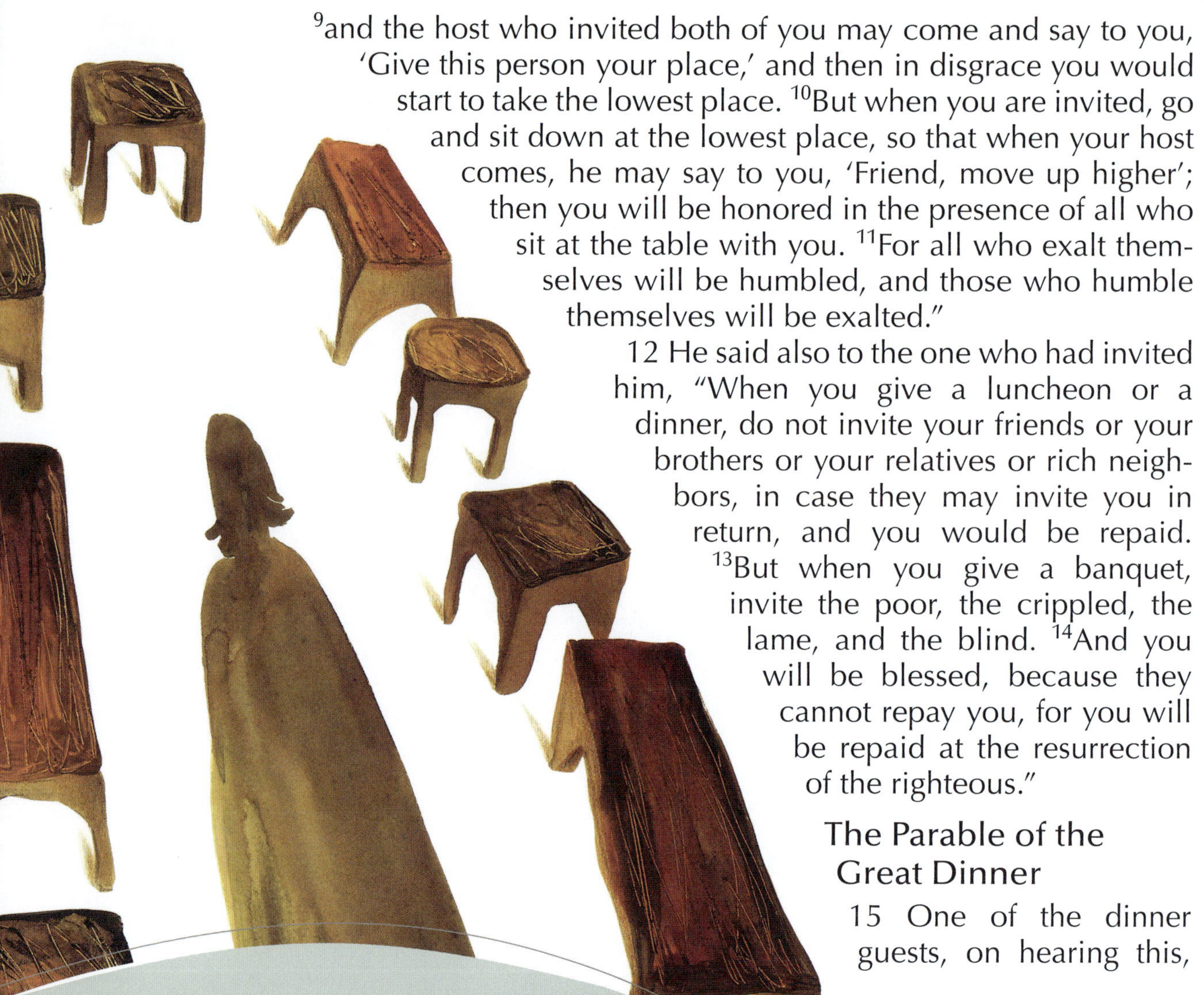

[9]and the host who invited both of you may come and say to you,
'Give this person your place,' and then in disgrace you would
start to take the lowest place. [10]But when you are invited, go
and sit down at the lowest place, so that when your host
comes, he may say to you, 'Friend, move up higher';
then you will be honored in the presence of all who
sit at the table with you. [11]For all who exalt themselves will be humbled, and those who humble
themselves will be exalted."

12 He said also to the one who had invited
him, "When you give a luncheon or a
dinner, do not invite your friends or your
brothers or your relatives or rich neighbors, in case they may invite you in
return, and you would be repaid.
[13]But when you give a banquet,
invite the poor, the crippled, the
lame, and the blind. [14]And you
will be blessed, because they
cannot repay you, for you will
be repaid at the resurrection
of the righteous."

The Parable of the Great Dinner

15 One of the dinner
guests, on hearing this,

said to him, "Blessed is anyone who will eat bread in the kingdom of God!"
16 Then Jesus[e] said to him, "Someone gave a great dinner and invited many.
17 At the time for the dinner he sent his slave to say to those who
had been invited, 'Come; for everything is ready now.' 18 But
they all alike began to make excuses. The first said to
him, 'I have bought a piece of land, and I must go
out and see it; please accept my regrets.' 19 Another
said, 'I have bought five yoke of oxen, and I am
going to try them out; please accept my regrets.'
20 Another said, 'I have just been married, and therefore I cannot come.' 21 So
the slave returned and reported this to
his master. Then the owner of the house
became angry and said to his slave, 'Go
out at once into the streets and lanes of
the town and bring in the poor, the crippled, the blind, and the lame.' 22 And
the slave said, 'Sir, what you ordered
has been done, and there is still room.'
23 Then the master said to the slave,
'Go out into the roads and lanes, and
compel people to come in, so that my
house may be filled. 24 For I tell you,[f]
none of those who were invited will taste
my dinner.'"

14:18–20 Why would anyone refuse such a wonderful invitation?

People often get caught up in all the things that need to be done each day or are simply okay with the way things are and fail to recognize God's invitation as the most important moment in their lives.

14:23 Why was the owner of the house so set on having his hall filled?

God does not need our company, but he wishes to share all he is with as many people as possible. This is the mystery of God's love: that it is so abundant that it calls every single person to him.

e **14.16** Gk *he*
f **14.24** The Greek word for *you* here is plural

The Cost of Discipleship

25 Now large crowds were traveling with him; and he turned and said to
them, 26 "Whoever comes to me and does not hate father and mother, wife and
children, brothers and sisters, yes, and even life itself, cannot be my disciple.
27 Whoever does not carry the cross and follow me cannot be my disciple.
28 For which of you, intending to build a tower, does not first sit down and
estimate the cost, to see whether he has enough to complete it? 29 Otherwise,
when he has laid a foundation and is not able to finish, all who see it will
begin to ridicule him, 30 saying, 'This fellow began to build and was not able
to finish.' 31 Or what king, going out to wage war against another king, will not
sit down first and consider whether he is able with ten thousand to oppose
the one who comes against him with twenty thousand? 32 If he cannot, then,
while the other is still far away, he sends a delegation and asks for the terms of
peace. 33 So therefore, none of you can become my disciple
if you do not give up all your possessions.

About Salt

34 "Salt is good; but if salt has lost its taste,
how can its saltiness be restored?[g] 35 It is fit
neither for the soil nor for the manure pile;
they throw it away. Let anyone
with ears to hear listen!"

g **14.34** Or *how can it be used for seasoning?*

The Parable of the Lost Sheep

15 Now all the tax collectors and sinners were
coming near to listen to him. 2And the Pharisees
and the scribes were grumbling and saying, "This
fellow welcomes sinners and eats with them."
3 So he told them this parable:[4] "Which one
of you, having a hundred sheep and losing
one of them, does not leave the ninety-nine in
the wilderness and go after the one that is lost
until he finds it? 5When he has found it, he
lays it on his shoulders and rejoices. 6And
when he comes home, he calls together his
friends and neighbors, saying to them, 'Rejoice
with me, for I have found my sheep that was lost.'
7Just so, I tell you, there will be more joy in heaven
over one sinner who repents than over ninety-nine
righteous persons who need no repentance.

The Parable of the Lost Coin

8 "Or what woman having ten silver coins,[h] if she loses
one of them, does not light a lamp, sweep the house, and
search carefully until she finds it? 9When she has found
it, she calls together her friends and neighbors, saying,
'Rejoice with me, for I have found the coin that I had lost.'
10Just so, I tell you, there is joy in the presence of the angels
of God over one sinner who repents."

15:4 I would have left the one sheep, after all he still had ninety-nine!
This parable is not meant to make the one more important than the ninety-nine. Rather, it is meant to emphasize just how important each one of us is to God.

15:8 Coins
"Drachmas," the coins of the day, were very small and could easily be lost.

h **15.8** Gk *drachmas*, each worth about a day's wage for a laborer

The Parable of the Prodigal and His Brother

11 Then Jesus[i] said, "There was a man who had two sons. 12The younger
of them said to his father, 'Father, give me the share of the property that
will belong to me.' So he divided his property between them. 13A few days
later the younger son gathered all he had and traveled to a distant country, and there he squandered his property in dissolute
living. 14When he had spent everything, a severe famine took
place throughout that country, and he began to be in need. 15So
he went and hired himself out to one of the citizens of that country,
who sent him to his fields to feed the pigs. 16He would gladly have
filled himself with[j] the pods that the pigs were eating; and
no one gave him anything. 17But when he came to himself he said, 'How many of my father's hired hands
have bread enough and to spare, but here I am
dying of hunger! 18I will get up and go to my
father, and I will say to him, "Father, I have
sinned against heaven and before you; 19I am
no longer worthy to be called your son; treat
me like one of your hired hands."' 20So he
set off and went to his father. But while he
was still far off, his father saw him and was
filled with compassion; he ran and put his
arms around him and kissed him. 21Then the
son said to him, 'Father, I have sinned against
heaven and before you; I am no longer worthy
to be called your son.'[k] 22But the father said to
his slaves, 'Quickly, bring out a robe—the best
one—and put it on him; put a ring on his finger

15:22 Do you think the father heard his son's words about being unworthy to be his son?

Yes, and these words signaled to the father that his son was sorry for what he had done. The father loved his son all along and was thrilled to welcome him back not as a hired hand but as his beloved son.

i **15.11** Gk *he*

j **15.16** Other ancient authorities read *filled his stomach with*

k **15.21** Other ancient authorities add *Treat me like one of your hired servants*

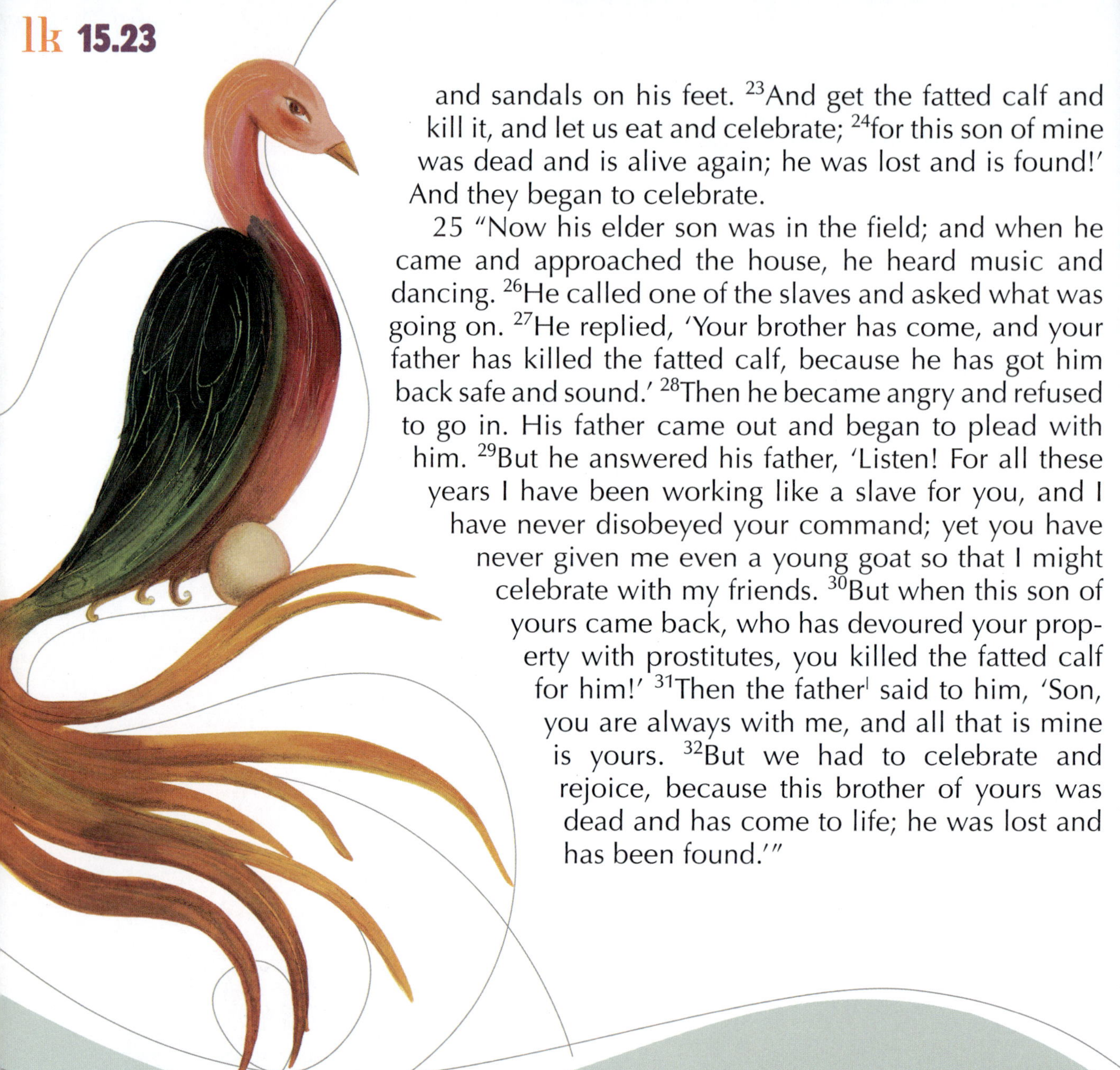

and sandals on his feet. 23 And get the fatted calf and
kill it, and let us eat and celebrate; 24 for this son of mine
was dead and is alive again; he was lost and is found!'
And they began to celebrate.
25 "Now his elder son was in the field; and when he
came and approached the house, he heard music and
dancing. 26 He called one of the slaves and asked what was
going on. 27 He replied, 'Your brother has come, and your
father has killed the fatted calf, because he has got him
back safe and sound.' 28 Then he became angry and refused
to go in. His father came out and began to plead with
him. 29 But he answered his father, 'Listen! For all these
years I have been working like a slave for you, and I
have never disobeyed your command; yet you have
never given me even a young goat so that I might
celebrate with my friends. 30 But when this son of
yours came back, who has devoured your property with prostitutes, you killed the fatted calf
for him!' 31 Then the father[l] said to him, 'Son,
you are always with me, and all that is mine
is yours. 32 But we had to celebrate and
rejoice, because this brother of yours was
dead and has come to life; he was lost and
has been found.'"

l **15.31** Gk *he*

The Parable of the Dishonest Manager

16 Then Jesus[m] said to the disciples, "There was a rich man who had a
manager, and charges were brought to him that this man was squandering
his property. 2So he summoned him and said to him, 'What is this that I
hear about you? Give me an accounting of your management, because
you cannot be my manager any longer.' 3Then the manager said to
himself, 'What will I do, now that my master is taking the position
away from me? I am not strong enough to dig, and I am ashamed
to beg. 4I have decided what to do so that, when I
am dismissed as manager, people may welcome
me into their homes.' 5So, summoning his master's debtors one by one, he asked the first, 'How
much do you owe my master?' 6He answered, 'A
hundred jugs of olive oil.' He said to him, 'Take
your bill, sit down quickly, and make it fifty.'
7Then he asked another, 'And how much
do you owe?' He replied, 'A hundred
containers of wheat.' He said to him,
'Take your bill and make it eighty.'
8And his master commended the
dishonest manager because he had
acted shrewdly; for the children
of this age are more shrewd in
dealing with their own generation

m **16.1** Gk *he*

than are the children of light. 9And I tell you,
make friends for yourselves by means of dishonest wealth[n] so that when it is gone, they
may welcome you into the eternal homes.[o]
10 "Whoever is faithful in a very little is faithful
also in much; and whoever is dishonest in a very
little is dishonest also in much. 11If then you have
not been faithful with the dishonest wealth,[p] who
will entrust to you the true riches? 12And if you have
not been faithful with what belongs to another, who
will give you what is your own? 13No slave can serve
two masters; for a slave will either hate the one and
love the other, or be devoted to the one and despise the
other. You cannot serve God and wealth."[q]

The Law and the Kingdom of God

14 The Pharisees, who were lovers of money, heard all
this, and they ridiculed him. 15So he said to them, "You
are those who justify yourselves in the sight of others;
but God knows your hearts; for what is prized by human
beings is an abomination in the sight of God.
16 "The law and the prophets were in effect until John
came; since then the good news of the kingdom of God
is proclaimed, and everyone tries to enter it by force.[r]
17But it is easier for heaven and earth to pass away, than
for one stroke of a letter in the law to be dropped.
18 "Anyone who divorces his wife and marries
another commits adultery, and whoever marries a
woman divorced from her husband commits adultery.

16:13 Wealth
The Greek term used is "mammon."

n **16.9** Gk *mammon*
o **16.9** Gk *tents*
p **16.11** Gk *mammon*
q **16.13** Gk *mammon*
r **16.16** Or *everyone is strongly urged to enter it*

The Rich Man and Lazarus

19 "There was a rich man who was dressed
in purple and fine linen and who feasted
sumptuously every day. 20And at his gate lay a
poor man named Lazarus, covered with sores,
21who longed to satisfy his hunger with what fell
from the rich man's table; even the dogs would
come and lick his sores. 22The poor man died and
was carried away by the angels to be with Abraham.[s]
The rich man also died and was buried. 23In Hades,
where he was being tormented, he looked up and
saw Abraham far away with Lazarus by his side.[t]
24He called out, 'Father Abraham, have mercy on
me, and send Lazarus to dip the tip of his finger in
water and cool my tongue; for I am in agony in these
flames.' 25But Abraham said, 'Child, remember that
during your lifetime you received your good things,
and Lazarus in like manner evil things; but now he
is comforted here, and you are in agony. 26Besides
all this, between you and us a great chasm has been
fixed, so that those who might want to pass from here
to you cannot do so, and no one can cross from there

16:18 Adultery, divorce

Two words related to marriage. The first indicates the betrayal of one of the two spouses. The second is comparable to current day divorce. It is God's will that we do all we can to not do either of them.

16:19 Purple and linen

Beautiful and luxurious clothes used mainly by the wealthy.

s **16.22** Gk *to Abraham's bosom*
t **16.23** Gk *in his bosom*

to us.' 27 He said, 'Then, father, I beg you to send him to my father's house—
28 for I have five brothers—that he may warn them, so that they will not also
come into this place of torment.' 29 Abraham replied, 'They have Moses and
the prophets; they should listen to them.' 30 He said, 'No, father Abraham; but
if someone goes to them from the dead, they will repent.'
31 He said to him, 'If they do not listen to Moses and
the prophets, neither will they be convinced even
if someone rises from the dead.'"

16:31 Why would people not be convinced by someone raised from the dead?

Sometimes not! Great miracles may surprise people but, after a while, some people forget and go back to their way of life.

Some Sayings of Jesus

17 Jesus[u] said to his disciples,
"Occasions for stumbling are bound to
come, but woe to anyone by whom
they come! 2 It would be better for you
if a millstone were hung around your
neck and you were thrown into the
sea than for you to cause one of these
little ones to stumble. 3 Be on your
guard! If another disciple[v] sins, you
must rebuke the offender, and if there
is repentance, you must forgive. 4 And if
the same person sins against you seven
times a day, and turns back to you seven
times and says, 'I repent,' you must forgive."
5 The apostles said to the Lord, "Increase
our faith!" 6 The Lord replied, "If you had faith
the size of a[w] mustard seed, you could say to
this mulberry tree, 'Be uprooted and planted
in the sea,' and it would obey you.

u **17.1** Gk *He*
v **17.3** Gk *your brother*
w **17.6** Gk *faith as a grain of*

7 "Who among you would say to your slave who has just
come in from plowing or tending sheep in the field,
'Come here at once and take your
place at the table'? [8]Would you not
rather say to him, 'Prepare supper
for me, put on your apron and serve
me while I eat and drink; later you
may eat and drink'? [9]Do you thank the
slave for doing what was commanded?
[10]So you also, when you have done all
that you were ordered to do, say, 'We are
worthless slaves; we have done only what
we ought to have done!'"

17:6 How big is a mustard seed?
It is very small, smaller than the head of a pin. Even just a little faith suffices to do great things!

Jesus Cleanses Ten Lepers

11 On the way to Jerusalem Jesus[x] was going
through the region between Samaria and Galilee.
[12]As he entered a village, ten lepers[y] approached
him. Keeping their distance, [13]they called out,
saying, "Jesus, Master, have mercy on us!" [14]When he
saw them, he said to them, "Go and show yourselves
to the priests." And as they went, they were made clean.
[15]Then one of them, when he saw that he was healed,

x **17.11** Gk *he*
y **17.12** The terms *leper* and *leprosy* can refer to several diseases

turned back, praising God with a loud voice. 16 He prostrated
himself at Jesus'[z] feet and thanked him. And he was a
Samaritan. 17 Then Jesus asked, "Were not ten made
clean? But the other nine, where are they? 18 Was
none of them found to return and give praise to
God except this foreigner?" 19 Then he said to
him, "Get up and go on your way; your faith
has made you well."

The Coming of the Kingdom

20 Once Jesus[a] was asked by the
Pharisees when the kingdom of God
was coming, and he answered, "The
kingdom of God is not coming with
things that can be observed; 21 nor will
they say, 'Look, here it is!' or 'There it
is!' For, in fact, the kingdom of God is
among[b] you."

22 Then he said to the disciples,
"The days are coming when you will
long to see one of the days of the Son of
Man, and you will not see it. 23 They will
say to you, 'Look there!' or 'Look here!' Do
not go, do not set off in pursuit. 24 For as the
lightning flashes and lights up the sky from
one side to the other, so will the Son of Man

17:16 Why did you tell us the nationality of this man?

According to the Jews, a Samaritan could not glorify God. But here, the Samaritan did and thus showed everyone that God's salvation is available to everyone who recognizes and responds to it.

17:21 Among us, where?

When we are Jesus' friends we already experience the kingdom of God. The disciples who lived with him understood this expression very well. You too can see signs of the presence of the kingdom in all those people who live and love like Jesus.

z **17.16** Gk *his*
a **17.20** Gk *he*
b **17.21** Or *within*

be in his day.[c] 25But first he must endure much
suffering and be rejected by this generation.
26Just as it was in the days of Noah, so too
it will be in the days of the Son of Man.
27They were eating and drinking, and
marrying and being given in marriage,
until the day Noah entered the ark, and
the flood came and destroyed all of
them. 28Likewise, just as it was in the
days of Lot: they were eating and
drinking, buying and selling, planting
and building, 29but on the day that Lot left
Sodom, it rained fire and sulfur from heaven
and destroyed all of them 30—it will be like
that on the day that the Son of Man is revealed.
31On that day, anyone on the housetop who has
belongings in the house must not come down to
take them away; and likewise anyone in the field must
not turn back. 32Remember Lot's wife. 33Those who try to
make their life secure will lose it, but those who lose their life will keep it. 34I
tell you, on that night there will be two in one bed; one will be taken and the
other left. 35There will be two women grinding meal together; one will be
taken and the other left."[d] 37Then they asked him, "Where, Lord?" He said to
them, "Where the corpse is, there the vultures will gather."

17:27 Eating, drinking, marrying . . . they did nothing wrong!
That is true. But they were so distracted by the tasks of daily life that they forgot about God.

c **17.24** Other ancient authorities lack *in his day*
d **17.35** Other ancient authorities add verse 36, *"Two will be in the field; one will be taken and the other left."*

18:1 Pray always, without getting tired . . . that is boring!

If for you "prayer" means "saying many words" over and over, then it might be boring . . . but Jesus was thinking of another kind of prayer where one continually expresses their hopes and desires to God . . .

The Parable of the Widow and the Unjust Judge

18 Then Jesus[e] told them a parable about their need
to pray always and not to lose heart. 2He said, "In a
certain city there was a judge who neither feared God
nor had respect for people. 3In that city there was a
widow who kept coming to him and saying, 'Grant
me justice against my opponent.' 4For a while he
refused; but later he said to himself, 'Though I
have no fear of God and no respect for anyone,
5yet because this widow keeps bothering me, I
will grant her justice, so that she may not wear
me out by continually coming.'"[f] 6And the Lord
said, "Listen to what the unjust judge says. 7And
will not God grant justice to his chosen ones who
cry to him day and night? Will he delay long in
helping them? 8I tell you, he will quickly grant justice
to them. And yet, when the Son of Man comes, will he
find faith on earth?"

The Parable of the Pharisee and the Tax Collector

9 He also told this parable to some who trusted in themselves that they were righteous and regarded others with
contempt: 10"Two men went up to the temple to pray, one a
Pharisee and the other a tax collector. 11The Pharisee,
standing by himself, was praying thus, 'God, I thank
you that I am not like other people: thieves, rogues,

e **18.1** Gk *he*
f **18.5** Or *so that she may not finally come and slap me in the face*

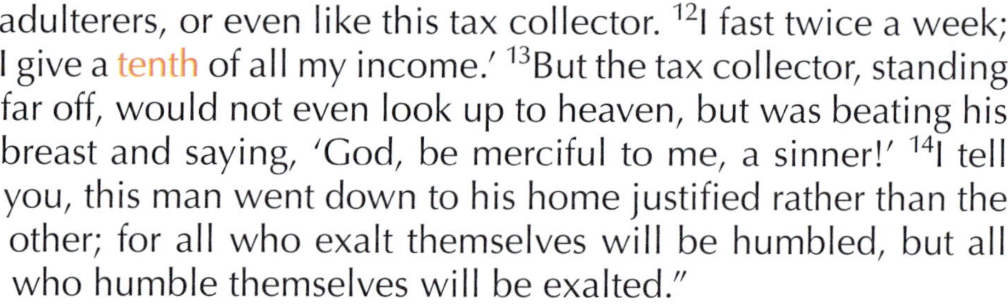

adulterers, or even like this tax collector. 12 I fast twice a week;
I give a tenth of all my income.' 13 But the tax collector, standing
far off, would not even look up to heaven, but was beating his
breast and saying, 'God, be merciful to me, a sinner!' 14 I tell
you, this man went down to his home justified rather than the
other; for all who exalt themselves will be humbled, but all
who humble themselves will be exalted."

18:12 Tenth
Pious Jews gave the Temple a tenth of their earnings. This is sometimes also referred to as tithing.

Jesus Blesses Little Children

15 People were bringing even infants to him that he might
touch them; and when the disciples saw it, they sternly
ordered them not to do it. 16 But Jesus called for them and
said, "Let the little children come to me, and do not stop
them; for it is to such as these that the kingdom of God
belongs. 17 Truly I tell you, whoever does not receive
the kingdom of God as a little child will never enter it."

The Rich Ruler

18 A certain ruler asked him, "Good Teacher, what
must I do to inherit eternal life?" 19 Jesus said to him,
"Why do you call me good? No one is good but God
alone. 20 You know the commandments: 'You shall
not commit adultery; You shall not murder; You shall
not steal; You shall not bear false witness; Honor your
father and mother.'" 21 He replied, "I have kept all these
since my youth." 22 When Jesus heard this, he said to
him, "There is still one thing lacking. Sell all that you
own and distribute the money[g] to the poor, and you will

g **18.22** Gk lacks *the money*

have treasure in heaven; then come, follow me." [23]But
when he heard this, he became sad; for he was very
rich. [24]Jesus looked at him and said, "How hard
it is for those who have wealth to enter the
kingdom of God! [25]Indeed, it is
easier for a camel to go through
the eye of a needle than for
someone who is rich to enter
the kingdom of God."

26 Those who heard it said,
"Then who can be saved?"
[27]He replied, "What is
impossible for mortals is
possible for God."

28 Then Peter said, "Look,
we have left our homes and
followed you." [29]And he
said to them, "Truly I tell
you, there is no one who has
left house or wife or brothers
or parents or children, for the
sake of the kingdom of God,
[30]who will not get back very much
more in this age, and in the age to
come eternal life."

18:21 He seems disappointed in Jesus' answer.

Yes, because he expected to hear of new teachings he could put into practice. Instead Jesus offers above all his friendship and invites all people to leave everything to be with him.

18:28 But how does one who leaves everything for the Lord manage to live?

This is also Peter's objection. Jesus points out that one who gives up everything for Him loses nothing, but gains his friendship which is worth way more than that which one left behind.

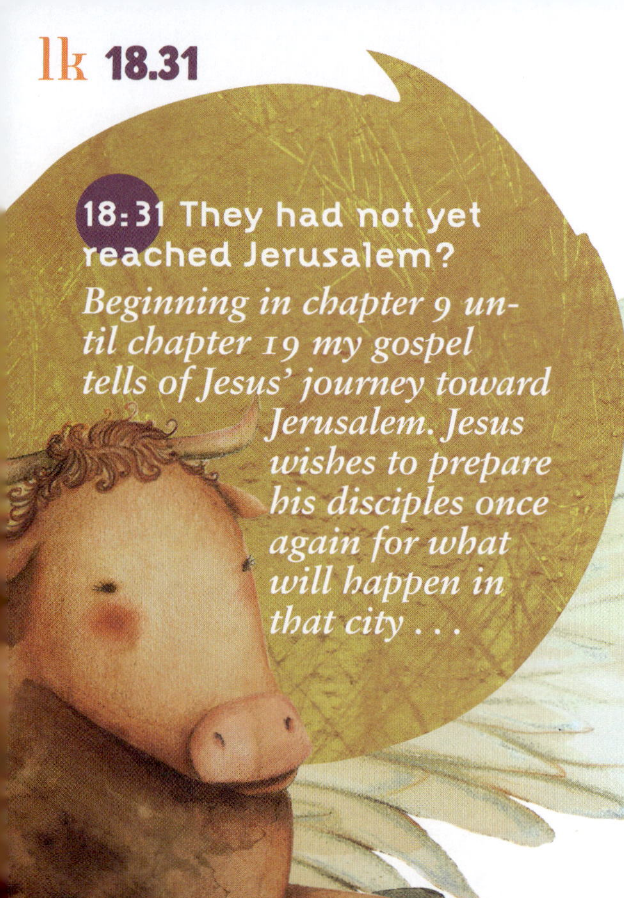

A Third Time Jesus Foretells His Death and Resurrection

31 Then he took the twelve aside and
said to them, "See, we are going up
to Jerusalem, and everything that is
written about the Son of Man by
the prophets will be accomplished.
32 For he will be handed over to the
Gentiles; and he will be mocked
and insulted and spat upon. 33 After
they have flogged him, they will
kill him, and on the third day he
will rise again." 34 But they understood nothing about all these things;
in fact, what he said was hidden from
them, and they did not grasp what was
said.

Jesus Heals a Blind Beggar Near Jericho

35 As he approached Jericho, a blind man
was sitting by the roadside begging. 36 When
he heard a crowd going by, he asked what
was happening. 37 They told him, "Jesus of Nazareth[h] is passing by." 38 Then
he shouted, "Jesus, Son of David, have mercy on me!" 39 Those who were

h **18.37** Gk *the Nazorean*

in front sternly ordered him to be quiet; but he shouted even more loudly,
"Son of David, have mercy on me!" 40Jesus stood still and ordered the man to
be brought to him; and when he came near, he asked him, 41"What do you
want me to do for you?" He said, "Lord, let me see again." 42Jesus said to him,
"Receive your sight; your faith has saved you." 43Immediately he regained his
sight and followed him, glorifying God; and all the people, when they saw it,
praised God.

Jesus and Zacchaeus

19 He entered Jericho and was passing through it.
2A man was there named Zacchaeus; he was a chief
tax collector and was rich. 3He was trying to see
who Jesus was, but on account of the crowd he
could not, because he was short in stature. 4So
he ran ahead and climbed a sycamore tree
to see him, because he was going to pass
that way. 5When Jesus came to the place,
he looked up and said to him, "Zacchaeus,
hurry and come down; for I must stay at
your house today." 6So he hurried down
and was happy to welcome him. 7All who
saw it began to grumble and said, "He has
gone to be the guest of one who is a sinner."
8Zacchaeus stood there and said to the Lord,
"Look, half of my possessions, Lord, I will give

19:2 What does the name Zacchaeus mean?

"God remembered." And that is exactly the meaning of this scene. Jesus does not forget anyone, not even the least—those who are sinners or thieves. On the contrary, he goes to their house for dinner!

to the poor; and if I have defrauded anyone of anything, I will
pay back four times as much." 9Then Jesus said to him, "Today
salvation has come to this house, because he too is a son of
Abraham. 10For the Son of Man came to seek out and to save
the lost."

19:13 Pounds
Called "mina" in Greek, these were ancient gold coins worth three months wages.

The Parable of the Ten Pounds

11 As they were listening to this, he went on to
tell a parable, because he was near Jerusalem, and
because they supposed that the kingdom of God was
to appear immediately. 12So he said, "A nobleman
went to a distant country to get royal power for himself and then return. 13He summoned ten of his slaves,
and gave them ten pounds,[i] and said to them, 'Do business with these until I come back.' 14But the citizens of
his country hated him and sent a delegation after him,
saying, 'We do not want this man to rule over us.' 15When
he returned, having received royal power, he ordered these
slaves, to whom he had given the money, to be summoned so that he might find out what they had gained
by trading. 16The first came forward and said, 'Lord,
your pound has made ten more pounds.' 17He said
to him, 'Well done, good slave! Because you
have been trustworthy in a very small
thing, take charge of ten cities.'

i **19.13** The mina, rendered here by *pound,* was about three months' wages for a laborer

18Then the second came, saying, 'Lord, your pound
has made five pounds.' 19He said to him, 'And you,
rule over five cities.' 20Then the other came, saying,
'Lord, here is your pound. I wrapped it up in a piece
of cloth, 21for I was afraid of you, because you are a
harsh man; you take what you did not deposit, and reap
what you did not sow.' 22He said to him, 'I will judge
you by your own words, you wicked slave! You knew,
did you, that I was a harsh man, taking what I did not
deposit and reaping what I did not sow?
23Why then did you not put my money
into the bank? Then when I returned, I
could have collected it with interest.'
24He said to the bystanders, 'Take the
pound from him and give it to the one
who has ten pounds.' 25(And they said
to him, 'Lord, he has ten pounds!') 26'I
tell you, to all those who have, more
will be given; but from those who
have nothing, even what they have
will be taken away. 27But as for these
enemies of mine who did not want me
to be king over them—bring them here
and slaughter them in my presence.'"

19:27 Was this a real king?

He was a real king. His name was Archelaeus, son of Herod the Great, and he did exactly what my story says. With this parable Jesus emphasized how important it is to utilize the gifts he has given us to plentifully and generously bear fruit.

The Jerusalem Ministry: "Blessed is the king who comes" (Lk19:29–21:38)

Jesus' long journey ends with a triumphant entrance into the city of Jerusalem. Among the jubilant cries of the people, however, one hears a low cry. It is the Lord, who knows the abyss in which the city will plunge, when the last person, the only Son, sent by the owner of the vineyard is killed (20.9–15). Jesus, however, does not give up. Once inside the city, he heads straight to its heart, the Temple. Here he spends every minute of his last days teaching the people and enduring more and more attacks by the chief priests and scribes. Jesus prepares himself for his ultimate sacrifice by giving himself to everyone in the Temple by day and praying to the Father by night on the Mount of Olives (21.37).

Jesus' Triumphal Entry into Jerusalem

28 After he had said this, he went on ahead, going up to Jerusalem.
29 When he had come near Bethphage and Bethany, at the place called
the Mount of Olives, he sent two of the disciples, 30 saying, "Go
into the village ahead of you, and as you enter it you will
find tied there a colt that has never been ridden. Untie
it and bring it here. 31 If anyone asks you, 'Why are
you untying it?' just say this, 'The Lord needs it.'"
32 So those who were sent departed and found it
as he had told them. 33 As they were untying the
colt, its owners asked them, "Why are you
untying the colt?" 34 They said, "The Lord
needs it." 35 Then they brought it to Jesus;
and after throwing their cloaks on the colt,
they set Jesus on it. 36 As he rode along,
people kept spreading their cloaks on the

19:36 Why did they spread their cloaks on the ground

The cloak was a precious article of clothing, especially at night and during the winter. By spreading their cloaks the people were recognizing that an important person was approaching.

road. [37]As he was now approaching the path
down from the Mount of Olives, the whole multitude of the disciples began to praise God joy-
fully with a loud voice for all the deeds of power
that they had seen, [38]saying,

"Blessed is the king
who comes in the name of the Lord!
Peace in heaven,
and glory in the highest heaven!"

[39]Some of the Pharisees in the crowd said to
him, "Teacher, order your disciples to stop." [40]He
answered, "I tell you, if these were silent, the stones
would shout out."

Jesus Weeps over Jerusalem

41 As he came near and saw the city, he wept over
it, [42]saying, "If you, even you, had only recognized
on this day the things that make for peace! But now
they are hidden from your eyes. [43]Indeed, the days
will come upon you, when your enemies will set up
ramparts around you and surround you, and hem you
in on every side. [44]They will crush you to the ground,
you and your children within you, and they will not leave within you one
stone upon another; because you did not recognize the time of your visita-
tion from God."[j]

j **19.44** Gk lacks *from God*

Jesus Cleanses the Temple

45 Then he entered the temple and began to drive out those who
were selling things there; 46 and he said, "It is written,

'My house shall be a house of prayer';
but you have made it a den of robbers."

47 Every day he was teaching in the temple. The
chief priests, the scribes, and the leaders of the
people kept looking for a way to kill him; 48 but
they did not find anything they could do, for all
the people were spellbound by what they heard.

The Authority of Jesus Questioned

20 One day, as he was teaching the people in
the temple and telling the good news, the chief
priests and the scribes came with the elders
2 and said to him, "Tell us, by what authority are
you doing these things? Who is it who gave you
this authority?" 3 He answered them, "I will also
ask you a question, and you tell me: 4 Did the baptism of John come from heaven, or was it of human
origin?" 5 They discussed it with one another, saying,
"If we say, 'From heaven,' he will say, 'Why did you
not believe him?' 6 But if we say, 'Of human origin,' all the
people will stone us; for they are convinced that John was a
prophet." 7 So they answered that they did not know where it came
from. 8 Then Jesus said to them, "Neither will I tell you by what authority I
am doing these things."

20:8 Why does Jesus not answer the question?

Jesus knew that the Pharisees were being deceitful. They did not want to know him better. They only wanted to make trouble for him.

The Parable of the Wicked Tenants

9 He began to tell the people this parable: "A man planted a vineyard, and
leased it to tenants, and went to another country for a long time. [10]When
the season came, he sent a slave to the tenants in order that they might give
him his share of the produce of the vineyard; but the tenants beat him and
sent him away empty-handed. [11]Next he sent another slave; that one also
they beat and insulted and sent away empty-handed. [12]And
he sent still a third; this one also they wounded
and threw out. [13]Then the owner of the vineyard said, 'What shall I do? I will send my
beloved son; perhaps they will respect
him.' [14]But when the tenants saw him,
they discussed it among themselves
and said, 'This is the heir; let us kill him
so that the inheritance may be ours.'
[15]So they threw him out of the vineyard
and killed him. What then will the owner
of the vineyard do to them? [16]He will come
and destroy those tenants and give the vineyard to others." When they heard this, they said,
"Heaven forbid!" [17]But he looked at them and said,
"What then does this text mean:

'The stone that the builders rejected
has become the cornerstone'?[k]

k **20.17** Or *keystone*

18 Everyone who falls on that stone will be broken to
pieces; and it will crush anyone on whom it falls."
19 When the scribes and chief priests realized that he had
told this parable against them, they wanted to lay hands
on him at that very hour, but they feared the people.

The Question about Paying Taxes

20 So they watched him and sent spies who pretended
to be honest, in order to trap him by what he said, so
as to hand him over to the jurisdiction and authority of
the governor. 21 So they asked him, "Teacher, we know
that you are right in what you say and teach, and you
show deference to no one, but teach the way of God
in accordance with truth. 22 Is it lawful for us to pay
taxes to the emperor, or not?" 23 But he perceived their
craftiness and said to them, 24 "Show me a denarius.
Whose head and whose title does it bear?" They said,
"The emperor's." 25 He said to them, "Then give to
the emperor the things that are the emperor's, and
to God the things that are God's." 26 And they were
not able in the presence of the people to trap him by
what he said; and being amazed by his answer, they
became silent.

The Question about the Resurrection

27 Some Sadducees, those who say there is no
resurrection, came to him 28 and asked him a question, "Teacher, Moses wrote for us that if a man's
brother dies, leaving a wife but no children, the man[l]
shall marry the widow and raise up children for his

20:23 Craftiness
Here the word refers to the attitude of those who act with deception or for ulterior motives.

20:27 Sadducees
A group of Israelites at the time of Jesus who were connected to the priests of the Temple in Jerusalem.

l **20.28** Gk *his brother*

20:32 Maybe the woman was just unlucky.

No. The Sadducees made up this particular case (perhaps referring to the story of Tobiah and Sarah in the book of Tobit) to try and argue with Jesus about the resurrection of the dead. Jesus affirms the resurrection and explains a famous passage from the book of Exodus.

brother. 29 Now there were seven brothers; the
first married, and died childless; 30 then the
second 31 and the third married her, and so
in the same way all seven died childless.
32 Finally the woman also died. 33 In the
resurrection, therefore, whose wife will
the woman be? For the seven had married her."

34 Jesus said to them, "Those who
belong to this age marry and are given
in marriage; 35 but those who are considered worthy of a place in that age and
in the resurrection from the dead neither
marry nor are given in marriage. 36 Indeed
they cannot die anymore, because they are
like angels and are children of God, being
children of the resurrection. 37 And the fact that
the dead are raised Moses himself showed, in
the story about the bush, where he speaks of the
Lord as the God of Abraham, the God of Isaac, and
the God of Jacob. 38 Now he is God not of the dead,
but of the living; for to him all of them are alive." 39 Then
some of the scribes answered, "Teacher, you have spoken
well." 40 For they no longer dared to ask him another question.

The Question about David's Son

41 Then he said to them, "How can they say that
the Messiah[m] is David's son? 42For David himself says in the book of Psalms,

'The Lord said to my Lord,
"Sit at my right hand,
43 until I make your enemies
your footstool."'

44David thus calls him Lord; so how can
he be his son?"

20:42–43 What does Jesus mean with this psalm verse?
Jesus wanted to make it clear that he was more than just a descendant of David. He is the Lord, the one and only Son of God.

Jesus Denounces the Scribes

45 In the hearing of all the people he said
to the[n] disciples, 46"Beware of the scribes,
who like to walk around in long robes,
and love to be greeted with respect in the
marketplaces, and to have the best seats in
the synagogues and places of honor at banquets. 47They devour widows' houses and for
the sake of appearance say long prayers.
They will receive the greater condemnation."

m **20.41** Or *the Christ*
n **20.45** Other ancient authorities read *his*

The Widow's Offering

21 He looked up and saw rich people putting their gifts into
the treasury; 2 he also saw a poor widow put in two small
copper coins. 3 He said, "Truly I tell you, this poor
widow has put in more than all of them; 4 for all of
them have contributed out of their abundance,
but she out of her poverty has put in all she had
to live on."

21:2 Are not two little coins worth little?

Very little, but that woman gave all that she had to the Lord. Jesus praises her over those who gave more money because of this.

The Destruction of the Temple Foretold

5 When some were speaking about the
temple, how it was adorned with beautiful
stones and gifts dedicated to God, he said,
6 "As for these things that you see, the days
will come when not one stone will be left
upon another; all will be thrown down."

Signs and Persecutions

7 They asked him, "Teacher, when will this be,
and what will be the sign that this is about to take
place?" 8 And he said, "Beware that you are not led
astray; for many will come in my name and say, 'I am
he!'[o] and, 'The time is near!'[p] Do not go after them.

o **21.8** Gk *I am*
p **21.8** Or *at hand*

9 "When you hear of wars and insurrections, do not be terrified; for these
things must take place first, but the end will not follow immediately." [10]Then
he said to them, "Nation will rise against nation, and kingdom against
kingdom; [11]there will be great earthquakes, and in various places famines and
plagues; and there will be dreadful portents and great signs from heaven.

12 "But before all this occurs, they will arrest you and persecute you;
they will hand you over to synagogues and prisons, and you will
be brought before kings and governors
because of my name. [13]This will give you
an opportunity to testify. [14]So make up your
minds not to prepare your defense in
advance; [15]for I will give you words[q] and a
wisdom that none of your opponents will
be able to withstand or contradict. [16]You
will be betrayed even by parents and
brothers, by relatives and friends; and
they will put some of you to death. [17]You
will be hated by all because of my name.
[18]But not a hair of your head will perish.
[19]By your endurance you will gain your
souls.

21:12 I do not want to be persecuted!

No one wants to suffer, not even Jesus! He reminds us, however, that suffering is a reality and invites us to not be afraid. Instead we should entrust ourselves, like he does, to God the Father.

q **21.15** Gk *a mouth*

The Destruction of Jerusalem Foretold

20 "When you see Jerusalem surrounded by armies, then know
that its desolation has come near.[r] 21 Then those in Judea must
flee to the mountains, and those inside the city must leave it,
and those out in the country must not enter it; 22 for these are
days of vengeance, as a fulfillment of all that is written. 23 Woe
to those who are pregnant and to those who are nursing
infants in those days! For there will be great distress on
the earth and wrath against this people; 24 they will
fall by the edge of the sword and be taken away as
captives among all nations; and Jerusalem will be
trampled on by the Gentiles, until the times of
the Gentiles are fulfilled.

21:20–24 Did these things happen?
Yes, about forty years later. When I heard of Jerusalem's fall, Jesus' words came immediately to mind.

The Coming of the Son of Man

25 "There will be signs in the sun, the moon,
and the stars, and on the earth distress among
nations confused by the roaring of the sea and
the waves. 26 People will faint from fear and fore-
boding of what is coming upon the world, for the
powers of the heavens will be shaken. 27 Then they
will see 'the Son of Man coming in a cloud' with
power and great glory. 28 Now when these things begin
to take place, stand up and raise your heads, because
your redemption is drawing near."

r **21.20** Or *is at hand*

The Lesson of the Fig Tree

29 Then he told them a parable: "Look at the fig tree and all the trees; [30]as
soon as they sprout leaves you can see for yourselves and know that summer
is already near. [31]So also, when you see these things taking place, you know
that the kingdom of God is near. [32]Truly I tell you, this generation will not pass
away until all things have taken place. [33]Heaven and earth will pass away, but
my words will not pass away.

Exhortation to Watch

34 "Be on guard so that your hearts are not weighed down with dissipation
and drunkenness and the worries of this life, and that day
does not catch you unexpectedly, [35]like a trap. For it will
come upon all who live on the face of the whole earth.
[36]Be alert at all times, praying that you may have the
strength to escape all these things that will take
place, and to stand before the Son of Man."

37 Every day he was teaching in the
temple, and at night he would go out and
spend the night on the Mount of Olives, as
it was called. [38]And all the people would
get up early in the morning to listen to him
in the temple.

21:34 Why do these three things weigh down our heart?

When someone wastes their existence by forgetting who they are and what they are doing, and busying themselves about what is not essential, they end up living badly, so that their heart becomes hardened and unable to love.

The Passion: See How a Son Dies (Lk 22:1–23:56)

The pages of Luke dedicated to the Passion narrative are what earned him the traditional title "scribe of Christ's meekness." The evangelist cushions the more violent tones of the story and presents us with a compassionate Jesus, who is capable of forgiving his own killers and has trustingly surrendered himself into the hands of the Father. Compared to the accounts of Mark and Matthew, there are more references in Luke of Jesus' sonship and of God's paternity. This strong bond is typical of Luke's account and of his personal understanding of Christ and of the Christian.

22:1 Why is the feast of Passover called that of Unleavened Bread?

During that week Jews only eat bread made without leaven, thus it is called "unleavened."

The Plot to Kill Jesus

22 Now the festival of Unleavened Bread,
which is called the Passover, was near. 2 The
chief priests and the scribes were looking
for a way to put Jesus[s] to death, for they
were afraid of the people.
3 Then Satan entered into Judas called
Iscariot, who was one of the twelve; 4 he
went away and conferred with the chief
priests and officers of the temple police
about how he might betray him to them.
5 They were greatly pleased and agreed to
give him money. 6 So he consented and
began to look for an opportunity to betray
him to them when no crowd was present.

s **22.2** Gk *him*

The Preparation of the Passover

7 Then came the day of Unleavened Bread, on which the Passover lamb had
to be sacrificed. 8So Jesus[t] sent Peter and John, saying, "Go and prepare the
Passover meal for us that we may eat it." 9They asked him, "Where do you
want us to make preparations for it?" 10"Listen," he said to them, "when you
have entered the city, a man carrying a jar of water
will meet you; follow him into the house he
enters 11and say to the owner of the house,
'The teacher asks you, "Where is the guest
room, where I may eat the Passover with
my disciples?"' 12He will show you a large
room upstairs, already furnished. Make
preparations for us there." 13So they went
and found everything as he had told them;
and they prepared the Passover meal.

The Institution of the Lord's Supper

14 When the hour came, he took his place
at the table, and the apostles with him.
15He said to them, "I have eagerly desired
to eat this Passover with you before I suffer;
16for I tell you, I will not eat it[u] until it is fulfilled in the kingdom of God." 17Then he took
a cup, and after giving thanks he said, "Take
this and divide it among yourselves; 18for I tell
you that from now on I will not drink of the fruit of

22:15 Did Jesus want to die?
Absolutely not! Jesus wanted, however, to love his friends and all people with his whole heart, even at the cost of his life. Above all, Jesus wanted to do the will of God the Father.

t **22.8** Gk *he*
u **22.16** Other ancient authorities read *never eat it again*

the vine until the kingdom of God comes." 19 Then he took a
loaf of bread, and when he had given thanks, he broke it
and gave it to them, saying, "This is my body, which
is given for you. Do this in remembrance of me."
20 And he did the same with the cup after supper,
saying, "This cup that is poured out for you is the
new covenant in my blood.[v] 21 But see, the one
who betrays me is with me, and his hand is on
the table. 22 For the Son of Man is going as it
has been determined, but woe to that one by
whom he is betrayed!" 23 Then they began to
ask one another which one of them it could
be who would do this.

22:19–20 These words are also said during Mass.

Exactly. The priest repeats them during the moment of "consecration," when we remember the passion, death, and resurrection of Jesus under the appearances of bread and wine.

The Dispute about Greatness

24 A dispute also arose among them as to
which one of them was to be regarded as
the greatest. 25 But he said to them, "The kings
of the Gentiles lord it over them; and those in
authority over them are called benefactors. 26 But
not so with you; rather the greatest among you
must become like the youngest, and the leader like
one who serves. 27 For who is greater, the one who is at
the table or the one who serves? Is it not the one at the table?
But I am among you as one who serves.
28 "You are those who have stood by me in my trials; 29 and I confer on

v **22.20** Other ancient authorities lack, in whole or in part, verses 19b–20 (*which is given . . . in my blood*)

you, just as my Father has conferred on me, a kingdom, 30 so
that you may eat and drink at my table in my kingdom,
and you will sit on thrones judging the twelve tribes
of Israel.

Jesus Predicts Peter's Denial

31 "Simon, Simon, listen! Satan has
demanded[w] to sift all of you like wheat,
32 but I have prayed for you that your
own faith may not fail; and you,
when once you have turned back,
strengthen your brothers." 33 And
he said to him, "Lord, I am ready
to go with you to prison and to
death!" 34 Jesus[x] said, "I tell you,
Peter, the cock will not crow this
day, until you have denied three
times that you know me."

Purse, Bag, and Sword

35 He said to them, "When I sent
you out without a purse, bag, or
sandals, did you lack anything?"
They said, "No, not a thing." 36 He
said to them, "But now, the one who
has a purse must take it, and likewise a
bag. And the one who has no sword must

22:32 What does "strengthen your brothers" mean?

Jesus gave Peter the task of supporting the other disciples, to help them remain faithful to Jesus and his teaching.

22:36, 38 First he tells them to buy a sword, then he refuses two?

Jesus speaks of the sword to make his friends understand that it is a decisive moment. He does not intend to react violently. That is why he rejects the actual swords that are offered.

w **22.31** Or *has obtained permission*
x **22.34** Gk *He*

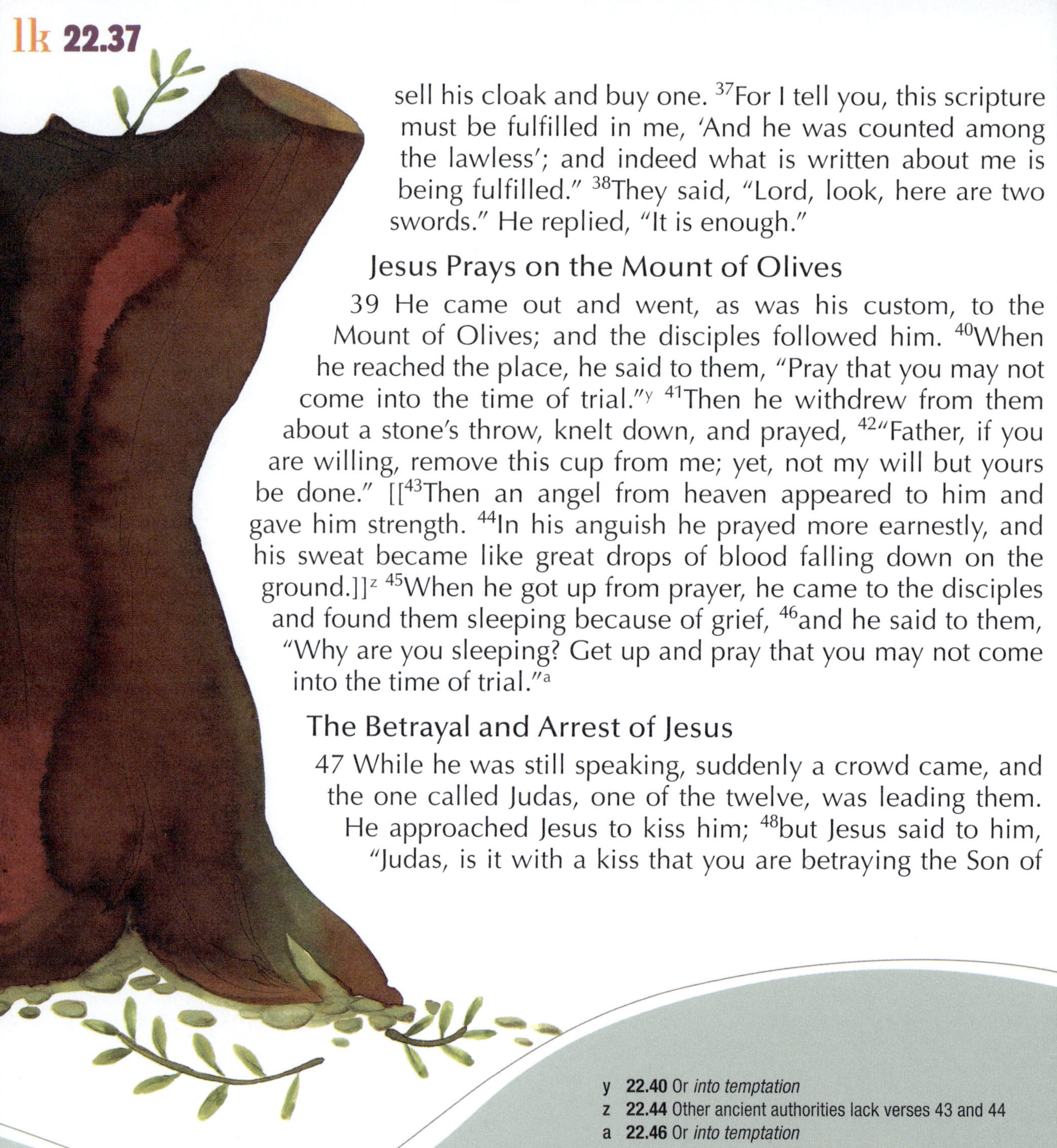

sell his cloak and buy one. [37]For I tell you, this scripture
must be fulfilled in me, 'And he was counted among
the lawless'; and indeed what is written about me is
being fulfilled." [38]They said, "Lord, look, here are two
swords." He replied, "It is enough."

Jesus Prays on the Mount of Olives

39 He came out and went, as was his custom, to the
Mount of Olives; and the disciples followed him. [40]When
he reached the place, he said to them, "Pray that you may not
come into the time of trial."[y] [41]Then he withdrew from them
about a stone's throw, knelt down, and prayed, [42]"Father, if you
are willing, remove this cup from me; yet, not my will but yours
be done." [[[43]Then an angel from heaven appeared to him and
gave him strength. [44]In his anguish he prayed more earnestly, and
his sweat became like great drops of blood falling down on the
ground.]][z] [45]When he got up from prayer, he came to the disciples
and found them sleeping because of grief, [46]and he said to them,
"Why are you sleeping? Get up and pray that you may not come
into the time of trial."[a]

The Betrayal and Arrest of Jesus

47 While he was still speaking, suddenly a crowd came, and
the one called Judas, one of the twelve, was leading them.
He approached Jesus to kiss him; [48]but Jesus said to him,
"Judas, is it with a kiss that you are betraying the Son of

y **22.40** Or *into temptation*
z **22.44** Other ancient authorities lack verses 43 and 44
a **22.46** Or *into temptation*

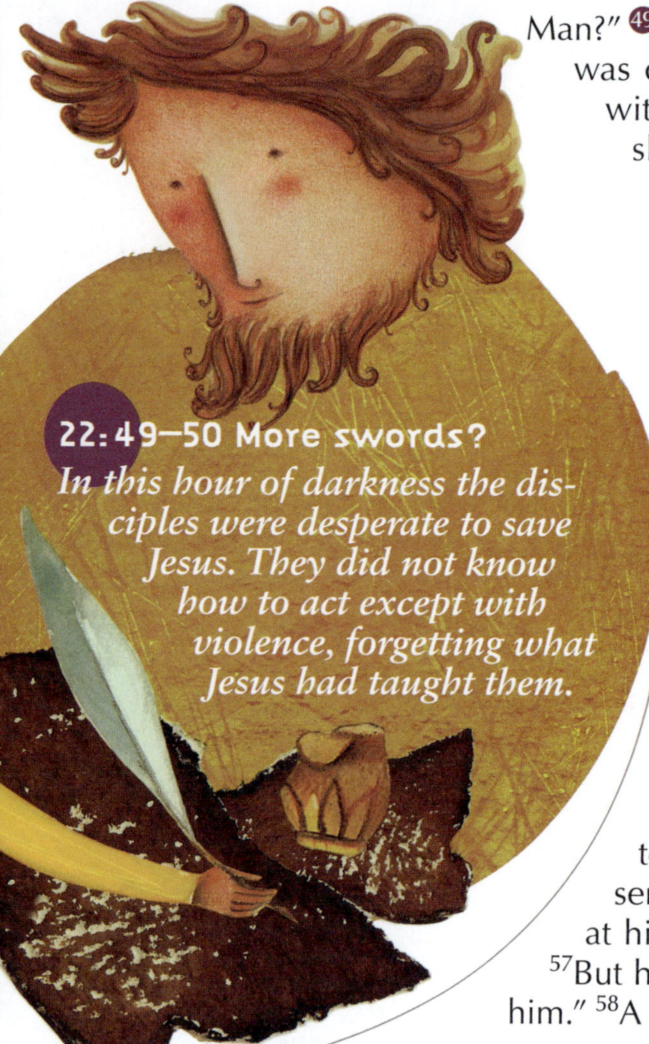

22:49–50 More swords?
In this hour of darkness the disciples were desperate to save Jesus. They did not know how to act except with violence, forgetting what Jesus had taught them.

Man?" 49When those who were around him saw what
was coming, they asked, "Lord, should we strike
with the sword?" 50Then one of them struck the
slave of the high priest and cut off his right
ear. 51But Jesus said, "No more of this!" And
he touched his ear and healed him. 52Then
Jesus said to the chief priests, the officers of
the temple police, and the elders who had
come for him, "Have you come out with
swords and clubs as if I were a bandit?
53When I was with you day after day in
the temple, you did not lay hands on
me. But this is your hour, and the power
of darkness!"

Peter Denies Jesus

54 Then they seized him and led him
away, bringing him into the high priest's
house. But Peter was following at a distance.
55When they had kindled a fire in
the middle of the courtyard and sat down
together, Peter sat among them. 56Then a
servant-girl, seeing him in the firelight, stared
at him and said, "This man also was with him."
57But he denied it, saying, "Woman, I do not know
him." 58A little later someone else, on seeing him, said,

"You also are one of them." But Peter said, "Man, I am not!" 59Then about an
hour later still another kept insisting, "Surely this man also was with him; for
he is a Galilean." 60But Peter said, "Man, I do not know what you are talking
about!" At that moment, while he was still speaking, the cock crowed. 61The
Lord turned and looked at Peter. Then Peter remembered the word of the
Lord, how he had said to him, "Before the cock crows today, you will deny
me three times." 62And he went out and wept bitterly.

The Mocking and Beating of Jesus

63 Now the men who were holding Jesus began to mock him and beat him;
64they also blindfolded him and kept asking him, "Prophesy! Who is it that
struck you?" 65They kept heaping many other insults on him.

Jesus before the Council

66 When day came, the assembly of the elders of
the people, both chief priests and scribes, gathered
together, and they brought him to their council.
67They said, "If you are the Messiah,[b] tell us." He
replied, "If I tell you, you will not believe; 68and if I
question you, you will not answer. 69But from now
on the Son of Man will be seated at the right hand
of the power of God." 70All of them asked, "Are you,
then, the Son of God?" He said to them, "You say that
I am." 71Then they said, "What further testimony do
we need? We have heard it ourselves from his own
lips!"

22:66 Council
They were also known as the Sanhedrin. At the time of Jesus, it was the highest court of the Jews and the high priest presided over it.

b **22.67** Or *the Christ*

23:1 Pilate
He was the Roman governor, the emperor's representative in Jerusalem. He was the only one who could order a death sentence.

23:2 It is a lie! Earlier Jesus said to give to the emperor the things that are the emperor's.

I see you remember what Jesus said in chapter 20. The priests, however, looked for an accusation that would interest Pilate, who was the emperor's representative.

Jesus before Pilate

23 Then the assembly rose as a body and
brought Jesus[c] before Pilate. 2 They began to accuse
him, saying, "We found this man perverting our
nation, forbidding us to pay taxes to the emperor,
and saying that he himself is the Messiah, a king."[d]
3 Then Pilate asked him, "Are you the king of the
Jews?" He answered, "You say so." 4 Then Pilate
said to the chief priests and the crowds, "I find
no basis for an accusation against this man." 5 But
they were insistent and said, "He stirs up the
people by teaching throughout all Judea, from
Galilee where he began even to this place."

Jesus before Herod

6 When Pilate heard this, he asked whether
the man was a Galilean. 7 And when he
learned that he was under Herod's jurisdiction, he sent him off to Herod, who was
himself in Jerusalem at that time. 8 When
Herod saw Jesus, he was very glad, for
he had been wanting to see him for a
long time, because he had heard about
him and was hoping to see him perform
some sign. 9 He questioned him at some
length, but Jesus[e] gave him no answer.
10 The chief priests and the scribes stood

c **23.1** Gk *him*
d **23.2** Or *is an anointed king*
e **23.9** Gk *he*

by, vehemently accusing him. 11 Even Herod with his soldiers treated him
with contempt and mocked him; then he put an elegant robe on him, and
sent him back to Pilate. 12 That same day Herod and Pilate
became friends with each other; before this they had
been enemies.

Jesus Sentenced to Death

13 Pilate then called together the chief
priests, the leaders, and the people, 14 and
said to them, "You brought me this man
as one who was perverting the people;
and here I have examined him in your
presence and have not found this man
guilty of any of your charges against
him. 15 Neither has Herod, for he sent
him back to us. Indeed, he has done
nothing to deserve death. 16 I will therefore have him flogged and release him."[f]
18 Then they all shouted out together,
"Away with this fellow! Release Barabbas
for us!" 19 (This was a man who had been put
in prison for an insurrection that had taken place
in the city, and for murder.) 20 Pilate, wanting to
release Jesus, addressed them again; 21 but they kept
shouting, "Crucify, crucify him!" 22 A third time he said to
them, "Why, what evil has he done? I have found in him no ground for the
sentence of death; I will therefore have him flogged and then release him."

23:18 They preferred to save a murderer rather than Jesus?
Sad but true. The giver of life dies and the one who ends life is saved.

f **23.16** Here, or after verse 19, other ancient authorities add verse 17, *Now he was obliged to release someone for them at the festival*

[23]But they kept urgently demanding with loud shouts that he should be crucified; and their voices prevailed. [24]So Pilate gave his verdict that their demand
should be granted. [25]He released the man they asked for, the one who had
been put in prison for insurrection and murder, and he handed Jesus over as
they wished.

The Crucifixion of Jesus

26 As they led him away, they seized a
man, Simon of Cyrene, who was coming
from the country, and they laid the
cross on him, and made him carry it
behind Jesus. [27]A great number of the
people followed him, and among them
were women who were beating their
breasts and wailing for him. [28]But Jesus
turned to them and said, "Daughters
of Jerusalem, do not weep for me, but
weep for yourselves and for your children. [29]For the days are surely coming
when they will say, 'Blessed are the
barren, and the wombs that never bore,
and the breasts that never nursed.' [30]Then
they will begin to say to the mountains, 'Fall
on us'; and to the hills, 'Cover us.' [31]For if
they do this when the wood is green, what
will happen when it is dry?"

23:28 Why weep for your children?

Because humanity was about to do away with Jesus, the only hope and salvation for every person, as well as for the children of the women present there.

32 Two others also, who were criminals, were led
away to be put to death with him. 33When they
came to the place that is called The Skull, they
crucified Jesus[g] there with the criminals,
one on his right and one on his left.
[[34Then Jesus said, "Father, forgive
them; for they do not know what
they are doing."]][h] And they cast
lots to divide his clothing. 35And
the people stood by, watching;
but the leaders scoffed at him,
saying, "He saved others; let
him save himself if he is the
Messiah[i] of God, his chosen
one!" 36The soldiers also
mocked him, coming up and
offering him sour wine, 37and
saying, "If you are the King of
the Jews, save yourself!"
38There was also an inscription
over him,[j] "This is the King of
the Jews."

g **23.33** Gk *him*

h **23.34** Other ancient authorities lack the sentence *Then Jesus . . . what they are doing*

i **23.35** Or *the Christ*

j **23.38** Other ancient authorities add *written in Greek and Latin and Hebrew* (that is, *Aramaic*)

39 One of the criminals who were hanged there kept deriding[k] him and
saying, "Are you not the Messiah?[l] Save yourself and us!" 40But the other
rebuked him, saying, "Do you not fear God, since you are under the same
sentence of condemnation? 41And we indeed have been condemned justly,
for we are getting what we deserve for our deeds, but this
man has done nothing wrong." 42Then he said, "Jesus,
remember me when you come into[m] your kingdom."
43He replied, "Truly I tell you, today you will be
with me in Paradise."

23:42 Was the first person to enter heaven with Jesus a thief?

I do not know if he was absolutely the first one, but he certainly was among the first. He understood that the only thing that matters in life is to be remembered and loved by Jesus.

The Death of Jesus

44 It was now about noon, and darkness
came over the whole land[n] until three
in the afternoon, 45while the sun's light
failed;[o] and the curtain of the temple was
torn in two. 46Then Jesus, crying with a
loud voice, said, "Father, into your hands
I commend my spirit." Having said this,
he breathed his last. 47When the centurion
saw what had taken place, he praised God
and said, "Certainly this man was innocent."[p]
48And when all the crowds who had gathered
there for this spectacle saw what had taken place,
they returned home, beating their breasts. 49But all
his acquaintances, including the women who had
followed him from Galilee, stood at a distance, watching
these things.

k **23.39** Or *blaspheming*
l **23.39** Or *the Christ*
m **23.42** Other ancient authorities read *in*
n **23.44** Or *earth*
o **23.45** Or *the sun was eclipsed.* Other ancient authorities read *the sun was darkened*
p **23.47** Or *righteous*

23:56 What were the spices and ointments for?
In those days, anointing the body with perfumed oils and spices was the traditional way to prepare a body for burial.

The Burial of Jesus

50 Now there was a good and righteous man named Joseph, who,
though a member of the council,
51 had not agreed to their plan
and action. He came from the
Jewish town of Arimathea, and he
was waiting expectantly for the
kingdom of God. 52 This man went
to Pilate and asked for the body
of Jesus. 53 Then he took it down,
wrapped it in a linen cloth, and
laid it in a rock-hewn tomb where
no one had ever been laid. 54 It was
the day of Preparation, and the sabbath was beginning.[q] 55 The women
who had come with him from Galilee
followed, and they saw the tomb and
how his body was laid. 56 Then they
returned, and prepared spices and ointments.

On the sabbath they rested according to
the commandment.

q **23.54** Gk *was dawning*

The Passover: "Witnesses of the Risen One" (Lk 24:1–53)

Luke's touch is also visible in the resurrection account. The message of the event that happened on the road to Emmaus is very clear. Two disciples were traveling, but in the wrong direction. Disappointment drives them away from Jerusalem. For the disciples Jerusalem is the place where their dreams ended but in actuality it is the place of the final victory of the Son of Man. Jesus, however, makes himself present even when we are on the roads of failure, sadness, and disappointment. The disciples' path is now marked by the activity of the Lord who warms the heart through the Scriptures and is present in the breaking of the bread.

Then, in a perfect cycle, Luke brings the curtain down on Jerusalem's Temple, with the disciples praising God. The Temple marked the beginning of his story, was the center of attraction on every page, and is its conclusion. Though it is not really a conclusion—it does nothing other than give a prelude to the Apostles' future deeds as told by the evangelist in his second book, Acts of the Apostles.

The Resurrection of Jesus

24 But on the first day of the week, at early dawn,
they came to the tomb, taking the spices that they had
prepared. 2They found the stone rolled away from the
tomb, 3but when they went in, they did not find the
body.[r] 4While they were perplexed about this, suddenly two men in dazzling clothes stood beside them.
5The women[s] were terrified and bowed their faces to
the ground, but the men[t] said to them, "Why do you
look for the living among the dead? He is not here,
but has risen.[u] 6Remember how he told you, while
he was still in Galilee, 7that the Son of Man must
be handed over to sinners, and be crucified, and on
the third day rise again." 8Then they remembered his

r **24.3** Other ancient authorities add *of the Lord Jesus*

s **24.5** Gk *They*

t **24.5** Gk *but they*

u **24.5** Other ancient authorities lack *He is not here, but has risen*

words, [9]and returning from the tomb, they told all this
to the eleven and to all the rest. [10]Now it was Mary
Magdalene, Joanna, Mary the mother of James,
and the other women with them who told this
to the apostles. [11]But these words seemed to
them an idle tale, and they did not believe
them. [12]But Peter got up and ran to the
tomb; stooping and looking in, he saw the
linen cloths by themselves; then he went
home, amazed at what had happened.[v]

24:11 Why did they not they believe the women?

They brought news of what, at the time, was an absolutely unbelievable fact: the resurrection of a dead person. Another reason is tied to the fact that in Jesus' time women were considered as unreliable witnesses.

The Walk to Emmaus

13 Now on that same day two of them
were going to a village called Emmaus,
about seven miles[w] from Jerusalem,
[14]and talking with each other about all
these things that had happened. [15]While
they were talking and discussing, Jesus himself came near and went with them, [16]but their
eyes were kept from recognizing him. [17]And he
said to them, "What are you discussing with each
other while you walk along?" They stood still, looking
sad.[x] [18]Then one of them, whose name was Cleopas,
answered him, "Are you the only stranger in Jerusalem who
does not know the things that have taken place there in these

v **24.12** Other ancient authorities lack verse 12
w **24.13** Gk *sixty stadia;* other ancient authorities read *a hundred sixty stadia*
x **24.17** Other ancient authorities read *walk along, looking sad?"*

days?" 19 He asked them, "What things?" They
replied, "The things about Jesus of Nazareth,[y]
who was a prophet mighty in deed and word
before God and all the people, 20 and how
our chief priests and leaders handed him
over to be condemned to death and crucified him. 21 But we had hoped that he was
the one to redeem Israel.[z] Yes, and besides
all this, it is now the third day since these
things took place. 22 Moreover, some
women of our group astounded us. They
were at the tomb early this morning, 23 and
when they did not find his body there,
they came back and told us that they had
indeed seen a vision of angels who said
that he was alive. 24 Some of those who
were with us went to the tomb and found
it just as the women had said; but they
did not see him." 25 Then he said to them,
"Oh, how foolish you are, and how slow
of heart to believe all that the prophets
have declared! 26 Was it not necessary that
the Messiah[a] should suffer these things and
then enter into his glory?" 27 Then beginning
with Moses and all the prophets, he interpreted to them the things about himself in all
the scriptures.

y **24.19** Other ancient authorities read *Jesus the Nazorean*
z **24.21** Or *to set Israel free*
a **24.26** Or *the Christ*

28 As they came near the village to which they were going, he walked
ahead as if he were going on. 29But they urged him strongly, saying, "Stay
with us, because it is almost evening and the day is now nearly over." So he
went in to stay with them. 30When he was at the table with them, he took
bread, blessed and broke it, and gave it to them. 31Then their eyes were
opened, and they recognized him; and he vanished from
their sight. 32They said to each other, "Were not our
hearts burning within us[b] while he was talking to
us on the road, while he was opening the scriptures to us?" 33That same hour they got up and
returned to Jerusalem; and they found the
eleven and their companions gathered
together. 34They were saying, "The Lord
has risen indeed, and he has appeared to
Simon!" 35Then they told what had happened on the road, and how he had been
made known to them in the breaking of
the bread.

24:36 What did the disciples feel when they saw that Jesus was truly alive?

A mixture of many emotions: amazement, fright, agitation, doubts, and then great joy. They were living the most beautiful experience that can happen to a person.

Jesus Appears to His Disciples

36 While they were talking about this, Jesus
himself stood among them and said to
them, "Peace be with you."[c] 37They were
startled and terrified, and thought that
they were seeing a ghost. 38He said to
them, "Why are you frightened, and why
do doubts arise in your hearts? 39Look
at my hands and my feet; see that it is
I myself. Touch me and see; for a ghost

b **24.32** Other ancient authorities lack *within us*

c **24.36** Other ancient authorities lack *and said to them, "Peace be with you."*

does not have flesh and bones as you see that I have." 40And when he had
said this, he showed them his hands and his feet.[d] 41While in their joy they
were disbelieving and still wondering, he said to them, "Have you anything
here to eat?" 42They gave him a piece of broiled fish, 43and he took it and ate
in their presence.

44 Then he said to them, "These are my words that I spoke to you
while I was still with you—that everything written about me in
the law of Moses, the prophets, and the psalms must be
fulfilled." 45Then he opened their minds to understand
the scriptures, 46and he said to them, "Thus it is
written, that the Messiah[e] is to suffer and to rise
from the dead on the third day, 47and that repentance
and forgiveness of sins is to be proclaimed
in his name to all nations, beginning from
Jerusalem. 48You are witnesses[f] of these things.
49And see, I am sending upon you what my
Father promised; so stay here in the city until
you have been clothed with power from on
high."

The Ascension of Jesus

50 Then he led them out as far as Bethany, and,
lifting up his hands, he blessed them. 51While he
was blessing them, he withdrew from them and was
carried up into heaven.[g] 52And they worshiped him,
and[h] returned to Jerusalem with great joy; 53and they
were continually in the temple blessing
God.[i]

d **24.40** Other ancient authorities lack verse 40
e **24.46** Or *the Christ*
f **24.48** Or *nations. Beginning from Jerusalem* [48]*you are witnesses*
g **24.51** Other ancient authorities lack *and was carried up into heaven*
h **24.52** Other ancient authorities lack *worshiped him, and*
i **24.53** Other ancient authorities add *Amen*

THE GOSPEL ACCORDING TO John

AUTHOR: THE "BELOVED DISCIPLE," TRADITIONALLY IDENTIFIED AS JOHN, SON OF ZEBEDEE

AUDIENCE: SECOND GENERATION CHRISTIANS

TIME AND PLACE: 75–90 AD, WRITTEN PERHAPS IN EPHESUS

THEMES: JESUS IS THE WORD MADE FLESH;
JESUS, REVELATION OF THE FATHER;
THE HOLY SPIRIT, GUIDE TOWARD FAITH AND GIVER OF LIFE;
THE CHURCH, THE COMMUNITY OF BELIEVERS

Look with New Eyes . . .

I was young when I met the Lord, and I was one of the first persons who decided to follow him. I was fascinated by Jesus' ability to see beyond a person's appearance and to go into their heart. As you might imagine, I was drawn to Jesus and then a very strong bond of friendship was immediately born between him and me. The other disciples started poking fun at me, calling me Jesus' "favorite." Then, they started coming to me every time they had to ask him something important. I learned a lot from Jesus: his words, his gestures, his presence taught me to look at everything as he did and to recognize what is really important in life.

It has been many years since my time with Jesus, and now I am old. My eyes are tired and do not see as clearly as they used to. Despite the passing of time, I am still deeply aware of how precious Jesus' teachings are. So, after spending my life meditating on all that Jesus taught us, I decided to write down everything I remember. That way you can share in the gifts the Lord has given to me. When you read my Gospel with an open heart, you will learn to look at the world with different eyes—the eyes of faith—and everything will become clearer to you. You will find a light even in the darkest night, and you will remember God's presence every day of your life. With the eyes of faith I was able to see Jesus' peaceful love for humanity on the cross, to identify the proof of his resurrection in his empty tomb, and to recognize the Resurrected Lord on the Sea of Tiberias. When you look with the eyes of faith at the world, you will see that death does not exist anymore. There is only life now.

Evangelist John

A Difficult Gospel?

To read the Gospel of John is to go on an adventure that might intimidate some people and excite others. John—the "theologian" evangelist and author of the "Spiritual Gospel"—is symbolically associated with an eagle. The eagle is known for flying high in the sky and for its keen eyesight (symbolic of John seeing Jesus as the Word made flesh), and for its mythical ability to stare straight into the sun (symbolic of John looking at Jesus' divinity without flinching). Even though the author wrote this Gospel for beginners, sometimes people think it is too difficult. It is good, then, to clarify some things that tend to confuse people.

~ Every evangelist is a theologian, a person who studies religious faith, practice, and experience. It is incorrect to assume that because John is called the "theologian" that the other Gospels of Matthew, Mark, and Luke (known as the synoptic gospels) do not contain theology. Each evangelist has combined the story of events and intentional reflection, history, and faith to explain why each believed Jesus was and is the Messiah. Moreover, recent studies recognize John's Gospel contains chronological and geographical details that only an eyewitness could have reported. Some of the information found in the synoptics was witnessed but passed on by word of mouth. Because the person who wrote the information down had not seen the events himself, some of the exact details are less reliable than in John's Gospel.

~ Secondly, the style of the fourth Gospel can confuse the reader. It is different because it gives away the ending. The author always keeps in mind the reality of Easter Sunday when he writes about Jesus. In this way, John dives in beyond the details of specific events to the true meaning of Jesus' actions and words which can only be understood from the perspective of the resurrection. To do this, John uses irony, words that express something other than and especially the opposite of the literal meaning.

~ The language of the fourth Gospel is extremely dense and can be understood on different—but not difficult—levels. The vocabulary John uses comes directly from the everyday experiences of the people of his day, but is also understood by later generations. The images of light and darkness; of life and death; of bread, wine, and water—these are things the people were then and are now very familiar with. These simple and timeless symbols infuse the Gospel with an extraordinary and supernatural communicative power. The language in this Gospel is symbolic, not because it is unreal or trying to hide anything, but because it is rich in meaning, and it speaks about the reality of Jesus in very powerful ways.

Blessed Are We!

Once we as readers overcome these difficulties, we can jump into the fourth Gospel's world and its uniqueness. This Gospel was written to call people to decisively move forward as a disciple of Christ. John's testimony becomes a promise of happiness and life for his readers. The fourth evangelist was thinking of us and dedicated the Risen One's last words to us, "Blessed are those who have not seen and yet have come to believe" (20:29). We are blessed, because John's recognition that Christ is the Word—or "Logos"—made flesh helps us to understand that we can encounter, listen to, see, even touch Jesus in the Sacred Scriptures. John lends us his eyes so that we can see what even Jesus' contemporaries were not able to see. This blessing is forever linked to the pages of this book, which will remain forever until the Lord comes again (21:22).

The Structure of the Gospel

John's Gospel can be divided into four parts: the prologue, the "Book of Signs," the "Book of Glory," and the epilogue. The prologue or the beginning of the fourth Gospel refers all the way back to the first day of creation. The epilogue or the end of the Gospel connects Christ to us and the end of history. So, the prologue and the epilogue root the story of Jesus' earthly life within God's eternal plan of salvation. In the part traditionally called the "Book of Signs," the evangelist chooses seven of Jesus' miracles to present to the reader as proofs, or "signs," of Jesus' divine identity and reasons to believe in Jesus. In the part traditionally called the "Book of Glory," John narrates the climax of Jesus' life—the hour of his passion, death, and resurrection. Here the signs from the Book of Signs are brought to fulfillment. The cross represents the truth and endurance of God's love and the life that Jesus came to give to every man, woman, and child.

Prologue: "In the beginning . . ." (Jn 1:1–18)
~ Book of Signs (Jn 1:19–12:50)
~ Book of Glory (Jn 13:1–20:31)
Epilogue: "After these things . . ." (Jn 21:1–25)

THE GOSPEL ACCORDING TO John

Prologue: "In the beginning . . ." (Jn 1:1–18)

The opening words of John's Gospel echo those with which the Hebrew Scriptures begin: "In the beginning when God created the heavens and the earth" (Gen 1: 1). Matthew's and Luke's writings are mostly concerned with narrating Jesus' historical background—the announcement of his birth, the stories of Christmas and his childhood—and the preaching of Jesus. John chooses, rather, to immediately present Jesus as the eternal Son of God, present alongside the Father before and at creation. He shows Jesus to be divine Wisdom who becomes flesh in order to pierce the world's darkness with the light of God's life-giving love. The poetic form of this evangelical page follows the same form of ancient hymns found in the books of the Old Testament up to the Book of Wisdom and reveals its probable liturgical use in the early Johannine Christian communities.

1:1 Word

The Latin word *verbum* means "word." The Word pronounced by God is a person: Jesus, his Son.

The Word Became Flesh

1 In the beginning was the Word, and the
Word was with God, and the Word was God.
2He was in the beginning with God. 3All things
came into being through him, and without him

a **1.4** Or [3]*through him. And without him not one thing came into being that has come into being.* [4]*In him was life*
b **1.9** Or *He was the true light that enlightens everyone coming into the world*
c **1.11** Or *to his own home*

not one thing came into being. What has
come into being 4 in him was life,[a] and
the life was the light of all people. 5The
light shines in the darkness, and the
darkness did not overcome it.
6 There was a man sent from
God, whose name was John. 7He
came as a witness to testify to the
light, so that all might believe
through him. 8He
himself was not
the light, but he
came to testify
to the light. 9 The
true light, which
enlightens everyone,
was coming into the world.[b]
10 He was in the world, and
the world came into being
through him; yet the world did
not know him. 11He came to what
was his own,[c] and his own people

1:4, 9, 12, 17 Life, light, children of God, truth, and grace . . . these are all beautiful things!

Certainly! This is God's plan for human beings. It will not fail even when the world does not welcome him nor when it seems that darkness is prevailing.

1:6 Is that you, John?

No, that is John the Baptist—Jesus' greatest witness. He pointed Jesus out to the people of his day.

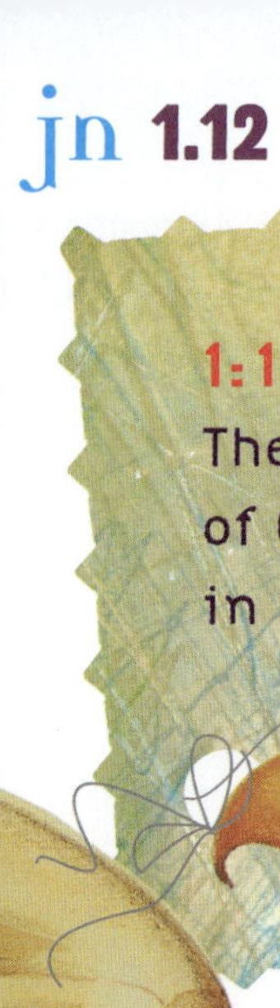

1:14 Glory
The manifestation of God's presence in history

did not accept him. [12]But to all who received him,
who believed in his name, he gave power to
become children of God, [13]who were born, not of
blood or of the will of the flesh or of the will of
man, but of God.
14 And the Word became flesh and lived
among us, and we have seen his glory, the glory
as of a father's only son,[d] full of grace and truth.
[15](John testified to him and cried out, "This
was he of whom I said, 'He who comes after
me ranks ahead of me because he was before
me.' ") [16]From his fullness we have all
received, grace upon grace. [17]The law
indeed was given through Moses; grace
and truth came through Jesus Christ.
[18]No one has ever seen God. It is God
the only Son,[e] who is close to the
Father's heart,[f] who has made him
known.

1:14 A Word that becomes flesh? What does that mean?
When God wanted to make himself definitively present among us he decided to make himself a man—Jesus, the Son of God "incarnate," which means in the flesh.

d **1.14** Or *the Father's only Son*
e **1.18** Other ancient authorities read *It is an only Son, God,* or *It is the only Son*
f **1.18** Gk *bosom*

Book of Signs (Jn 1:19–12:50)

The first twelve chapters of John's Gospel present Jesus as a preacher and worker of miracles, or "signs," which told the men and women of his time in Galilee, Samaria, and Jerusalem that Jesus is the Messiah. The evangelist describes Jesus' public ministry as taking place over a three-year period, using Jewish holidays of the time to help his readers understand the flow of time: three Passovers (2:13; 6:4; 11:55), "a festival of the Jews" (5:1) probably during Pentecost (feast of the Weeks), the "festival of Booths" (7:2), and the "festival of the Dedication" (10:22). In telling the narrative, the evangelist chose to highlight five images to show who Jesus is.

Jesus, Bridegroom and New Wine (Jn 1:19–2:12)

John begins his narration in the first week of Jesus' ministry, a week marked by the call of the first disciples and crowned by the miracle during the wedding at Cana when he changed water into wine. This miracle, the author informs us, is the first of the signs (2:11) that proves Jesus' divinity. Since it is the first it is also very important, symbolically speaking. Jesus is presented as humanity's spouse, "bridegroom," as well as the wine of the New Covenant. From the narrative point of view, Jesus is introduced through the testimony of John the Baptist, who immediately identifies Jesus as "the Lamb of God" (1:29, 36) and "Son of God" (1:34). The concept of testimony or witness is key for the fourth evangelist. It will be picked up again in crucial moments (19:35; 21:24).

The Testimony of John the Baptist

19 This is the testimony given by John when the Jews
sent priests and Levites from Jerusalem to ask him,
"Who are you?" 20He confessed and did not deny it, but

1:21 Elijah
The Jews considered him the greatest prophet in the Old Testament and believed that he would reappear just before the coming of the Messiah.

1:26, 33 What is the difference between baptism with water and Baptism with the Holy Spirit?
The first one, the one from John the Baptist, was a baptism to ask for the forgiveness of one's sins. The second, the one which comes from Jesus and the one Christians today receive, is a sign of our new life as the children of God, given to us in the paschal mystery of Jesus and made possible by the Holy Spirit.

confessed, "I am not the Messiah."[g]
21 And they asked him, "What then?
Are you Elijah?" He said, "I am not."
"Are you the prophet?" He answered,
"No." 22 Then they said to him, "Who
are you? Let us have an answer for
those who sent us. What do you say
about yourself?" 23 He said,

"I am the voice of one crying out in
the wilderness,
'Make straight the way of the Lord,'"
as the prophet Isaiah said.

24 Now they had been sent from the
Pharisees. 25 They asked him, "Why
then are you baptizing if you are
neither the Messiah,[h] nor Elijah,
nor the prophet?" 26 John
answered them, "I baptize with
water. Among you stands one
whom you do not know, 27 the
one who is coming after me; I
am not worthy to untie the thong
of his sandal." 28 This took place
in Bethany across the Jordan
where John was baptizing.

g **1.20** Or *the Christ*
h **1.25** Or *the Christ*

The Lamb of God

29 The next day he saw Jesus coming toward him
and declared, "Here is the Lamb of God who
takes away the sin of the world! 30This is he of
whom I said, 'After me comes a man who ranks
ahead of me because he was before me.' 31I
myself did not know him; but I came baptizing
with water for this reason, that he might be
revealed to Israel." 32And John testified, "I saw
the Spirit descending from heaven like a dove,
and it remained on him. 33I myself did not know
him, but the one who sent me to baptize with
water said to me, 'He on whom you see the Spirit
descend and remain is the one who baptizes with the
Holy Spirit.' 34And I myself have seen and have testified that this is the Son of God."[i]

1:29 Are these words spoken at Mass?

Yes, when the consecrated Host is shown to us before Communion! The words confirm our belief that in the consecrated Host God is fully present among us.

The First Disciples of Jesus

35 The next day John again was standing with two of
his disciples, 36and as he watched Jesus walk by, he
exclaimed, "Look, here is the Lamb of God!" 37The
two disciples heard him say this, and they followed
Jesus. 38When Jesus turned and saw them following,
he said to them, "What are you looking for?" They
said to him, "Rabbi" (which translated means

i **1.34** Other ancient authorities read *is God's chosen one*

1:39 Why did Jesus not answer their question?
To understand who Jesus is one must be near him and become his friend, not just know things about him.

1:41 The Messiah, Anointed
In Hebrew and Greek the word "anointed" is "Christ." God's Messiah, or the Christ, is given the task of carrying out God's promise to save his people (expressed in the sign of anointing).

1:42 Why did Jesus change Simon's name?
In the Bible, a significant change in a person's life is often marked by God changing the person's name. From this moment Simon's life has changed and he has received a new mission.

Teacher), "where are you staying?" 39He said to
them, "Come and see." They came and saw
where he was staying, and they remained
with him that day. It was about four o'clock
in the afternoon. 40One of the two who
heard John speak and followed him was
Andrew, Simon Peter's brother. 41He first
found his brother Simon and said to him,
"We have found the Messiah" (which
is translated Anointed).[j] 42He brought
Simon[k] to Jesus, who looked
at him and said, "You are
Simon son of John. You are to
be called Cephas" (which is
translated Peter[l]).

Jesus Calls Philip and Nathanael

43 The next day Jesus decided to
go to Galilee. He found Philip and
said to him, "Follow me." 44Now
Philip was from Bethsaida, the city
of Andrew and Peter. 45Philip found
Nathanael and said to him, "We have
found him about whom Moses in the

j **1.41** Or *Christ*
k **1.42** Gk *him*
l **1.42** From the word for *rock* in Aramaic (*kepha*) and Greek (*petra*), respectively

law and also the prophets wrote, Jesus son of Joseph
from Nazareth." 46Nathanael said to him, "Can anything good come out of Nazareth?" Philip said to
him, "Come and see." 47When Jesus saw Nathanael
coming toward him, he said of him, "Here is truly
an Israelite in whom there is no deceit!" 48Nathanael
asked him, "Where did you get to know me?" Jesus
answered, "I saw you under the fig tree before Philip
called you." 49Nathanael replied, "Rabbi, you are
the Son of God! You are the King of Israel!" 50Jesus
answered, "Do you believe because I told you that
I saw you under the fig tree? You will see greater
things than these." 51And he said to him, "Very
truly, I tell you,[m] you will see heaven opened and
the angels of God ascending and descending
upon the Son of Man."

1:43 Galilee
A region of northern Palestine that borders Lebanon

1:51 Did Nathanael ever see what Jesus said he would?
Yes. In seeing and knowing Jesus, Nathanael witnesses the meeting place of heaven and earth, where God reveals himself to people.

m **1.51** Both instances of the Greek word for *you* in this verse are plural

The Wedding at Cana

2 On the third day there was a wedding
in Cana of Galilee, and the mother of Jesus
was there. 2 Jesus and his disciples had also
been invited to the wedding. 3 When the
wine gave out, the mother of Jesus said to
him, "They have no wine." 4 And Jesus said to
her, "Woman, what concern is that to you and
to me? My hour has not yet come." 5 His mother
said to the servants, "Do whatever he
tells you." 6 Now standing there
were six stone water jars for the
Jewish rites of purification, each
holding twenty or thirty gallons.
7 Jesus said to them, "Fill the jars
with water." And they filled them
up to the brim. 8 He said to them,
"Now draw some out, and take it
to the chief steward." So they took it.
9 When the steward tasted the water that
had become wine, and did not know where

2:4 Hour

This is a key word in John's Gospel. It points to the events of the Easter Triduum, the moment in which the mystery of God's salvation will be fulfilled by Jesus.

it came from (though the servants who had drawn
the water knew), the steward called the bridegroom 10 and said to him, "Everyone serves the
good wine first, and then the inferior wine
after the guests have become drunk. But
you have kept the good wine until now."
11 Jesus did this, the
first of his signs,
in Cana of Gal-
ilee, and revealed
his glory; and his
disciples believed in
him.
12 After this he went down
to Capernaum with his mother,
his brothers, and his disciples; and
they remained there a few days.

2:10 He saved the wedding celebration for this couple! *His mother asked him to help the couple and then, through his gestures, Jesus showed that those who acknowledge him and do what he says, will be welcomed to the great feast in heaven.*

2:11 Signs

In this Gospel, the author emphasizes that Jesus' miracles are "signs" which tell his followers who he really is. Jesus performs these signs not to amaze people, but to reveal his true identity and thus help faith be formed in the disciples.

Jesus, Source of Living Water (Jn 2:13–4:54)

Jesus heads to Jerusalem for the Passover feast. His presence does not go unnoticed and many people begin to believe in him (2:23). Even one of the Pharisees is interested in Jesus and secretly visits him at night to ask questions. Because of his encounter, Nicodemus acknowledges Jesus as a teacher "come from God" (3:2). In the next chapter, another person proclaims a higher profession of faith. This time the Samaritan woman states, though uncertainly, that Jesus is "the Messiah" (4:29). Jesus had read her heart and offered her "living water" (4:10) which, for the people of Israel, had always been an image of Wisdom, of the Torah, and of God. The section closes with the second sign worked by the Lord in Cana of Galilee: the healing of the son of a pagan (a royal official).

Jesus Cleanses the Temple

13 The Passover of the Jews was near, and
Jesus went up to Jerusalem. 14 In the temple
he found people selling cattle, sheep,
and doves, and the money changers
seated at their tables. 15 Making a whip
of cords, he drove all of them out of
the temple, both the sheep and the
cattle. He also poured out the coins
of the money changers and overturned
their tables. 16 He told those who were
selling the doves, "Take these things out
of here! Stop making my Father's house a
marketplace!" 17 His disciples remembered
that it was written, "Zeal for your house will

2:14 Why was there a marketplace in the Temple?

At that time it was normal that within the various buildings and courtyards that made up the Temple of Jerusalem, merchants and money changers would sell what was needed for sacrificial and ritual offerings.

consume me." [18]The Jews then said to him, "What sign can
you show us for doing this?" [19]Jesus answered them,
"Destroy this temple, and in three days I will raise it
up." [20]The Jews then said, "This temple has been
under construction for forty-six years, and will
you raise it up in three days?" [21]But he was
speaking of the temple of his body. [22]After
he was raised from the dead, his disciples
remembered that he had said this; and
they believed the scripture and the word
that Jesus had spoken.

23 When he was in Jerusalem during
the Passover festival, many believed in his
name because they saw the signs that he
was doing. [24]But Jesus on his part would
not entrust himself to them, because he
knew all people [25]and needed no one to
testify about anyone; for he himself knew what was in
everyone.

2:21 Why does Jesus speak of his body as being a temple?

Because he is the place where we meet God and where the true and ultimate sacrifice is fulfilled.

Nicodemus Visits Jesus

3 Now there was
a Pharisee named Nico-
demus, a leader of the
Jews. [2]He came to Jesus[n]

n **3.2** Gk *him*
o **3.3** Or *born anew*
p **3.6** The same Greek word means both *wind* and *spirit*
q **3.7** The Greek word for *you* here is plural
r **3.7** Or *anew*
s **3.8** The same Greek word means both *wind* and *spirit*
t **3.11** The Greek word for *you* here and in verse 12 is plural

by night and said to him, "Rabbi, we know that you are
a teacher who has come from God; for no one can do
these signs that you do apart from the presence of God."
3Jesus answered him, "Very truly, I tell you, no one
can see the kingdom of God without being born
from above."[o] 4 4Nicodemus said to him, "How can
anyone be born after having grown old? Can one
enter a second time into the mother's womb
and be born?" 5Jesus answered, "Very truly,
I tell you, no one can enter the kingdom of
God without being born of water and Spirit.
6What is born of the flesh is flesh, and what
is born of the Spirit is spirit.[p] 7Do not be
astonished that I said to you, 'You[q] must be
born from above.'[r] 8The wind[s] blows where
it chooses, and you hear the sound of it,
but you do not know where it comes from
or where it goes. So it is with everyone
who is born of the Spirit." 9Nicodemus
said to him, "How can these things be?"
10Jesus answered him, "Are you a teacher
of Israel, and yet you do not understand
these things?

11 "Very truly, I tell you, we speak of what
we know and testify to what we have seen; yet
you[t] do not receive our testimony. 12If I have told

3:4 Nicodemus was right. How is it possible to be born twice?

Jesus was speaking about rebirth from above—of water and the Spirit—and not physical life. Through the sacrament of Baptism we are reborn as children of God.

you about earthly things and you do not believe, how can you believe if I tell
you about heavenly things? 13No one has ascended into heaven except the
one who descended from heaven, the Son of Man.[u] 14And just as Moses lifted
up the serpent in the wilderness, so must the Son of Man be lifted up, 15that
whoever believes in him may have eternal life.[v]

16 "For God so loved the world that he gave his only Son, so that everyone
who believes in him may not perish but may have eternal life.

17 "Indeed, God did not send the Son into the world
to condemn the world, but in order that the world
might be saved through him. 18Those who believe
in him are not condemned; but those who do
not believe are condemned already, because
they have not believed in the name of the
only Son of God. 19And this is the judgment, that the light has come into the
world, and people loved darkness rather
than light because their deeds were evil.
20For all who do evil hate the light and do
not come to the light, so that their deeds
may not be exposed. 21But those who do
what is true come to the light, so that it
may be clearly seen that their deeds have
been done in God."[w]

3:14 Where does the Son of man have to be lifted up?

On the cross, where, out of love for the world, Jesus gave his life for us. Every human being must take a stance before the cross to be a believer or not. No one can remain indifferent.

u **3.13** Other ancient authorities add *who is in heaven*

v **3.15** Some interpreters hold that the quotation concludes with verse 15

w **3.21** Some interpreters hold that the quotation concludes with verse 15

Jesus and John the Baptist

22 After this Jesus and his disciples went into the
Judean countryside, and he spent some time there
with them and baptized. 23 John also was baptizing
at Aenon near Salim because water was abundant
there; and people kept coming and were being
baptized 24—John, of course, had not yet been
thrown into prison.

25 Now a discussion about purification
arose between John's disciples and a Jew.[x]
26 They came to John and said to him,
"Rabbi, the one who was with you across
the Jordan, to whom you testified, here he
is baptizing, and all are going to him."
27 John answered, "No one can receive anything except what has been given from
heaven. 28 You yourselves are my witnesses
that I said, 'I am not the Messiah,[y] but I have
been sent ahead of him.' 29 He who has the
bride is the bridegroom. The friend of the
bridegroom, who stands and hears him,
rejoices greatly at the bridegroom's voice. For
this reason my joy has been fulfilled. 30 He must
increase, but I must decrease."[z]

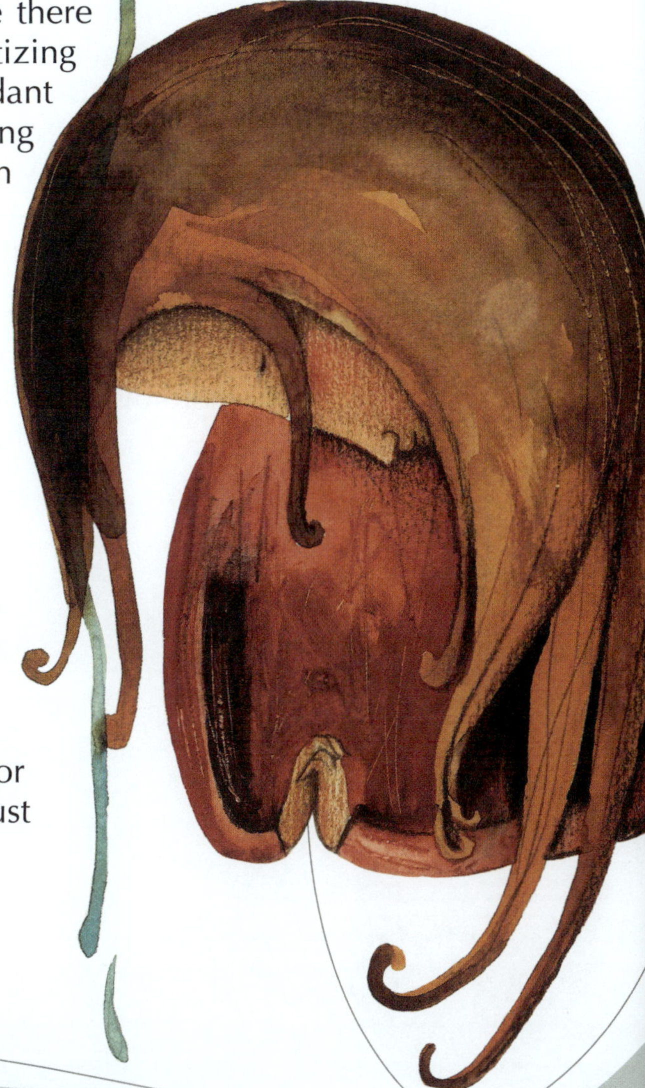

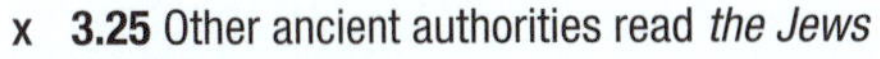

x **3.25** Other ancient authorities read *the Jews*

y **3.28** Or *the Christ*

z **3.30** Some interpreters hold that the quotation continues through verse 36

The One Who Comes from Heaven

31 The one who comes from above is above all; the one who is of the earth
belongs to the earth and speaks about earthly things. The one who comes
from heaven is above all. 32He testifies to what he has seen and heard, yet
no one accepts his testimony. 33Whoever has accepted his testimony has
certified[a] this, that God is true. 34He whom God has sent speaks the words of
God, for he gives the Spirit without measure. 35The Father loves the Son and
has placed all things in his hands. 36Whoever believes in the Son has eternal
life; whoever disobeys the Son will not see life, but must endure God's wrath.

Jesus and the Woman of Samaria

4 Now when Jesus[b] learned that the Pharisees had heard, "Jesus is making
and baptizing more disciples than John" 2—although it was not Jesus himself
but his disciples who baptized— 3he left Judea
and started back to Galilee. 4But he had to go
through Samaria. 5So he came to a Samaritan
city called Sychar, near the plot of ground that
Jacob had given to his son Joseph. 6Jacob's well
was there, and Jesus, tired out by his journey,
was sitting by the well. It was about noon.

7 A Samaritan woman came to draw water,
and Jesus said to her, "Give me a drink." 8(His
disciples had gone to the city to buy food.)
9The Samaritan woman said to him, "How is
it that you, a Jew, ask a drink of me, a
woman of Samaria?" (Jews do not share
things in common with Samaritans.)[c]

4:4 Samaria
This region north of Judea was inhabited by people of Hebrew origin. The Samaritans lived apart from the Jews because of political and religious reasons (verse 20).

a **3.33** Gk *set a seal to*
b **4.1** Other ancient authorities read *the Lord*
c **4.9** Other ancient authorities lack this sentence

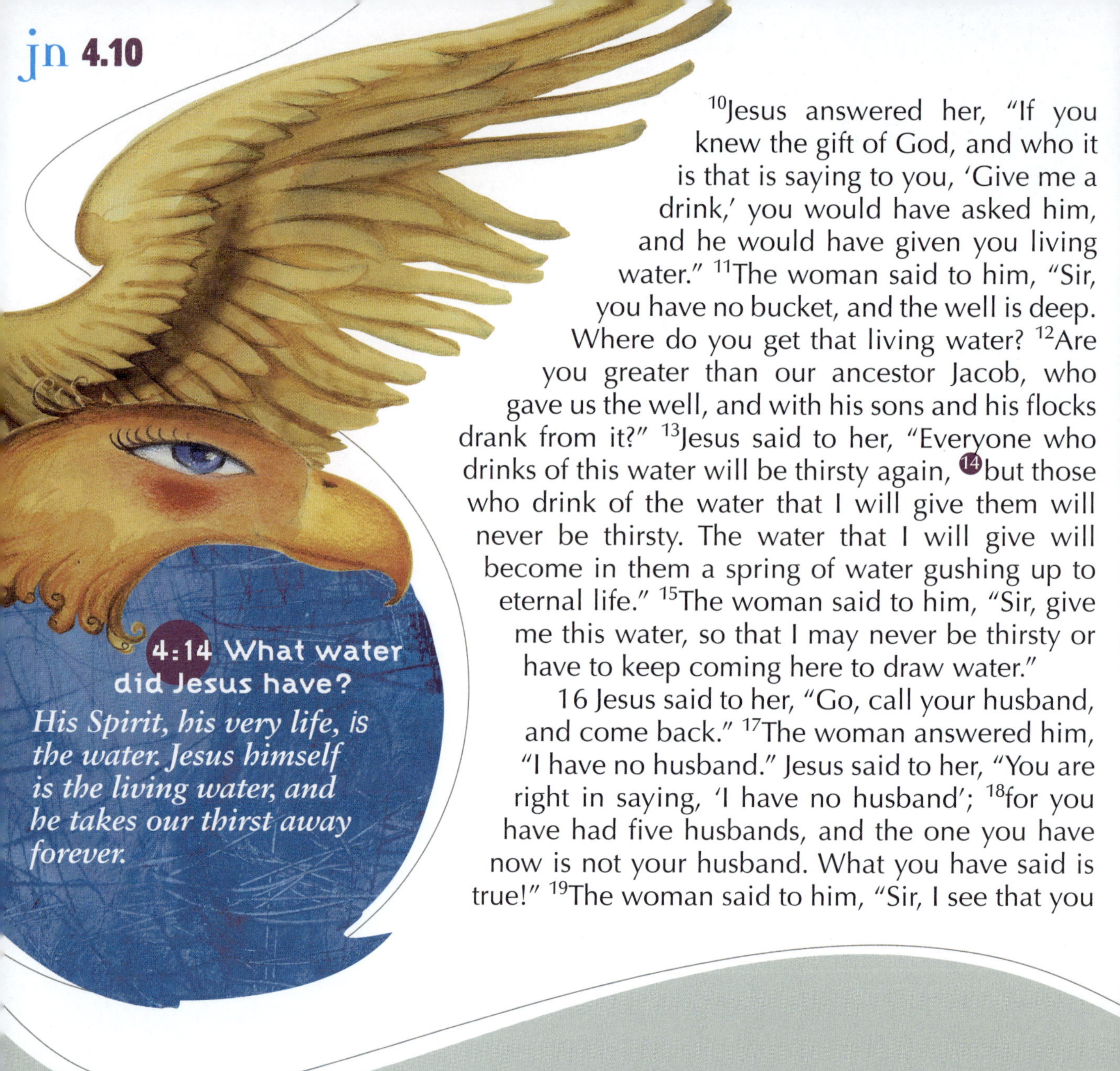

4:14 What water did Jesus have?

His Spirit, his very life, is the water. Jesus himself is the living water, and he takes our thirst away forever.

10 Jesus answered her, "If you
knew the gift of God, and who it
is that is saying to you, 'Give me a
drink,' you would have asked him,
and he would have given you living
water." 11 The woman said to him, "Sir,
you have no bucket, and the well is deep.
Where do you get that living water? 12 Are
you greater than our ancestor Jacob, who
gave us the well, and with his sons and his flocks
drank from it?" 13 Jesus said to her, "Everyone who
drinks of this water will be thirsty again, 14 but those
who drink of the water that I will give them will
never be thirsty. The water that I will give will
become in them a spring of water gushing up to
eternal life." 15 The woman said to him, "Sir, give
me this water, so that I may never be thirsty or
have to keep coming here to draw water."
16 Jesus said to her, "Go, call your husband,
and come back." 17 The woman answered him,
"I have no husband." Jesus said to her, "You are
right in saying, 'I have no husband'; 18 for you
have had five husbands, and the one you have
now is not your husband. What you have said is
true!" 19 The woman said to him, "Sir, I see that you

are a prophet. 20Our ancestors worshiped
on this mountain, but you[d] say that the
place where people must worship is
in Jerusalem." 21Jesus said to her,
"Woman, believe me, the hour is
coming when you will worship
the Father neither on this mountain nor in Jerusalem. 22You
worship what you do not
know; we worship what we
know, for salvation is from the
Jews. 23But the hour is coming,
and is now here, when the true
worshipers will worship the
Father in spirit and truth, for the
Father seeks such as these to worship him. 24God is spirit, and those
who worship him must worship in
spirit and truth." 25The woman said to
him, "I know that Messiah is coming"
(who is called Christ). "When he comes,
he will proclaim all things to us." 26Jesus said
to her, "I am he,[e] the one who is speaking to
you."

4:23 What does it mean to worship God in spirit and truth?

Because of Jesus, people can pray to God anywhere and in a manner that makes sense to them. Jesus invites us to see the true face of the Father and calls us to spend time making a good relationship with God.

d **4.20** The Greek word for *you* here and in verses 21 and 22 is plural
e **4.26** Gk *I am*

27 Just then his disciples came. They were astonished that he was speaking
with a woman, but no one said, "What do you want?" or, "Why are you
speaking with her?" 28Then the woman left her water jar and went back to the
city. She said to the people, 29"Come and see a man who told me everything
I have ever done! He cannot be the Messiah,[f] can he?" 30They left the city and
were on their way to him.

31 Meanwhile the disciples were
urging him, "Rabbi, eat something."
32But he said to them, "I have food
to eat that you do not know
about." 33So the disciples said
to one another, "Surely no one
has brought him something to
eat?" 34Jesus said to them,
"My food is to do the will of
him who sent me and to
complete his work. 35Do you
not say, 'Four months more,
then comes the harvest'? But I
tell you, look around you, and
see how the fields are ripe for
harvesting. 36The reaper is
already receiving[g] wages and is
gathering fruit for eternal life, so
that sower and reaper may rejoice

f **4.29** Or *the Christ*
g **4.36** Or [35]*. . . the fields are already ripe for harvesting.* [36]*The reaper is receiving*

together. [37]For here the saying holds true, 'One sows and another reaps.' [38]I
sent you to reap that for which you did not labor. Others have labored, and
you have entered into their labor."

39 Many Samaritans from that city believed in him
because of the woman's testimony, "He told me
everything I have ever done." [40]So when the
Samaritans came to him, they asked him to
stay with them; and he stayed there two
days. [41]And many more believed because
of his word. [42]They said to the woman,
"It is no longer because of what you
said that we believe, for we have
heard for ourselves, and we know that
this is truly the Savior of the world."

Jesus Returns to Galilee

43 When the two days were over, he
went from that place to Galilee [44](for
Jesus himself had testified that a prophet
has no honor in the prophet's own
country). [45]When he came to Galilee,
the Galileans welcomed him, since
they had seen all that he had done in
Jerusalem at the festival; for they too had
gone to the festival.

Jesus Heals an Official's Son

46 Then he came again to Cana in Galilee where he had changed the water
into wine. Now there was a royal official whose son lay ill in Capernaum.
47When he heard that Jesus had come from Judea to
Galilee, he went and begged him to come down and
heal his son, for he was at the point of death.
48Then Jesus said to him, "Unless you[h] see
signs and wonders you will not believe."
49The official said to him, "Sir, come
down before my little boy dies." 50Jesus
said to him, "Go; your son will live."
The man believed the word that Jesus
spoke to him and started on his way.
51As he was going down, his slaves
met him and told him that his child
was alive. 52So he asked them the
hour when he began to recover, and
they said to him, "Yesterday at one in
the afternoon the fever left him." 53The
father realized that this was the hour
when Jesus had said to him, "Your son
will live." So he himself believed, along
with his whole household. 54Now this was
the second sign that Jesus did after coming
from Judea to Galilee.

4:50 I do not know if I would have believed on his word alone.

As Jesus says, people often want extraordinary signs. Here, instead, the official trusts Jesus' authoritative word and later has his trust confirmed by the news of his son's recovery.

h **4.48** Both instances of the Greek word for *you* in this verse are plural

Jesus, Bread to Eat (Jn 5:1–6:71)

In this section, two Jewish festivals and three of Jesus' miracles are described. Chapter 5 presents Jesus Master going to Jerusalem for a feast—it is unknown if it is Pentecost or the feast of Tabernacles (5:1). While in Jerusalem he heals a sick man at the pool of Beth-zatha on the Sabbath. Chapter 6 returns us to Galilee, where Jesus remains despite the approaching Passover (6:4). Here John introduces the miracles of the multiplication of the loaves and fish and Jesus walking on the waters of the Sea of Tiberias. The heart of this section is where Jesus teaches that he is the bread of life come down from heaven (6:35, 38, 41, 48, 51). The sacramental theme of the Eucharist introduced here will not be taken up again until the Last Supper.

Jesus Heals on the Sabbath

5 After this there was a festival of the Jews,
and Jesus went up to Jerusalem.
2 Now in Jerusalem by the Sheep Gate
there is a pool, called in Hebrew[i] Beth-
zatha,[j] which has five porticoes. 3In
these lay many invalids—blind,
lame, and paralyzed. [k] 5One man
was there who had been ill for
thirty-eight years. 6When Jesus
saw him lying there and knew that
he had been there a long time, he
said to him, "Do you want to be

5:3–5 Why was verse 4 removed?

Because a writer, other than the original evangelist, added the line. Since it is not from John, some translations of the Bible do not include it.

i 5.2 That is, *Aramaic*

j 5.2 Other ancient authorities read *Bethesda*, others *Bethsaida*

k 5.3 Other ancient authorities add, wholly or in part, *waiting for the stirring of the water; 4for an angel of the Lord went down at certain seasons into the pool, and stirred up the water; whoever stepped in first after the stirring of the water was made well from whatever disease that person had.*

5:14 Is it not necessary to stop sinning before being cured?

Humans sometimes think wrongly that salvation must be earned. But with Jesus it is just the opposite—salvation is a free gift. When a person truly receives this gift into their heart, it converts and changes them so that, over time, they desire to do good more than to sin.

made well?" 7The sick man answered him,
"Sir, I have no one to put me into the pool
when the water is stirred up; and while I am
making my way, someone else steps down
ahead of me." 8Jesus said to him, "Stand
up, take your mat and walk." 9At once
the man was made well, and he took up
his mat and began to walk.

Now that day was a sabbath. 10So
the Jews said to the man who had
been cured, "It is the sabbath; it is not
lawful for you to carry your mat."
11But he answered them, "The man
who made me well said to me, 'Take
up your mat and walk.'" 12They asked
him, "Who is the man who said to you,
'Take it up and walk'?" 13Now the man
who had been healed did not know who
it was, for Jesus had disappeared in[l] the
crowd that was there. 14Later Jesus found
him in the temple and said to him, "See,
you have been made well! Do not sin any
more, so that nothing worse happens to you."
15The man went away and told the Jews that it

l **5.13** Or *had left because of*

was Jesus who had made him well. 16 Therefore the Jews started persecuting
Jesus, because he was doing such things on the sabbath. 17 But Jesus answered
them, "My Father is still working, and I also am working." 18 For this reason
the Jews were seeking all the more to kill him, because he was
not only breaking the sabbath, but was also calling God
his own Father, thereby making himself equal to
God.

The Authority of the Son

19 Jesus said to them, "Very truly, I tell you,
the Son can do nothing on his own, but
only what he sees the Father doing; for
whatever the Father[m] does, the Son does
likewise. 20 The Father loves the Son and
shows him all that he himself is doing;
and he will show him greater works than
these, so that you will be astonished.
21 Indeed, just as the Father raises the
dead and gives them life, so also the Son
gives life to whomever he wishes. 22 The
Father judges no one but has given
all judgment to the Son, 23 so that
all may honor the Son just as

5:19 Who is this Son?

It is Jesus. He does the will of God the Father, is loved by him, and is, in a word, one with him. The mystery of the Trinity is a relationship of love, in the Spirit, between the Father and the Son.

m **5.19** Gk *that one*

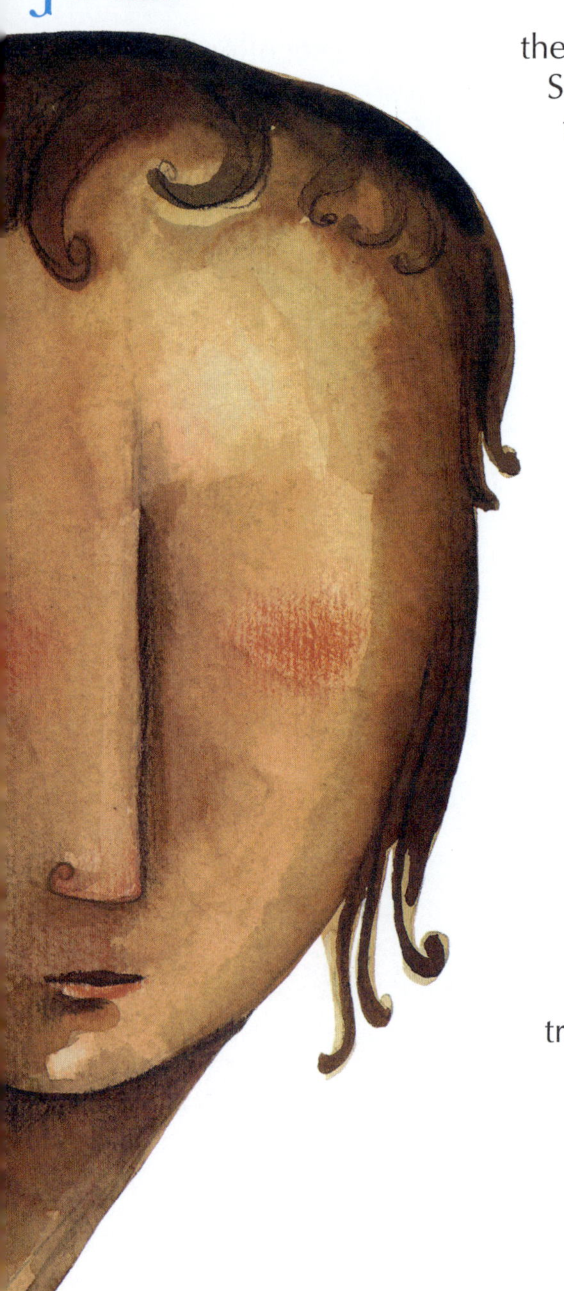

they honor the Father. Anyone who does not honor the
Son does not honor the Father who sent him. [24]Very
truly, I tell you, anyone who hears my word and
believes him who sent me has eternal life, and does
not come under judgment, but has passed from
death to life.

25 "Very truly, I tell you, the hour is coming,
and is now here, when the dead will hear the
voice of the Son of God, and those who hear will
live. [26]For just as the Father has life in himself, so
he has granted the Son also to have life in himself; [27]and he has given him authority to execute
judgment, because he is the Son of Man. [28]Do
not be astonished at this; for the hour is coming
when all who are in their graves will hear his
voice [29]and will come out—those who have
done good, to the resurrection of life, and those
who have done evil, to the resurrection of condemnation.

Witnesses to Jesus

30 "I can do nothing on my own. As I hear, I judge;
and my judgment is just, because I seek to do not
my own will but the will of him who sent me.

31 "If I testify about myself, my testimony is not
true. [32]There is another who testifies on my behalf,

and I know that his testimony to me is true. [33]You sent messengers to John,
and he testified to the truth. [34]Not that I accept such human testimony, but I
say these things so that you may be saved. [35]He was a burning and shining
lamp, and you were willing to rejoice for a while in his light. [36]But I have a
testimony greater than John's. The works that the Father has given me to complete, the very works that I am doing, testify on my behalf that the Father has
sent me. [37]And the Father who sent me has himself testified on my behalf.
You have never heard his voice or seen his form, [38]and you do
not have his word abiding in you, because you do not
believe him whom he has sent.

39 "You search the scriptures because you
think that in them you have eternal life; and it
is they that testify on my behalf. [40]Yet you
refuse to come to me to have life. [41]I do
not accept glory from human beings.
[42]But I know that you do not have the
love of God in[n] you. [43]I have come in
my Father's name, and you do not
accept me; if another comes in his
own name, you will accept him.
[44]How can you believe when you
accept glory from one another and
do not seek the glory that comes from

n **5.42** Or *among*

the one who alone is God? (45) Do not think that I will
accuse you before the Father; your accuser is Moses, on
whom you have set your hope. 46If you believed Moses,
you would believe me, for he wrote about me. 47But if
you do not believe what he wrote, how will you believe
what I say?"

Feeding the Five Thousand

6 After this Jesus went to the other side of the Sea of
Galilee, also called the Sea of Tiberias.[o] 2A large
crowd kept following him, because they saw the
signs that he was doing for the sick. 3Jesus went
up the mountain and sat down there with his
disciples. 4Now the Passover, the festival of
the Jews, was near. 5When he looked up
and saw a large crowd coming toward
him, Jesus said to Philip, "Where are we
to buy bread for these people to eat?"
6He said this to test him, for he himself
knew what he was going to do. 7Philip
answered him, "Six months' wages[p]
would not buy enough bread for each
of them to get a little." 8One of his
disciples, Andrew, Simon Peter's
brother, said to him, (9) "There is a

5:45 What does Moses have to do with it?

In rejecting Jesus the Jews reveal that they do not really believe the words of Moses. Moses was considered the author of the first five books of Scripture (vs. 46–47), in which the faithful can see the foreshadowing of the coming of Jesus.

boy here who has five barley loaves and two fish.
But what are they among so many people?"
10Jesus said, "Make the people sit down."
Now there was a great deal of grass in
the place; so they[q] sat down, about
five thousand in all. 11Then Jesus took
the loaves, and when he had given
thanks, he distributed them to those
who were seated; so also the fish,
as much as they wanted. 12When
they were satisfied, he told his disciples, "Gather up the fragments
left over, so that nothing may be
lost." 13So they gathered them up,
and from the fragments of the five
barley loaves, left by those who
had eaten, they filled twelve baskets. 14When the people saw the
sign that he had done, they began
to say, "This is indeed the prophet
who is to come into the world."
15 When Jesus realized that they
were about to come and take him by
force to make him king, he withdrew again
to the mountain by himself.

6:9 Did Jesus need the boy's food to perform the miracle?

Technically, no but Jesus always wants to work with what we all, even children, have to offer in his works of salvation.

6:13 Were the people not hungry?

The people definitely ate their fill. The twelve baskets of left-overs show how generous God is, not just in meeting our needs but giving us more than we need. The number twelve is also symbolic of the twelve tribes of Israel in the Old Testament.

o **6.1** Gk *of Galilee of Tiberias*

p **6.7** Gk *Two hundred denarii*; the denarius was the usual day's wage for a laborer

q **6.10** Gk *the men*

Jesus Walks on the Water

16 When evening came, his disciples went down to
the sea, 17got into a boat, and started across the sea
to Capernaum. It was now dark, and Jesus had not
yet come to them. 18The sea became rough because
a strong wind was blowing. 19When they had rowed
about three or four miles,[r] they saw Jesus walking on
the sea and coming near the boat, and they were
terrified. 20But he said to them, "It is I;[s] do not be
afraid." 21Then they wanted to take him into the
boat, and immediately the boat reached the land
toward which they were going.

The Bread from Heaven

22 The next day the crowd that had stayed
on the other side of the sea saw that there
had been only one boat there. They also
saw that Jesus had not got into the boat
with his disciples, but that his disciples
had gone away alone. 23Then
some boats from Tiberias came near
the place where they had eaten the
bread after the Lord had given thanks.[t]
24So when the crowd saw that neither
Jesus nor his disciples were there,

r **6.19** Gk *about twenty-five or thirty stadia*
s **6.20** Gk *I am*
t **6.23** Other ancient authorities lack *after the Lord had given thanks*

they themselves got into the boats and went to Capernaum
looking for Jesus.

25 When they found him on the other side of
the sea, they said to him, "Rabbi, when did you
come here?" [26]Jesus answered them, "Very
truly, I tell you, you are looking for me, not
because you saw signs, but because you ate
your fill of the loaves. [27]Do not work for the
food that perishes, but for the food that
endures for eternal life, which the Son of
Man will give you. For it is on him that
God the Father has set his seal." [28]Then
they said to him, "What must we do to
perform the works of God?" [29]Jesus
answered them, "This is the work of God,
that you believe in him whom he has sent."
[30]So they said to him, "What sign are you
going to give us then, so that we may see it
and believe you? What work are you performing? [31]Our ancestors ate the manna in the
wilderness; as it is written, 'He gave them bread
from heaven to eat.'" [32]Then Jesus said to them,
"Very truly, I tell you, it was not Moses who gave
you the bread from heaven, but it is my Father who

6:31 Manna
It was the food that, along with quails, God sent Moses and the people of Israel daily during their forty years of wandering in the desert.

gives you the true bread from heaven. 33For the bread of God is that which[u]
comes down from heaven and gives life to the world." 34They said to him,
"Sir, give us this bread always."
35 Jesus said to them, "I am the bread of life. Whoever comes to me will
never be hungry, and whoever believes in me will never be
thirsty. 36But I said to you that you have seen me and
yet do not believe. 37Everything that the Father
gives me will come to me, and anyone who
comes to me I will never drive away; 38for I
have come down from heaven, not to do
my own will, but the will of him who
sent me. 39And this is the will of him
who sent me, that I should lose nothing
of all that he has given me, but raise it
up on the last day. 40This is indeed
the will of my Father, that all who
see the Son and believe in him may
have eternal life; and I will raise
them up on the last day."

6:35 What an amazing statement!

You are absolutely right. Jesus began with a sign—the multiplication of the loaves and fish—to prepare the people for the shocking statement that he is the true Bread that satisfies every person.

u **6.33** Or *he who*

41 Then the Jews began to complain about him because he
said, "I am the bread that came down from heaven." 42They
were saying, "Is not this Jesus, the son of Joseph, whose father
and mother we know? How can he now say, 'I have come
down from heaven'?" 43Jesus answered
them, "Do not complain among yourselves.
44No one can come to me
unless drawn by the Father who sent
me; and I will raise that person up
on the last day. 45It is written in the
prophets, 'And they shall all be
taught by God.' Everyone who has
heard and learned from the Father
comes to me. 46Not that anyone has
seen the Father except the one who
is from God; he has seen the Father.
47Very truly, I tell you, whoever
believes has eternal life. 48I am the
bread of life. 49Your ancestors ate the
manna in the wilderness, and they died.
50This is the bread that comes down from
heaven, so that one may eat of it and not
die. 51I am the living bread that came down
from heaven. Whoever eats of this bread will
live forever; and the bread that I will give for the
life of the world is my flesh."

6:41 Why did the Jews complain about Jesus?

They thought of Jesus as someone who could solve people's everyday problems, like physical hunger (that is why, at one point, they wanted to make him their king). They did not think of him as anything more and so became upset when he declared himself to be the Son of God.

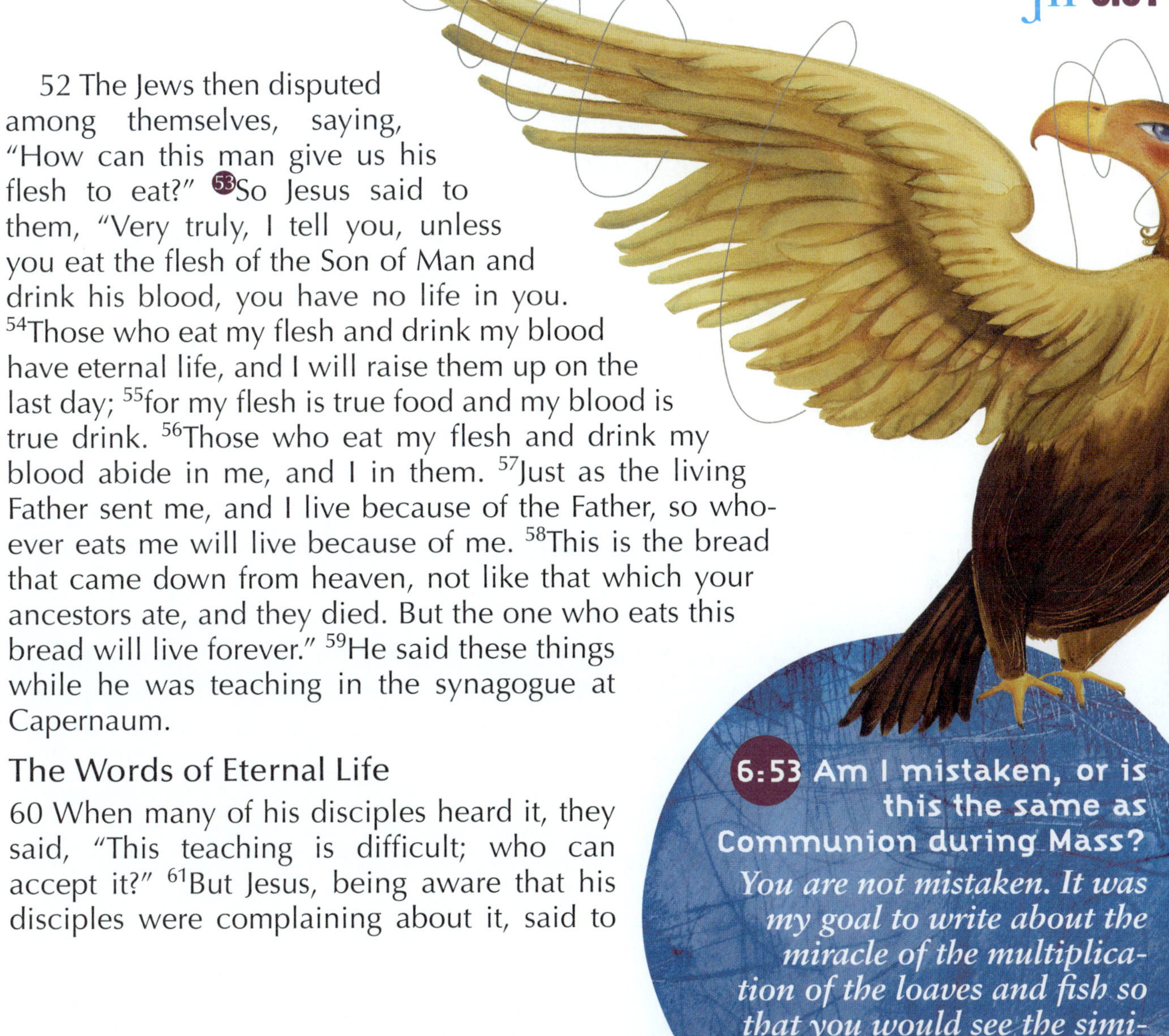

52 The Jews then disputed
among themselves, saying,
"How can this man give us his
flesh to eat?" 53 So Jesus said to
them, "Very truly, I tell you, unless
you eat the flesh of the Son of Man and
drink his blood, you have no life in you.
54 Those who eat my flesh and drink my blood
have eternal life, and I will raise them up on the
last day; 55 for my flesh is true food and my blood is
true drink. 56 Those who eat my flesh and drink my
blood abide in me, and I in them. 57 Just as the living
Father sent me, and I live because of the Father, so whoever eats me will live because of me. 58 This is the bread
that came down from heaven, not like that which your
ancestors ate, and they died. But the one who eats this
bread will live forever." 59 He said these things
while he was teaching in the synagogue at
Capernaum.

The Words of Eternal Life

60 When many of his disciples heard it, they
said, "This teaching is difficult; who can
accept it?" 61 But Jesus, being aware that his
disciples were complaining about it, said to

6:53 Am I mistaken, or is this the same as Communion during Mass?

You are not mistaken. It was my goal to write about the miracle of the multiplication of the loaves and fish so that you would see the similarities between it and the Eucharist.

6:69 Holy One of God
Another way of saying "consecrated," sent by God

them, "Does this offend you? 62 Then what if you were
to see the Son of Man ascending to where he was
before? 63 It is the spirit that gives life; the flesh is useless. The words that I have spoken to you are spirit
and life. 64 But among you there are some who do not
believe." For Jesus knew from the first who were the
ones that did not believe, and who was the one that
would betray him. 65 And he said, "For this reason I
have told you that no one can come to me unless it
is granted by the Father."

66 Because of this many of his disciples turned
back and no longer went about with him. 67 So Jesus
asked the twelve, "Do you also wish to go away?"
68 Simon Peter answered him, "Lord, to whom can
we go? You have the words of eternal life. 69 We have
come to believe and know that you are the Holy
One of God."[v] 70 Jesus answered them, "Did I not
choose you, the twelve? Yet one of you is a devil."
71 He was speaking of Judas son of Simon Iscariot,[w]
for he, though one of the twelve, was going to betray
him.

v **6.69** Other ancient authorities read *the Christ, the Son of the living God*

w **6.71** Other ancient authorities read *Judas Iscariot son of Simon;* others, *Judas son of Simon from Karyot* (Kerioth)

Jesus, Light for the Believer (Jn 7:1–10:21)

The previous section ended with the departure of many of Jesus' disciples and with Peter's profession of faith. As Jesus continues to proclaim that he is the Son of God, some of his followers become upset and leave him while the Jews increasingly dislike him. The evangelist begins this section with another journey toward Jerusalem, this time for the feast of Tabernacles (7:2). While in the city, Jesus runs into more trouble with the Pharisees, the chief priests, and the scribes. Jesus calls himself the "light of the world" (8:12; 9:5), "I am" (8:58), "gate for the sheep" (10:7), and the "good shepherd" (10:11). The section ends with the miraculous healing of a man who was blind from birth. By that point, however, two groups had formed with their opinions about Jesus' miracles: for those who believe, they are a clear sign of God's love (9:38); for those who do not believe, they are reasons for scandal, rejection, and hatred of Jesus (8:59; 9:18, 34, 41; 10:20).

The Unbelief of Jesus' Brothers

7 After this Jesus went about in Galilee. He did not wish[x]
to go about in Judea because the Jews were looking for an
opportunity to kill him. 2Now the Jewish festival of Booths[y]
was near. 3So his brothers said to him, "Leave here and go
to Judea so that your disciples also may see the works you
are doing; 4for no one who wants[z] to be widely known acts
in secret. If you do these things, show yourself to the world."

x **7.1** Other ancient authorities read *was not at liberty*
y **7.2** Or *Tabernacles*
z **7.4** Other ancient authorities read *wants it*

5(For not even his brothers believed in him.) 6Jesus said to them, "My time
has not yet come, but your time is always here. 7The world cannot hate you,
but it hates me because I testify against it that its works are evil. 8Go to the
festival yourselves. I am not[a] going to this festival, for my time has not yet fully
come." 9After saying this, he remained in Galilee.

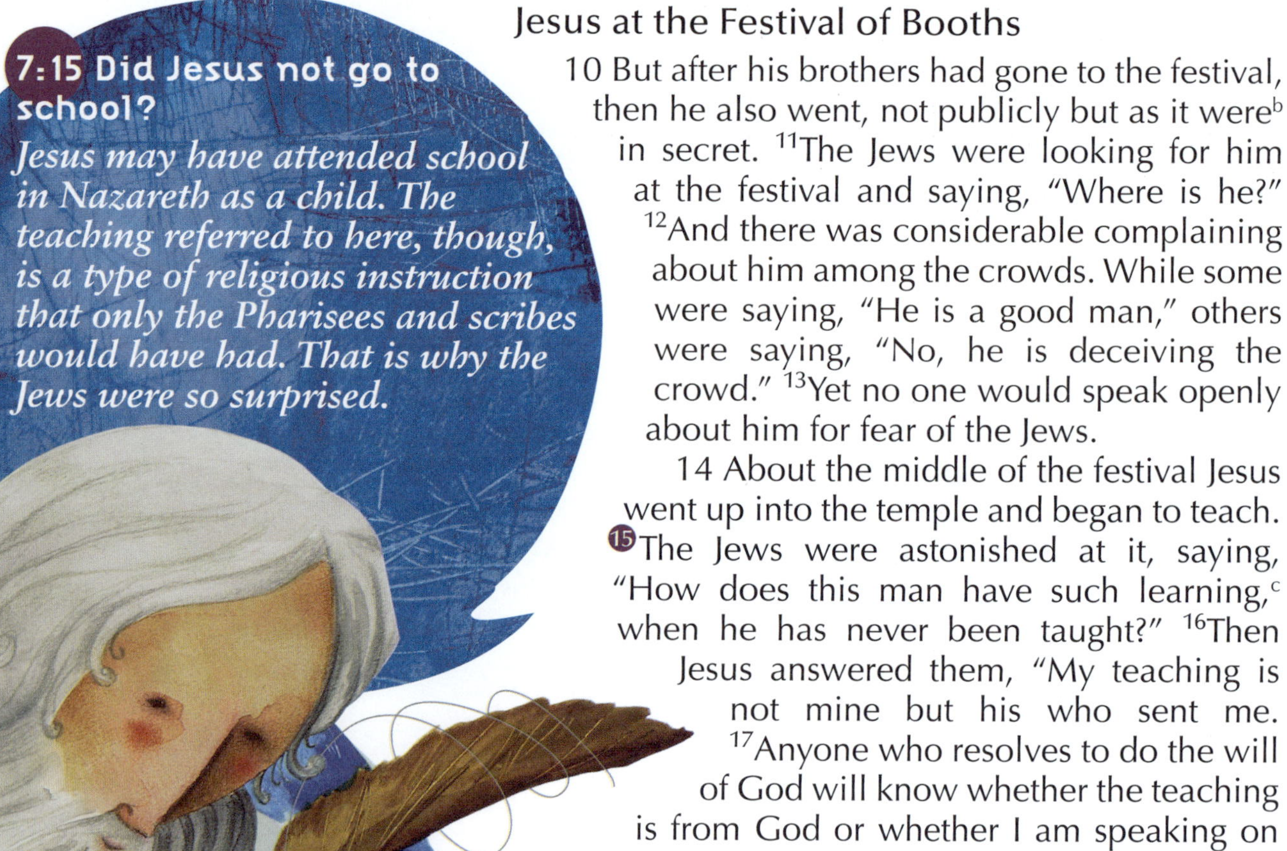

Jesus at the Festival of Booths

10 But after his brothers had gone to the festival,
then he also went, not publicly but as it were[b]
in secret. 11The Jews were looking for him
at the festival and saying, "Where is he?"
12And there was considerable complaining
about him among the crowds. While some
were saying, "He is a good man," others
were saying, "No, he is deceiving the
crowd." 13Yet no one would speak openly
about him for fear of the Jews.

14 About the middle of the festival Jesus
went up into the temple and began to teach.
15The Jews were astonished at it, saying,
"How does this man have such learning,[c]
when he has never been taught?" 16Then
Jesus answered them, "My teaching is
not mine but his who sent me.
17Anyone who resolves to do the will
of God will know whether the teaching
is from God or whether I am speaking on

my own. [18]Those who speak on their own seek their own glory;
but the one who seeks the glory of him who sent him is true,
and there is nothing false in him.

19 "Did not Moses give you the law? Yet none of you
keeps the law. Why are you looking for an opportunity to
kill me?" [20]The crowd answered, "You have a demon! Who
is trying to kill you?" [21]Jesus answered them, "I performed
one work, and all of you are astonished. [22]Moses gave you
circumcision (it is, of course, not from Moses, but from the
patriarchs), and you circumcise a man on the sabbath. [23]If a
man receives circumcision on the sabbath in order that
the law of Moses may not be broken, are you angry
with me because I healed a man's whole body
on the sabbath? [24]Do not judge by appearances, but judge with right judgment."

Is This the Christ?

25 Now some of the people of Jerusalem
were saying, "Is not this the man whom they
are trying to kill? [26]And here he is, speaking
openly, but they say nothing to him! Can
it be that the authorities really know that
this is the Messiah?[d] [27]Yet we know where
this man is from; but when the Messiah[e]
comes, no one will know where he is from."
[28]Then Jesus cried out as he was teaching in the
temple, "You know me, and you know where I am from.

a **7.8** Other ancient authorities add *yet*
b **7.10** Other ancient authorities lack *as it were*
c **7.15** Or *this man know his letters*
d **7.26** Or *the Christ*
e **7.27** Or *the Christ*

I have not come on my own. But the one who sent me is true, and you do not
know him. [29]I know him, because I am from him, and he sent me." [30]Then
they tried to arrest him, but no one laid hands on him, because his hour had
not yet come. [31]Yet many in the crowd believed in him and were saying,
"When the Messiah[f] comes, will he do more signs than this man has done?"[g]

Officers Are Sent to Arrest Jesus

32 The Pharisees heard the crowd muttering such things about
him, and the chief priests and Pharisees sent temple police to
arrest him. [33]Jesus then said, "I will be with you a little while
longer, and then I am going to him who sent me. [34]You will
search for me, but you will not find me; and where I am,
you cannot come." [35]The Jews said to one another,
"Where does this man intend to go that we will not
find him? Does he intend to go to the Dispersion
among the Greeks and teach the Greeks? [36]What
does he mean by saying, 'You will search for
me and you will not find me' and 'Where I
am, you cannot come'?"

Rivers of Living Water

37 On the last day of the festival, the great day, while Jesus
was standing there, he cried
out, "Let anyone who is thirsty
come to me, [38]and let the one

7:34 Was Jesus going somewhere secret?

It was no secret. Jesus was referring to his return to God the Father that would happen after his death and resurrection.

f **7.31** Or *the Christ*
g **7.31** Other ancient authorities read *is doing*

who believes in me drink. As[h] the scripture has
said, 'Out of the believer's heart[i] shall flow
rivers of living water.'" 39 Now he said this
about the Spirit, which believers in him
were to receive; for as yet there was no
Spirit,[j] because Jesus was not yet glorified.

Division among the People

40 When they heard these words,
some in the crowd said, "This is
really the prophet."
41 Others said,
"This is the Messiah."[k] But some
asked, "Surely the Messiah[l] does not
come from Galilee, does he?
42 Has not
the scripture said that the Messiah[m] is
descended from David and comes from
Bethlehem, the village where David lived?"
43 So there was a division in the crowd because
of him.
44 Some of them wanted to arrest him, but
no one laid hands on him.

7:39 When was Jesus glorified?
On the cross, when he sacrificed his life and gave the Spirit to everyone

The Unbelief of Those in Authority

45 Then the temple police went back to the chief
priests and Pharisees, who asked them, "Why did you not
arrest him?"
46 The police answered, "Never has anyone

h **7.38** Or *come to me and drink.* [38] *The one who believes in me, as*

i **7.38** Gk *out of his belly*

j **7.39** Other ancient authorities read *for as yet the Spirit* (others, *Holy Spirit*) *had not been given*

k **7.41** Or *the Christ*

l **7.41** Or *the Christ*

m **7.42** Or *the Christ*

spoken like this!" 47Then the Pharisees replied,
"Surely you have not been deceived too, have you?
48Has any one of the authorities or of the Pharisees
believed in him? 49But this crowd, which does not
know the law—they are accursed." 50Nicodemus, who
had gone to Jesus[n] before, and who was one of them,
asked, 51"Our law does not judge people without first
giving them a hearing to find out what they are doing,
does it?" 52They replied, "Surely you are not also from
Galilee, are you? Search and you will see that no
prophet is to arise from Galilee."

The Woman Caught in Adultery

[[53Then each of them went home,
8 while Jesus went to the Mount of Olives.
2Early in the morning he came again to the
temple. All the people came to him and he sat
down and began to teach them. 3The scribes
and the Pharisees brought a woman who
had been caught in adultery; and making
her stand before all of them, 4they said to
him, "Teacher, this woman was caught in
the very act of committing adultery. 5Now
in the law Moses commanded us to stone
such women. Now what do you say?"
6They said this to test him, so that they

8:3 Adultery
A serious sin that a man or woman commits by cheating on his or her spouse.

n **7.50** Gk *him*
o **8.8** Other ancient authorities add *the sins of each of them*
p **8.11** Or *Lord*
q **8.11** The most ancient authorities lack 7.53—8.11; other authorities add the passage here or after 7.36 or after 21.25 or after Luke 21.38, with variations of text; some mark the passage as doubtful.

might have some charge to bring against
him. Jesus bent down and wrote with his
finger on the ground. 7When they kept on
questioning him, he straightened up and
said to them, "Let anyone among you who
is without sin be the first to throw a stone
at her." 8And once again he bent down and
wrote on the ground.[o] 9When they heard it,
they went away, one by one, beginning with
the elders; and Jesus was left alone with the
woman standing before him. 10Jesus straightened up and said to her, "Woman, where are
they? Has no one condemned you?" 11She
said, "No one, sir."[p] And Jesus said, "Neither do I condemn you. Go your way,
and from now on do not sin again."]][q]

Jesus the Light of the World

12 Again Jesus spoke to them,
saying, "I am the light of the world.
Whoever follows me will never
walk in darkness but will have the
light of life." 13Then the Pharisees
said to him, "You are testifying on
your own behalf; your testimony

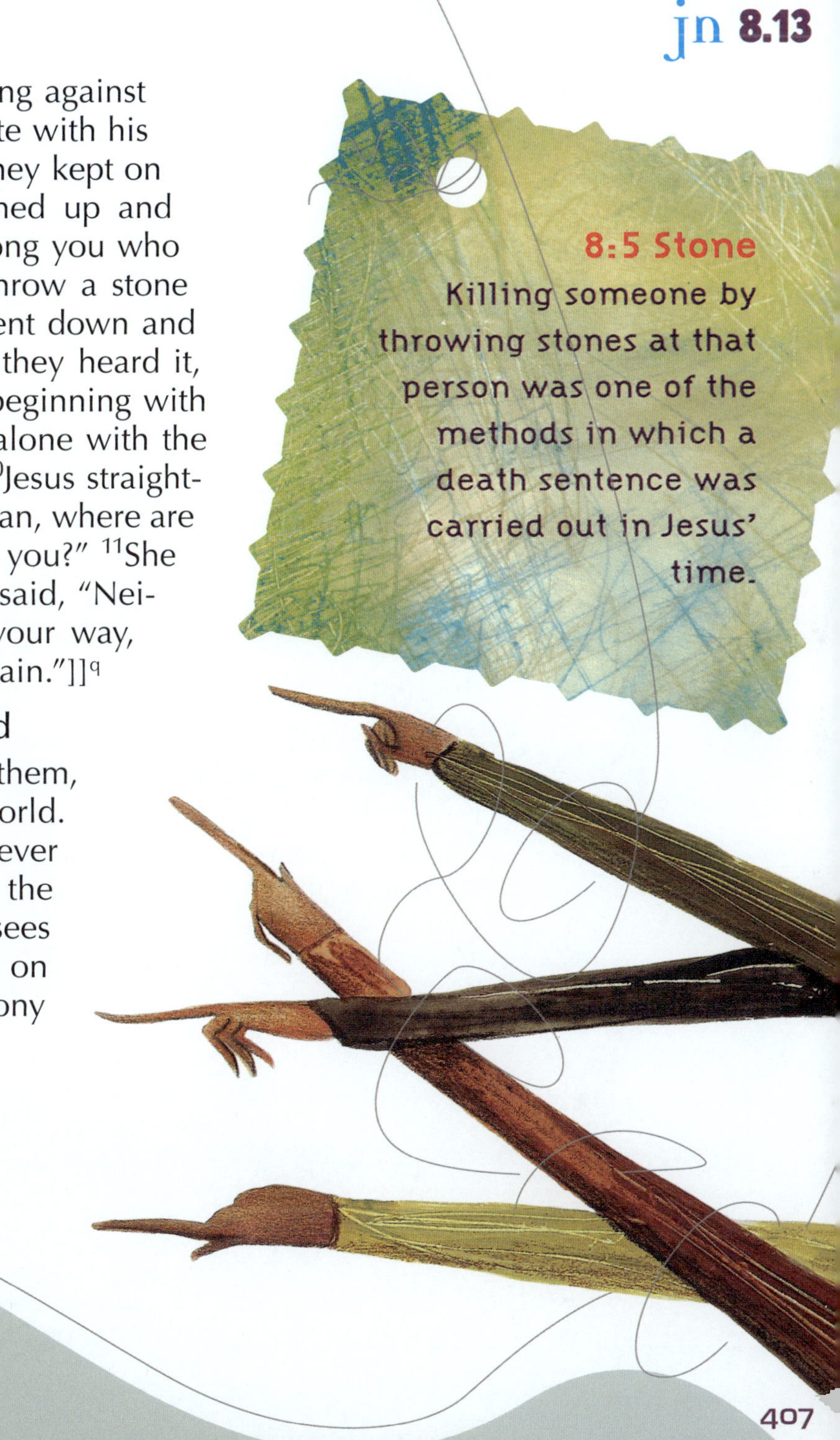

is not valid." [14]Jesus answered, "Even if I testify
on my own behalf, my testimony is valid because
I know where I have come from and where I am
going, but you do not know where I come from or
where I am going. [15]You judge by human standards;[r] I
judge no one. [16]Yet even if I do judge, my judgment is
valid; for it is not I alone who judge, but I and the Father[s]
who sent me. [17]In your law it is written that the testimony
of two witnesses is valid. [18]I testify on my own behalf, and
the Father who sent me testifies on my behalf." [19]Then they
said to him, "Where is your Father?" Jesus answered, "You
know neither me nor my Father. If you knew me, you would
know my Father also." [20]He spoke these words while he was
teaching in the treasury of the temple, but no one arrested him,
because his hour had not yet come.

Jesus Foretells His Death

21 Again he said to them, "I am going away, and you will search
for me, but you will die in your sin. Where I am going, you cannot
come." [22]Then the Jews said, "Is he going to kill himself? Is that
what he means by saying, 'Where I am going, you cannot come'?"
[23]He said to them, "You are from below, I am from above; you are

r **8.15** Gk *according to the flesh*
s **8.16** Other ancient authorities read *he*
t **8.24** Gk *I am*
u **8.25** Or *What I have told you from the beginning*
v **8.28** Gk *I am*

of this world, I am not of this world. 24I told you that you
would die in your sins, for you will die in your sins unless
you believe that I am he."[t] 25They said to him, "Who
are you?" Jesus said to them, "Why do I speak to
you at all?[u] 26I have much to say about you and
much to condemn; but the one who
sent me is true, and I declare to the
world what I have heard from him."
27They did not understand that he was
speaking to them about the Father. 28So
Jesus said, "When you have lifted up
the Son of Man, then you will realize
that I am he,[v] and that I do nothing on
my own, but I speak these things as the
Father instructed me. 29And the one who
sent me is with me; he has not left me
alone, for I always do what is pleasing
to him." 30As he was saying these things,
many believed in him.

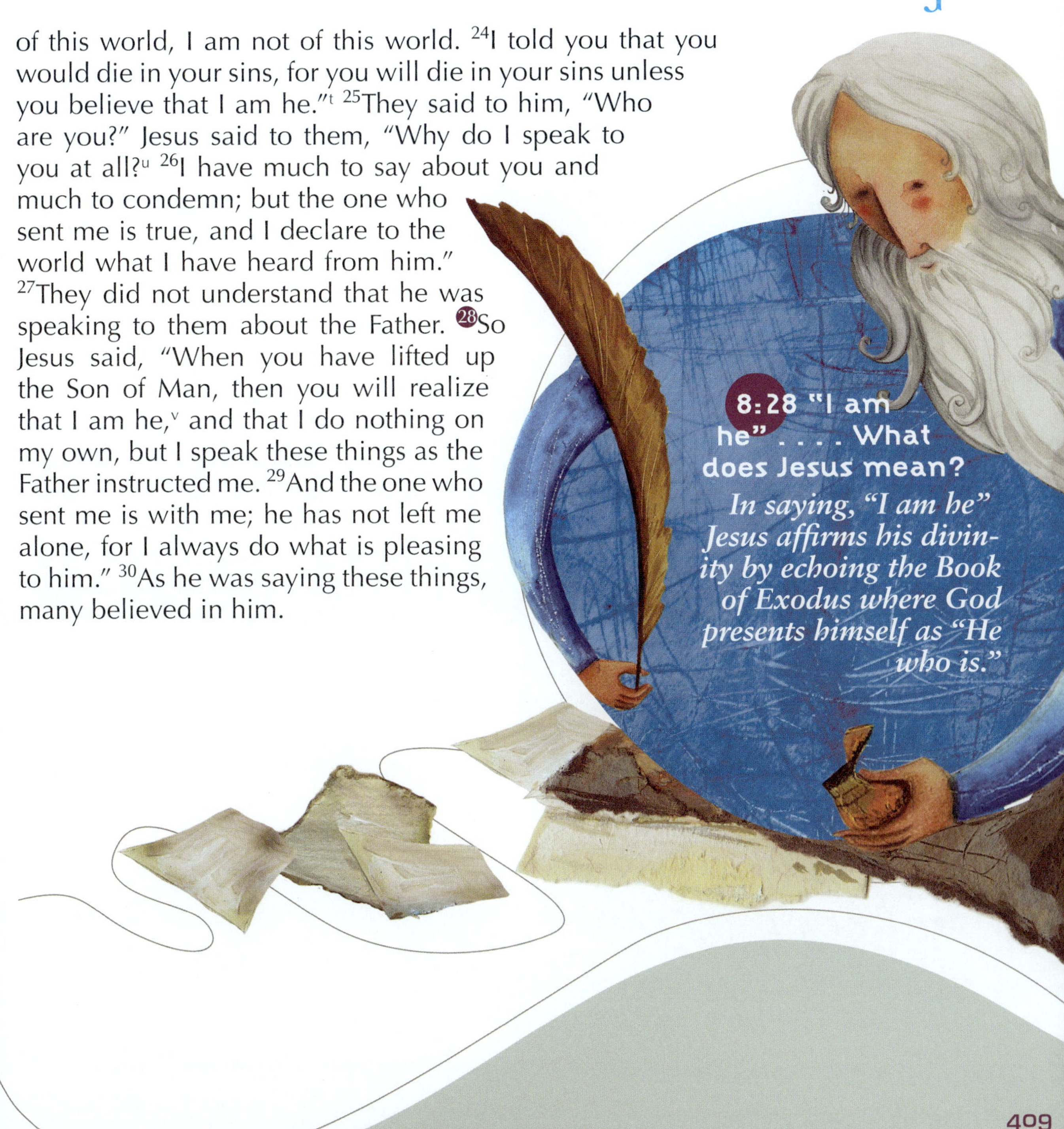

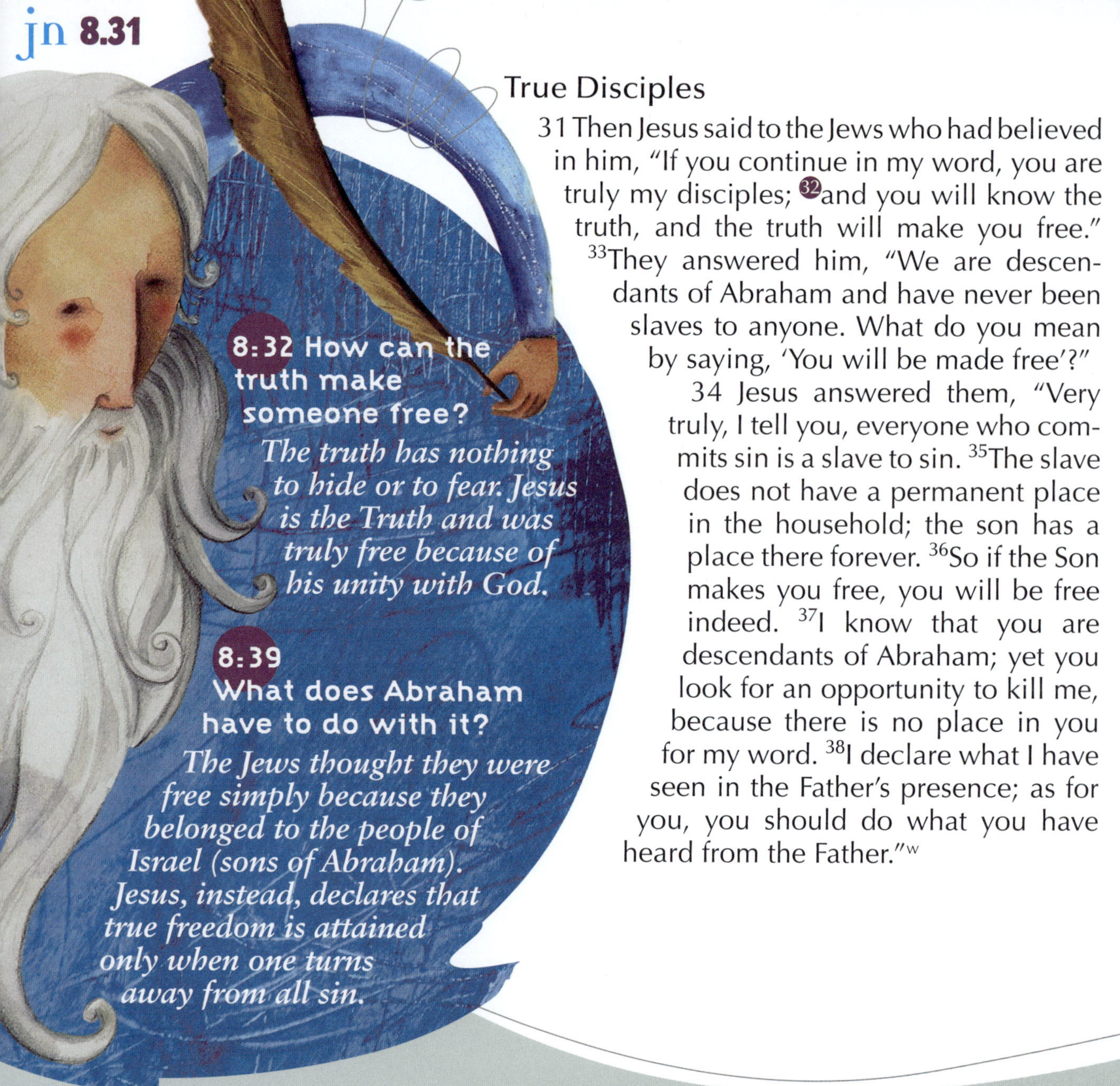

True Disciples

31 Then Jesus said to the Jews who had believed
in him, "If you continue in my word, you are
truly my disciples; 32 and you will know the
truth, and the truth will make you free."
33 They answered him, "We are descendants of Abraham and have never been
slaves to anyone. What do you mean
by saying, 'You will be made free'?"
34 Jesus answered them, "Very
truly, I tell you, everyone who commits sin is a slave to sin. 35 The slave
does not have a permanent place
in the household; the son has a
place there forever. 36 So if the Son
makes you free, you will be free
indeed. 37 I know that you are
descendants of Abraham; yet you
look for an opportunity to kill me,
because there is no place in you
for my word. 38 I declare what I have
seen in the Father's presence; as for
you, you should do what you have
heard from the Father."[w]

w **8.38** Other ancient authorities read *you do what you have heard from your father*

Jesus and Abraham

39 They answered him, "Abraham is our father." Jesus said
to them, "If you were Abraham's children, you would be
doing[x] what Abraham did, 40but now you are trying to
kill me, a man who has told you the truth that I heard
from God. This is not what Abraham did. 41You are
indeed doing what your father does." They said to
him, "We are not illegitimate children; we have
one father, God himself." 42Jesus said to them, "If
God were your Father, you would love me, for
I came from God and now I am here. I did not
come on my own, but he sent me. 43Why do you
not understand what I say? It is because you
cannot accept my word. 44You are from your
father the devil, and you choose to do your
father's desires. He was a murderer from the
beginning and does not stand in the truth,
because there is no truth in him. When
he lies, he speaks according to his own
nature, for he is a liar and the father of
lies. 45But because I tell the truth, you do
not believe me. 46Which of you convicts
me of sin? If I tell the truth, why do you not
believe me? 47Whoever is from God hears
the words of God. The reason you do not
hear them is that you are not from God."

x **8.39** Other ancient authorities read *If you are Abraham's children, then do*

48 The Jews answered him, "Are we not right in
saying that you are a Samaritan and have a
demon?" 49Jesus answered, "I do not have a
demon; but I honor my Father, and you dishonor
me. 50Yet I do not seek my own glory; there is
one who seeks it and he is the judge. 51Very
truly, I tell you, whoever keeps my word will
never see death." 52The Jews said to him, "Now
we know that you have a demon. Abraham
died, and so did the prophets; yet you say,
'Whoever keeps my word will never taste
death.' 53Are you greater than our father
Abraham, who died? The prophets also died.
Who do you claim to be?" 54Jesus answered,
"If I glorify myself, my glory is nothing. It is
my Father who glorifies me, he of whom you
say, 'He is our God,' 55though you do not
know him. But I know him; if I would say that
I do not know him, I would be a liar like you.
But I do know him and I keep his word. 56Your
ancestor Abraham rejoiced that he would see
my day; he saw it and was glad." 57Then the
Jews said to him, "You are not yet fifty years old,

and have you seen Abraham?"[y] 58Jesus said to them,
"Very truly, I tell you, before Abraham was, I
am." 59So they picked up stones to throw at
him, but Jesus hid himself and went out of
the temple.

A Man Born Blind Receives Sight

9 As he walked along, he saw a
man blind from birth. 2His disciples asked him, "Rabbi, who
sinned, this man or his parents, that he was born blind?"
3Jesus answered, "Neither
this man nor his parents
sinned; he was born blind
so that God's works might
be revealed in him. 4We[z]
must work the works of him
who sent me[a] while it is day;
night is coming when no one
can work. 5As long as I am in the
world, I am the light of the world."

9:2 Why does it have to be someone's fault if a person is born blind?

At the time people believed that blindness and other disabilities were a sign of divine punishment for sin. Jesus, however, says this is not true. God does not punish anyone with diseases or misfortunes.

9:5 What does it mean to say that Jesus is the light of the world?

It means that, as his disciples, we can recognize Jesus as the Son of God. With this understanding we can see the truth of things, and also what path God wants us to take in life without fear of tripping or falling.

y **8.57** Other ancient authorities read *has Abraham seen you?*
z **9.4** Other ancient authorities read *I*
a **9.4** Other ancient authorities read *us*

6When he had said this, he spat on the ground
and made mud with the saliva and spread the
mud on the man's eyes, 7saying to him, "Go,
wash in the pool of Siloam" (which means
Sent). Then he went and washed and
came back able to see. 8The neighbors
and those who had seen him before as a
beggar began to ask, "Is this not the man
who used to sit and beg?" 9Some were
saying, "It is he." Others were saying,
"No, but it is someone like him." He
kept saying, "I am the man." 10But they
kept asking him, "Then how were your
eyes opened?" 11He answered, "The
man called Jesus made mud, spread
it on my eyes, and said to me, 'Go to
Siloam and wash.' Then I went and
washed and received my sight." 12They
said to him, "Where is he?" He said, "I do
not know."

The Pharisees Investigate the Healing

13 They brought to the Pharisees the man who
had formerly been blind. 14Now it was a sabbath
day when Jesus made the mud and opened his
eyes. 15Then the Pharisees also began to ask him
how he had received his sight. He said to them,

"He put mud on my eyes. Then I washed, and now I see."
16 Some of the Pharisees said, "This man is not from God,
for he does not observe the sabbath." But others said,
"How can a man who is a sinner perform such
signs?" And they were divided. 17 So they said
again to the blind man, "What do you say
about him? It was your eyes he opened."
He said, "He is a prophet."
18 The Jews did not believe that he
had been blind and had received his
sight until they called the parents of
the man who had received his sight
19 and asked them, "Is this your son,
who you say was born blind? How
then does he now see?" 20 His parents answered, "We know that this
is our son, and that he was born
blind; 21 but we do not know how it is
that now he sees, nor do we know
who opened his eyes. Ask him; he is of
age. He will speak for himself." 22 His
parents said this because they were afraid
of the Jews; for the Jews had already agreed
that anyone who confessed Jesus[b] to be the
Messiah[c] would be put out of the synagogue.
23 Therefore his parents said, "He is of age; ask him."

9:16–17 First Jesus is called a "man," then a "prophet." Which is it?

If you take a pencil and underline all the words the healed man uses to describe Jesus, you will discover that over time he understands more and more who Jesus is, to the point of acknowledging him as the Lord of his life. This is the fruit of the Lord's healing.

b **9.22** Gk *him*
c **9.22** Or *the Christ*

24 So for the second time they called the man who had been blind, and
they said to him, "Give glory to God! We know that this man is a sinner."
25He answered, "I do not know whether he is a sinner. One thing I do know,
that though I was blind, now I see." 26They said to him, "What did he do to
you? How did he open your eyes?" 27He answered them, "I have told you
already, and you would not listen. Why do you want to hear it again? Do
you also want to become his disciples?" 28Then they reviled him,
saying, "You are his disciple, but we are disciples of Moses.
29We know that God has spoken to Moses, but as for this
man, we do not know where he comes from." 30The man
answered, "Here is an astonishing thing! You do not
know where he comes from, and yet he opened my
eyes. 31We know that God does not listen to sinners, but he does listen to one who worships him
and obeys his will. 32Never since the world
began has it been heard that anyone
opened the eyes of a person born blind.
33If this man were not from God, he
could do nothing." 34They answered
him, "You were born entirely in sins,
and are you trying to teach us?" And
they drove him out.

Spiritual Blindness

35 Jesus heard that they had driven him out, and when he found him, he said,
"Do you believe in the Son of Man?"[d] 36 He answered,
"And who is he, sir?[e] Tell me, so that I may believe
in him." 37 Jesus said to him, "You have seen him,
and the one speaking with you is he." 38 He
said, "Lord,[f] I believe." And he worshiped
him. 39 Jesus said, "I came into this world
for judgment so that those who do not
see may see, and those who do see may
become blind." 40 Some of the Pharisees
near him heard this and said to him,
"Surely we are not blind, are we?"
41 Jesus said to them, "If you were blind,
you would not have sin. But now that
you say, 'We see,' your sin remains.

9:39 So, Jesus not only heals blindness, he also causes it?

Jesus speaks of two types of being blind: physically, as in not being able to see with one's eyes, and spiritually, as in not being able to see that Jesus is the Son of God. The man born blind is healed of both physical and spiritual blindness. The Pharisees, however, who think that they can see are shown to be spiritually blind because of their sin.

Jesus the Good Shepherd

10 "Very truly, I tell you,
anyone who does not enter the
sheepfold by the gate but climbs
in by another way is a thief and a
bandit. 2 The one who enters by the gate
is the shepherd of the sheep. 3 The gate-
keeper opens the gate for him, and the

d **9.35** Other ancient authorities read *the Son of God*
e **9.36** *Sir* and *Lord* translate the same Greek word
f **9.38** *Sir* and *Lord* translate the same Greek word

sheep hear his voice. He calls his own
sheep by name and leads them out.
[4]When he has brought out all his
own, he goes ahead of them, and
the sheep follow him because
they know his voice. [5]They will
not follow a stranger, but they
will run from him because
they do not know the voice
of strangers." [6]Jesus used
this figure of speech with
them, but they did not
understand what he was
saying to them.
7 So again Jesus said to
them, "Very truly, I tell you, I
am the gate for the sheep.
[8]All who came before me are
thieves and bandits; but the
sheep did not listen to them. (9) I
am the gate. Whoever enters by me
will be saved, and will come in and
go out and find pasture. [10]The thief
comes only to steal and kill and destroy. I
came that they may have life, and have it abundantly.

10:9, 11 How did Jesus manage to be both "gate" and "shepherd"?

Jesus unites two images in this one parable. With the symbol of the gate, Jesus tells the listener that only through him can we find salvation. With the symbol of the shepherd, Jesus states that he loves us so much that he knows us personally and gives his life so we may live.

10:12 Hired hand
A term used here to indicate persons who will do any work—not caring whether they believe in what they are doing or not—as long as they are paid. They lack conviction and are without faith.

11 "I am the good shepherd. The good
shepherd lays down his life for the sheep.
12The hired hand, who is not the shepherd
and does not own the sheep, sees the wolf
coming and leaves the sheep and runs
away—and the wolf snatches them and
scatters them. 13The hired hand runs
away because a hired hand does not
care for the sheep. 14I am the good
shepherd. I know my own and my own
know me, 15just as the Father knows me
and I know the Father. And I lay down
my life for the sheep. 16I have other
sheep that do not belong to this fold. I
must bring them also, and they will
listen to my voice. So there will be one
flock, one shepherd. 17For this reason the
Father loves me, because I lay down my life in order to take
it up again. 18No one takes[g] it from me, but I lay it down of my own
accord. I have power to lay it down, and I have power to take it up
again. I have received this command from my Father."
19 Again the Jews were divided because of these words. 20Many of them
were saying, "He has a demon and is out of his mind. Why listen to him?"
21Others were saying, "These are not the words of one who has a demon. Can
a demon open the eyes of the blind?"

g **10.18** Other ancient authorities read *has taken*

Jesus, the True New Life (Jn 10:22–12:50)

This last section in the "Book of Signs" opens in Jerusalem with the feast of the Dedication of the Temple. None of Jesus' miracles have brought all of the Jews to believe that he is the Messiah (10:24). Many did come to believe when they witnessed the most incredible miracle recorded in the fourth Gospel—the resurrection of Lazarus from the dead (11:45). This same sign, however, was the final reason the Jewish authorities used to explain why they wanted to kill Jesus (11:53). John makes it clear that those who close their heart to Christ will not believe, even if they see or hear about his great miracles (12:37–42). This bitter note is the end of the Book of Signs and seems to say Jesus' mission—from an earthly perspective—has been unsuccessful. The reader, however, has already been foretold the hopeful events of Easter. The end of the Book of Signs is the end of Jesus' earthly work (11:55), and he is presented to the world as "the resurrection and the life" (11:25).

Jesus Is Rejected by the Jews

22 At that time the festival of the Dedication
took place in Jerusalem. It was winter, 23and
Jesus was walking in the temple, in the portico of Solomon. 24So the Jews gathered
around him and said to him, "How long
will you keep us in suspense? If you are the
Messiah,[h] tell us plainly." 25Jesus answered,
"I have told you, and you do not believe.
The works that I do in my Father's name
testify to me; 26but you do not believe,
because you do not belong to my sheep.
27My sheep hear my voice. I know them,

10:22 Festival of the Dedication

This celebration recalls the re-consecration of the Temple. In 164 B.C., Judas Maccabeus expelled the Syrians from Jerusalem and reclaimed the Temple for the Jews. (You can read this story in the two books of Maccabees found in the Old Testament).

h **10.24** Or *the Christ*

and they follow me. 28 I give them eternal life, and they will never perish.
No one will snatch them out of my hand. 29 What my Father has given me is
greater than all else, and no one can snatch it out of the Father's hand.[i] 30 The
Father and I are one."
31 The Jews took up stones again to stone him.
32 Jesus replied, "I have shown you many good
works from the Father. For which of these are
you going to stone me?" 33 The Jews
answered, "It is not for a good work that
we are going to stone you, but for blasphemy, because you, though only a
human being, are making yourself
God." 34 Jesus answered, "Is it not
written in your law,[j] 'I said, you
are gods'? 35 If those to whom
the word of God came were
called 'gods'—and the scripture cannot be annulled—
36 can you say that the one whom
the Father has sanctified and sent
into the world is blaspheming
because I said, 'I am God's Son'? 37 If I
am not doing the works of my Father,
then do not believe me. 38 But if I do them,
even though you do not believe me, believe
the works, so that you may know and

10:33 But how does one come to understand that Jesus is the Messiah?

In this event, Jesus points out two ways to understand who he is. Jesus' disciples must read and know Scripture. They must also observe and believe the works he accomplishes. In both these ways Jesus shows that he is the Son of God.

i **10.29** Other ancient authorities read *My Father who has given them to me is greater than all, and no one can snatch them out of the Father's hand*

j **10.34** Other ancient authorities read *in the law*

understand[k] that the Father is in me and I am
in the Father." 39Then they tried to arrest him
again, but he escaped from their hands.
40 He went away again across the
Jordan to the place where John had been
baptizing earlier, and he remained
there. 41Many came to him, and they
were saying, "John performed no sign,
but everything that John said about
this man was true." 42And many
believed in him there.

The Death of Lazarus

11 Now a certain man was ill,
Lazarus of Bethany, the village of
Mary and her sister Martha. 2Mary
was the one who anointed the Lord
with perfume and wiped his feet with her
hair; her brother Lazarus was ill. (3) 3So the
sisters sent a message to Jesus,[l] "Lord, he
whom you love is ill." 4But when Jesus
heard it, he said, "This illness does not lead
to death; rather it is for God's glory, so that the Son of
God may be glorified through it." 5Accordingly, though Jesus
loved Martha and her sister and Lazarus, 6after having heard that Lazarus[m] was ill, he stayed two days longer in the place where he was.

11:3, 33, 35 Jesus had friends?
Certainly, and Lazarus was one of the closest! Because of their close friendship Jesus returned to Judea even though his life was in danger.

k **10.38** Other ancient authorities lack *and understand*; others read *and believe*
l **11.3** Gk *him*
m **11.6** Gk *he*

7 Then after this he said to the disciples, "Let us go to Judea again." 8The
disciples said to him, "Rabbi, the Jews were just now trying to stone you, and
are you going there again?" 9Jesus answered, "Are there not twelve hours of
daylight? Those who walk during the day do not stumble,
because they see the light of this world. 10But those
who walk at night stumble, because the light is
not in them." 11After saying this, he told them,
"Our friend Lazarus has fallen asleep, but I
am going there to awaken him." 12The disciples said to him, "Lord, if he has fallen
asleep, he will be all right." 13Jesus,
however, had been speaking about his
death, but they thought that he was
referring merely to sleep. 14Then Jesus
told them plainly, "Lazarus is dead.
15For your sake I am glad I was not
there, so that you may believe. But let
us go to him." 16Thomas, who was
called the Twin,[n] said to his fellow disciples, "Let us also go, that we may die
with him."

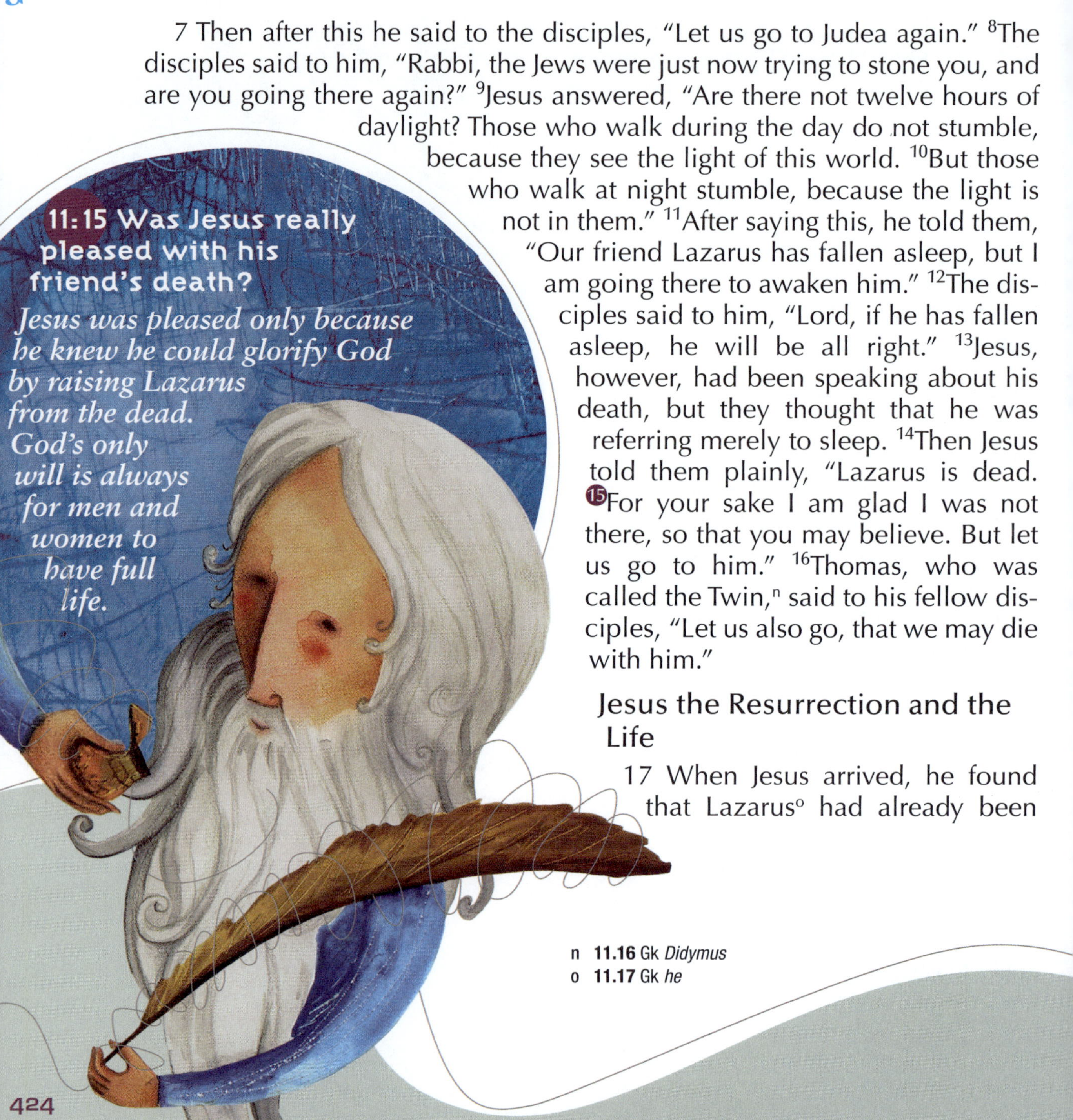

Jesus the Resurrection and the Life

17 When Jesus arrived, he found
that Lazarus[o] had already been

n **11.16** Gk *Didymus*
o **11.17** Gk *he*

in the tomb four days. [18]Now Bethany was near
Jerusalem, some two miles[p] away, [19]and many
of the Jews had come to Martha and Mary
to console them about their brother.
[20]When Martha heard that Jesus was
coming, she went and met him, while
Mary stayed at home. [21]Martha said
to Jesus, "Lord, if you had been
here, my brother would not have
died. [22]But even now I know that
God will give you whatever you ask
of him." [23]Jesus said to her, "Your
brother will rise again." [24]Martha
said to him, "I know that he will
rise again in the resurrection
on the last day." [25]Jesus said to
her, "I am the resurrection and
the life.[q] Those who believe in
me, even though they die, will
live, [26]and everyone who lives
and believes in me will never die.
Do you believe this?" [27]She said to
him, "Yes, Lord, I believe that you are
the Messiah,[r] the Son of God, the one
coming into the world."

11:25–26 It seems to me that Christians die just like everyone else.

It is true that a Christian's earthly life will end like everyone else. But those who believe in Jesus, who is the resurrection and the life, know that death is not the end of everything. Jesus gives a life that never ends to his friends who, because of their Baptism, are now children of God.

p **11.18** Gk *fifteen stadia*
q **11.25** Other ancient authorities lack *and the life*
r **11.27** Or *the Christ*

Jesus Weeps

28 When she had said this, she went back and called her
sister Mary, and told her privately, "The Teacher is here
and is calling for you." 29And when she heard it, she
got up quickly and went to him. 30Now Jesus had not
yet come to the village, but was still at the place where
Martha had met him. 31The Jews who were with her in the
house, consoling her, saw Mary get up quickly and go out.
They followed her because they thought that she was going to
the tomb to weep there. 32When Mary came where Jesus was
and saw him, she knelt at his feet and said to him, "Lord,
if you had been here, my brother would not have died."
33When Jesus saw her weeping, and the Jews who came
with her also weeping, he was greatly disturbed in spirit and
deeply moved. 34He said, "Where have you laid him?" They
said to him, "Lord, come and see." 35Jesus began to
weep. 36So the Jews said, "See how
he loved him!" 37But some of them
said, "Could not he who opened
the eyes of the blind man have
kept this man from dying?"

Jesus Raises Lazarus to Life

38 Then Jesus, again greatly disturbed, came to the tomb.
It was a cave, and a stone was lying against it. [39]Jesus said,
"Take away the stone." Martha, the sister of the dead
man, said to him, "Lord, already there is a stench
because he has been dead four days." [40]Jesus
said to her, "Did I not tell you that if you
believed, you would see the glory of
God?" [41]So they took away the stone.
And Jesus looked upward and said,
"Father, I thank you for having heard
me. [42]I knew that you always hear
me, but I have said this for the sake
of the crowd standing here, so that
they may believe that you sent
me." [43]When he had said this, he
cried with a loud voice, "Lazarus,
come out!" [44]The dead man came
out, his hands and feet bound with
strips of cloth, and his face wrapped
in a cloth. Jesus said to them, "Unbind
him, and let him go."

11:42 Why did Jesus say this prayer if he did not need to?
With this sign, Jesus not only wanted to restore Lazarus to life, but to show everyone that he was sent to do the Father's will.

The Plot to Kill Jesus

45 Many of the Jews therefore, who had come
with Mary and had seen what Jesus did, believed
in him. [46]But some of them went to the Pharisees
and told them what he had done. [47]So the chief

s **11.48** Or *our temple*; Greek *our place*
t **11.57** Gk *he*

priests and the Pharisees called a meeting of the council, and said, "What
are we to do? This man is performing many signs. 48If we let him go on like
this, everyone will believe in him, and the Romans will come and destroy
both our holy place[s] and our nation." 49But one of them, Caiaphas, who was
high priest that year, said to them, "You know nothing at all! 50You do not
understand that it is better for you to have one man die for the people than to
have the whole nation destroyed." 51He did not say this on his own, but being
high priest that year he prophesied that Jesus was about to die for the nation,
52and not for the nation only, but to gather into one the
dispersed children of God. 53So from that day on they
planned to put him to death.

54 Jesus therefore no longer walked about
openly among the Jews, but went from there
to a town called Ephraim in the region near
the wilderness; and he remained there
with the disciples.

55 Now the Passover of the Jews was
near, and many went up from the country
to Jerusalem before the Passover to purify
themselves. 56They were looking for
Jesus and were asking one another as
they stood in the temple, "What do you
think? Surely he will not come to the festival, will he?" 57Now the chief priests and
the Pharisees had given orders that anyone
who knew where Jesus[t] was should let them
know, so that they might arrest him.

11:49–52 So, without realizing it, Caiaphas spoke the truth!

Exactly. The death of Jesus—the "one man"—accomplishes the salvation of all humanity—the "nation."

Mary Anoints Jesus

12 Six days before the Passover Jesus came to Bethany, the home
of Lazarus, whom he had raised from the
dead. 2 There they gave a dinner for him.
Martha served, and Lazarus was one of those
at the table with him. 3 Mary took a pound of
costly perfume made of pure nard, anointed
Jesus' feet, and wiped them[u] with her hair.
The house was filled with the fragrance of
the perfume. 4 But Judas Iscariot, one of
his disciples (the one who was about
to betray him), said, 5 "Why was this
perfume not sold for three hundred
denarii[v] and the money given to the
poor?" 6 (He said this not because he
cared about the poor, but because
he was a thief; he kept the common
purse and used to steal what was put
into it.) 7 Jesus said, "Leave her alone.
She bought it[w] so that she might keep
it for the day of my burial. 8 You always
have the poor with you, but you do not
always have me."

12:3–5 How much is 300 denari worth?

That was how much a worker earned in a year. Mary made a truly generous gesture in this expression of her affection for Jesus Master.

12:7 Did Jesus know he was going to die?

Yes. This is why he spoke of his burial during the Last Supper, giving a somber feeling to the meal.

u **12.3** Gk *his feet*

v **12.5** Three hundred denarii would be nearly a year's wages for a laborer

w **12.7** Gk lacks *She bought it*

The Plot to Kill Lazarus

9 When the great crowd of the Jews learned that he was there, they came not
only because of Jesus but also to see Lazarus, whom he had raised from the
dead. 10So the chief priests planned to put Lazarus to death as well, 11since
it was on account of him that many of the Jews were deserting
and were believing in Jesus.

Jesus' Triumphal Entry into Jerusalem

12 The next day the great crowd that had come to the festival heard that Jesus was coming to Jerusalem.
13So they took branches of palm trees and went
out to meet him, shouting,

"Hosanna!
Blessed is the one who comes in the name
of the Lord—
the King of Israel!"

14Jesus found a young donkey and sat on it; as
it is written:

15 "Do not be afraid, daughter of Zion.
Look, your king is
coming,
sitting on a
donkey's colt!"

16His disciples did not
understand these things
at first; but when Jesus was

glorified, then they remembered that these things had been written of
him and had been done to him. [17]So the crowd that had been with
him when he called Lazarus out of the tomb and raised him from the
dead continued to testify.[x] [18]It was also because they heard that he
had performed this sign that the crowd went to meet him.
[19]The Pharisees then said to one another, "You see,
you can do nothing. Look, the world has gone after
him!"

Some Greeks Wish to See Jesus

20 Now among those who went up
to worship at the festival were some
Greeks. [21]They came to Philip, who
was from Bethsaida in Galilee, and
said to him, "Sir, we wish to see
Jesus." [22]Philip went and told
Andrew; then Andrew and Philip
went and told Jesus. [23]Jesus
answered them, "The hour has
come for the Son of Man to be
glorified. [24]Very truly, I tell you,
unless a grain of wheat falls into
the earth and dies, it remains
just a single grain; but if it dies, it
bears much fruit. [25]Those who love
their life lose it, and those who hate
their life in this world will keep it for
eternal life. [26]Whoever serves me must

12:20 What were the Greeks doing in Jerusalem?

They were pagan converts to Judaism who went there for the feast of Passover. I wanted to remember this detail to show that the salvation offered by Jesus, the fulfillment of his hour, was truly given for all humanity.

x **12.17** Other ancient authorities read *with him began to testify that he had called . . . from the dead*

follow me, and where I am, there will my servant be also. Whoever serves me, the Father will honor.

Jesus Speaks about His Death

27 "Now my soul is troubled. And what should
I say—'Father, save me from this hour'? No,
it is for this reason that I have come to this
hour. 28Father, glorify your name." Then
a voice came from heaven, "I have
glorified it, and I will glorify it again."
29The crowd standing there heard it
and said that it was thunder. Others
said, "An angel has spoken to
him." 30Jesus answered, "This
voice has come for your sake,
not for mine. 31Now is the
judgment of this world; now
the ruler of this world will
be driven out. 32And I,
when I am lifted up from
the earth, will draw all
people[y] to myself." 33He
said this to indicate the kind
of death he was to die. 34The
crowd answered him, "We
have heard from the law that the
Messiah[z] remains forever. How can

12:27 Was Jesus afraid to die?

Certainly. Even though he had just stated that life is most fruitful only when it is given, Jesus felt in his body all the dread and the anguish of his coming death.

12:31 What judgment is Jesus speaking about?

God's judgment, which took place on the cross. It accomplished the expulsion of the world's evil and the reunification of God and all humanity.

y **12.32** Other ancient authorities read *all things*
z **12.34** Or *the Christ*

you say that the Son of Man must be lifted up? Who is this Son of Man?"
35Jesus said to them, "The light is with you for a little longer. Walk while you
have the light, so that the darkness may not overtake you. If you walk in the
darkness, you do not know where you are going. 36While you have the light,
believe in the light, so that you may become children of light."

The Unbelief of the People

After Jesus had said this, he departed and hid from them.
37Although he had performed so many signs in their
presence, they did not believe in him. 38This was to
fulfill the word spoken by the prophet Isaiah:
"Lord, who has believed our message,
and to whom has the arm of the Lord
been revealed?"
39And so they could not believe, because
Isaiah also said,
40 "He has blinded their eyes
and hardened their heart,
so that they might not look with
their eyes,
and understand with their heart
and turn—
and I would heal them."
41Isaiah said this because[a] he saw
his glory and spoke about him.
42Nevertheless many, even of the
authorities, believed in him. But

12:37, 43 That seems a bit harsh.

I am sad to say it, but what I wrote is true. Earlier in my Gospel, when I recounted the signs accomplished by Jesus, I stressed that many people did not trust him.

a **12.41** Other ancient witnesses read *when*

because of the Pharisees they did
not confess it, for fear that they
would be put out of the synagogue;
43for they loved human glory more
than the glory that comes from God.

Summary of Jesus' Teaching

44 Then Jesus cried aloud: "Whoever
believes in me believes not in me but in
him who sent me. 45And whoever sees
me sees him who sent me. 46I have come
as light into the world, so that everyone
who believes in me should not remain
in the darkness. 47I do not judge anyone
who hears my words and does not keep
them, for I came not to judge the world,
but to save the world. 48The one who
rejects me and does not receive my word
has a judge; on the last day the word that
I have spoken will serve as judge, 49for I
have not spoken on my own, but the Father
who sent me has himself given me a commandment about what to say and what to
speak. 50And I know that his commandment
is eternal life. What I speak, therefore, I speak
just as the Father has told me."

Book of Glory (Jn 13:1–20, 31)

The second part of John's Gospel begins with chapter 13. This part shows the perfect fulfillment of the love that Jesus came to bring to the world (13:1). The Book of Glory begins with a great discourse, or speech. The Lord and Master prepares his disciples for the events of his passion, death, and resurrection. In the first half of the Gospel, the Book of Signs, Jesus addresses all of humankind with his signs and words. In this second part, he speaks to a much smaller group—the disciples who believe in him. Here, Jesus begins to describe his messianic identity, his role, and his bond of communion with the Father. The perfect fulfillment of the Son's mission is represented by the cross, as is emphasized by Jesus' last words before he died, "It is finished" (19:30).

The Last Supper: "If you know these things, you are blessed if you do them." (Jn 13:1–38)

The Johannine account—that means John's Gospel—of the Last Supper is different from the synoptic Gospels. The difference is that instead of the institution of the Eucharist, John depicts Jesus washing the Apostles' feet. This gesture represents for the fourth evangelist the only way to understand Easter. By stripping himself of his robes (13:4) and putting himself at the service of his disciples (13:5), Jesus shows the radically different kind of Lordship he has come to establish in the world. He also provides the means by which the disciple is to understand the cross. Those who do not see the servant-Lord, see the Crucified Christ as a heartbreaking image of total failure. Only those who keep their eyes on the servant-Lord will be able to look at the Crucified Christ and see a glorious witness of unwavering love that is strong enough to conquer death. This is the experience of the "beloved disciple," the exceptional witness who—with this title—makes his appearance at the Last Supper (13:23) and who will play a key role in the whole second part of the work.

Jesus Washes the Disciples' Feet

13 Now before the festival of the
Passover, Jesus knew that his hour
had come to depart from this world
and go to the Father. Having loved
his own who were in the world, he
loved them to the end. [2]The devil
had already put it into the heart
of Judas son of Simon Iscariot to
betray him. And during supper
[3]Jesus, knowing that the Father had
given all things into his hands, and
that he had come from God and was
going to God, [4]got up from the table,[b] took
off his outer robe, and tied a towel around
himself. [5]Then he poured water into a basin and
began to wash the disciples' feet and to wipe
them with the towel that was tied around
him. [6]He came to Simon Peter, who said
to him, "Lord, are you going to wash my

13:6 Why does Peter not want to have his feet washed?

This service was normally done by the lowest servant in the house, not by the master of the house. Peter could not imagine his Lord performing such a demeaning task.

b **13.4** Gk *from supper*

feet?" [7]Jesus answered, "You do not know now what I am doing, but later
you will understand." [8]Peter said to him, "You will never wash my feet." Jesus
answered, "Unless I wash you, you have no share with me." [9]Simon Peter
said to him, "Lord, not my feet only but also
my hands and my head!" [10]Jesus said to him,
"One who has bathed does not need to wash,
except for the feet,[c] but is entirely clean. And
you[d] are clean, though not all of you." [11]For he
knew who was to betray him; for this reason he
said, "Not all of you are clean."

12 After he had washed their feet, had put on
his robe, and had returned to the table, he said to
them, "Do you know what I have done to you?
[13]You call me Teacher and Lord—and you are
right, for that is what I am. (14) So if I, your
Lord and Teacher, have washed your feet,
you also ought to wash one another's
feet. [15]For I have set you an example,
that you also should do as I have
done to you. [16]Very truly, I tell you,
servants[e] are not greater than their
master, nor are messengers greater

13:14 Must I wash others' feet too?

Try not to take this too literally. One of our characteristics as Christians is we are called to be servants of one another. We must do this all the time. To know why, read verses 34 and 35 of this chapter.

c **13.10** Other ancient authorities lack *except for the feet*
d **13.10** The Greek word for *you* here is plural
e **13.16** Gk *slaves*

13:21 Why was Jesus troubled instead of angry?
Jesus cared deeply for Judas, and the thought of being betrayed by a friend made him troubled him and made him sad.

than the one who sent them. 17If you know
these things, you are blessed if you do
them. 18I am not speaking of all of you;
I know whom I have chosen. But it is
to fulfill the scripture, 'The one who
ate my bread[f] has lifted his heel
against me.' 19I tell you this now,
before it occurs, so that when it
does occur, you may believe that I
am he.[g] 20Very truly, I tell you,
whoever receives one whom I send
receives me; and whoever receives
me receives him who sent me."

Jesus Foretells His Betrayal

21 After saying this Jesus was troubled
in spirit, and declared, "Very truly, I tell
you, one of you will betray me." 22The
disciples looked at one another, uncertain
of whom he was speaking. 23One of his disciples—the one whom Jesus loved—was reclining
next to him; 24Simon Peter therefore motioned to him to ask
Jesus of whom he was speaking. 25So while reclining next to Jesus, he asked
him, "Lord, who is it?" 26Jesus answered, "It is the one to whom I give this
piece of bread when I have dipped it in the dish."[h] So when he had dipped

f **13.18** Other ancient authorities read *ate bread with me*
g **13.19** Gk *I am*
h **13.26** Gk *dipped it*

the piece of bread, he gave it to Judas son of Simon
Iscariot.[i] 27 After he received the piece of bread,[j]
Satan entered into him. Jesus said to him,
"Do quickly what you are going to do."
28 Now no one at the table knew why he
said this to him. 29 Some thought that,
because Judas had the common
purse, Jesus was telling him, "Buy
what we need for the festival";
or, that he should give something to the poor. 30 So, after
receiving the piece of bread,
he immediately went out. And
it was night.

The New Commandment

31 When he had gone
out, Jesus said, "Now the
Son of Man has been glorified, and God has been
glorified in him. 32 If God
has been glorified in him,[k]
God will also glorify him in

13:27 Was it an evil piece of bread?

No, food and objects cannot be evil! It was a critical moment when Jesus identifies Judas as his betrayer, by giving him the piece of bread. Judas had to choose between Jesus and Satan. He chose Satan.

13:31 How can someone who is betrayed and killed be glorified?

Jesus accomplished the Father's mission through his sacrifice on the cross. Jesus' perseverance, even to death, shows fully the glory of God.

i **13.26** Other ancient authorities read *Judas Iscariot son of Simon*; others, *Judas son of Simon from Karyot* (Kerioth)
j **13.27** Gk *After the piece of bread*
k **13.32** Other ancient authorities lack *If God has been glorified in him*

himself and will glorify him at once. 33Little children, I am with you only a
little longer. You will look for me; and as I said to the Jews so now I say to you,
'Where I am going, you cannot come.' 34I give you a new commandment,
that you love one another. Just as I have loved you, you also should love one
another. 35By this everyone will know that you are my disciples, if you have
love for one another."

Jesus Foretells Peter's Denial

36 Simon Peter said to him, "Lord, where are
you going?" Jesus answered, "Where I am
going, you cannot follow me now; but
you will follow afterward." 37Peter said to
him, "Lord, why can I not follow you
now? I will lay down my life for you."
38Jesus answered, "Will you lay down
your life for me? Very truly, I tell you,
before the cock crows, you will have
denied me three times.

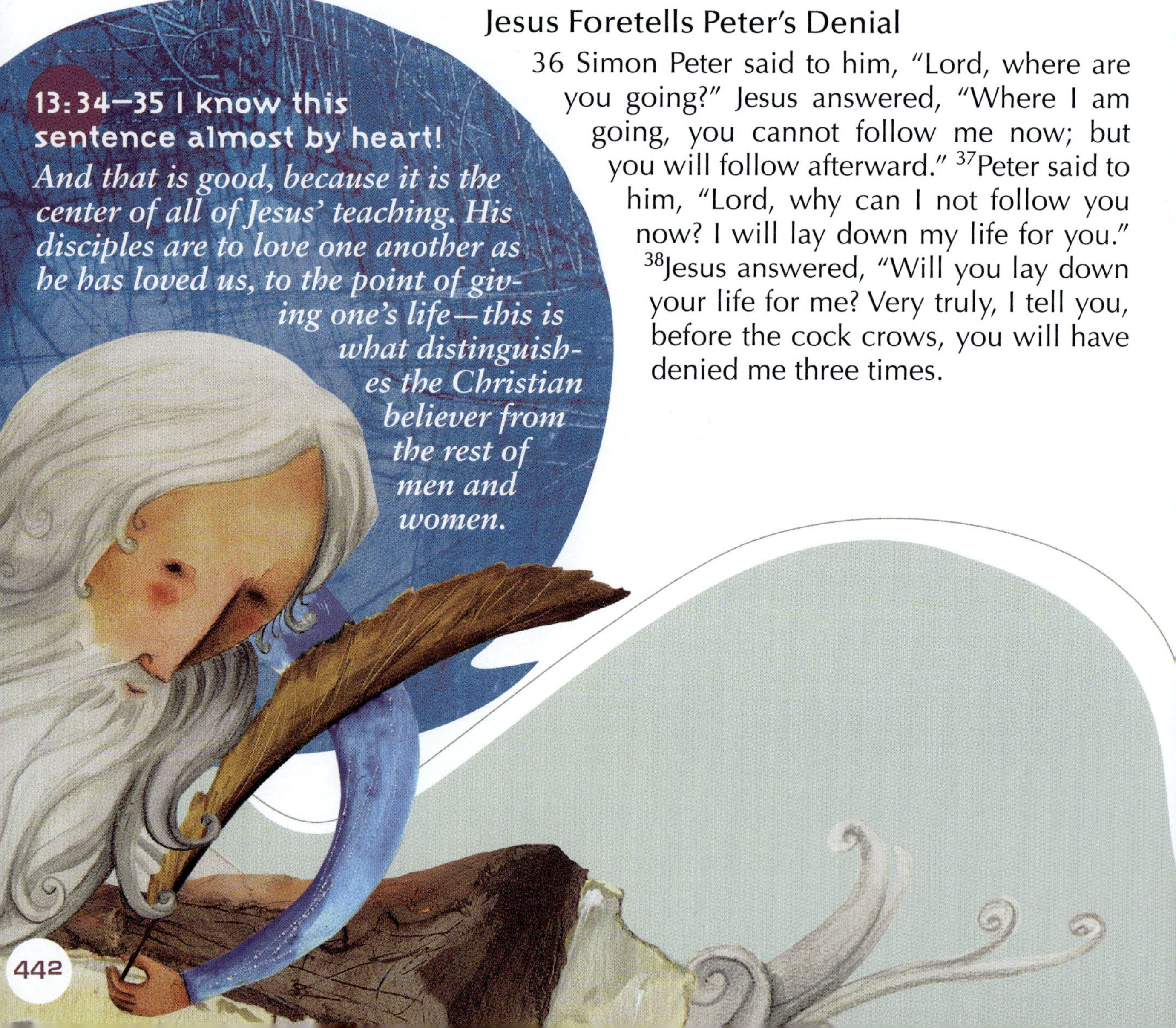

The Last Discourse to the Disciples: "The hour has come . . ."

(Jn 14:1–17:26)

John's writing in these chapters reaches very great heights. Because of this, in the Christian tradition he has been depicted symbolically as an eagle. In this very long and intense discourse, or speech, Jesus entrusts himself to the Father, promises the Spirit, and invites the disciples into that exchange of love that binds together the three persons of the Trinity. The major themes of the fourth Gospel are taken up and intertwined: love, faith, observance of the commandments, truth, peace, unity, life. This speech is like a long pause slowing down the pace of the story, giving the disciple-reader time to prepare for the last act of the Gospel: the great dramatic act of the passion.

Jesus the Way to the Father

14 "Do not let your hearts be troubled. Believe[l] in God, believe also in
me. 2In my Father's house there are many
dwelling places. If it were not so, would
I have told you that I go to prepare a
place for you?[m] 3And if I go and prepare a
place for you, I will come again and will
take you to myself, so that where I am,
there you may be also. 4And you know
the way to the place where I am going."[n]
5Thomas said to him, "Lord, we do not
know where you are going. How can
we know the way?" 6Jesus said to him,
"I am the way, and the truth, and the
life. No one comes to the Father except

l 14.1 Or *You believe*

m 14.2 Or *If it were not so, I would have told you; for I go to prepare a place for you*

n 14.4 Other ancient authorities read *Where I am going you know, and the way you know*

14:8 Philip's wish was beautiful. Why did Jesus scold him?

In everyone's heart there is the desire, even if hidden, to see God. Jesus explained the way to satisfy this desire, but Philip still did not understand. A disciple of Jesus sees the Father when he or she looks at and follows Jesus, who defined himself as the Way, the Truth, and the Life.

14:13 Can I even pray for my team to win the championship?

This isn't quite what Jesus was talking about. To ask in Jesus' name does not mean simply to add his name to every wish that goes through our head. Jesus wants us to desire as he desires and to ask for that which he asks. That is, we should strive to always do the Father's will.

through me. 7If you know me, you will know[o] my
Father also. From now on you do know him and
have seen him."
8 Philip said to him, "Lord, show us
the Father, and we will be satisfied."
9Jesus said to him, "Have I been with
you all this time, Philip, and you
still do not know me? Whoever
has seen me has seen the Father.
How can you say, 'Show us the
Father'? 10Do you not believe
that I am in the Father and the
Father is in me? The words that
I say to you I do not speak on
my own; but the Father who
dwells in me does his works.
11Believe me that I am in the
Father and the Father is in me;
but if you do not, then believe
me because of the works themselves.
12Very truly, I tell you, the
one who believes in me will also
do the works that I do and, in fact,
will do greater works than these,
because I am going to the Father. 13I
will do whatever you ask in my name,
so that the Father may be glorified in the
Son. 14If in my name you ask me[p] for anything, I will do it.

o **14.7** Other ancient authorities read *If you had known me, you would have known*

p **14.14** Other ancient authorities lack *me*

The Promise of the Holy Spirit

15 "If you love me, you will keep[q] my commandments. [16]And I will ask the
Father, and he will give you another Advocate,[r] to be with you forever. [17]This
is the Spirit of truth, whom the world cannot receive, because it neither sees
him nor knows him. You know him, because he abides with you, and he will
be in[s] you.

18 "I will not leave you orphaned; I am coming to
you. [19]In a little while the world will no longer
see me, but you will see me; because I
live, you also will live. [20]On that day you
will know that I am in my Father, and
you in me, and I in you. [21]They who
have my commandments and keep
them are those who love me; and those
who love me will be loved by my
Father, and I will love them and reveal
myself to them." [22]Judas (not Iscariot)
said to him, "Lord, how is it that you
will reveal yourself to us, and not to
the world?" [23]Jesus answered him,
"Those who love me will keep my word,
and my Father will love them, and we will
come to them and make our home with
them. [24]Whoever does not love me does not
keep my words; and the word that you hear is
not mine, but is from the Father who sent me.

q **14.15** Other ancient authorities read *me, keep*
r **14.16** Or *Helper*
s **14.17** Or *among*

14:27 Why is Jesus' peace different from the world's peace?

The world thinks of peace as simply the absence of war—which is often caused by fear. God's peace, instead, is a gift that converts the heart of the individual to trust him above all things and so changes the world one person at a time.

14:30 Ruler of this world

The devil, who can reign in people's hearts, is opposed to Jesus. By dying on the cross, however, the Lord conquered and condemned him, just when the opposite seemed to be happening.

25 "I have said these things to you while I am
still with you. 26 But the Advocate,[t] the Holy
Spirit, whom the Father will send in my
name, will teach you everything, and
remind you of all that I have said to
you. 27 Peace I leave with you; my
peace I give to you. I do not give to
you as the world
gives. Do not let
your hearts be
troubled, and do
not let them be
afraid. 28 You heard me
say to you, 'I am going
away, and I am coming
to you.' If you loved me,
you would rejoice that I am
going to the Father, because
the Father is greater than I. 29 And
now I have told you this before it
occurs, so that when it does occur, you
may believe. 30 I will no longer talk much
with you, for the ruler of this world is
coming. He has no power over me; 31 but I
do as the Father has commanded me, so
that the world may know that I love the
Father. Rise, let us be on our way.

t **14.26** Or *Helper*
u **15.2** The same Greek root refers to pruning and cleansing
v **15.3** The same Greek root refers to pruning and cleansing
w **15.8** Or *be*

Jesus the True Vine

15 "I am the true vine, and my Father is the vinegrower. 2He removes
every branch in me that bears no fruit. Every branch that bears fruit he
prunes[u] to make it bear more fruit. 3You have
already been cleansed[v] by the word that I
have spoken to you. 4Abide in me as I
abide in you. Just as the branch cannot
bear fruit by itself unless it abides in
the vine, neither can you unless
you abide in me. 5I am the vine,
you are the branches. Those who
abide in me and I in them bear
much fruit, because apart from
me you can do nothing. 6Who-
ever does not abide in me is
thrown away like a branch
and withers; such branches
are gathered, thrown into
the fire, and burned. 7If
you abide in me, and my
words abide in you, ask for
whatever you wish, and it
will be done for you. 8My
Father is glorified by this,
that you bear much fruit and
become[w] my disciples. 9As
the Father has loved me,

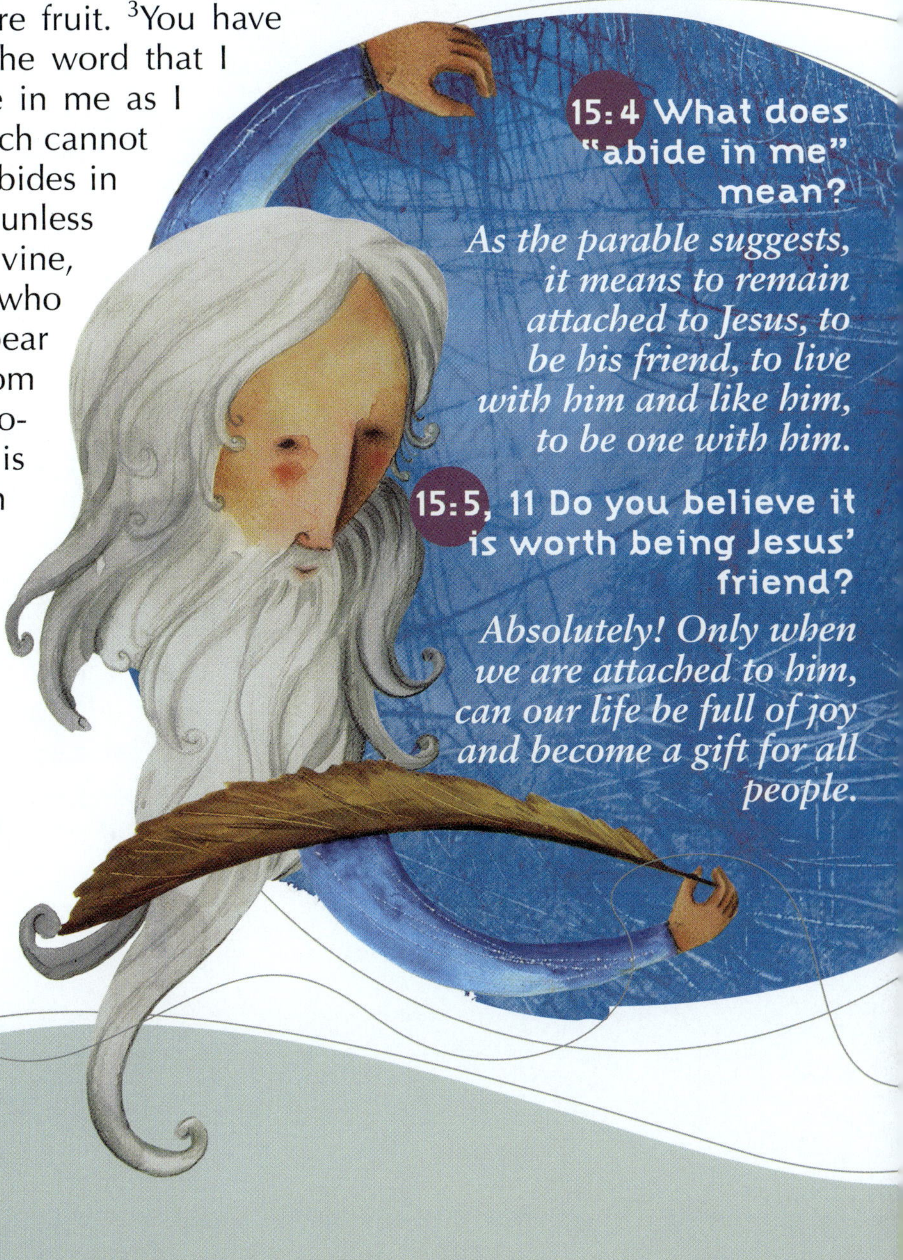

15:4 What does "abide in me" mean?

As the parable suggests, it means to remain attached to Jesus, to be his friend, to live with him and like him, to be one with him.

15:5, 11 Do you believe it is worth being Jesus' friend?

Absolutely! Only when we are attached to him, can our life be full of joy and become a gift for all people.

so I have loved you; abide in
my love. 10If you keep my commandments, you will abide in
my love, just as I have kept my
Father's commandments and abide in
his love. 11I have said these things to you
so that my joy may be in you, and that your
joy may be complete.

12 "This is my commandment, that you
love one another as I have loved you. 13No one
has greater love than this, to lay down one's life
for one's friends. 14You are my friends if you do
what I command you. 15I do not call you servants[x] any longer, because the servant[y] does
not know what the master is doing; but I
have called you friends, because I have
made known to you everything that I have
heard from my Father. 16You did not
choose me but I chose you. And I
appointed you to go and bear fruit, fruit
that will last, so that the Father will give
you whatever you ask him in my name. 17I
am giving you these commands so that you
may love one another.

x **15.15** Gk *slaves*
y **15.15** Gk *slave*

The World's Hatred

18 "If the world hates you, be aware that it hated
me before it hated you. 19 If you belonged to the
world,[z] the world would love you as its own.
Because you do not belong to the world,
but I have chosen you out of the world—
therefore the world hates you. 20 Remember
the word that I said to you, 'Servants[a] are not
greater than their master.' If they persecuted
me, they will persecute you; if they kept my
word, they will keep yours also. 21 But they
will do all these things to you on account
of my name, because they do not know him
who sent me. 22 If I had not come and spoken
to them, they would not have sin; but now they
have no excuse for their sin. 23 Whoever hates
me hates my Father also. 24 If I had not done among
them the works that no one else did, they would not
have sin. But now they have seen and hated both me
and my Father. 25 It was to fulfill the word that is written
in their law, 'They hated me without a cause.'

26 "When the Advocate[b] comes, whom I will send
to you from the Father, the Spirit of truth who comes
from the Father, he will testify on my behalf. 27 You also
are to testify because you have been with me from the
beginning.

15:18 Does the world really hate Christians?
In using the word "world" here, I was thinking of the people hostile to God and incapable of seeing what Jesus has done. When people are hostile to God, they refuse Jesus and his friends.

z **15.19** Gk *were of the world*
a **15.20** Gk *Slaves*
b **15.26** Or *Helper*

16:2 Did what Jesus predict really happen?

Yes. Just as I was writing my Gospel, Christians were expelled from the synagogues and persecuted. If you pay attention to the news, you will discover that even today in some parts of the world Jesus' disciples are persecuted and even martyred.

16:5 I would have asked the question. Where did Jesus want to go?

He wanted to return to the Father. Jesus has not abandoned us, in fact, he has given us his Holy Spirit to guide us in God's ways.

16 "I have said these things to you to
keep you from stumbling. 2They will put
you out of the synagogues. Indeed, an
hour is coming when those who kill
you will think that by doing so they
are offering worship to God. 3And
they will do this because they
have not known the Father or
me. 4But I have said these
things to you so that when
their hour comes you may
remember that I told you
about them.

The Work of the Spirit

"I did not say these things
to you from the beginning,
because I was with you. 5But
now I am going to him who
sent me; yet none of you asks
me, 'Where are you going?'
6But because I have said these
things to you, sorrow has filled
your hearts. 7Nevertheless I tell you
the truth: it is to your advantage that

I go away, for if I do not go away, the Advocate[c] will not come
to you; but if I go, I will send him to you. 8And when he comes,
he will prove the world wrong about[d] sin and righteousness and
judgment: 9about sin, because they do not believe in me; 10about
righteousness, because I am going to the Father and you will see
me no longer; 11about judgment, because the ruler of this world
has been condemned.

12 "I still have many things to say to you, but you cannot bear
them now. 13When the Spirit of truth comes, he will guide you
into all the truth; for he will not speak on his own, but will speak
whatever he hears, and he will declare to you the things that
are to come. 14He will glorify me, because he will take
what is mine and declare it to you. 15All that the Father
has is mine. For this reason I said that he will take
what is mine and declare it to you.

Sorrow Will Turn into Joy

16 "A little while, and you will no longer see
me, and again a little while, and you will
see me." 17Then some of his disciples said
to one another, "What does he mean by
saying to us, 'A little while, and you
will no longer see me, and again
a little while, and you will see

16:16 What did Jesus mean by this?

If you read the following verses, you will find out that we too had a hard time understanding these words. They are a reference to Jesus' death and resurrection. This is explained also through the image of the woman in labor (verse 21).

c **16.7** Or *Helper*
d **16.8** Or *convict the world of*

me'; and 'Because I am going to the
Father'?" [18]They said, "What does he
mean by this 'a little while'? We do not
know what he is talking about." [19]Jesus
knew that they wanted to ask him, so he
said to them, "Are you discussing among
yourselves what I meant when I said, 'A little
while, and you will no longer see me, and again
a little while, and you will see me'? [20]Very truly,
I tell you, you will weep and mourn, but the world
will rejoice; you will have pain, but your pain will
turn into joy. [21]When a woman is in labor, she has pain,
because her hour has come. But when her child is born,
she no longer remembers the anguish because of the joy
of having brought a human being into the world. [22]So you
have pain now; but I will see you again, and your hearts will
rejoice, and no one will take your joy from you. [23]On that
day you will ask nothing of me.[e] Very truly, I tell you, if you
ask anything of the Father in my name, he will give it to you.[f]
[24]Until now you have not asked for anything in my name. Ask
and you will receive, so that your joy may be complete.

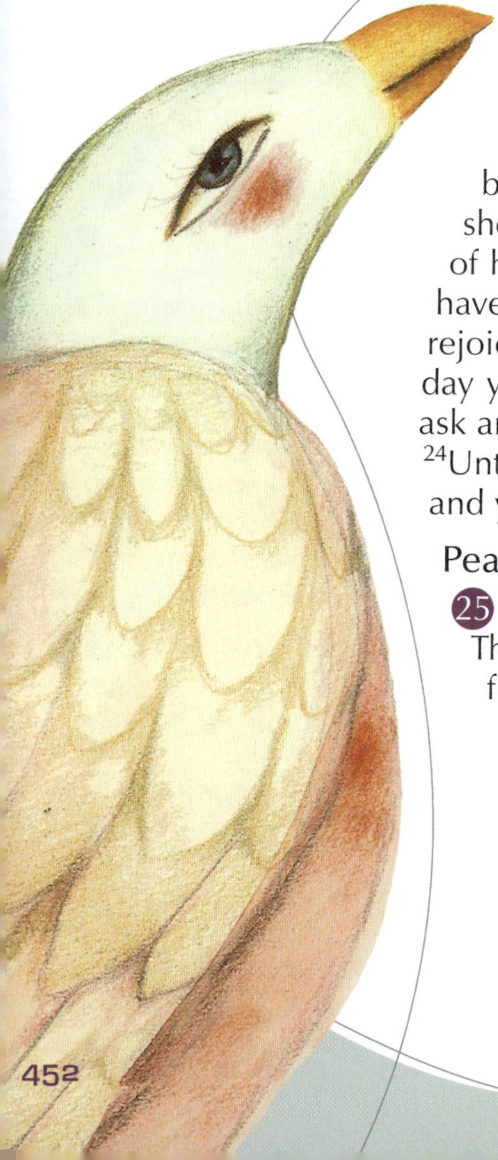

Peace for the Disciples

25 "I have said these things to you in figures of speech.
The hour is coming when I will no longer speak to you in
figures, but will tell you plainly of the Father. [26]On that

e **16.23** Or *will ask me no question*

f **16.23** Other ancient authorities read *Father, he will give it to you in my name*

g **16.27** Other ancient authorities read *the Father*

day you will ask in my name. I do not say to you
that I will ask the Father on your behalf; 27for
the Father himself loves you, because you
have loved me and have believed that
I came from God.[g] 28I came from the
Father and have come into the world;
again, I am leaving the world and
am going to the Father."

29 His disciples said, "Yes, now
you are speaking plainly, not in
any figure of speech! 30Now we
know that you know all things,
and do not need to have anyone
question you; by this we believe
that you came from God."
31Jesus answered them, "Do you
now believe? 32The hour is
coming, indeed it has come,
when you will be scattered, each
one to his home, and you will leave
me alone. Yet I am not alone because
the Father is with me. 33I have said this
to you, so that in me you may have
peace. In the world you face persecution. But take courage; I have conquered the world!"

16:25 What does "in figures of speech" mean?

Up until now, Jesus has used stories to express difficult concepts. Now, his love will be plain to see on the cross.

16:32 I would never leave Jesus alone!

That's what we thought too, but when they arrested him, we were all filled with fear and fled.

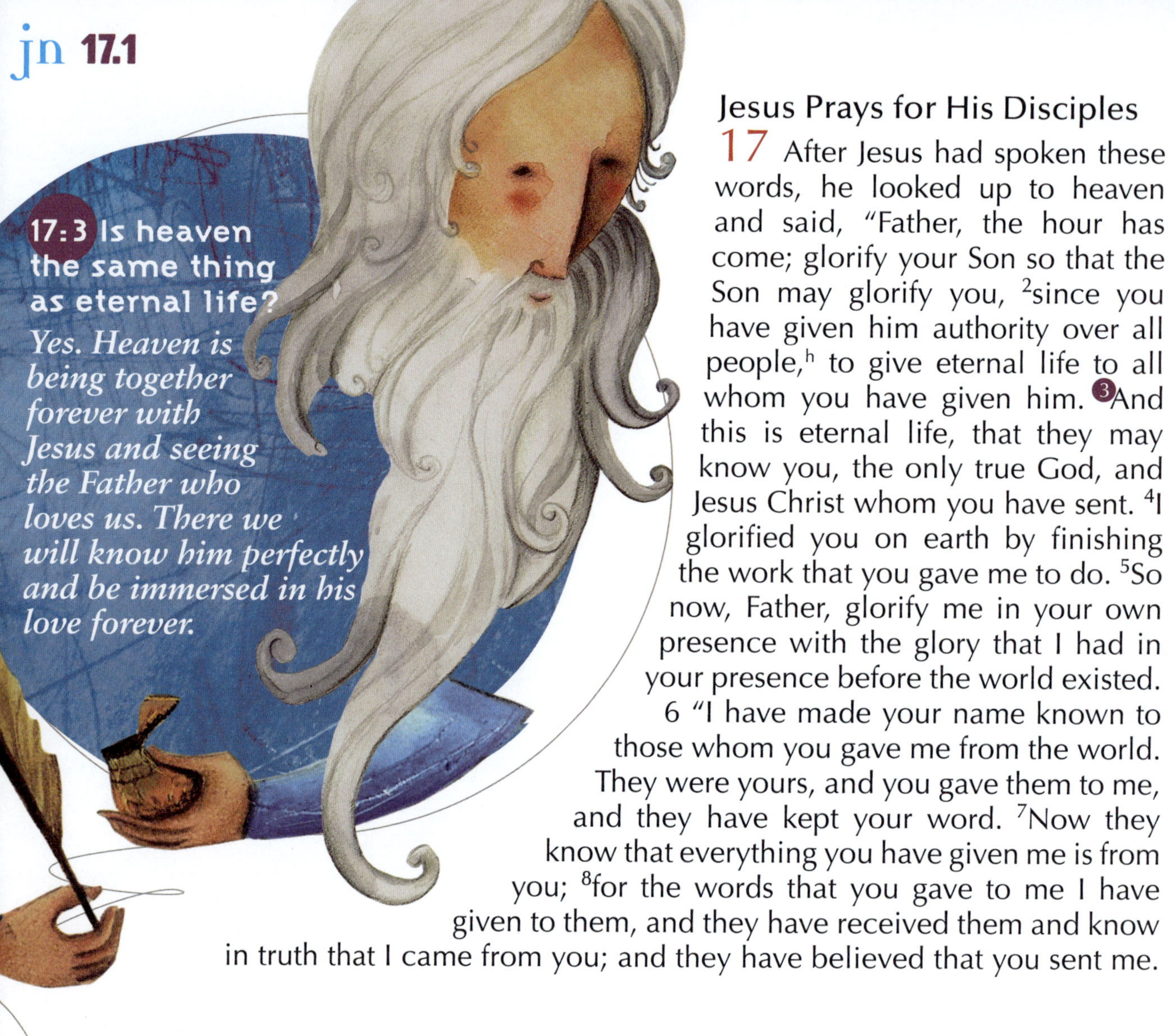

17:3 Is heaven the same thing as eternal life?
Yes. Heaven is being together forever with Jesus and seeing the Father who loves us. There we will know him perfectly and be immersed in his love forever.

Jesus Prays for His Disciples

17 After Jesus had spoken these
words, he looked up to heaven
and said, "Father, the hour has
come; glorify your Son so that the
Son may glorify you, [2]since you
have given him authority over all
people,[h] to give eternal life to all
whom you have given him. (3)And
this is eternal life, that they may
know you, the only true God, and
Jesus Christ whom you have sent. [4]I
glorified you on earth by finishing
the work that you gave me to do. [5]So
now, Father, glorify me in your own
presence with the glory that I had in
your presence before the world existed.
6 "I have made your name known to
those whom you gave me from the world.
They were yours, and you gave them to me,
and they have kept your word. [7]Now they
know that everything you have given me is from
you; [8]for the words that you gave to me I have
given to them, and they have received them and know
in truth that I came from you; and they have believed that you sent me.

h **17.2** Gk *flesh*

[9]I am asking on their behalf; I am not asking on behalf of the world, but on
behalf of those whom you gave me, because they are yours. [10]All mine are
yours, and yours are mine; and I have been glorified in them.
[11]And now I am no longer in the world, but they are in
the world, and I am coming to you. Holy Father,
protect them in your name that you have given
me, so that they may be one, as we are one.
[12]While I was with them, I protected them in
your name that[i] you have given me. I guarded
them, and not one of them was lost except
the one destined to be lost,[j] so that the scripture might be fulfilled. [13]But now I am
coming to you, and I speak these things in
the world so that they may have my joy
made complete in themselves.[k] (14) I have
given them your word, and the world
has hated them because they do
not belong to the world, just as I
do not belong to the world. [15]I
am not asking you to take them out of
the world, but I ask you to protect them
from the evil one.[l] [16]They do not belong to
the world, just as I do not belong to the world.
[17]Sanctify them in the truth; your word is truth.
[18]As you have sent me into the world, so I have
sent them into the world. [19]And for their sakes I
sanctify myself, so that they also may be sanctified
in truth.

17:14 Are Catholic Christians of the world or not?

Jesus' friends live in the world, but do not embrace its lifestyles. For example, they do not seek success, wealth, or pleasure as the most important things in their life. Rather Jesus' disciples seek first to do God's will—the good of every creature, following Jesus' own example.

i **17.12** Other ancient authorities read *protected in your name those whom*
j **17.12** Gk *except the son of destruction*
k **17.13** Or *among themselves*
l **17.15** Or *from evil*

20 "I ask not only on behalf of these, but also on behalf of
those who will believe in me through their word, [21]that they may
all be one. As you, Father, are in me and I am in you, may they
also be in us,[m] so that the world may believe that you have sent
me. [22]The glory that you have given me I have given them, so
that they may be one, as we are one, [23]I in them and you in me,
that they may become completely one, so that the world
may know that you have sent me and have loved them
even as you have loved me. [24]Father, I desire that
those also, whom you have given me, may be with
me where I am, to see my glory, which you have
given me because you loved me before the
foundation of the world.

25 "Righteous Father, the world does
not know you, but I know you; and these
know that you have sent me. [26]I made
your name known to them, and I will
make it known, so that the love
with which you have loved me
may be in them, and I in
them."

17:20 He was praying for me too!

Yes. And do you see what he asked for you and for Christians of every age? He prays for the gift of unity, the grace to be one despite differences, all united in and through the Holy Trinity.

m **17.21** Other ancient authorities read *be one in us*

The Account of the Passion: "It is finished." (Jn 18:1–19:42)

We have before us John's account of Jesus' passion, the beating heart of every Gospel. The Johannine Jesus has absolute mastery of every situation—Jesus is never depicted as weak or as a failure. While being judged, condemned, and raised on the cross, Jesus always displays the demeanor and dignity of a true king. Pilate unknowingly confirms this with the triple inscription he had placed on the cross (19:19–22). The cross is usually seen as an instrument of torture. However, for the fourth evangelist the cross is really the throne of glory from which Christ rules the world. It is from there that the Son of God completes the Father's universal salvific plan (19:30). Lastly, the beloved disciple's presence at the crucifixion is essential to the credibility of the testimony on which the fourth Gospel is based (19:35).

The Betrayal and Arrest of Jesus

18 After Jesus had spoken these words,
he went out with his disciples across the
Kidron valley to a place where there was
a garden, which he and his disciples
entered. [2]Now Judas, who betrayed
him, also knew the place, because
Jesus often met there with his disciples. [3]So Judas brought a detachment
of soldiers together with police from
the chief priests and the Pharisees,
and they came there with lanterns
and torches and weapons. [4]Then Jesus,
knowing all that was to happen to him,
came forward and asked them, "Whom
are you looking for?" [5]They answered, "Jesus of

18:2, 5
How terrible to be known as the one who "betrayed" one's own teacher.
I chose to write it twice to help you understand that in that moment Judas made a very bad decision.

18:6 Why did they fall to the ground? *When Jesus said, "I am he," it reminded them of how God called himself before Moses in Exodus. It reminded the soldiers that God was present and they were frightened.*

18:8 Jesus did not seem to be afraid. *I wanted to emphasize this characteristic of Jesus in my Gospel. Jesus is the master of what is happening. In this way Jesus shows that he freely chose to allow what was about to happen to him.*

Nazareth."[n] Jesus replied, "I am he."[o] Judas, who betrayed
him, was standing with them. 6 When Jesus[p] said to
them, "I am he,"[q] they stepped back and fell to
the ground. 7 Again he asked them, "Whom
are you looking for?" And they said, "Jesus
of Nazareth."[r] 8 Jesus answered, "I told you
that I am he.[s] So if you are looking for
me, let these men go." 9 This was to fulfill
the word that he had spoken, "I did not
lose a single one of those whom you
gave me." 10 Then Simon Peter, who
had a sword, drew it, struck the high
priest's slave, and cut off his right ear.
The slave's name was Malchus. 11 Jesus
said to Peter, "Put your sword back
into its sheath. Am I not to drink the
cup that the Father has given me?"

Jesus before the High Priest

12 So the soldiers, their officer, and the
Jewish police arrested Jesus and bound
him. 13 First they took him to Annas, who
was the father-in-law of Caiaphas, the high
priest that year. 14 Caiaphas was the one who
had advised the Jews that it was better to have
one person die for the people.

n **18.5** Gk *the Nazorean*
o **18.5** Gk *I am*
p **18.6** Gk *he*
q **18.6** Gk *I am*
r **18.7** Gk *the Nazorean*
s **18.8** Gk *I am*

Peter Denies Jesus

15 Simon Peter and another disciple followed Jesus. Since that disciple was known to the high priest, he went with Jesus into the courtyard of the high priest, [16]but Peter was standing outside at the gate. So the other disciple, who was known to the high priest, went out, spoke to the woman who guarded the gate, and brought Peter in. [17]The woman said to Peter, "You are not also one of this man's disciples, are you?" He said, "I am not." [18]Now the slaves and the police had made a charcoal fire because it was cold, and they were standing around it and warming themselves. Peter also was standing with them and warming himself.

The High Priest Questions Jesus

19 Then the high priest questioned Jesus about his disciples and about his teaching. [20]Jesus answered, "I have spoken openly to the world; I have always taught in synagogues and in the temple, where all the Jews come together. I have said

18:12 Who was Annas?

Annas is only found in my Gospel. He was a very powerful Jewish man who carried out a kind of pre-interrogation of Jesus.

nothing in secret. [21]Why do you ask me?
Ask those who heard what I said to them;
they know what I said." [22]When he had
said this, one of the police standing
nearby struck Jesus on the face, saying,
"Is that how you answer the high
priest?" [23]Jesus answered, "If I have
spoken wrongly, testify to the wrong.
But if I have spoken rightly, why do
you strike me?" [24]Then Annas sent him
bound to Caiaphas the high priest.

Peter Denies Jesus Again

25 Now Simon Peter was standing and
warming himself. They asked him, "You
are not also one of his disciples, are
you?" He denied it and said, "I am not."
[26]One of the slaves of the high priest, a
relative of the man whose ear Peter had
cut off, asked, "Did I not see you in the
garden with him?" [27]Again Peter denied it,
and at that moment the cock crowed.

18:25–27 Was Peter ashamed of himself for having denied being Jesus' disciple?

In that moment Peter was very afraid of being arrested and tortured and wanted to save himself. It was only days later, when speaking with the risen Jesus, that Peter had an opportunity to say to Jesus what he really thought about the Lord (chapter 21).

t **18.28** Gk *the praetorium*
u **18.28** Gk *the praetorium*
v **18.33** Gk *the praetorium*

Jesus before Pilate

28 Then they took Jesus from Caiaphas to
Pilate's headquarters.[t] It was early in the
morning. They themselves did not enter the
headquarters,[u] so as to avoid ritual defile-
ment and to be able to eat the Passover. 29So
Pilate went out to them and said, "What accusation do you bring against this man?" 30They
answered, "If this man were not a criminal,
we would not have handed him over to you."
31Pilate said to them, "Take him yourselves
and judge him according to your law." The Jews
replied, "We are not permitted to put anyone to
death." 32(This was to fulfill what Jesus had said
when he indicated the kind of death he was
to die.)
33 Then Pilate entered the headquarters[v] again, summoned Jesus, and asked
him, "Are you the King of the Jews?"
34Jesus answered, "Do you ask this on
your own, or did others tell you about
me?" 35Pilate replied, "I am not a
Jew, am I? Your own nation and the
chief priests have handed you over
to me. What have you done?" 36Jesus
answered, "My kingdom is not from
this world. If my kingdom were from

18:28 Headquarters

This is also known as the Praetorium, where the Roman governor, who represented the emperor in Jerusalem, carried out daily business. Because it belonged to pagans and the enemy of Israel, the Jews did not want to enter this building.

18:33–37 Was Jesus a king or not?

Pilate wanted to know if Jesus identified himself as an earthly king to determine whether he should condemn Jesus or not. The Lord responded that he was a king—but a king altogether different from what Pilate or anyone else had in mind.

this world, my followers would be fighting to keep
me from being handed over to the Jews. But as it is,
my kingdom is not from here." 37Pilate asked him,
"So you are a king?" Jesus answered, "You say that
I am a king. For this I was born, and for this I came
into the world, to testify to the truth. Everyone who
belongs to the truth listens to my voice." 38Pilate
asked him, "What is truth?"

Jesus Sentenced to Death

After he had said this, he went out to the Jews again
and told them, "I find no case against him. 39But
you have a custom that I release someone for you at
the Passover. Do you want me to release for you the
King of the Jews?" 40They shouted in reply, "Not this
man, but Barabbas!" Now Barabbas was a bandit.
19 Then Pilate took Jesus and had him flogged.
2And the soldiers wove a crown of thorns and
put it on his head, and they dressed him in a
purple robe. 3They kept coming up to him,
saying, "Hail, King of the Jews!" and striking
him on the face. 4Pilate went out again and
said to them, "Look, I am bringing him out to
you to let you know that I find no case against
him." 5So Jesus came out, wearing the crown of
thorns and the purple robe. Pilate said to them,
"Here is the man!" 6When the chief priests and the
police saw him, they shouted, "Crucify him! Crucify him!" Pilate said to them, "Take him yourselves

and crucify him; I find no case
against him." 7The Jews answered
him, "We have a law, and according
to that law he ought to die because he
has claimed to be the Son of God."
8 Now when Pilate heard this, he
was more afraid than ever. 9He entered
his headquarters[w] again and asked
Jesus, "Where are you from?" But
Jesus gave him no answer. 10Pilate
therefore said to him, "Do you
refuse to speak to me? Do you not
know that I have power to release
you, and power to crucify you?"
11Jesus answered him, "You
would have no power over me
unless it had been given you
from above; therefore the one
who handed me over to you is
guilty of a greater sin." 12From
then on Pilate tried to release
him, but the Jews cried out, "If
you release this man, you are no
friend of the emperor. Everyone who
claims to be a king sets himself
against the emperor."

19:5 Did Pilate realize the significance of his own words?

No. Pilate probably hoped the Jews would have thought Jesus had been punished enough and be willing to spare his life. But Pilate has no idea how right he is—Jesus, who suffers out of love for us, is the perfect man.

19:12 Was Pilate the emperor's friend?

In those days to be a "friend of the emperor" meant having an honorary title. The Jews used this phrase to corner Pilate into doing what they wanted.

w **19.9** Gk *the praetorium*

19:14–15 I do not understand. It seems that the roles have been reversed.

In a way, yes. It is Pilate, a pagan, who proclaims that Jesus truly is the King of the Jews. Meanwhile the Jews state that their only king is the Roman emperor, which means that they denied that God was their king. So, the Jews refuse the kingship of the Father by refusing the Son, Jesus.

19:17 Does anyone help Jesus?

The fourth Gospel leaves out the detail of Simon of Cyrene (Mt 27:32). In this way, John hopes to depict Jesus as the Lord and Savior who does not need help on the way to his death.

13 When Pilate heard these words, he brought Jesus outside and sat[x] on the judge's bench at a place called The Stone Pavement, or in Hebrew[y]
Gabbatha. 14 Now it was the day of Preparation for the Passover; and it was about noon. He said to the Jews, "Here is your King!"
15 They cried out, "Away with him! Away with him! Crucify him!" Pilate asked them, "Shall I crucify your King?" The chief priests answered, "We have no king but the emperor."
16 Then he handed him over to them to be crucified.

The Crucifixion of Jesus

So they took Jesus;
17 and carrying the cross by himself, he went out to what is called The Place of the Skull, which in Hebrew[z] is called Golgotha.
18 There they crucified him, and with him two others, one on either side, with Jesus between them.
19 Pilate also had an inscription written and put on the cross. It read,

x **19.13** Or *seated him*
y **19.13** That is, *Aramaic*
z **19.17** That is, *Aramaic*

"Jesus of Nazareth,[a] the King of the Jews."
[20]Many of the Jews read this inscription,
because the place where Jesus was
crucified was near the city; and it was
written in Hebrew,[b] in Latin, and
in Greek. [21]Then the chief priests
of the Jews said to Pilate, "Do not
write, 'The King of the Jews,' but,
'This man said, I am King of the
Jews.' " [22]Pilate answered, "What I
have written I have written." [23]When
the soldiers had crucified Jesus, they
took his clothes and divided them
into four parts, one for each soldier.
They also took his tunic; now the tunic
was seamless, woven in one piece from
the top. [24]So they said to one another, "Let
us not tear it, but cast lots for it to see who
will get it." This was to fulfill what the scripture says,

"They divided my clothes among
themselves,
and for my clothing they cast lots."

19:19–22 So Pilate wrote the truth?
Exactly. On the cross—his throne—Jesus fully reveals himself as the King of the Jews while his people, once again, reject him.

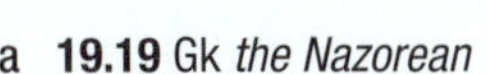

a **19.19** Gk *the Nazorean*
b **19.20** That is, *Aramaic*

19:26 It is nice to know that Jesus remembered his mother before he died.

By saying those words and calling her "woman," Jesus told Mary that she would now be not only his mother, but the mother of every disciple.

19:30 Gave up his spirit

There are two meanings here. The first is to physically die. Death is understood as separation of body and soul. The second is to exhale. Dying, Jesus breathed out his Holy Spirit giving it to all people.

25 And that is what the soldiers did.
Meanwhile, standing near the cross of
Jesus were his mother, and his mother's
sister, Mary the wife of Clopas, and
Mary Magdalene. 26 When Jesus saw
his mother and the disciple whom he
loved standing beside her, he said to
his mother, "Woman, here is your
son." 27 Then he said to the disciple,
"Here is your mother." And from that
hour the disciple took her into his
own home.
28 After this, when Jesus knew that
all was now finished, he said (in order to
fulfill the scripture), "I am thirsty." 29 A jar
full of sour wine was standing there. So
they put a sponge full of the wine on a
branch of hyssop and held it to his mouth.
30 When Jesus had received the wine, he
said, "It is finished." Then he bowed his
head and gave up his spirit.

19:31 Day of Preparation
Also known as *Parasceve*, it is the solemn vigil of the feast of Passover.

Jesus' Side Is Pierced

31 Since it was the day of Preparation, the Jews
did not want the bodies left on the cross during the
sabbath, especially because that sabbath was a day
of great solemnity. So they asked Pilate to have the
legs of the crucified men broken and the bodies
removed. 32 Then the soldiers came and broke the
legs of the first and of the other who had been crucified with him. 33 But when they came to Jesus and
saw that he was already dead, they did not break
his legs. 34 Instead, one of the soldiers pierced
his side with a spear, and at
once blood and water came
out. 35 (He who saw this has
testified so that you also may
believe. His testimony is true,
and he knows[c] that he tells the
truth.) 36 These things occurred
so that the scripture might be
fulfilled, "None of his bones
shall be broken." 37 And again
another passage of scripture says,
"They will look on the one whom
they have pierced."

19:31 Why break the legs of the crucified persons?
It prevented the condemned from lifting themselves up to breathe easier and thus sped up their death.

c **19.35** Or *there is one who knows*

The Burial of Jesus

38 After these things, Joseph of Arimathea,
who was a disciple of Jesus, though a
secret one because of his fear of the
Jews, asked Pilate to let him take away
the body of Jesus. Pilate gave him permission; so he came and removed
his body. 39Nicodemus, who had
at first come to Jesus by night, also
came, bringing a mixture of myrrh
and aloes, weighing about a hundred pounds. 40They took the body
of Jesus and wrapped it with the
spices in linen cloths, according
to the burial custom of the Jews.
41Now there was a garden in the
place where he was crucified,
and in the garden there was a new
tomb in which no one had ever
been laid. 42And so, because it
was the Jewish day of Preparation,
and the tomb was nearby, they
laid Jesus there.

19:34 If I fall and scrape my knee, only blood comes out, not water!

I emphasized this detail to remind believers that the dying of Jesus (blood) gave life to all (water).

19:39 Myrrh and aloes

Perfumes used by the Jews to prepare the bodies for burial.

jn **20.1**

The Resurrection Accounts: "Blessed are those who have not seen and yet have come to believe . . ." (Jn 20:1–31)

That first day of the week (20:1, 19) marked the end of one era and the beginning of another. The traditional Jewish week had as its climax the Sabbath/shabbat. Now the resurrection of Jesus opens up a new day for worshipping God. It is a time given directly by Jesus which the first Christians received as "the day of the Lord." The accounts of the resurrection in chapter 20 both take place on a Sunday, or "first day of the week" (20:1, 19, 26). They bring together the themes of seeing and believing—already addressed in the "Book of Signs." So far, throughout the Gospel of John, belief came after seeing the events and miracles of Jesus (20:8, 18, 25, 29a). But what about future generations? They would not be able to witness Jesus! In verse 29b, Jesus states that they will be even more blessed because they will believe based on hearing the testimony of those who saw. Instead of seeing Jesus with their eyes, which can become clouded and blind, they can trust the beloved disciple's acute eyes, whose testimony is preserved in the pages of the fourth Gospel.

20:1, 5, 7
Stones removed, linen wrappings on the ground, the head cloth rolled up. What happened in Jesus' tomb?

No one saw what happened, but Jesus' body was no longer there. The only things that remained were the signs that something great and unique had occurred.

The Resurrection of Jesus

20 Early on the first day of the
week, while it was still dark, Mary
Magdalene came to the tomb and
saw that the stone had been removed
from the tomb. 2So she ran and went to
Simon Peter and the other disciple, the
one whom Jesus loved, and said to them,

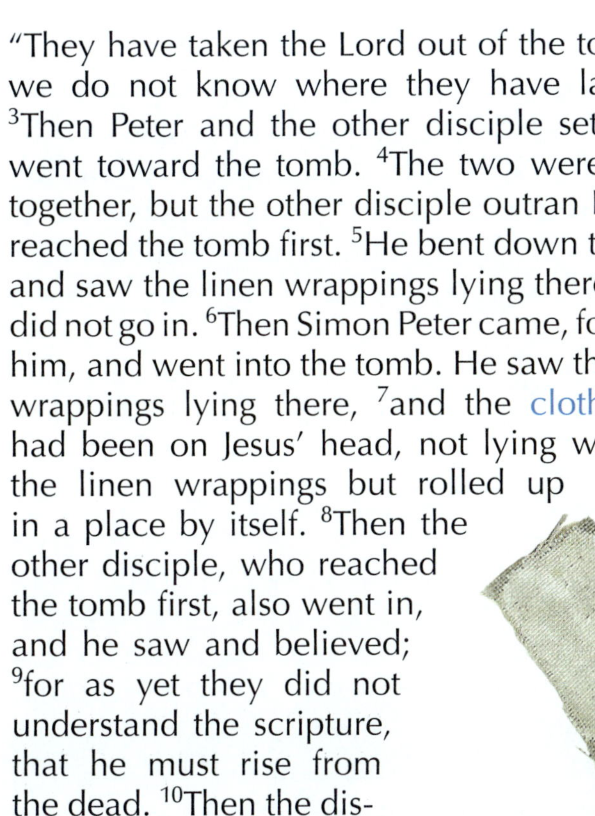

"They have taken the Lord out of the tomb, and
we do not know where they have laid him."
3Then Peter and the other disciple set out and
went toward the tomb. 4The two were running
together, but the other disciple outran Peter and
reached the tomb first. 5He bent down to look in
and saw the linen wrappings lying there, but he
did not go in. 6Then Simon Peter came, following
him, and went into the tomb. He saw the linen
wrappings lying there, 7and the cloth that
had been on Jesus' head, not lying with
the linen wrappings but rolled up
in a place by itself. 8Then the
other disciple, who reached
the tomb first, also went in,
and he saw and believed;
9for as yet they did not
understand the scripture,
that he must rise from
the dead. 10Then the dis-
ciples returned to their
homes.

20:7 Cloth
The veil that was placed on the face of the corpse before burial

20:14 Why did Mary Magdalene not recognize Jesus?

First, she did not expect to see Jesus alive. Second, the risen Jesus' body was not exactly the same as that which she had known. She recognized him when he called her by her name.

Jesus Appears to Mary Magdalene

11 But Mary stood weeping outside the tomb.
As she wept, she bent over to look[d] into the
tomb; 12and she saw two angels in white, sitting where the body of Jesus had been lying,
one at the head and the
other at the feet. 13They
said to her, "Woman, why
are you weeping?" She said
to them, "They have taken
away my Lord, and I do not
know where they have laid
him." 14When she had said this,
she turned around and saw Jesus
standing there, but she did not
know that it was Jesus. 15Jesus said to
her, "Woman, why are you weeping?
Whom are you looking for?" Supposing
him to be the gardener, she said to him, "Sir,
if you have carried him away, tell me where you
have laid him, and I will take him away." 16Jesus

d **20.11** Gk lacks *to look*

said to her, "Mary!" She turned and said to him in Hebrew,[e] "Rabbouni!" (which means Teacher). 17Jesus said to her, "Do not hold on to me, because I have not yet ascended to the Father. But go to my brothers and say to them, 'I am ascending to my Father and your Father, to my God and your God.'" 18Mary Magdalene went and announced to the disciples, "I have seen the Lord"; and she told them that he had said these things to her.

Jesus Appears to the Disciples

19 When it was evening on that day, the first day of the week, and the doors of the house where the disciples had met were locked for fear of the Jews, Jesus came and stood among them and said, "Peace be with you."

20:15 Was Jesus moved by Mary's tears?

Yes. Jesus knows and accepts his disciples' pain. In this case he used her pain to open Mary to the hope of the resurrection.

20:19 Jesus appeared to the Apostles on Sunday?

Exactly! That is why, since then, Christians commemorate Jesus' passion, death, and resurrection by gathering together and celebrating the Eucharist every Sunday, the day of the risen Lord.

e **20.16** That is, *Aramaic*

20 After he said this, he showed them his hands
and his side. Then the disciples rejoiced when
they saw the Lord. 21 Jesus said to them again,
"Peace be with you. As the Father has sent
me, so I send you." 22 When he had said
this, he breathed on them and said to them,
"Receive the Holy Spirit. 23 If you forgive the
sins of any, they are forgiven them; if you
retain the sins of any, they are retained."

Jesus and Thomas

24 But Thomas (who was called the Twin[f]),
one of the twelve, was not with them
when Jesus came. 25 So the other disciples
told him, "We have seen the Lord." But he
said to them, "Unless I see the mark of the
nails in his hands, and put my finger in the
mark of the nails and my hand in his side, I
will not believe."

26 A week later his disciples were again
in the house, and Thomas was with them.
Although the doors were shut, Jesus came and

f **20.24** Gk *Didymus*

stood among them and said, "Peace be with
you." [27]Then he said to Thomas, "Put your finger
here and see my hands. Reach out your hand and
put it in my side. Do not doubt but believe."
[28]Thomas answered him, "My Lord and my God!"
[29]Jesus said to him, "Have you believed because
you have seen me? Blessed are those who have
not seen and yet have come to believe."

The Purpose of This Book

30 Now Jesus did many other signs in
the presence of his disciples, which are
not written in this book. [31]But these
are written so that you may come to
believe[g] that Jesus is the Messiah,[h]
the Son of God, and that through
believing you may have life in his
name.

g **20.31** Other ancient authorities read *may continue to believe*
h **20.31** Or *the Christ*

Epilogue: "Follow me . . ." (Jn 21:1–25)

The disciples return to Galilee and to the comfort of their old life as fishermen. After the fatigue of a fruitless night's work, the Risen One appears and gives abundant life. Once again, the eyes of the beloved disciple are the first to recognize the Lord. It is he who notifies Peter, who in turn dives into the water and reaches the Risen One. The Lord asks a question to Peter three times, a question that seeks to penetrate Peter's heart: "Simon son of John, do you love me more than these?" (21:15, 16, 17). That love which was first denied (18:17, 25, 27) is now sorrowfully reaffirmed and leads to Peter's life work of loving the Lord by caring for and serving the small but growing community of believers. In this strenuous mission, however, Peter will not be alone. The beloved disciple will remain at his side. And better yet John's testimony will not cease until the Lord returns at the end of time (21:22). The book that we have in our hands is therefore the last gift of the Risen One to us, a precious gift as it gives us the possibility of knowing him, of believing in his love, and of receiving his life.

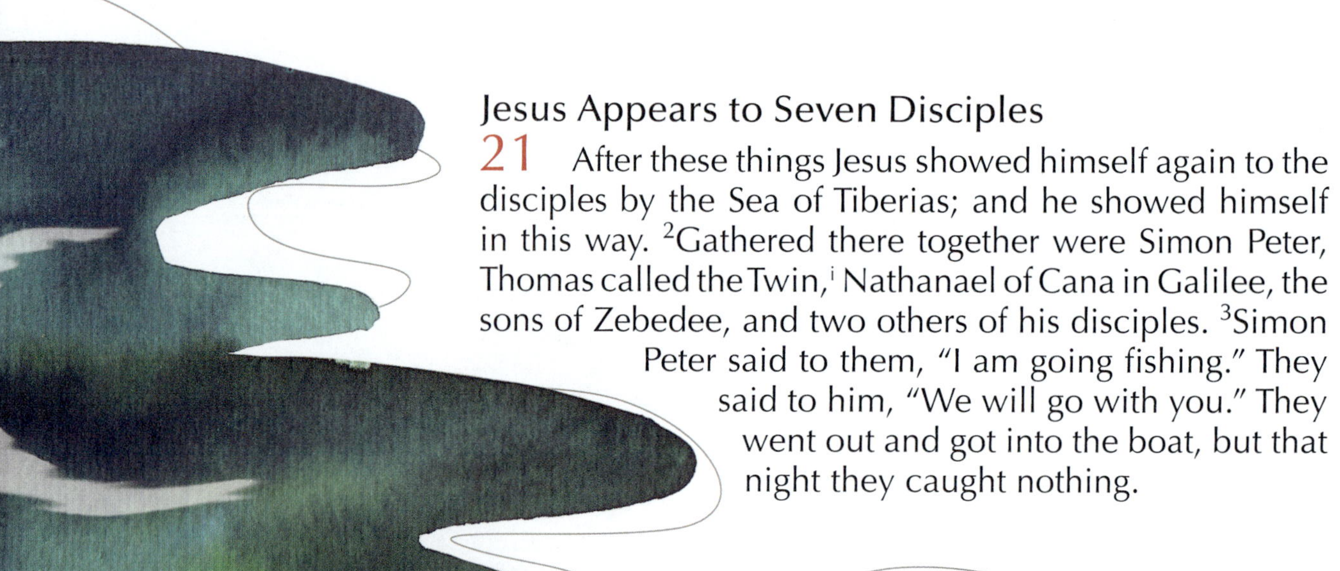

Jesus Appears to Seven Disciples

21 After these things Jesus showed himself again to the
disciples by the Sea of Tiberias; and he showed himself
in this way. 2Gathered there together were Simon Peter,
Thomas called the Twin,[i] Nathanael of Cana in Galilee, the
sons of Zebedee, and two others of his disciples. 3Simon
Peter said to them, "I am going fishing." They
said to him, "We will go with you." They
went out and got into the boat, but that
night they caught nothing.

i **21.2** Gk *Didymus*

4 Just after daybreak, Jesus stood on the
beach; but the disciples did not know that
it was Jesus. 5 Jesus said to them, "Children,
you have no fish, have you?" They answered
him, "No." 6 He said to them, "Cast the net
to the right side of the boat, and you will find
some." So they cast it, and now they were
not able to haul it in because there were
so many fish. 7 That disciple whom Jesus
loved said to Peter, "It is the Lord!"
When Simon Peter heard that it was
the Lord, he put on some clothes,
for he was naked, and jumped
into the sea. 8 But the other disciples came in the boat, drag-
ging the net full of fish, for they
were not far from the land,
only about a hundred yards[j]
off.

j **21.8** Gk *two hundred cubits*

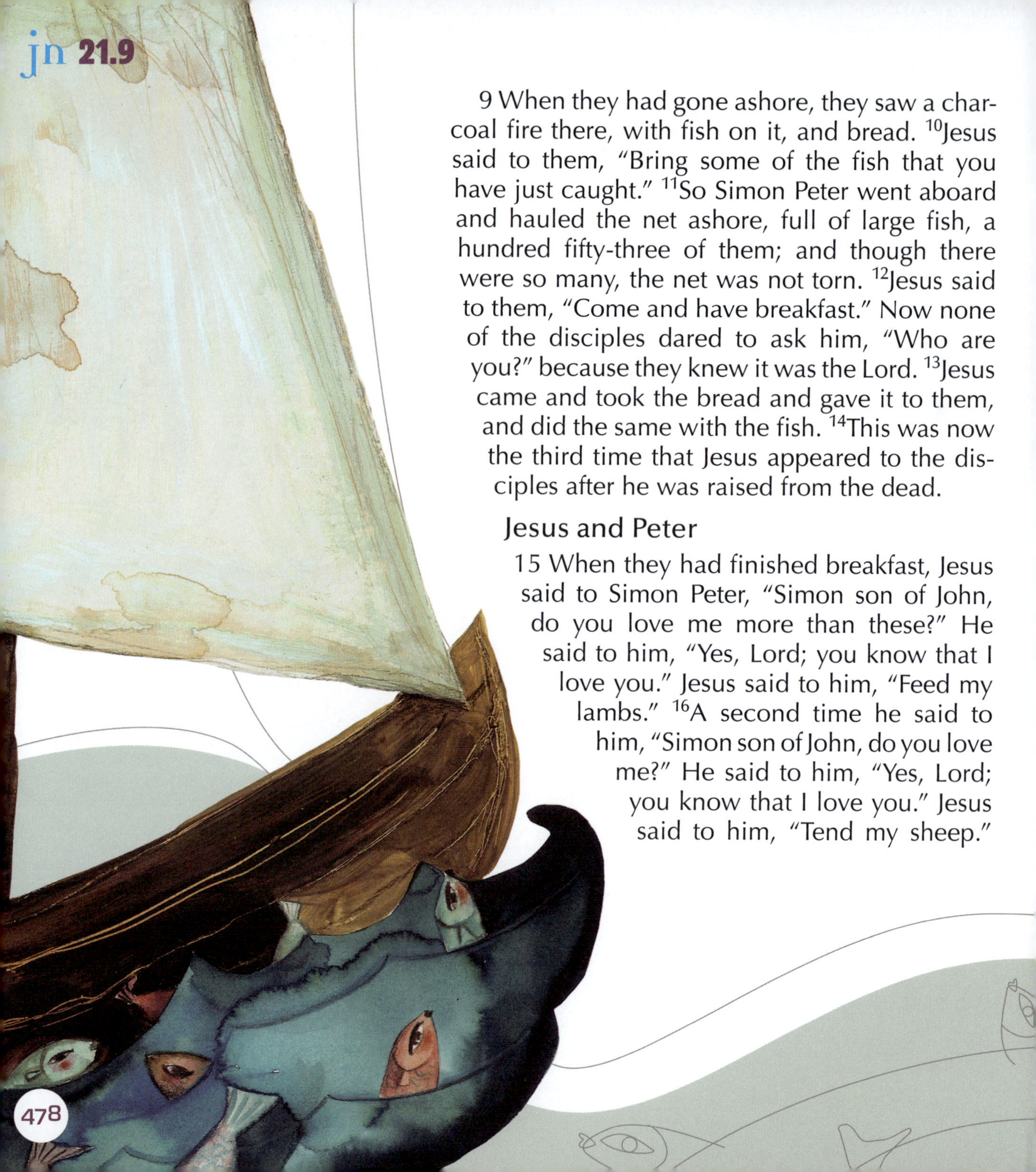

9 When they had gone ashore, they saw a charcoal fire there, with fish on it, and bread. 10Jesus
said to them, "Bring some of the fish that you
have just caught." 11So Simon Peter went aboard
and hauled the net ashore, full of large fish, a
hundred fifty-three of them; and though there
were so many, the net was not torn. 12Jesus said
to them, "Come and have breakfast." Now none
of the disciples dared to ask him, "Who are
you?" because they knew it was the Lord. 13Jesus
came and took the bread and gave it to them,
and did the same with the fish. 14This was now
the third time that Jesus appeared to the disciples after he was raised from the dead.

Jesus and Peter

15 When they had finished breakfast, Jesus
said to Simon Peter, "Simon son of John,
do you love me more than these?" He
said to him, "Yes, Lord; you know that I
love you." Jesus said to him, "Feed my
lambs." 16A second time he said to
him, "Simon son of John, do you love
me?" He said to him, "Yes, Lord;
you know that I love you." Jesus
said to him, "Tend my sheep."

21:20, 24 Who is this disciple whom Jesus loved?
It is me who told you the many wonderful and great things Jesus did and said. But it is also every person who, loved by him, recognizes Jesus as "Lord" of his or her life.

17 He said to him the third time,
"Simon son of John, do you love
me?" Peter felt hurt because
he said to him the third time,
"Do you love me?" And he
said to him, "Lord, you know
everything; you know that I
love you." Jesus said to him,
"Feed my sheep. 18 Very
truly, I tell you, when you
were younger, you used to
fasten your own belt and to
go wherever you wished.
But when you grow old, you
will stretch out your hands,
and someone else will fasten
a belt around you and take
you where you do not wish to
go." 19 (He said this to indicate
the kind of death by which he
would glorify God.) After this he
said to him, "Follow me."

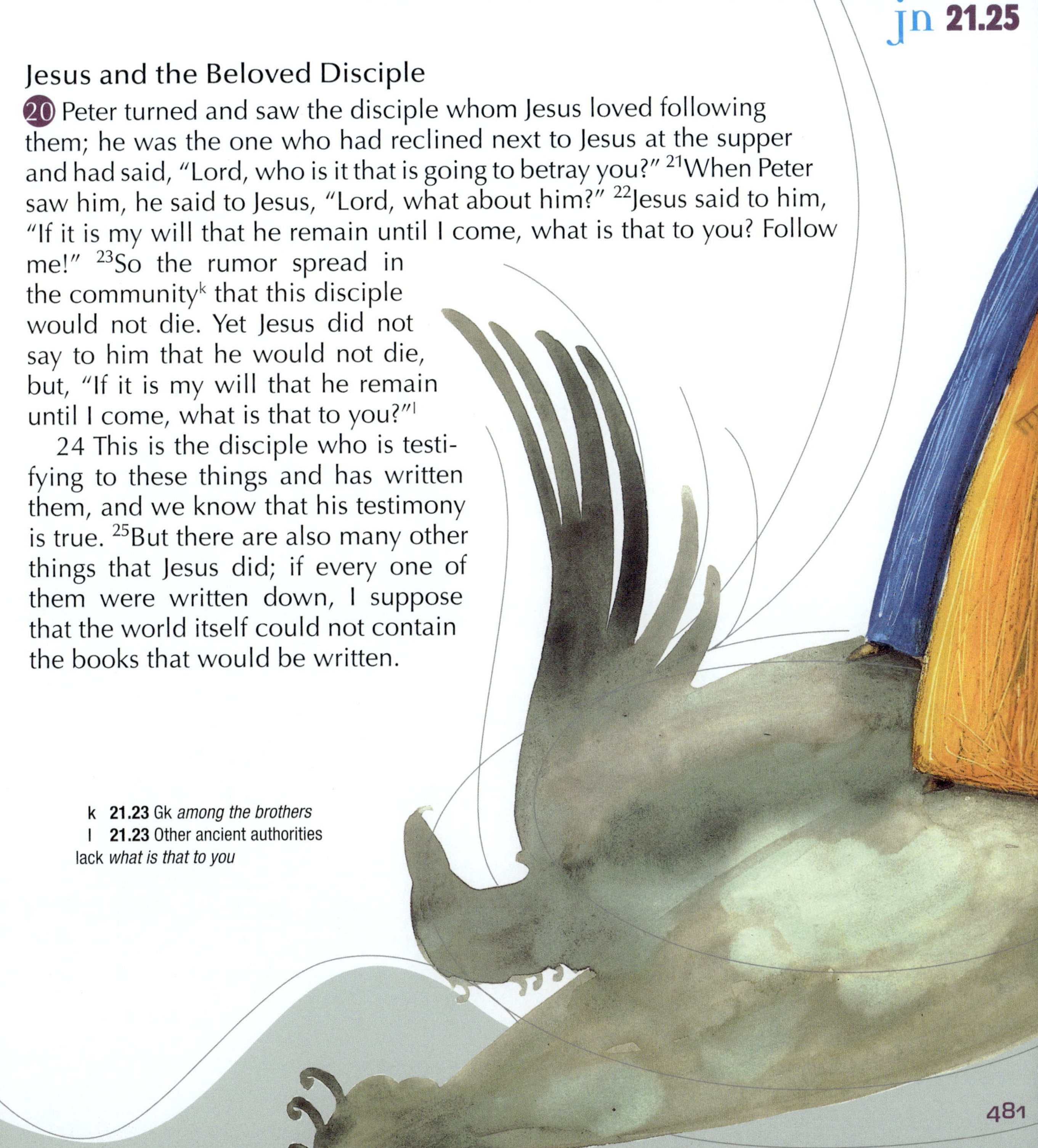

Jesus and the Beloved Disciple

20 Peter turned and saw the disciple whom Jesus loved following
them; he was the one who had reclined next to Jesus at the supper
and had said, "Lord, who is it that is going to betray you?" [21]When Peter
saw him, he said to Jesus, "Lord, what about him?" [22]Jesus said to him,
"If it is my will that he remain until I come, what is that to you? Follow
me!" [23]So the rumor spread in
the community[k] that this disciple
would not die. Yet Jesus did not
say to him that he would not die,
but, "If it is my will that he remain
until I come, what is that to you?"[l]

24 This is the disciple who is testifying to these things and has written
them, and we know that his testimony
is true. [25]But there are also many other
things that Jesus did; if every one of
them were written down, I suppose
that the world itself could not contain
the books that would be written.

k **21.23** Gk *among the brothers*
l **21.23** Other ancient authorities lack *what is that to you*

Appendices

A Little History

Jesus lived in a particular time and place. He would have witnessed many of the historical events of first-century Palestine. At the time, the Roman Empire dominated the world, but there were many people who had some control in the Roman provinces. Here are some examples:

In the days of ***King Herod of Judea . . .*** (Lk 1:5)

In those days a decree went out from ***Emperor Augustus*** that all the world should be counted. This was the first registration and was taken while ***Herod the Great*** was king of Judea and ***Quirinius*** was ***governor of Syria*** (Lk 2:1–2).

In the fifteenth year of the reign of ***Emperor Tiberius***, when ***Pontius Pilate*** was governor of Judea; and ***Herod Antipas*** (son of Herod the Great) was ***ruler of Galilee***; and his brother ***Philip*** was ruler of the region of Ituraea and Trachonitis; and Lysanias was ruler of ***Abilene***; during the high priesthoods of Annas and Caiaphas, the word of God came to John (Lk 3:1–2).

They bound Jesus, led him away, and handed him over to Pilate, the governor. (Mt 27:2).

Pilate asked whether the man was a Galilean. And when Pilate learned that Jesus was under Herod's jurisdiction, Pilate sent him off to Herod Antipas, who was himself in Jerusalem at that time (Lk 23:6–7).

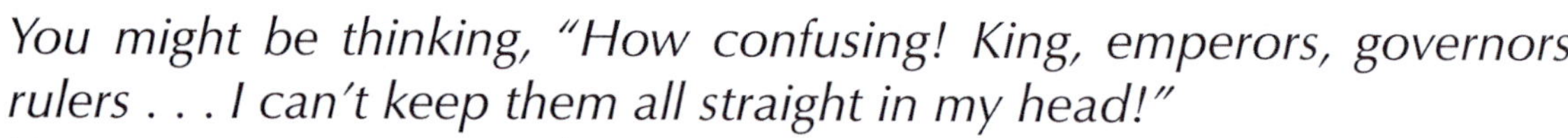

You might be thinking, "How confusing! King, emperors, governors, rulers . . . I can't keep them all straight in my head!"

You are not wrong. To better understand these historical terms you need a basic understanding of the political situation of the world—so very different from ours—in which Jesus was born, lived, worked, and died. This is the purpose of this appendix. Happy reading!

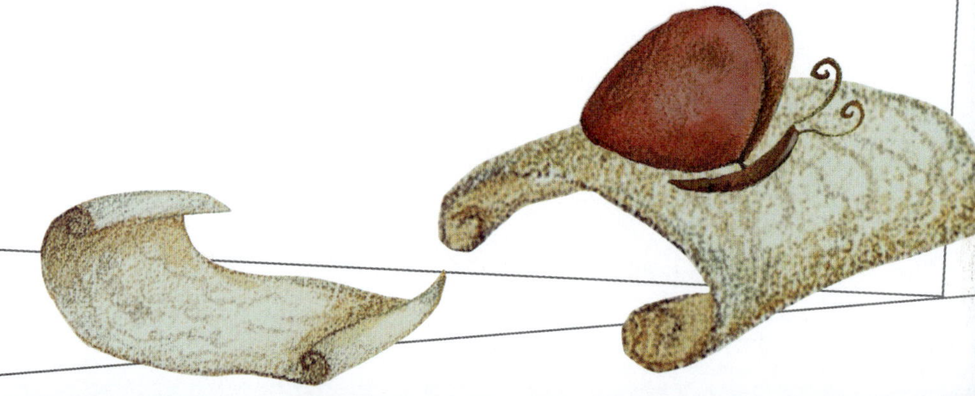

The Roman Empire

For a long time Rome had been a republic—a nation governed by a group of elected officials and senators. However, over time, political power was gradually put into the hands of one man, who had authority even over the assembly of senators. One of the first of these men with almost unchecked power was Octavius, who had defeated his rival Anthony in the naval battle of Actium in 31 BC. The Senate recognized him as the highest authority over Rome in 27 BC. At that time, he was given the title of ***princeps***, which is Latin for prince or leader. **Octavius** then added Augustus, which means "sublime," to his name. This title was only meant for deities (gods), but Octavius wanted to be addressed that way anyway. Then, the Senate gave Octavius two more titles. One

was the highest priestly office—that of ***pontifex maximus***—and the other named him ***pater patriae*** or "father of the fatherland." His government provided a long era of peace, which lasted even after his death in AD 14. ***Octavius Augustus*** was succeeded by his adopted son Tiberius. At the age of fifty-six, **Tiberius** was an expert commander and a wise politician. He was able to continue the enlightened work of his father. When he died in AD 37, Caligula became emperor. Unlike Octavius and Tiberius, the emperor **Caligula** was immoral and incredibly cruel. His actions gained the hatred of many. Then, several people plotted to kill him and succeeded in AD 41.

After Caligula's death, his uncle Claudius became the emperor. He was an honest and intelligent man, who was genuinely concerned about the empire's problems. Unfortunately, **Claudius** was poisoned in AD 54 by his wife Agrippina, who wanted her seventeen-year-old son **Nero** to ascend the throne. It was under Nero that the first mass persecution of Roman Christians broke out. Nero was an evil and irresponsible emperor, who caused many people a lot of suffering. Knowing that people were plotting his death, Nero committed suicide in AD 68. With the death of Nero, the reign of Flavius began.

The Provinces of the Empire

Over time, the large number of territories that Rome conquered were governed in different ways.

The oldest and more peaceful areas were called ***senatorial provinces***: they willingly listened to the Senate and therefore Rome did not need to send soldiers there to keep order. The ***imperial provinces*** were recently conquered territories. The people in these territories often revolted and were controlled by military legions which were stationed in these areas by the emperor, who was the head of the army. The political life of these imperial provinces was then entrusted to senators, who took the title of **governors**. Some of the secondary imperial provinces—such as Palestine where Jesus lived—were governed by **prefects** and were called **prefectures**.

Christian communities first started growing in the ***imperial province of Syria*** to which belonged the prefecture of Judea.

Palestine

The political situation in Palestine at the time of Jesus' birth was dominated by **Herod the Great**. In 40 BC he made the long journey to Rome in order to have himself appointed as the king of Judea. There Anthony and Octavius—who at that time governed the empire together—greeted Herod as friend to the emperor and ally of the Roman people. Once Herod had gained the title, he still had to re-conquer Judea because it was, at that time, under the rule of a people called the Parthians and not under Jewish rule. In 37 BC, after a long war with the help of Roman troops, Herod finally succeeded in reclaiming Jerusalem. From then on, the throne was his. He regained the favor of the Jews—who had been very critical of him because of his alliance with Rome and because he was a violent man—by rebuilding the Temple in Jerusalem.

Herod the Great ruled until his death in 4 BC. The kingdom was then divided between his three sons according to the provisions of Herod's will and approved by Emperor Octavius Augustus. The situation of Palestine after Herod's death was as follows:

- **Archelaus** governed the largest areas of the kingdom from 4 BC to AD 6 (Judea, Idumea, and Samaria). Upon his death the territories went under the direct control of Rome, which assigned governors (sometimes called prefects). We know the governor Pontius Pilate remained in office in Judea from 26 to AD 36 (see Mt 27:2, 11, 15, 17).
- **Herod Antipas** reigned from 4 BC to AD 39 as ruler, or tetrarch, of Galilee (an area to the north of Samaria) and of Perea (a long, narrow region east of the Jordan River). It was he who ordered the beheading of John the Baptist at the fortress of Machaerus (see Mk 6:15–30) and who met Jesus during his ministry and during his trial in Jerusalem (see Lk 13:31–32; 23:7–12).
- **Philip** governed two northern regions—Trachonitis and Iturea—as tetrarch until AD 34. Only a small number of Jews had settled in this territory; Jesus and his disciples stayed in this region for only a short period of time (see Mk 8:27).

Reference Dates

40 BC	The Roman Senate appoints **Herod the Great** as King of Judea.
37 BC	**Herod the Great** conquers Jerusalem, driving out the Parthians.
31 BC	**Octavius** defeats Anthony at Actium; this is the end of the Republic and the beginning of the principality of Rome.
20 BC	The reconstruction of the Temple in Jerusalem by **Herod the Great** begins.
6 BC ca.	**Jesus** is born.
4 BC	**Herod the Great** dies and his kingdom is divided: **Archelaus** governs the regions of Judea, Idumea, and Samaria.Herod Antipas, becomes the ruler of Galilee and Perea.Philip, becomes the tetrarch of Trachonitis and Iturea.
AD 6	**Archelaus** dies and Rome takes direct control of Judea, Idumea, and Samaria. **Jesus**, is in **Jerusalem among the doctors in the Temple**.
AD 14	Emperor **Octavius Augustus** dies. **Tiberius** takes the imperial throne.
AD 26	**Pontius Pilate** is appointed governor of Judea.
AD 28	**Herod Antipas** has **John the Baptist** beheaded. **Jesus begins his public life and the calls the first disciples**.
AD 30	**Jesus' passion, death (probably Friday, April 7), and resurrection of occurs.**

Appendix 2

The Miracles of Jesus

Jesus Heals Illnesses of Body and of Spirit

	MATTHEW	MARK	LUKE	JOHN
Cleanses a Leper	8:1–84	1:40–45	5:12–16	
Heals a Centurion's Servant	8:5–13		7:1–10	
Heals Peter's Mother-in-Law	8:14–15	1:30–31	4:38–39	
Other Healings in Capernaum	8:16–17	1:32–34	4:40–41	
Heals Two Possessed Men	8:28–34	5:1–20	8:26–39	
Heals a Paralytic	9:2–8	2:1–12	5:17–26	
Heals a Woman with a Hemorrhage	9:18–26	5:25–34	8:43–48	
Heals Two Blind Men	9:27–31			
Heals a Mute	9:32–34			
Heals a Man with a Withered Hand	12:9–14	3:1–6	6:6–11	

	MATTHEW	MARK	LUKE	JOHN
Other Healings in Galilee	12:15–21	3:7–12	6:17–19	
Heals a Blind and Mute Man Possessed by a Demon	12:22			
Healings in Gennesaret		14:34–36	6:53–56	
Heals the Possessed Daughter of a Canaanite Woman	15:21–28	7:24–30		
Cures the Lame, Crippled, Blind, and Deaf	15:29–31	7:31–37		
Cures a Boy with a Demon	17:14–21	9:14–29	9:37–43a	
Heals Two Blind Men in Jericho	20:29–34	10:46–52	18:35–43	
Cures a Man with an Unclean Spirit in the Synagogue		1:21–28	4:31–37	
Heals a Deaf Man with Speech Impediment		7:31–37		
Heals Blind Man of Bethsaida		8:22–26		
Heals a Crippled Woman on the Sabbath			13:10–17	

	MATTHEW	MARK	LUKE	JOHN
Jesus Heals the Man with Dropsy			14:1–4	
Cleanses Ten Lepers			17:11–19	
Heals the High Priest's Servant's Ear			22:50–51	
Heals a Royal Official's Dying Son				4:46–54
Heals a Sick Man at the Pool of Bethzatha				5:1–18
Heals a Man Born Blind				9:1–41

Jesus Intervenes on Nature

	MATTHEW	MARK	LUKE	JOHN
Changes Water into Wine at Cana				2:1–11
Stills a Storm	8:23–27	4:35–41	8:22–25	
Walks on Water	14:22–33	6:45–52		6:15–21
Feeds the Five Thousand	14:13–21	6:30–44	9:10–17	6:1–14

	MATTHEW	MARK	LUKE	JOHN
Feeds the Four Thousand	15:32–39	8:1–10		
Tells Peter to Find a Coin in a Fish's Mouth	17:24–27			
Makes a Fig Tree Dry Up	21:18–22	11:12–14, 20–25		
First Miraculous Catch of Fish			5:4–7	
Second Miraculous Catch of Fish				21:1–14

Jesus Brings the Dead Back to Life

	MATTHEW	MARK	LUKE	JOHN
Brings Jairus' Daughter Back to Life	9:18–19, 23–26	5:21–24, 35–43	8:40–42, 49–56	
Brings Back to Life the Widow's Son in Nain			7:11–17	
Raises His Friend, Lazarus, from the Dead				11:1–44

Parables of Jesus

	MATTHEW	MARK	LUKE	JOHN
Salt	5:13	9:50	14:34–35	
Lamp under a Bushel Basket	5:14–16	4:21–23	8:16–17; 11:33	
House Built on Rock	7:24–27		6:47–49	
Narrow Gate	7:13–14		13:24	
New Patch on Old Cloak	9:16	2:21	5:36	
New Wine in Old Wineskins	9:17	2:22	5:37–38	
Playing Flute and Song of Mourning	11:16–17		7:31–32	
A Tree and Its Fruit	7:15–20; 12:33		6:43–44	
The Sower	13:3–9	4:1–9	8:4–8	
Weeds among the Wheat	13:24–30			
Mustard Seed	13:31–32	4:30–32	13:18–19	
Yeast	13:33		13:20–21	

	MATTHEW	MARK	LUKE	JOHN
The Hidden Treasure	13:44			
The Pearl	13:45–46			
The Fishing Net	13:47–50			
Treasures New and Old	13:52			
The Lost Sheep	18:10–14		15:1–7	
The Unforgiving Servant	18:21–35			
Laborers in the Vineyard	20:1–16			
The Two Sons	21:28–32			
The Wicked Tenants	21:33–46	12:1–12	20:9–19	
The Wedding Banquet	22:1–14			
The Fig Tree	24:32–36	13:28–32	21:29–33	
The Trusted Servant	24:45–51		12:41–48	
Ten Bridesmaids	25:1–13			
The Talents	25:14–30		19:11–27	
Sheep or Goats	25:32–33			

	MATTHEW	MARK	LUKE	JOHN
The Growing Seed		4:26–29		
The Closed Door			13:25–29	
The Creditor and Two Debtors			7:41–43	
The Good Samaritan			10:30–37	
Persevering Friend			11:5–8	
The Rich Fool			12:16–21	
The Watchful Servants			12:35–40	
The Barren Fig Tree			13:6–9	
The Place of Honor			14:7–11	
The Great Dinner			14:15–24	
The Prudent Builder			14:28–30	
The Prudent King			14:31–32	
The Lost Coin			15:8–10	

	MATTHEW	MARK	LUKE	JOHN
The Prodigal Son and His Brother			15:11–32	
The Dishonest Manager			16:1–8	
The Rich Man and Lazarus			16:19–31	
The Master and the Servant			17:7–10	
The Widow and the Unjust Judge			18:1–8	
The Pharisee and the Tax Collector			18:9–14	
The Wind				3:8
Friend of the Bridegroom				3:29
Gate to the Sheepfold				10:1–6
The Good Shepherd				10:11–15
The Grain of Wheat				12:24
The Vine and the Branches				15:1–8
The Woman in Labor				16:21

Appendix 4

Symbols and Gestures in the Sacraments of Christian Initiation

SACRAMENT Baptism

SYMBOLS AND GESTURES Naming of the Person

MEANING The gift of faith and of new life in Christ is given to each of us personally. Jesus knows each of us and we belong to him. We often read in the Bible that when God invites someone to follow him, he gives that person a new name.

PASSAGES FOR REFERENCE

Mt 16:17–18
Mk 3:16–17
Jn 1:42

In the Rest of the Bible

Gn 17:5, 15; 32:28–30
Is 62:2

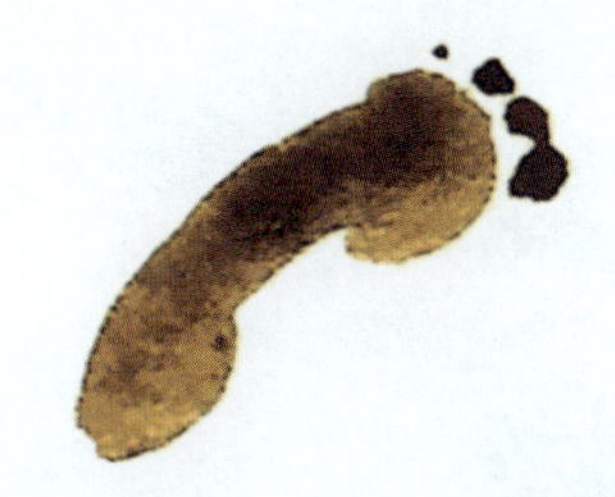

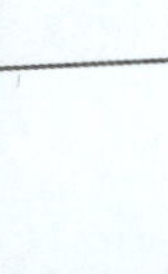

Sacrament Baptism

Symbols and Gestures The Sign of the Cross on the Forehead

Meaning Jesus' cross is the source of salvation. To be a Christian means to follow Jesus on the path he traced out for us by his passion, death, and resurrection.

Passages for Reference

Mt 16:21, 24–25; 27:32–54
Jn 19:28–30

In the Rest of the Bible

Ez 9:4
Rom 6:6
Eph 2:16
Col 1:20
1 Pt 2:24

Sacrament **Baptism**

Symbols and Gestures **Baptism with Water**

Meaning

The people of Israel were saved from slavery by passing through the waters of the Red Sea. Jesus was baptized in the waters of the Jordan River and was consecrated by the Holy Spirit. While on the cross, blood and water flowed from Jesus' pierced side. Water generates life; it renews and purifies. It recalls new life in Christ and cleanses us from sin.

Passages for Reference

Mt 28:19–20
Mk 1:4–11; 16:16
Jn 1:19–34; 3:5–8; 4:10–14; 19:33–34

In the Rest of the Bible

Ex 14:21–31
Ps 23:2–3
Is 12:3
Acts 2:38

Sacrament Baptism

Symbols and Gestures Clothing with the White Garment

Meaning It is the sign of the new dignity of the believer, who is now clothed in Christ. The color of the robe recalls Jesus' resurrection.

Passages for Reference

Mt 17:2

Mk 9:2–3; 16:5

Lk 9:29

In the Rest of the Bible

Rev 6:11; 7:14; 22:14

Sacrament **Baptism**

Symbols and Gestures **Lit Candle**

Meaning It is a paschal, or Easter, sign which recalls the column of fire that guided the Israelites through the desert.

Christ is the light of the world. Those who believe in him should live in Christ's light, guarding and increasing their faith.

Passages for Reference

Mt 5:14–16

Lk 1:78–79

Jn 1:9; 3:19–21; 8:12; 9:5

In the Rest of the Bible

Ex 13:21–22

1 Jn 2:8–11

Sacrament Baptism and Confirmation

Symbols and Gestures Anointing with Chrism Oil

Meaning In the tradition of Israel, oil was used to anoint the priests and the king. The Church uses oil to signify the gift of the Holy Spirit and our belonging to Christ.

Passages for Reference

Mk 14:3–9

Lk 4:18–19

Jn 19: 39–40

In the Rest of the Bible

Ex 30:22–32

1 Sm 16:1–13

1 Chr 11:3

Is 61:1

1 Jn 2:20, 27

Sacrament # Confirmation

Symbols and Gestures **Laying on of Hands**

Meaning

Confirmation is a blessing which signifies the giving of a particular gift or the assignment of an important task. In the New Testament, it is often a gesture of consecration that is linked to the gift of the Holy Spirit.

Passages for Reference

Mk 6:5; 7:32; 10:16; 16:17–18

Lk 4:40

In the Rest of the Bible

Gn 48:13–16

Nu 27:18–19

Acts 8:15–17; 13:1–3

2 Tim 1:6

SACRAMENT

Eucharist

SYMBOLS AND GESTURES

Bread Becomes the Body of Christ

MEANING

Bread is a symbol of the nourishment a person needs to live. Jesus transformed the bread he blessed and broke into his Body, and gave his Body and his own life for the sake of the world. Christ is the living Bread come down from heaven.

PASSAGES FOR REFERENCE

Mt 26:26
Mk 14:22
Lk 22:19; 24:30, 35
Jn 6:11, 26–35

In the Rest of the Bible

Ex 16:4
Acts 2:42
1 Cor 10:16–17

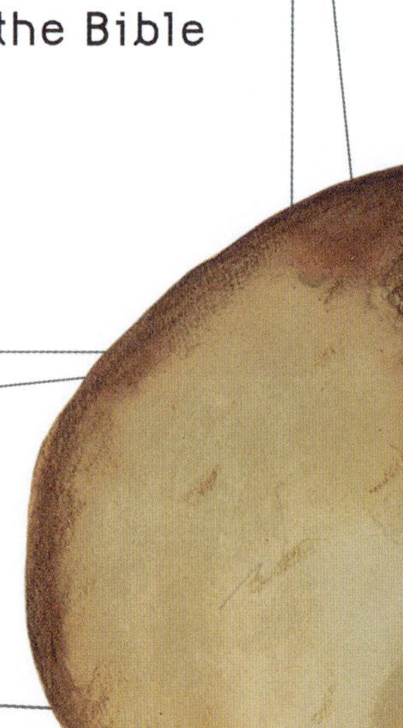

Sacrament **Eucharist**

Symbols and Gestures **Wine Becomes the Blood of Christ**

Meaning Wine is a symbol of celebration and joy. Jesus transforms wine into his Blood which he shed for us. By doing this he formed the new and everlasting covenant between God and humanity.

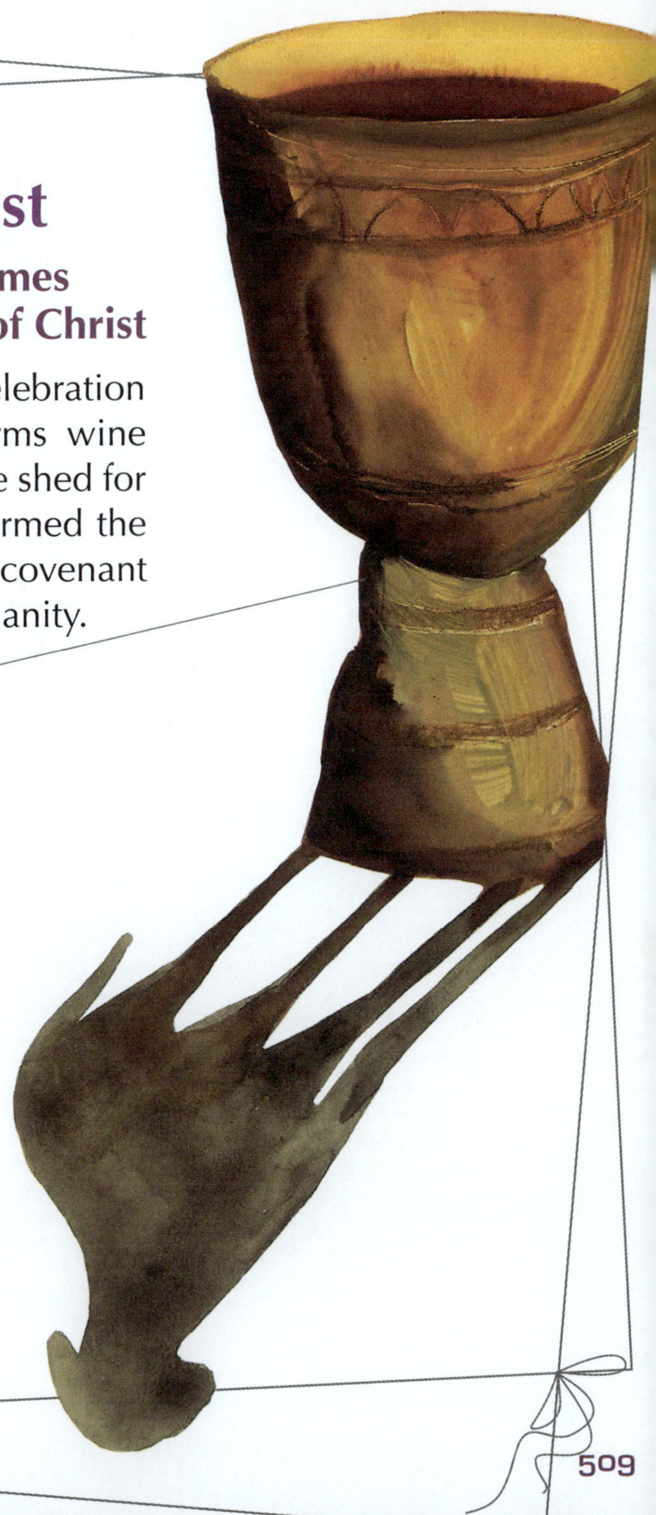

Passages for Reference

Mt 26:27–28

Mk 14:23–24

LK 22:20

Jn 19:34

In the Rest of the Bible

Ex 12:7; 24:8

Acts 20:28

Eph 1:7

Heb 9–10; 13:12, 20

Gospels for Sundays and Feast Days

The evangelical accounts that we hear on Sundays during the Mass are not chosen at random. Each feast has its own passage. The festival cycle repeats every three years, because it dedicates a whole year to each of the three gospels so-called "synoptics" (Matthew, Mark, and Luke). The year in which the Gospel of Matthew is read is referred to as year A. The year in which Mark's Gospel is read is known as year B. And year C is the year in which the Gospel of Luke is read. What follows is a table with the gospel passages for all the Sundays of Ordinary Time and those for the principle feasts of the liturgical year. If before going to Mass you read the corresponding gospel passage with your mother and father, you will be better able to follow the reading the priest will proclaim in church and understand more deeply the message that Jesus wants you to receive.

Roman Rite

SUNDAYS AND SOLEMNITIES	YEAR A	YEAR B	YEAR C
1st Sunday of Advent	Mt 24:37–44	Mk 13:33–37	Lk 21:25–28, 34–36
2nd Sunday of Advent	Mt 3:1–12	Mk 1:1–8	Lk 3:1–6
3rd Sunday of Advent	Mt 11:2–11	Jn 1:6–8	Lk 3:10–18
4th Sunday of Advent	Mt 1:18–24	Lk 1:26–38	Lk 1:39–45
Christmas (the same readings every year)	Mass in the evening: Mt 1:1–25 Mass at midnight: Lk 2:1–14 Mass at dawn: Lk 2:15–20 Mass during the day: Jn 1:1–18		
Holy Family (Sunday within the octave of Christmas)	Mt 2:13–15, 19–23	Lk 2:22–40	Lk 2:41–52
Epiphany		Mt 2:1–12	
Baptism of the Lord (Sunday after Epiphany)	Mt 3:13–17	Mk 1:7–11	Lk 3:15–16, 21–22
1st Sunday of Lent	Mt 4:1–11	Mk 1:12–15	Lk 4:1–13
2nd Sunday of Lent	Mt 17:1–9	Mk 9:2–10	Lk 9:28b–36
3rd Sunday of Lent	Jn 4:5–42	Jn 2:13–25	Lk 13:1–9
4th Sunday of Lent	Jn 9:1–41	Jn 3:14–21	Lk 15:1–3, 11–32
5th Sunday of Lent	Jn 11:1–45	Jn 12:20–33	Jn 8:1–11
Palm Sunday	Mt 26:14–27:66	Mk 14:1–15:47	Lk 22:14–23:56

SUNDAYS AND SOLEMNITIES	YEAR A	YEAR B	YEAR C
Holy Thursday		Jn 13:1–15	
Good Friday		Jn 18:1–19:42	
Easter Vigil Mass	Mt 28:1–10	Mk 16:1–8	Lk 24:1–12
Mass during the day		Jn 20:1–18	
Evening Mass		Lk 24:13–35	
2nd Sunday of Easter		Jn 20:19–31	
3rd Sunday of Easter	Lk 24:13–35	Lk 24:35–48	Jn 21:1–19
4th Sunday of Easter	Jn 10:1–10	Jn 10:11–18	Jn 10:27–30
5th Sunday of Easter	Jn 14:1–12	Jn 15:1–8	Jn 13:1, 31–33a, 34–35
6th Sunday of Easter	Jn 14:15–21	Jn 15:9–17	Jn 14:23–29
Ascension of the Lord 7th Sunday of Easter or Thursday after 6th Sunday of Easter	Mt 28:16–20	Mk 16:15–20	Lk 24:46–53
7th Sunday of Easter In dioceses where Ascension is celebrated on Thursday	Jn 17:1–11a	Jn 17:11b–19	Jn 17:20–26
Pentecost	Jn 20:19–23	Jn 15:26–27; 16:12–15	Jn 14:15–16, 23b–26
Trinity Sunday (1st Sunday after Pentecost)	Jn 3:16–18	Mt 28:16–20	Jn 16:12–15
Corpus Christi (2nd Sunday after Pentecost)	Jn 6:51–59	Mk 14:12–16, 22–26	Lk 9:11b–17
2nd Sunday of O.T.* (the 2nd Sunday after Epiphany)	Jn 1:29–34	Jn 1:35–42	Jn 2:1–12
3rd Sunday of O.T.	Mt 4:12–23	Mk 1:14–20	Lk 1:1–4; 4:14–21

*O.T.= Ordinary Time

SUNDAYS AND SOLEMNITIES	YEAR A	YEAR B	YEAR C
4th Sunday of O.T.	Mt 5:1–12	Mk 1:21–28	Lk 4:21–30
5th Sunday of O.T.	Mt 5:13–16	Mk 1:29–39	Lk 5:1–11
6th Sunday of O.T.	Mt 5:17–37	Mk 1:40–45	Lk 6:27–38
7th Sunday of O.T.	Mt 5:38–48	Mk 2:1–12	Lk 6:27–38
8th Sunday of O.T.	Mt 6:24–34	Mk 2:18–22	Lk 6:39–45
9th Sunday of O.T.	Mt 7:21–27	Mk 2:23–28; 3:1–6	Lk 7:1–10
10th Sunday of O.T.	Mt 9:9–13	Mk 3:20–35	Lk 7:11–17
11th Sunday of O.T.	Mt 9:36–38; 10:1–8	Mk 4:26–34	Lk 7:36–50; 8:1–3
12th Sunday of O.T.	Mt 10:26–33	Mk 4:35–41	Lk 9:18–24
13th Sunday of O.T.	Mt 10:37–42	Mk 5:21–43	Lk 9:51–62
14th Sunday of O.T.	Mt 11:25–30	Mk 6:1–6	Lk 10:1–12, 17–20
15th Sunday of O.T.	Mt 13:1–23	Mk 6:7–13	Lk 10:25–37
16th Sunday of O.T.	Mt 13:24–43	Mk 6:30–34	Lk 10:38–42
17th Sunday of O.T.	Mt 13:44–52	Jn 6:1–15	Lk 11:1–13
18th Sunday of O.T.	Mt 14:13–21	Jn 6:24–35	Lk 12:13–21
19th Sunday of O.T.	Mt 14:22–33	Jn 6:41–51	Lk 12:32–48
20th Sunday of O.T.	Mt 15:21–28	Jn 6:51–58	Lk 12:49–53
21st Sunday of O.T.	Mt 16:13–20	Jn 6:53, 60–69	Lk 13:22–30
22nd Sunday of O.T.	Mt 16:21–27	Mk 7:1–8, 14–15, 21–23	Lk 14:1, 7–14
23rd Sunday of O.T.	Mt 18:15–20	Mk 7:31–37	Lk 14:25–33

SUNDAYS AND SOLEMNITIES	YEAR A	YEAR B	YEAR C
24th Sunday of O.T.	Mt 18:21–35	Mk 8:27–35	Lk 15:1–32
25th Sunday of O.T.	Mt 20:1–16	Mk 9:30–37	Lk 16: 1–13
26th Sunday of O.T.	Mt 21:28–32	Mk 9:38–43, 45, 47–48	Lk 16:19–31
27th Sunday of O.T.	Mt 21:33–43	Mk 10:2–16	Lk 17:5–10
28th Sunday of O.T.	Mt 22:1–14	Mk 10:17–30	Lk 17:11–19
29th Sunday of O.T.	Mt 22:15–21	Mk 10:35–45	Lk 18:1–8
30th Sunday of O.T.	Mt 22:34–40	Mk 10:46–52	Lk 18:9–14
31st Sunday of O.T.	Mt 23:1–12	Mk 12:28–34	Lk 19:1–10
32nd Sunday of O.T.	Mt 25:1–13	Mk 12:38–44	Lk 20:27–38
33rd Sunday of O.T.	Mt 25:14–30	Mk 13:24–32	Lk 21:5–19
Christ the King (last Sunday of liturgical year)	Mt 25:31–46	Jn 18:33b–37	Lk 23:35–43

Gospel Readings for Other Feast Days in the Liturgical Year

* indicates holy day of obligation for Canada and United States

** indicates holy day of obligation in United States only

December 8	**Immaculate Conception of the Blessed Virgin Mary, Patroness of the United States	Lk 1:26–38
December 12	Our Lady of Guadalupe, Patroness of the Americas	Lk 1:39–47
January 1	*Mary, Mother of God	Lk 2:16–21

January 25	Conversion of Saint Paul	Mk 16:15–18
February 2	Presentation of the Lord World Day of Prayer for Consecrated Life	Lk 2:22–40
Wednesday before 1st Sunday of Lent	Ash Wednesday	Mt 6:1–6, 16–18
March 19	Saint Joseph, Patron of Canada	Mt 1:16, 18–21, 24a or Lk 2:41–51a
March 25	Annunciation of the Lord	Lk 1:26–38
Monday after Pentecost	Mary, Mother of the Church	Jn 19:25–27
Friday following 2nd Sunday after Pentecost	Most Sacred Heart of Jesus	Mt 11:25–30
Saturday following 2nd Sunday after Pentecost	Immaculate Heart of Blessed Virgin Mary	Lk 2:41–51
June 24	Nativity of John the Baptist	Lk 1:57–66, 80
June 29	Saints Peter and Paul	Mt 16:13–19
August 15	**Assumption of the Blessed Virgin Mary	Lk 1:39–56
August 22	Queenship of the Blessed Virgin Mary	Mt 23:1–12
September 8	Nativity of the Blessed Virgin Mary	Mt 1:1–16, 18–23
September 14	Exaltation of the Holy Cross	Jn 3:13–17
September 15	Our Lady of Sorrows	Lk 2:33–35 or Jn 19:25–27
November 1	**All Saints' Day	Mt 5:1–12a
November 2	All Souls' Day	Mt 25:31–46
November 21	Presentation of the Blessed Virgin Mary	Mary Lk 2:22–40

Other holy days of obligation in the United States and Canada are Christmas and the Ascension of the Lord, regardless of which day of the week it falls upon.

How to Pray with Scripture: *Lectio Divina*

A very ancient way of praying with the Bible is called "holy reading," or Lectio Divina. It helps the reader "hear" and "understand" what God is saying to the person. It has five simple steps.

Step One: Lectio (reading)

Before reading, ask the Holy Spirit to speak to you through the Scripture you are about to read.

Then, read the passage you have selected slowly, perhaps more than once. Take notice of any word, phrase, or image that catches your attention.

Step Two: Meditatio (meditation)

The second step is to reread the same passage and reflect on what God is saying to you through the word, phrase, or image that attracted you. Is God challenging you? Asking something of you? Consoling or encouraging you? Reflect on how you can put God's invitation into practice. Resolve to do it throughout the day.

Step Three: Oratio (verbal prayer)

In the third step, you may choose to reread the passage again, or not. Having "heard" God speak, it is now your chance to respond. You can use your own words, or words from the Scripture passage you have been praying with. Enter into a conversation with God. Ask for help and tell him what is in your heart.

Step Four: Contemplatio (contemplation)

Remember the word, phrase, or image that touched you. You can silently repeat it throughout the day and carry God's word to you into your life. This will also help you to maintain your resolution to act on God's invitation.

Important Dates

YEAR	CYCLE	1ST SUNDAY OF LENT	EASTER
2020	A	March 1	April 12
2021	B	February 21	April 4
2022	C	March 6	April 17
2023	A	February 26	April 9
2024	B	February 18	March 31
2025	C	March 9	April 20
2026	A	February 22	April 5
2027	B	February 14	March 28
2028	C	March 5	April 16
2029	A	February	18 April 1
2030	B	March 10	April 21
2031	C	March 2	April 13

YEAR	CYCLE	PENTECOST	1ST SUNDAY OF ADVENT
2020	A	May 31	November 29
2021	B	May 23	November 28
2022	C	June 5	November 27
2023	A	May 28	December 3
2024	B	May 19	December 1
2025	C	June 8	November 30
2026	A	May 24	November 29
2027	B	May 16	November 28
2028	C	June 4	December 3
2029	A	May 20	December 2
2030	B	June 9	December 1
2031	C	June 1	November 30

palestine at the time of jesus
Chorazin
Mount of Beatitudes
Bethsaida Julia
Capernaum
Dalmanutha (Tabgha)
Bethsauda
Magdala
Mount Arbel
Gergesa
Sea of Galilee
(Lake of Gennesaret)
Tiberias
Hippos
Sennabris
Jordan River

Sidon
Damascus
Sarepta (Zarephath)
ITUREA
SYRO-
PHOENICIA
Caesarea Philippi
Tyre
TRACHONITIS
ULATHA
Sea of Galilee
(Lake of Gennesaret)
GALILEA
BATANAEA
Capernaum
Bethsaida
Ptolemais
Canatha
Magdala
Hippos
Tiberias
Cana
Dion
AURANITIS
Abila
Sepphoris
Nazareth
Mount Tabor
Gadara
Nain
Scythopolis
Judaea under
Pontius Pilate
Pella
Caesarea
SAMARIA
DECAPOLIS
Tetrarchy of
Herod Antipas
Territory of the Decapolis
Sebaste
Gerasa
Tetrarchy of Philip
Sychar
Jordan River
Roman province of Syria
Mediterranean
Sea
Mount Arbel
Ex-territory of Salome
Philadelphia
Territory with special
status in the province
of Syria
Joppa
Arimathea
Bethel
Lydda
Phasaelis
Jericho
Cities of the Decapolis
JUDEA
Bethphage
Jerusalem
Bethany
PEREA
Azotus
Ein Karem
Qumran
Bethlehem
Ascalon
Herodium
Machaerus
Dead
Sea
Hebron
Gaza
IDUMEA
Masada
Beersheba

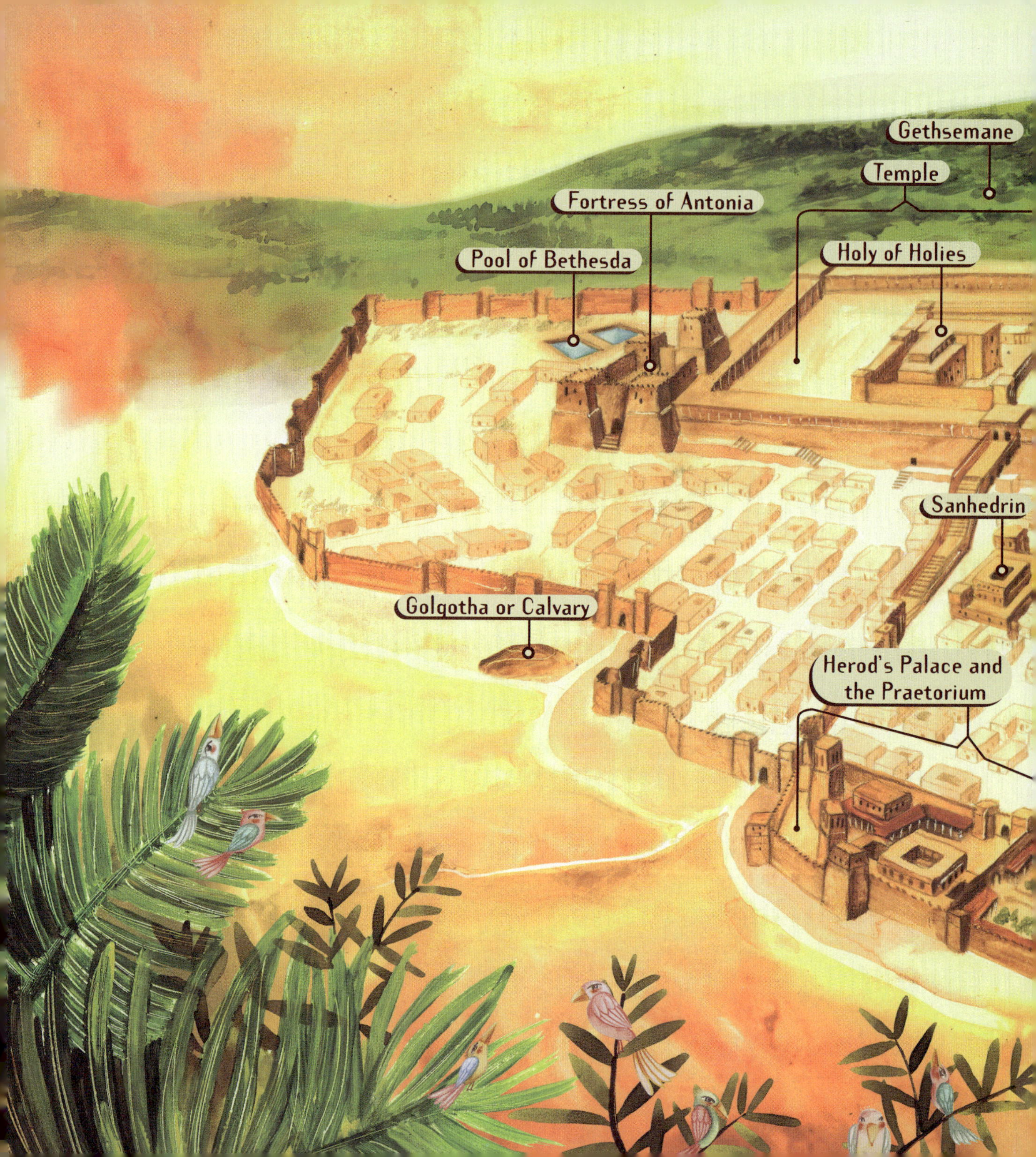
Gethsemane
Temple
Fortress of Antonia
Pool of Bethesda
Holy of Holies
Sanhedrin
Golgotha or Calvary
Herod's Palace and
the Praetorium

Jerusalem in the first century
Mount of Olives
Pool of Siloam
Cenacle
GLIFO DESIGN

Who are the Daughters of St. Paul?

Pauline KIDS

We are Catholic sisters with a mission. Our task is to bring the love of Jesus to everyone like Saint Paul did. You can find us in over 50 countries. Our founder, Blessed James Alberione, showed us how to reach out to the world through the media. That's why we publish books, make movies and apps, record music, broadcast on radio, perform concerts, help people at our bookstores, visit parishes, host JClub book fairs, use social media and the Internet, and pray for all of you.

The Daughters of St. Paul operate book and media centers at the following addresses. Visit, call, or write the one nearest you today, or find us at www.paulinestore.org.

CALIFORNIA
3908 Sepulveda Blvd, Culver City, CA 90230 — 310-397-8676
3250 Middlefield Road, Menlo Park, CA 94025 — 650-562-7060

FLORIDA
145 SW 107th Avenue, Miami, FL 33174 — 305-559-6715

HAWAII
1143 Bishop Street, Honolulu, HI 96813 — 808-521-2731

ILLINOIS
172 North Michigan Avenue, Chicago, IL 60601 — 312-346-4228

LOUISIANA
4403 Veterans Memorial Blvd, Metairie, LA 70006 — 504-887-7631

MASSACHUSETTS
885 Providence Hwy, Dedham, MA 02026 — 781-326-5385

MISSOURI
9804 Watson Road, St. Louis, MO 63126 — 314-965-3512

NEW YORK
115 E. 29th Street, New York City, NY 10016 — 212-754-1110

SOUTH CAROLINA
243 King Street, Charleston, SC 29401 — 843-577-0175

TEXAS
No book center; for parish exhibits or outreach evangelization, contact: 210-569-0500 or SanAntonio@paulinemedia.com or P.O. Box 761416, San Antonio, TX 78245

VIRGINIA
1025 King Street, Alexandria, VA 22314 — 703-549-3806

CANADA
3022 Dufferin Street, Toronto, ON M6B 3T5 — 416-781-9131